The Secret Wife of KING GEORGE IV

Diane Haeger

ST. MARTIN'S GRIFFIN ✹ NEW YORK

www.stmartins.com

Design by Patrice Sheridan

Library of Congress Cataloging-in-Publication Data

Haeger, Diane.
    The secret wife of King George IV / Diane Haeger.
        p. cm.
    ISBN 0-312-24420-7 (hc)
    ISBN 0-312-27477-7 (pbk)
    1. Fitzherbert, Maria Anne, 1756–1837—Fiction.   2. George IV, King of
    Great Britain, 1762–1830—Marriage—Fiction.   3. Great Britain—
    History—George IV, 1820–1830—Fiction.   I. Title.
PS3558.A32125 S43   2000
813'.54—dc21   99-089862
                                                                    CIP

First St. Martin's Griffin Edition: April 2001

10 9 8 7 6 5 4 3 2 1

The Secret Wife
of
KING
GEORGE IV

To Fran Measley,
for the many you inspired.
Most especially,
for the encouragement you long ago gave to me.

ACKNOWLEDGMENTS

THERE ARE SEVERAL PEOPLE TO whom I owe an enormous debt of gratitude in helping me finally bring this complex true story to life: Hannelore Lixenburg and the staff at the Brighton Pavilion, for their generosity of time and their interest in revealing to me various elements of George IV's life at his beach side haven; the staff at Richmond Hill House for their particular assistance to me at Maria's early home; the exceptional research staff at California State University, Long Beach Library, for always leading me to the right historical treasure; Marlene Fried and Richard Hanke, again and always, for their attention to detail, and for reading and re-reading every word I write; my incredibly supportive cyber contingent for their humor, their love of books, and for their unwavering interest in my stories — Ruth Brooks, Dave Dennehy, Judy Dils, Cliff Leach, and Nora Guyer; Joan Duncan and Laurie Lambie for care and concern in an area that has made my work so much easier. I admire you both!; my agent, Irene Goodman, who believed in this book, and in me, from the first.

And last, but not in any way least, my wonderful husband, Ken Haeger, who gives me the strength, the encouragement, and the space, every single day to believe that there is a place for these true love stories from history . . . and who shows me in everything he does that real heros still do very much exist.

The Secret Wife
of
KING
GEORGE IV

PROLOGUE

June 1830

She came slowly from the shadows like an apparition, a mysterious woman veiled in a whisper of black gauze. The bells of Windsor's village churches continued to toll as two Yeoman of the Guard held aside their burning flambeaux and dropped in a reverent bow to the woman whose face they could not see. Then each opened a panel of the huge carved doors to the State Apartments.

No one who had come to mourn at Windsor Castle should see her or even suspect her presence. That would only ignite old scandals, open old wounds. So, as quickly as they had been opened, the doors were sealed behind her. The echo clapped like thunder in the huge paneled hollow. Then there was the silence.

For the longest time she stood in the black-draped, incense-clouded apartment that housed his coffin. *Chinese incense*. Yes, George would have liked that touch.

When she could manage it, she ran a slim hand, now spotted with age, along the smooth burled wood surface of his elegant coffin. The ivory inlay. Handles dipped in gold. Fragrant roses filling two grand Sevres vases. Elegant to the end, she smiled and raised the dark veil,

1

not a hair out of place. She was glad for the single wooden chair that waited near her like a dutiful servant, and she sank gratefully between its carved oak arms. Her tired eyes filled with tears as her mind was filled with memories.

George's valet had told her, with excruciating honesty, about the locket that England's King still wore, and would, for all eternity—the locket bearing her image. His wife, but never his Queen.

And so the old wound was made raw yet one more time. So many missed opportunities. So much wasted time. Even as the years had pressed on, there had never been a time when she had not looked for his face in a crowd, when she had not thought of him as she lay alone in a bed they once had shared.

William had been exceedingly kind since George's death. The new King had sent a messenger to tell her that she was entitled to wear widow's black. He had also arranged for her to have this private time here before the funeral, and His Highness hoped that she would come to dinner when she felt able. William had been a good friend. Like Frederick and Edward, he understood what she had meant to their elder brother—that she had been so very much more than the mistress that the rest of the world believed.

Slowly, and with all of the effort she possessed, she rose. Her legs were weak and unsteady. Her vision was blurred by the steady stream of tears.

You still can make me cry, you bastard, she thought. *Even now when you are gone, you are still the only one who can do that. Ah, but then there never was anyone like you, George Augustus. Nor, I imagine, shall there ever be again.*

She surprised herself when the thought made her smile. The tears began to dry, and for a moment, at least that one moment, the pain was not so great.

You spoiled me for anyone else, didn't you? I think it was from that very first moment on the Mall when you smiled at me so brazenly. Oh, how I did blush then! You looked as if you owned the entire world that day, and I did not know it then but I wanted nothing more in life than to be a part of that world. Your world. To be swept up in your brilliant light...and for a time, I was. Oh yes indeed, how I was...

Part One

M‌RS. FITZHERBERT IS ARRIVED IN

LONDON FOR THE SEASON.

—*MORNING HERALD*

MARCH 20, 1784

CHAPTER ONE

"MARIA, *REALLY!*"

The lacquered red phaeton clicked over the smooth pavement down from Piccadilly, across toward Pall Mall, as Maria Fitzherbert languidly waved a painted Chinese fan before the soft features of her face. She was trying her best not to look so disinterested. Still, her dark, cocoa eyes fluttered half closed against the sooty London sky as Isabella Sefton tossed her a look of reproach.

After an interminable pause, Isabella then began happily to chatter again. "Now. As I was saying. Tonight we shall go to Almack's. Of course simply everyone who is anyone shall be there. Then tomorrow at four, we are receiving the Duchess of Gordon and Lady Cowper. At eight, as soon as we manage to be rid of everyone, we shall go on to the King's Theater, where you know of course that your uncle and I are among the privileged few who have a box..."

Maria shifted impatiently on the opposite blue-silk cushion as their carriage crossed St. James's Street. She could not help herself. It was an incessant jabbing, that voice, sharp like a razor, and her perfume, the scent of jasmine daubed too liberally into the decolletage of a tastefully styled pistachio silk gown.

"Perhaps it is too soon for me to go to a place like Almack's."

"Oh, rubbish!" Isabella huffed. "The Assembly rooms are just the place for you. Thomas has been dead nearly a year already and you simply *must* begin again. Beauty doesn't last forever, you know!"

"But to enter it all so boldly—"

"Darling, is there really any other way?" Isabella asked, laughed an incisive little laugh, then tossed back her dark hair with coltish aplomb.

The driver slowed, vying for room on the crowded street, which narrowed steadily among a tangle of elegant phaetons, tandems, and post chaises filled with the "smart set" out for the afternoon ritual. It was an endless procession of horses' hooves and large iron coach wheels. See and be seen.

None of the fashionable ever did much of anything before the hour of four. Now, as the bells of Christopher Wren's Church of St. James's struck five, the streets and shops along St. James's Street and Bond Street were choked with the most elegantly dressed, the most notable of London society.

"Now then," Isabella began again, her shrill voice slicing the stale air. "Have you a proper new gown for tonight? And not that uninspired apricot atrocity you last wore to Vauxhall. I have heard gossip that none other than the Duchess of Devonshire herself shall be among us, and they say that the woman is an absolute slave to fashion."

As they turned onto the Mall, Maria gazed beyond the glass window. Low-slung branches whispered shades of pale green, white, and pale pink in the afternoon breeze. Bright rhododendron, like puffs of pink snow dotted with green, tipped their stalks toward the crowded street.

Again their carriage slowed to a stop as Isabella chattered on.

At first she did not notice the two riders galloping wildly across the green directly toward them. Two men in tight white breeches that set off long, muscled legs, their hair blown back by the wind. Both rode stallions. One was black and sleek, the other white and magnificent.

"Saints above!" Isabella cried. "They are positively out of their minds, racing with one another, here, in the city!"

Wild. Untamed. They were laughing, heads back, faces flushed. When they were but a breath from Isabella's carriage, the riders both pulled the bridles tightly and the horses halted. As Maria watched the two riders, her breath caught.

Both men were young and impeccably dressed, but it was the devilishly handsome face of the man with the high white cravat, red cutaway jacket, and windblown chestnut hair that took her breath away. A slash of sweat glistened on his forehead, and he had been laughing. Until he saw her.

The eyes that settled on Maria were the most startlingly blue eyes she had ever seen. He was as handsome as a god.

"Do you know who that is?" Isabella squealed with delight and pulled her from the curiosity of the moment with her rapacious hounding. "It is the Prince of Wales!"

Maria gave him a fleeting, elusive glance. She saw the Royal Crest, the gold lion and the unicorn around a golden crown, emblazoned on his saddle. Without knowing what else to do, she looked away.

Isabella was right. It was he.

As their coach remained at a standstill for a collection of well-dressed strollers to cross up toward the Mall, his gaze continued unflinching upon her. His full lips were turned up in a little half smile. And those eyes! *Sky blue*, as if they had no beginning and no end. His portraits did not begin to do them justice. They drilled and rooted her now so that she could not quite tell if he was flirting with her or mocking her.

When he nodded to her, still smiling, Maria could feel warm blood rush up from her neck and blossom like one of Isabella's prized camellias on her pale, un-rouged face. There was something dangerous, almost malevolent, in his expression, but Maria could no longer will herself to look away.

The carriage still did not move. Neither did the riders.

The two horses whinnied and pawed at the pavement. Maria felt her dry throat constrict. She could not swallow. She had heard the rumors like everyone else, that the king's eldest son was brash and impulsive—more like a rebel warrior than a prince.

Maria did her best to bite back a smile.

Then suddenly, the coach lurched and pulled them away from the moment, and on down the crowded Mall.

"Can you imagine it?" Isabella was saying, her eyes glittering like black currants as the carriage lurched forward and the steady clop of hooves began again. "The Prince of Wales was flirting brazenly with you! Ooh, is that not delicious!"

Maria opened her fan again and began to move the warm spring air, hoping that her uncle's wife would not see her trembling. "I wouldn't make too much of it, Isabella," she said with as much disinterest as she could gather. "I hear that the Prince of Wales flirts with positively everyone."

Lady Sefton looked away, her smooth face paled with concession, remembering from personal experience that on that score her husband's beautiful niece could not have been more correct.

"Pity," she muttered as she opened her fan.

THIS WAS NOT GOING TO be easy.

In fact, tonight, it seemed like the most difficult thing in the world. To face all of this again. Society. The amorous glances of interested men who did *not* interest her. The games everyone played. For position. For power. For the thrill of the chase.

Maria sat at her dressing table in a her underpetticoat of pale blue and white striped satin, gazing into the mirror and yet looking past her own image. It was nearly dusk, the sky beyond the long draperied windows was a bonfire of color, but she did not notice that either.

The tall ebony clock beside her dressing table chimed. Her heart sank. It was nearly time to dress.

She was forcing herself to attend the charade this evening for one reason and one reason alone. Isabella, wife of the ninth Viscount and first Earl of Sefton, knew positively "everyone who was anyone" in London. Her uncle's well-meaning wife was also the Smythe family's entrée into non-Catholic society, the more important majority in London, and in a manner all of her own, she missed no attempt to remind Maria of her influence.

But that, above all else, mattered to her ambitious brother, and so far this season, she had done her best to oblige him.

Now that Maria was widowed, Isabella had taken it upon herself, in an exhaustive round of parties and balls, to introduce her into the more exclusive society.

It truly was the only way, she harangued, to make a *really* important match. But marriage, a third for Maria, was not a priority. It was the first time in her life that she had felt the curious sensation of freedom. And she had begun to like it.

As the widow of Thomas Fitzherbert, Maria had a comfortable stipend, a house in London, and one in the country at Twickenham. At twenty-nine, she also had a newly kindled desire to do as she pleased.

She had decided before setting a solitary foot back in London, that if she did marry again this time she would do it differently. This time if—and only if—she consented to become another man's wife, it was not going to be for social position. It was going to be for the one experience that had always eluded her. *Love.*

Her unpainted lips turned up in a gentle smile. Now that really was a fantasy! In this society of nobility and dandies, and men like that ridiculous Prince of Wales, who only toyed with women...Ah, love. A needle in the proverbial haystack!

Pressing back a smile, she pursed her lips, picked up a silver scent flask, and daubed just the barest hint of rose water at her neck and wrists. Then finally she looked up. Her bare, unpainted face gazed back: Wide brown eyes, fair skin over a heart-shaped face, and a nose that was just a shade too imperfect to be called Greek.

Well, John did always say she had more elegance than true beauty, which perhaps was fortunate, since elegance was timeless. Beauty was not.

But there was something else. It was in her eyes and in the way she held her head. Their mother's stubborn pride, she thought.

Their father's temper, John said.

Come to think of it—she smiled again—there probably was not a man in all of London willing to do battle with that particularly heady combination!

By eight o'clock, the string of carriages that waited outside of Almack's club stretched down King Street and onto St. James's Street, almost to Piccadilly.

Maria and Isabella waited in their sweet-smelling party gowns while the white-gloved footman attended Maria's brother, John. He stepped from the carriage, dressed in an ash-gray tailcoat, knee

9

breeches, and silk stockings, and gave instructions to the driver. Ahead of them was a steady stream of meticulously costumed *beau monde* who, like themselves, had spent all of the morning at the details of their toilette.

The flow of partygoers now inched up the eight steps of white-veined marble, then through the neat Corinthian portico like a slowly moving snake.

When John had joined them once again, the trio moved into the crowded assembly rooms, already warm from the press of bodies. But that was Almack's; miserably warm, decoratively plain, and always overcrowded.

There were throngs of people chattering, bowing, and rustling about; the space around them dimmed white by a mist of scented hair powder. Maria and Isabella stood beneath a huge crystal chandelier that smoked and dripped candle wax onto the polished parquet floors as the air curled with a carefree Handel sonata.

Like everyone else, Maria and her companions conformed to the dictates of well-heeled society. Their hair was properly powdered, their faces painted and accentuated by the still very fashionable well-placed patch or two. John wore one beside his left eye in an attempt to draw attention to his most desirable feature. His eyes, like Maria's, were deep as melting chocolate and had long dark lashes.

Isabella and Maria each wore a single patch beneath the cheekbone. But it was Maria who had inspired the evening's one element of surprise. When the current mode was pastel, she had startled Isabella Sefton almost into silence by wearing a smashing gown of diaphanous indigo silk. A white lace fichu began low, was tied between her breasts, and framed her ivory shoulders. She wore her pale gold hair softly curled into ringlets and had ornamented it with tiny pink rosebuds.

"The first dance?" Maria's brother asked.

He extended his hand to his sister in an elegant gesture. All around the room men were choosing partners. She glanced at him, tall and naturally athletic looking with a slim waist, long legs, and broad shoulders. His hair was the same golden-blond shade as hers.

"Oh, do be a dear and ask me first since my Charles is not here," Isabella whined. She looked back from the dance floor and took

John's hand before he had a moment to object. "It is so awkward not to be asked for the first dance. Besides, I am not above bribery. If you dance with me first, I shall see that you are introduced to the Duchess of Devonshire directly afterward."

Maria smiled and nodded her approval, knowing that an introduction like that would mean as much to him as a moment's peace would mean to her.

She watched them glide away into a whirl of other dancers before she felt free to take a breath of relief. She had been with Isabella the entire day. They had even dressed together at Sefton House.

At least for a few merciful moments, the chatter would cease.

Maria watched them dance together, she small and graceful like a bird; he tall, lithe, and handsome — and she tried her level best not to look so bored by all of it as she felt.

Like hunting hounds drawn to the scent of blood, a collection of young men sensed Maria's disinterest and were attracted by it. They circled cautiously around her in their high collars and tight knee breeches, their tailcoats and their brilliantly embroidered waistcoats shimmering beneath.

Like everyone else, these men had powdered their hair and faces. Their patches had been strategically applied. But the competing fragrances of civet, ambergris, and musk, as they neared her, were noxious in the closed hall.

Maria ignored their collective movements forward. She leaned alone against a gilt column, her fan extended, watching her brother and Isabella dance.

"What great fortune, madam, that you as yet have no partner," said a tall, graceful young man as he bowed before her.

"My brother has requested that I dance only with him this evening, sir," she lied coolly, and looked back at the dancers.

"Jack Smythe is your brother?" he asked with smooth-voiced surprise, having seen them enter Almack's together. The honey-rich tone of his voice, along with his question, caused her to turn around.

"He is, sir."

The young man's expression broadened. "Then you are Mrs. Fitzherbert."

Maria nodded and smiled just enough to be civil, but not enough to be encouraging. Two other young men moved in behind him, and all at once she found herself encircled by a young and attractive assemblage of gentlemen all leaning toward her in apparent fascination.

"Surely old Jack shall make an exception in my case. Please allow me the honor of introducing myself. I am Francis Russell, Duke of Bedford," he said with another polite bow, his hands clasped behind his back.

Maria looked more closely past the rapt expression, at a face that was thin and angular and softened by a wealth of pale blond hair. But overall, his face was plain and his eyes were flecked with just enough muddy brown to make them dull.

"Your brother and I are old friends," he said with a soft smile. "We knew one another at Trinity College, in Cambridge." Maria felt her own pinched expression begin to fade. Her brother had indeed gone to school in Cambridge. This was not simply a petty attempt at flirtation.

"It is a pleasure," she conceded as an unconsciously beguiling smile turned the corners of her rosy lips.

"May I get you a glass of lemonade or perhaps some tea, Mrs. Fitzherbert?" asked another of the anxious young men whom she recognized as the eldest son of the Earl of Coventry.

She nodded. "Lemonade would be lovely."

Then, just when she had begun to feel the first hint of ease in Isabella's absence, the music ended. The dancers poured off the dance floor toward the wall of mirrors beneath the bandbox behind her.

"There she is!" Maria heard one of the young men near her whisper to another.

Like sunflowers in a June breeze, all of her aspiring suitors turned toward the refreshment table and a dramatic, bold-faced beauty in a heavily corseted lilac silk gown. Others stood on chairs and craned their necks to catch a glimpse of her.

Since her brother and Isabella had gone to her side directly from the dance floor, Maria knew that it was the infamous Duchess of Devonshire. The woman was not only confidante to the famous Whig leader Charles James Fox, but more scandalously, her name had been repeatedly linked to the wild Prince of Wales himself.

To be faced with such infamy all in one day, she mused, remembering the Prince's smile and his dangerous flirtation with her on the Mall that afternoon. Suddenly now, all of the men who had fawned after her so dramatically were shifting their attention to the Duchess. Only the captivated Duke of Bedford remained.

"Shall I ask your brother's permission to dance with you then?"

Maria looked back into the soft sensitive face and the lackluster eyes that studied her like a painting. It was the last thing she desired. She wanted to tell him so. But a lifetime of breeding forced her to say instead, "As you wish."

Pleased at what he saw as success, the Duke nodded, then turned to join the collection of other well-heeled noblemen who had gathered around the Duchess. How dull men could be! And how utterly predictable, Maria thought, her pride a little wounded in spite of her disinterest.

"Was that not Francis Russell?" John asked when he and Isabella returned.

"He came to ask me to dance."

"And you refused him? Great God, Maria, how could you have been so foolish? The man is worth a small fortune!"

"He said that you had been friends in Cambridge."

"That was generous of him, to say the least! We shared only a course or two together. He must be quite taken with you to have made it out to be more than that!" John smiled, and the gleam in his dark eyes, filled with expectation, made her cringe.

"I am going to call him over here right now so that you can apologize for your rudeness. We shall say that it is the heat in here," he said, fanning a hand before his flushed face. "He is bound to believe that."

"I'll not apologize! I told His Grace that he would need to ask your permission to dance with me. He made the decision to go fawning, like all of the others, after that Devonshire woman!"

"Oh, splendid! Simply splendid!" He grinned, ignoring her tone. "So then, tell me. Did he seem 'interested'? How did he ask you? Was his tone fair? Insistent? What?"

Maria tossed her head and the tight blond curls fell back on her softly powdered shoulders like honey-colored twists of silk. "He

13

asked me only for a dance, John. That was all. You musn't make it into anything more than that."

"And *you* musn't underestimate the Duke of Bedford. He is not one likely to dally when he sees something that catches his eye! He is a terribly intense fellow. Always has been. Knows precisely what he wants. That much about him was common knowledge at Trinity."

"John Smythe, really!" Isabella puffed, posing her hands on small, padded hips in mock anger. "You speak as if she were not your sister but an article of commerce!"

"My sister is a precious jewel, Isabella, and like all things of value, she too has her price."

Violin bows were drawn back again. Fingers loomed above piano keys. Horns, trumpets, and flutes were readied. The orchestra in a box above the dance floor struck up a new measure and another tune began to fill the stifling hall. Lady Sefton opened her fan, decorated with pink roses and little wisps of ivy.

"Here he comes," she said behind it. "Oh, he is rather plain, isn't he? ... But look at that, he's brought you a lemonade, taken it right out of the hands of the Earl of Coventry's son. How bold! He certainly doesn't look as if he would be. Your brother is right. At the very least, Maria, it is worth a dance."

They had collected beside the same long, sealed window, now opaque with steam, as John smiled and held up a welcoming hand. "Smythe!"

"Francis Russell! I thought that was you!"

"You never told me at school that you had such a beautiful sister," the young Duke declared, gleaming at Maria.

"When we were at school she wasn't nearly so beautiful."

"I was forced to hear about her here in London. Mrs. Fitzherbert's return has made all of the papers, you know."

"Well, Russell, whatever the means, at least you've discovered her. And, as they do say, it is better late than never!"

"I could not agree with you more."

After a flourish of similar and embarrassing banter instigated by her zealous brother, Maria and the Duke of Bedford were pushed out onto the dance floor with a wink and a nudge. She was not certain if she had ever been more embarrassed for and yet at the same time bored by anyone in her life.

14

"If I may say, you are far more beautiful up close than at a distance, Mrs. Fitzherbert," he stammered out a compliment.

"Your Grace is very kind but you needn't flatter me." Maria's dark eyes sparkled with anger in the light of the chandelier. "After all, you already have your dance."

"It was not flattery, Mrs. Fitzherbert, I assure you," he replied, his voice ringing with a thick, clotted sincerity. "It was simply the truth. That is one thing you shall always have from me."

When she looked up at him again, her anger beginning to fade, Maria saw that Francis Russell's slim, colorless face was perspiring. At the points of the dance when they came together, she could feel his hands trembling. Maria knew that he was trying to be charming, but he was trying too hard.

"Then I thank Your Grace for his candor," she finally said, as politely as she could manage.

"...And you must call me Francis. I rely on my title only with my servants and when trying to gain entry to places as popular as Almack's."

Or when you are trying to gain the favor of disinterested ladies, she longed to say. Instead she struggled for something that would sound more polite. "So tell me, Francis, do you spend a great deal of time in London?"

"Not nearly so much as I intend to if I shall be fortunate enough to find you here."

Maria grimaced.

When the last note of the tune came, the Duke of Bedford bowed and led Maria back to her brother and Isabella, who now were engaged in some deep conversation with Lord and Lady Cowper. As they neared, she could tell by her brother's mottled face, and Isabella's discreet yawn behind her fan, that the inevitable topic was politics.

The subjects were always the same. The Tories and the Whigs. The Prince of Wales and the King. One was a horrid villain, the other completely misunderstood. All of England had chosen sides, as had father and son, and no one could seem to get enough of the debate.

"You're absolutely wrong, Smythe, my good man," Lord Cowper was saying. "I tell you, those infernal Whigs only fan the flames that would be better left alone to extinguish!"

15

"And if the King's band of Tories are left on their own, as you say, their brand of corruption shall slowly bleed all of England dry, as certain as we are standing here tonight! No. I say the Prince of Wales was absolutely right to break with his father in this, King or no King."

"Ach," Lord Cowper scoffed into his sagging chin. "The Prince does nothing more than act like a willful child in it. He has made a Whig alliance for no other purpose than to defy his father!"

"Gentlemen, gentlemen, please," the Duke of Bedford interceded tactfully. His voice was pitched with strength as he moved between the two men. "Are we not here to dance?"

Maria looked at him with surprise. It was the first time that evening that she thought of Francis Russell as anything but uninspiring. Perhaps there was a spark of power there after all. After an awkward moment of clearing throats and averted gazes, she watched Lord Cowper's thick lips stretch into a smile.

"Quite right, dear boy," he said, slapping Francis on the back and nodding in agreement. "But political debate is difficult to avoid these days with our King and his heir at such great odds with one another."

"Lady Sefton," Francis interceded again with the same courteous bow he had given Maria. "If you are free for the next dance, I should be honored to accompany you."

"Oh, the pleasure would indeed be mine, sir," she cooed, folding away her fan and taking his arm.

"Well? What do you think?" John asked his sister before the young Duke had quite gotten out of earshot. "Is he not absolutely perfect for you?"

"John, please."

"Well really, Maria, you have been widowed for a year now. Isn't it about time you settle down again?"

"What I would like instead of your impertinence, brother dear," she replied, chuckling at the brother she adored, "is another glass of lemonade."

"If you promise to tell me every single thing that Russell said when I return, then I shall be glad to fetch it for you."

Maria kissed his cheek then nodded toward the refreshment table to urge him to go. As she did, she saw that just beyond the punch bowl the Duchess of Devonshire, wrapped in a froth of lilac silk, was still holding court. A group of young men was fanned out around her chair now like leaves around a brilliant rose.

What is this power she has? Maria wondered as once again she stood alone, leaning against the slim gilt column. Surely friendship with the Prince of Wales alone could not be sufficient to entice men like that. Yes, she was beautiful enough, tall and fair-skinned with hair the color of cinnamon in long cascading ringlets. Her face was cerused, rouged and powdered enough to resemble the perfection of youth...at least in the poorly lit assembly rooms of Almack's. And she was worldly enough, having been declared by the Prince of Wales to be the best bred woman in England. But there must be something more.

She had heard, as all of England had, that along with Charles James Fox, the Duchess of Devonshire exercised more influence over the Prince of Wales than even his mistresses. Looking at her now, completely dominating the room as she did, Maria began to believe that it was true—and she was glad she would never need to face that disingenuous nodding and smiling that so captivated everyone else but which had ruthlessness behind it.

When the dance ended, Isabella and the Duke of Bedford came and stood beside her once again. Now Isabella was fanning herself even more furiously, her carefully powdered face marred by a thin patina of perspiration.

"Why do they allow it to get so bloody warm in here?" she hissed as she dotted her glistening brow with the tip of a lace handkerchief.

Francis smiled. "Ah, Lady Sefton, but then Almack's would not be Almack's if it were a pleasure rather than an obligation."

Then, as suddenly as thunder rolling through a field, into the gentile atmosphere of lemonade, tea cakes, and civilized dances, three liveried footmen ushered in the two most brilliant and scandalous men of the Whig aristocracy. Red-faced and sodden, Charles James Fox slumped against his colleague, the dark-haired and customarily graceful Richard Brinsley Sheridan. Both of their jackets were disheveled and their velvet waistcoats stained beneath. But Fox was by far the more shocking in appearance. A corpulent man with dirty, pepper-colored hair and prominent beetle-brows, he was missing enough silver buttons on his grimy white shirt that his pale bare belly burst through from beneath. The two staggered together across the room.

"How dreadfully vulgar!" sniped Isabella.

"They must have started awfully early today over at Brook's," Bedford supposed.

"Earlier than usual," she said, her arms folded across her chest and her pert face wrinkled into a frown. "They ruin simply everything by coming here in that condition."

"At least one cannot say that Almack's is not amusing," Bedford said back, and his lips curved up with the faint suggestion of a smile.

"Well. I, for one, could use some air," Isabella announced with a little huff. "If you both shall be good enough to excuse me."

Maria caught her cousin by the ribbon-dotted sleeve as she turned away. "I shall go with you."

"Oh, no no. You must stay here and keep this dear man company until our John returns. I shall be no more than a moment."

Before she could object further, Isabella winked in the same unsubtle manner John had earlier. Then she disappeared into a swell of dancers who rushed to get away from the two newest and very drunk guests at Almack's.

"I am afraid my cousin is not very subtle," Maria said after another of the many awkward silences between them.

"Ah, but what Lady Sefton lacks in subtlety she more than makes up for in her discriminating sense of timing. I must confess that I am glad to have a moment alone with you."

She felt the warm, discomforting swell of blood rise up from her slim neck and blossom across her face for the second time that day. In a curious flash, she suddenly saw the image of the Prince of Wales smiling mischievously at her from his carriage. His tongue across his moist lips and the glitter of his brilliant, haunting eyes. But the image paled as quickly as it had appeared and the face of the good-natured Duke loomed before her more hopeful than before. She bit her lower lip and looked around impatiently for John.

"With your permission, madam, I should like to call on you tomorrow," he declared.

Maria turned back, her mind quickly whirling with ways to kindly reject him. Then she met again the dull, spaniel eyes and the slim face now marred with surprising apprehension.

"Would I be likely to find you at home tomorrow at five?" he forged ahead, and his voice cracked.

"Oh, I am sorry," Maria said, trying her best to make it sound sincere. "But I am afraid Lady Sefton has arranged for us to go the opera tomorrow evening. I shall be dressing at five."

She watched his face harden and his jaw begin to set in the face of her rejection. She wanted to leave it alone. Let him thank her for the dance and leave now. He was nice enough, but there was no fire between them, and she knew that there never would be. Still, for all of her disinterest, she could not be cruel enough to refuse him so completely. For that, John would never forgive her. Reluctantly she continued.

"But if your calendar is free at four," she forced herself to say, "you would find both myself and my brother at home and happy to receive you."

The Duke of Bedford grinned triumphantly and took her hand. "I shall count the hours."

With nothing left to say, now that she had done her duty to her brother by agreeing upon a second meeting, Maria turned back toward the crowded dance floor. She was trying not to look too desperate as she searched for John to take her home. But the notion of the sort of passionless connections that loomed before her in the example of the Duke of Bedford had begun to make her feel more than a little ill.

ACROSS THE STREET BEHIND THE elegant Corinthian pilasters and cornice of Brook's Club, George, Prince of Wales, gathered with an assembly of Whig nobles around a green baize gaming table. For more than four hours he had sat with his head hung low against the glowing candlelight. In one hand he held the cards and swatted a persistent fly with them. A continuously full cherry brandy occupied the other.

Faced with appalling losses at both faro and whist, his friends, Fox and Sheridan, had already given up the table to pursue the more reliable pleasures to be had at Almack's. But for George, the passion for women that enslaved his friends had paled. For the Heir to the Throne of England gambling and the company of friends was the only truly dependable mistress.

"No more cards for me, Your Highness. I am completely tapped out," yawned Lord Townshend.

"Nor me," seconded Lord Salisbury.

George looked up from his cards, his elegant square face peaked with surprise. The blue eyes that were usually as limpid as crystal were now, at this late hour, tinged crimson. And still his square, Hanoverian jaw fell with disappointment.

"Oh, do be a sport, Salisbury. Play us just one more round," he coaxed, and swatted the fly again. "It was all such fun."

"Sorry, Your Highness, my wife shall be positively wicked if I lose a single shilling more."

"I'm afraid that I am in the same fix, Your Highness."

Two of the other men surrounding the King's eldest son took this as a welcome cue and pushed their heavy velvet-covered chairs back from the table, preparing to stand.

"Not you as well?"

"It is late, Your Highness."

George looked across at the tall clock cased in ebony at the end of the hall, flickering in the last of the firelight. "It is not even midnight."

"Respectfully, Your Highness, it is after two."

George squinted and looked again at the clock hands. "Ah, yes. So it is...so it is. Very well then, one last wager. No cards. A gentlemen's bet."

Lord Townshend and Lord Salisbury glanced at one another.

Townshend and Salisbury were nearly to the door, it being held open by a very weary and willing doorman. "Tomorrow night, Your Highness?" Salisbury called to the Prince. "We shall all be here by seven."

"Alas, no." George sighed, taking another swill of brandy as he sank back in the overstuffed velvet chair. "Tomorrow night my little brother, Ernest, is dragging me to the opera again. Bloody bore it is, but I did promise."

They were the last to occupy Brook's long vermilion-colored drawing room. It was not the first time. The candles had been snuffed and the perfume-scented logs had fallen to ash. Only red embers glowed from behind the brass fire screen. But George always avoided returning home for as long as he could.

Out in the carriage, he lay his head against the brocade carriage seat, cold night air whistling past a crack in the door as he was whisked down St. James's Street and home toward Carlton House. Across from him sat his valet, Orlando Bridgeman, a slender young man with storm-gray eyes, an angular face, and oily black hair. He was trying desperately to stay awake. When his head fell to his chest, spilling strings of dark hair into his eyes, George looked away. It was all so pathetic at this hour of the morning: Bridgeman, the Prince's mounting debt and, in particular, the loneliness.

The flicker of street lamps traced a path down the deserted London streets and lit the early-morning mist that had settled against the carriage window. It washed the view like a watercolor painting.

George ran a hand across his face as they passed through the gates and past a long colonnaded screen that separated his house from Pall Mall. A device "to bar the gaze of the vulgar," his architect had said when he had proposed it. *A barrier to me,* George believed now.

It surprised him to realize that he had gone so long unshaven. His eyes stung from too much brandy and too little sleep. *I must look dreadful,* he thought, without much concern.

A quarter of an hour later, he stood alone in the center of the dark and impossibly gloomy Blue Salon, clutching an empty bottle of brandy. It was one of the still unrenovated drawing rooms at Carlton House, rooms he was trying to make habitable in spite of the King's calculated frugality.

It was so like his father not to want him to succeed, even at renovating a home into which he had insisted his son and heir relocate.

Just as George began to turn, he saw a shadowy figure near the fireplace, heading toward a door to the garden. The figure of a woman.

"Stop! You there! Who is it?"

After a moment, a short, thickly set woman moved back into the light holding a small dark object with both hands. In the shadow of the moonlight, George saw that it was Belle Pigot.

Memories filtered back when he saw that small, kind face, wrapped so with the lines of age but also with love for him. One memory in particular always came back when he saw her. A moment in his childhood that had changed him forever...

❖   ❖   ❖

21

"GEORGE, YOU MUSTN'T!"

"Oh, I just want to have a bit of fun, that's all. God knows there's precious little of *that* to be had around here!"

George Augustus, the nine-year-old Heir to the Throne of England and his younger brother Frederick scrambled away from the tray of silver-covered dishes that had been set out for supper near their Preceptor's desk. He had been gone from the royal nursery for only a few moments, but that had been long enough for two mischievous brothers.

"Dr. Markham will be furious!" Frederick whispered.

"But just imagine the look on his face when he sees it!"

"I think you should imagine the King's face when he hears of it!"

George playfully cuffed the side of his brother's head. "Oh relax, Freddie." He chuckled, full of a spirit that Prince Frederick found infectious. "You're far too much like the old goat as it is!"

They were two boys who mirrored one another in their ruddy complexions, moppish chestnut curls, and wide blue eyes. In the mind of their father the King of England, however, they were not at all alike. Frederick alone was the child of his heart. As the long paneled doors across the room closed with a click, William Markham, Bishop of Chester and Preceptor to the two eldest princes, strode back across the room.

"Remember now," George whispered. "Just as we planned it."

Markham loomed over the boys in powdered wig, a braided gray waistcoat, and tight black knee breeches. "Very well then. Back to our Latin, hmm?"

"Respectfully," Frederick fumbled, caught completely up now in his elder brother's delicious ruse. "Might we be allowed to stop for today? It is nearly eight o'clock and we have been at our studies since midday."

The Preceptor, lean and craggy-faced, frowned at the younger prince. "You both know full well that His Majesty was very clear when I accepted this position. An idle mind is a mind at risk. We must continue on at least until we finish with the chapter."

"Then hadn't we better eat something? I am certain our good King has no desire to see us starved," George reasoned, his face full of shining innocence as he sat erect in a stiff beechwood chair. "The servants brought supper while you stepped out, and we really should not leave it to get cold."

Markham cast an eye across the room at the linen-draped table covered with silver dishes and a full crystal decanter of wine. He looked back at the wide-eyed boys, still dressed by their father's command like the small children he wished them to remain. Rather embarrassingly instead of breeches and waistcoats, they wore cambric frocks with Valenciennes lace cuffs at their wrists. They were kept, for the most part like this, force-fed Latin, Greek, mathematics, religion, and philosophy for long hours.

They were taught the virtues of hard work and simplicity until they were bleary-eyed, and they were shut off from the excitement and wonders of the rich world that lay beyond the castle walls. One must feel a certain bit of sympathy for their unnatural circumstances, Markham reflected, even if they tended, on occasion, toward the rather high-spirited behavior that the pious King so despised.

The Preceptor inhaled through a long, veined nose, and breathed in the heady aroma of freshly cooked meat laced with thick, rich sauce. "Very well then. Perhaps a short respite for supper is in order."

"You will be dining with us won't you, Dr. Markham?" George asked sweetly. "They've certainly brought enough and I understand that the main course tonight is rabbit. Your favorite."

Markham inclined his head as Frederick shot a nervous glance at his brother. "Your Highness is most kind."

The three moved toward the table set up across the high-ceilinged chamber as two footmen in white gloves drew near to serve them. Markham drew a napkin across his lap. "It smells delightful."

But the moment the silver cover was lifted from the plate, a live gray rabbit sprung out from underneath and lunged at the Preceptor. "Ooh!" he wailed with surprise as he tumbled backward from his chair. The frightened animal leaped across his chest and onto the floor as George and Frederick pealed with laughter—until they saw the King.

Surrounded by his aides and the young Princesses Augusta and Charlotte, His Majesty, King George III, stood at the open door like a statue, firm and unyielding. Two of the footmen who did not see him enter the nursery still dashed across the room after the rabbit. Everything else fell to a hush. The King was a tall, foreboding man with beady coal-black eyes and full pale lips. His white wig contrasted a full face mottled red with anger.

23

Markham struggled to his feet and then bowed.

"Are you all right?" asked the King.

"Certainly, Your Majesty." He winced. "Just a show of high spirits. No harm done really."

"I do not pay you as entertainment for my sons, Dr. Markham," the King said coldly. "I pay you to educate them."

William Markham hung his head. "Yes, Your Majesty."

The King's footfalls were heavy as he moved in black leather shoes with silver buckles toward the two boys. Heads lowered and seemingly repentant, neither youth was laughing now, but it was only one who received the King's royal wrath.

"This was your doing once again, wasn't it, George?"

"No, father! Don't blame him. It was entirely my idea!" Frederick volunteered, stepping protectively out in front of his elder brother. "I brought the rabbit inside!"

"We both know better, my boy," the King replied and then softly patted his favorite son's mop of curly hair. As he looked back at George, his expression was intense and unforgiving. "So, what have you to say for yourself this time?"

George leered up defiantly, crystal blue eyes, his mother's eyes, sparkling in the light from the windows. "I have nothing to say... Your Majesty."

"You did this *only* to defy me. *Just* as you always do."

"It was my idea, father! Truly!" Frederick pleaded.

"Silence!... Markham, get your whip."

"Your Majesty, please. Perhaps I worked your sons too hard today, pushed them too far. After all, they are only just boys. And it was all really rather harmless."

"Silence, I say! Now get your whip!..." the King bellowed, his sharp command ringing in the heavy summer air. "Willful, petulant delinquent! I'll not have a son of mine, much less England's heir, behaving like a common street urchin! Now, raise your frock and bend over... Raise it, I say!"

When the prince would not comply, two of the footmen were summoned to hold down the frightened, struggling youth. "Very well then, Markham. Flog him!"

The Preceptor's face paled. "Respectfully, Your Majesty, I really do not think—"

"Flog him!"

Markham glanced at George. So defiant on the outside, he thought. So full of a need for the love and approval of his father just beneath the surface. Reluctantly, he drew back the whip. These boys were like sons to him. They were so often under his charge. And in spite of their boyish pranks, they loved him as well. He knew that.

Markham felt the pain even before he delivered the first blow. He watched the frightened prince writhe and struggle beneath the grasp of the two sinewy servants for only a moment. Finally, knowing no other choice in the presence of an arrogant King, he drew his hand back and pelted George's bare, ivory bottom with full force.

"Again!" the King cried as leather cracked against flesh. "Again, I say!"

Frederick hid his face in his hands and felt the tears fall between his fingers as his brother, the best and only friend he had been allowed in the world, was beaten until he bled. The Princesses Augusta and Elizabeth were rushed crying from the scene as George collapsed onto a priceless Chinese carpet.

"Now, so help me God, this time you shall agree to live by the will of our Lord and by the will of your King, not by your own design! Do you understand?"

George's eyes were downcast but his face was still filled with an insolence that infuriated his father.

"For the love of God, answer him!" Frederick pleaded as blood trickled from the open wounds down George's bare, milk-white legs.

"I asked you if you understood!"

"I understand only too well," he murmured.

"I did not hear you!"

"YES!"

The King held up a hand and a pale, shaken William Markham finally dropped the whip to the floor. He could not bear to look at what he had done to such a sweet and spirited boy. His Majesty moved toward Frederick and, with purposeful cruelty, brought his second son to his chest. He kissed the top of the boy's head with animated affection. "Very well, George. Now that you have learned your lesson, you may come and kiss your King good night as well."

William Markham closed his eyes as George staggered onto his knees like a wounded animal, then onto his feet.

25

He was unable, even for the risk, to keep the hostility from his voice. As he leered at his father, tears rained down his sweet, unmarred face. "Respectfully, 'Your Majesty,' I would rather burn in the fires of hell than press my lips against your flesh!"

"George!" Frederick gasped.

William Markham covered his mouth with his hand. But unexpectedly, the King began to laugh, loud and unrestrained, hands on hips. "Very well, little man. It is not an act of feigned affection which I relish any more than you. But for your vulgar mouth about it you will retire without your supper. You will learn restraint, by God in Heaven, if I have to beat you to death to do it!"

When the King had gone, George collapsed once again onto the carpet. Frederick raced to his side along with Markham and two footmen. "Oh, George, I'm so sorry," the boy said, and wept.

"Dear God, how I hate him! How I do so long to make him pay!"

"You mustn't say it, George! He's our father!"

"I'm not his son, Freddie," he whispered. "No amount of wanting will make it so. But someday he shall pay for how he has treated me, if I have to become the bane of his existence to do it. That I do swear!"

"You don't mean that, George! You're just hurt."

"I mean every word."

George looked up at Markham, who was standing over them, his face still pale and replete with guilt. It was an expression that pained George almost as much as the beating. He had only meant the jest as a bit of fun. This was a man he had not wished to see hurt.

"And about the rabbit, Dr. Markham," he said in a low voice. "I am sorry."

"It is already forgotten, my dear boy."

George let the two footmen who only moments before had held him captive now help him to his feet. It had been their duty. He understood that, and finally the wounds that at first had been numb now had begun to burn. He welcomed the excruciating sensation. He knew from experience that it was the only thing to make him forget the pain he felt in his heart.

When the servants had left the young prince alone in his dark bedchamber, a curved side door opened with a little squeal, then quietly closed again. A short, stocky woman dressed in pleated yellow silk and a white lace cap moved quietly toward the bed and sat down on the edge beside him. George lay prostrate on the embroidered bed-cover, weeping into his hands.

"Let me see, child," said Belle Pigot with a motherly tenderness.

"I cannot," George cried. "You're a woman."

"I am an old woman. Now let me see."

The woman who had worked for the royal family in some capacity most of her life lifted his frock gently and fought from gasping when she saw the long bloody slash marks across his bottom. It was as Markham had warned her. The poor child had been beaten like a dog, and all for showing the spirit of youth. Pitiful. Pitiful indeed. Did His Majesty not understand that with a boy like this it was bound to make him rebel all the more? She went to the basin at the end of the bed and rang a cloth through the water.

"I don't understand him, Belle," George pleaded as she carefully dotted his wounds. "...why he hates me so, and yet Freddie can do no wrong."

"You must never tell His Majesty I said so," she whispered, "for saying so might well cost me my life, but you have real spirit, child. I believe that frightens the King. He cannot be assured of the fate of the country if he cannot control his successor."

"His successor?" He laughed bitterly. "What of the fate of his son? He's supposed to love me, isn't he?"

"That he is, child." She sighed, stroking his chestnut curls with gentle fingers. "Unfortunately, things in this life are not always as they should be. But you can rise above this. I know, in spite of his neglect, that you have the will to become a great king one day. If you desire it, I believe you can leave a legacy far greater than your father's. Only, you must not let this anger destroy your life. Promise me, my dear sweet George, that you will not close yourself off to love...not let it be your undoing."

In his mind, George saw his father's hard face full of an expectation he would never be able to fulfill. Through the image he heard Belle's tender concern. But she did not understand. No one did. How could they comprehend what it was like to live without love, to live life as nothing more than an object to be groomed and cultivated into an image, with no thought for feeling or tenderness?

It was unfair and it was cruel. Young he might have been, that much George knew. Still, beside him sat Belle Pigot, a gentle and caring woman who had been a part of his life for as long as he could remember. He would not disappoint her. He could not.

"Promise me, child," she said again in a coaxing timbre.

Looking up at her sweet, heart-shaped face, eyes dark and deep and filled with concern, George knew that he must answer her. But he could never mean what she wanted him to say. The damage had already been done.

"I promise," he finally lied, and let her embrace him until the tears and the fearsome rage subsided.

THE MEMORY FADED AWAY, BACK into the corner of his mind where he kept all of the other vulnerabilities of his youth. All the little moments that had brought him to this tumultuous place in his life he occupied now. George leveled his gaze and looked straight into the sweet face of the woman who was both mother and friend.

"Why are you not home? It's nearly three," he asked as he came the rest of the way across the frayed blue and gold carpet to meet her. "And what have you got there?"

At first she did not answer him. Before anything else came into view he could see her eyes, deep dark soulful eyes rimmed with the shadows of age. He could tell that she had been crying.

"It is a vase. I took it from your bedchamber," she said, her face coloring with emotion. "I am sorry, George. I just did not know what else to do."

"What is it, Belle?" he asked, his resonant voice full of concern yet free of reproach as he put his arm around her.

"It is Charles."

"Your brother, Charles?"

She set the priceless vase down on a table and looked back at him. "He is ill. Very ill."

"I'm sorry," he said softly. "I didn't know."

"No one did. I thought at first that he would recover. I did all that I could. Now that my father is dead, George, Charlie is all that I have left in the world, and I cannot lose him. I cannot!"

"Here. Come and sit beside me," he said and led the woman he loved, as if she were his own mother, to sit with him on a faded blue settee. George hadn't a care that she had just confessed to stealing a priceless vase. He would have given her the world for what, as a boy, she had given to him.

"What has happened?"

"The doctors tell me that he needs to be sent to Madeira, where the air is pure, if he is to survive this."

George took her hand, fleshy and slightly cold, and squeezed it. "What can I do?"

"It is difficult to ask."

"Anything, Belle. I hope you know that."

"Your family has always been very generous through the years, but even though I have sold everything I have, I still don't have the sort of money it takes to send someone on an extended trip like the one he needs."

George rose to his feet, tall and so commanding. "Just see Southampton in the morning and tell him how much you need."

"Lord Southampton turned me down this afternoon."

Her words hung in the air between them for a moment until he realized what she had said. It could not be. Southampton would never…He had always understood the tie to Belle. Slowly, she too rose back up and faced him, so small, square and simply spoken. Her face was sweet and full in the moonlight, covered with a pale net of fine lines. Her small lips were soft pink, pursed like a rosebud.

"There must be some mistake. He knows how dear you are to me."

"He made himself quite clear, George. His precise words were that Your Highness was not in a position free enough at the moment to finance such a journey."

George pulled her to his chest. Yet one more burden when the King intentionally refused him ample money on which to live and finance a proper household. But no matter what the cost, Belle Pigot was the one person he could not see disappointed. Her brother's journey was one he would gladly finance. Somehow.

"Make your plans for Charles," he whispered as he held her.

"I'm so sorry about the vase. I just didn't know what else to do."

"You shall have your money by tomorrow."

She looked up at him with new tears glistening in her dark eyes. "You know that I shall never be able to repay you."

George hugged her again and then smiled. "Old friend, I was just going to say the same thing to you."

29

THOMAS KEATE LOOMED OVER THE grand canopied bed with the other servants of the bedchamber late the next morning just as the prince began to wake. The room was still darkened by the heavy damask draperies and he could not tell if it was day or night.

"What time is it?"

"Half past eleven, Your Highness," replied Keate, the prince's physician.

"Oh, my head is splitting. Do be merciful and let me be for another hour, will you, Southampton?" George whispered, turned on the satin bolster, and pulled the white Lyonnais silk sheet up over his head.

After his visit with Belle Pigot, he'd been awake most of the rest of the night trying to find an escape from his own financial worries, a maze that had trapped him for a long time now.

Charles Fitzroy, First Baron of Southampton, a small, brittle little man with clipped speech and hair almost as dark as his eyes, was undaunted. "Your Royal Highness has consented to attend tea at the Duchess of Devonshire's, and before that you've got your correspondence and your meeting with the new architects for Carlton House."

After a moment, George folded back the thin swanskin blankets and leered up at two Lords of the Bedchamber who stood beside his physician, Keate. One was holding a silk robe. A crystal snifter of brandy was held ready by the other.

"What time did you say it was, Keate?"

"Half past eleven, Your Highness."

Across the room, a footman drew back the long, green draperies. Looped on brass rods, they were folded into gold tassels as shafts of daylight bled into the room in an attempt to replicate a sunrise. At the same time, the incense burners, two elephants in cloisonné enamel, were lit, then the fire beside his bed. The scented wood cracked and popped in the heavy silence.

As George stood before a gilt mirror, Edward Bouverie, one of the two Grooms of the Chamber, guided one arm and then the other into the sleeves of the Prince's red Chinese robe.

"Very well, Charles. No doubt you've seen my Keeper of the Privy

Purse. Tell it to me straightaway then. How much did we lose last night?"

Lord Southampton hesitated by clearing his throat. George's lips thickened with disdain and he rolled his eyes impatiently.

"Straight, I say!"

"Five hundred pounds, Your Highness."

The King was withholding money again, so he had gone to Brook's Club initially hoping to make enough money at least to pay some of his servants, if not some of the repairs on the roof. Last evening had only made things worse. George ran a hand slowly across his face where a day old beard now darkened his pale skin. He felt the familiar sinking in the pit of his stomach.

"Perhaps Your Highness should not gamble for a while."

"And what other way than that do you propose I earn money on my own? Perhaps I should take a position pouring ale at DeBerry's!" he snapped. "You know very well that I have people depending on me, Charles! Servants with families to feed, and the King has left me this decrepit old house in constant need of repairs as punishment for trying to find some bit of independence! If I give up, I let him win, and that I cannot do!"

By trying to bring his dream of Carlton House to life and create something magnificent on his own which his father could not destroy, George had unwittingly dug his own regal grave. It was clear to him only now. The King had granted his son a separate dwelling—this old run-down place here in London, not only to be rid of him but to cruelly flaunt his authority. George needed his father, and he needed the royal purse.

It was all-out war, with money and power the King's heaviest weaponry.

Public humiliation of a cruel King was the only way the Prince of Wales saw that he had been left to retaliate. George had sworn since he was a boy that he would fight back. And so he had.

The father was pious, so the son dallied with women.

The father was a Tory. So the son became a Whig.

Handsome. Wild. Untamable... and impossibly lost.

"I understand that you refused Mrs. Pigot an advance of her salary," he said, leaning back at his dressing table and folding his arms across his chest.

"It pained me to do it, sir, but considering our present circumstances, I felt I had no other choice."

His voice was insistent and deep, his eyes coldly clear. "First thing this morning, I want you to see that one thousand pounds is sent to her house."

"Respectfully, Your Highness, you haven't one thousand pounds left to give. Which is precisely what I told the lady."

George heaved a heavy sigh and looked around the room. "Why did none of you tell me her brother was so ill when you know that he is the only family she has left?"

The men of George's staff glanced at one another. "Respectfully," Southampton began, "we felt certain that Your Highness had enough with which to contend these days. We had not wish to burden you further."

After a moment, he wiped a hand across his face. *Another day of it,* George thought bleakly, as he watched his valet preparing the ivory powder to brush clean his hair. The carefree appearance of royalty was nothing but an old and awful joke.

For a moment he felt as old and as tired as his father, and as bored with a life that most would have killed to have. If he hoped to help his dear Belle Pigot, it would be either with more gambling or by reasoning with the King. As of last evening, gambling had failed.

The sun moved behind the scudding clouds, and the bedchamber grayed, darkening the green lampas silk on the walls to black. Without waiting to be asked, Orlando Bridgeman poured another brandy for the Prince. He set it on the dressing table beside a collection of silver-topped bottles and jars, patch boxes, and little enamel snuffboxes.

Again George ran his hand across his face. This time more slowly. Then, as though trying to summon the energy, he took in a breath and forced himself to gaze up at the image reflected in the small gold-framed mirror. It surprised him that the vision before him was still young and vibrant when he felt so miserably old and disillusioned.

The stolid first Earl of Onslow, Lord of the Bedchamber, opened the long paned window beside the dressing table with a little click and George could feel the cool breeze begin to revive him. The fragrance of new spring roses rushed at him with almost noxious sweetness from the garden below.

"Your Highness has received another correspondence from Lady Campbell," Onslow said softly as George opened one of the crystal bottles and began to smooth oil of cacao across his face.

"Oh, splendid! That is all I need!"

"As you have now parted, Her Ladyship says that she wishes the return of the locket of hair she gave to you during your..." He stumbled for the word that would not offend the Prince at this sensitive hour of the day. "...courtship," he finally chose, pulling forth the small, fragrant missive.

George turned slowly, his eyes focusing on his aide. "Oh, she does, does she?"

To women, he was still a trophy to be fought over and won. England's prize.

His lips curled with the words and the pale dash of brows above his eyes narrowed. He was caught in his own web of problems, Belle's brother was dying, and that foolish, greedy woman for whom he had actually once begun to care—who cared nothing for him beyond his title, wished for something so banal as the return of a lock of her hair? She was like all the rest. In the end, she too had betrayed him.

She had sold their story for money to the *Morning Herald*, detailing everything between them. The wound had been deep and lethal. After a moment, George reached down and with powerful fingers pulled a black leather case from one of the drawers.

"Open it," he said in a chillingly even voice, as he selected another bottle from his dressing table.

Onslow, his face full and sallow complexioned, looked up at the Prince. Then he carefully took the case and pushed back the lid. Inside, wound in a tangle of faded pastel-colored ribbons in hues of gold, fire, and smoke, like tiny coiling creatures, were dozens of different locks of ladies' hair.

"Send the entire case to Lady Campbell," George said dryly, "and tell her to choose."

George turned back around and opened a jar of perfumed almond powder. Onslow and the others watched silently as he began lightly to dust his own face, having quickly put the image of Lady Augusta Campbell from his mind. There was something more important to consider. If he wished to see Belle Pigot have the money she

33

deserved, there was no other choice. God help him, but he would have to see the King.

TWO HOURS LATER, GEORGE MARCHED into his father's private drawing room at Buckingham House. Possessing a confidence that no one, especially the King, would be allowed to see through, the Prince of Wales had refused to be announced.

He knew how it irritated His Majesty.

Bathed in a tender blue light, the drawing room was filled with superb pieces of art, many of them from France. Gobelin tapestries warmed the walls, along with paintings by Vernet, Greuze, and Le Main. Cabinets and tables were stuffed with China and topped with bronzes and marble busts and countless gold clocks, girandoles, and incense burners.

How comfortably he did live, thought George, while his eldest son was forced to plead for absolutely everything.

The King, who was in the middle of a cello lesson, struggled to play a tune for his instructor as George stood watching. "I desire a word with Your Majesty."

The King did not stop playing. "It has been a long time since you and I have had anything to say to one another."

"Ever the magnanimous father, I see," George bristled.

His Majesty, still a forbidding presence, broad-shouldered and humorless in a short blue waistcoat, white silk shirt, and tight gray breeches, finally looked up. He heaved an aggravated sigh but he did not look directly at his son. "Very well. What is it this time, George?"

"I need money."

"How might I have known you would say that? But then you certainly don't come to me for anything else, do you?"

"Your Majesty has never given me much of a desire to come to you for anything else."

The King crooked an eyebrow and glanced at George for only a moment. "Ah. In the mood for sparring, are we?"

George clenched his hands into bloodless angry fists and then released them, trying to remind himself why he had come. *Think of Belle Pigot. Think of her need...*

34

"Your Majesty should know by now that I would not deign to come here groveling for myself. It is for the staff you assigned me."

The King rolled his eyes. "Oh, really George. Could you not come up with anything more original than that?"

The confession about Belle Pigot burned in his throat but he would not, could not, give his father the satisfaction of hearing about something—nor someone, who truly mattered to him.

"You have been given enough money to sustain your dwelling in modest terms, and to pay your staff *if* you spend wisely," the King continued on, looking away once again.

"Then give me a duty. Give me something to do! Let me earn the funds I need! I am your heir, for Lord's sake! I have a right to a function with some meaning!"

"Ah, so the delight in your renegade ways is finally paling a bit, is it?"

"Damn you!" George raged and slammed a powerful fist on a marble-topped table. "You love having me come to you like this at every turn! I think your greatest desire in the world is to see your own son fail!"

"I have wanted you to learn a lesson, George. You must learn to economize before I shall see you granted anything more. Even a duty would be too much reward at present...It is only that simple."

The same old argument in which they had engaged a dozen times came tumbling forth now, sliding across George's tongue on a hot bitter wave. "Paying my staff a decent wage and making that miserably run-down old house livable, since when is that so great a crime?"

The King shot him a second look, this one of contempt. "Oh, I know the sort of *living* you do! About your wild gambling with that pitiable sot, Fox!"

"I gamble so that I am able to pay the debts that *you* refuse to pay!"

"That is not what the papers and the caricatures all over London say!" the King taunted.

"Of course not! There is no story in ingenuity!"

They were face-to-face now, like two bulls, both red-faced, their muscular bodies tensed. "I'll not change my mind about this, George, so you may as well save your breath. One day when you agree to take an appropriate bride, then of course the matter shall be reconsidered."

"Now *that* is really at the heart of it, isn't it? Control! It is not a lesson at all. I have a staff, people counting on me to put bread on their plates, and you are still trying to control my life, my actions, and even my beliefs! It is just as it was when I was a child! Well finally, thank God in His Heaven, I am a child no longer!"

"Then quit behaving like one! You with your damnable defiance, your women, and your gambling! All just to embarrass me! Why can you not be more like Frederick?"

The remark stung. George stepped back.

Always Frederick. Second in line. First in their father's heart. It always had been. No matter what he did, no matter how he tried, he would never measure up to the King's favorite son. So long ago he had stopped trying. Publicly, he had cultivated an image of the man his father always believed he was. Willful. Spoiled. Useless. It was all part of the elegantly contrived deception. A shield to the disappointment.

"You could have spared us both from this," George said more softly. "If only just once, Father, you had made me feel that you loved me."

The King's eyes were cold and unforgiving. "You know the problem with you, George? You're weak. You have no spine! Love? Hah! You would never hear Frederick going on about such a thing!"

"That's because Freddie never needed to ask for it! To him it was always given freely!"

The King smiled sardonically, then rolled his dark eyes. "Really, George, are you quite finished?" There was a thick, painful pause between them before George watched his father, a stranger to him, poise the bow again.

The disappointment of childhood was open and raw on his smooth, elegant face as he said, "Your Highness has reminded me with characteristic cruelty that, as father and son, we were finished long ago. Rest assured, that is one fact I'll not forget again."

The King paused, then looked back at his cello. "As you wish."

George moved across the room in long strides, but then stopped when he reached the open door. "You know," he said as he pivoted back around, "I am not certain I ever realized fully what a hateful man you really are."

The King's lips twisted in a sneer as he glanced up. "George, my boy. You make it easy."

A DELICATE SÈVRES VASE OF blue and gold sat alone on a polished satinwood table in George's receiving room at Carlton House. A gift to his grandfather from the King of France, the vase was priceless, both in money and in sentiment. His grandfather had given it to him personally shortly before his own death. It was the same vase Belle had attempted to steal the night before, now returned to its place.

Bridgeman came into the room and closed the paneled double doors. "How was your visit with the King, sir?"

"Sell it." George pointed, ignoring the question.

"But the vase, sir, it is priceless!" gasped his valet, knowing not only the value but the history of it.

"That dear old woman is worth far more to me than a piece of china, Bridgeman."

"But is there no other way?"

"Apparently not. And I wish her to have the money."

Bridgeman waited a moment, considering whether or not to try and persuade him against it. In the end, he wisely chose not to. He knew how the Prince had always valued that vase. The rift with the King was old and deep. So were the wounds.

"Yes, sell it, Bridgeman, and as discretely as you can. I certainly do not need to add to London's already fertile gossip mill about my spending. When you have the money I wish you take it to Belle at once. And make no explanation of how it was obtained. Give her the thousand pounds she needs for her brother plus another five hundred pounds for herself. Then see the rest of the profit divided equally between my staff and their families for money they are owed."

"As Your Highness wishes," Orlando replied, watching the downward spiral of a handsome, misunderstood young prince to whom he was devoted, and entirely incapable of doing anything to stop it.

LATER THAT AFTERNOON, THE PRINCE of Wales stood outside of the Palladian Devonshire mansion facing Green Park. He was completely transformed from the angry young man who had gone to Buckingham House hoping to reach an unmoving King.

He would get over it. And, more important, he would survive. He would pay his devoted staff even if he had to sell every last stick of furniture and precious art in Carlton House.

George was through trying to reach a man with no heart.

As the prince's footman ran ahead to sound the brass door knocker, George lingered in a fresh costume of black velvet lined with gray satin and topped with his signature white cravat. His hair had been oiled, perfumed, curled, and powdered. His nails had been clipped and jewelry added to his short, powerful hands. The odor of brandy had been swilled away with a wash of peppermint and now he smelled pleasantly only of civet.

When the long black door was opened by a liveried servant, the laughter, the chatter of guests, and the rich sounds of music tumbled out from behind him. He was late. Fashionably late. Everyone else had arrived. But no matter. It was always better to make an entrance. That was one thing of value he had learned from his father. He steadied himself on a stylish malacca cane and stepped into the black and white marble foyer.

"Into the fire once again," George grumbled to himself with an imperceptible little sneer and the glib, seasoned boredom of a much older man.

He was half hidden by long powder-blue draperies as he removed his gloves and hat and handed them along with his cane to Georgiana's butler. Then he peered into the drawing room where London's most noble Whig members gathered. The political party that had nearly made a difference. The Duke of Portland whispering to Edmund Burke. There was Sheridan in the corner with a serving maid, which did not surprise him. Then he saw Fox. His paunchy, graceless companion was slouched against the fireplace hearth, a drink in one hand, the other groping none other than Elizabeth Armistead, one of George's own recently cast-off paramours, yet another woman who had betrayed him.

"Bloody opportunist," George muttered, feeling an unexpected spark of jealousy. This was not the first time the more prudent Fox had speedily advanced on one of his discards.

As he stood contemplating the coupling of his former mistress and his portly, round-faced friend, the Duchess of Devonshire spied him lingering in the foyer half hidden behind the velvet drapery. Instantly she broke her conversation with Lord Charlemont and flew across the crowded drawing room, her satin gown billowing out like a hyacinth-colored sail behind her.

"And precisely where have *you* been?" she asked, taking both of his hands, her slim face smoldering with irritation. "We were all becoming so worried!"

Despite the fact that Georgiana was his most intimate friend, it would have done him no good at all to tell her the truth about going to see the King. She had warned him not to do it, knowing full well where it would lead.

"I had an unexpected visitor at Carlton House," he lied. "But I concluded my business the moment I was able, and now I am ready to cast myself completely under your very potent spell."

Georgiana lowered her clever, sea-green eyes and smiled. "Do come in then and join the others," she said softly as she took his arm, the lines in her face having softened in the glow of the drawing-room candlelight.

"Ah, Your Highness. Good to see you again," said Georgiana's husband, the portly and ruddy-complexioned fifth Duke of Devonshire, as he came up behind them.

George smiled feebly, his mouth aching already from the predictability of it all. He scanned the room for someone, anyone, to rescue him from the tedious afternoon, which he knew from experience, lay ahead. Unfortunately, there were only the regulars. Fox still tête-à-tête with Elizabeth Armistead. Sheridan still watching the serving maid bend and stoop as she attended the other guests. And Lord and Lady Spencer, both parading back and forth before a long gold-framed mirror, admiring their own new summer costumes. He could not have felt more bored.

Circumstances within the Whig Party had not had the same energy for nearly a year. Since the shining hour of the Whigs' "Coalition Ministry" had come so abruptly to an end. Since Fox, that brilliant, unwieldy paradox had been forced from office, retaining only his place in Parliament. Yet they all still met like this, all the key players in that brilliant supplanting of the King's Tory government, with Georgiana Devonshire as their Helen of Troy. All of them still making plans, discussing strategy, for the time when they might rise up once again. The Prince of Wales, the most famous

Whig, despite his current difficulties, was obliged to be a part of their vision.

Just as he began to stifle a yawn, Georgiana squeezed his arm. She made an excuse to her husband and, hoping to see a spark of the old George she knew and loved, drew him aside "By the way, darling, I nearly forgot to mention something. I'm going to Bath again. I've heard that things are finished with you and...oh, what was her name?"

His eyes narrowed, remembering the betrayal. "Augusta."

"Ah, yes, wasn't it though. Well, I am afraid you shall simply have to muddle through for a few days here without me, and yet so soon on the heels of your separation with Fox's latest mistress over there."

He lifted a brow. "Elizabeth is his mistress already, is she?"

"Simply everyone is talking about them. Oh, didn't you know? Poor dear Armistead girl from the wrong side of London. She hasn't a chance, of course, of keeping anyone of *real* means, past what I should expect would be a few well-spent afternoons."

Georgiana was an acquired taste to be sure. But she had been a friend, a *good* friend. And that was what he tried to think about at moments like these. "When do you plan to return?"

"Not until the tenth of the month."

George felt himself stiffen. He didn't want it to matter, not with anyone. "You assured me you would be here to cohost the ball for the Whig Party at the end of the week."

"Well I know I did, darling. But plans change," she said blithely.

George stopped near a serpentine-fronted table, topped with a bust of her husband. He ran his finger down the tip of the marble nose. *So she means to try it again,* he thought.

Lately, whenever she sensed that he needed her friendship most, Georgiana would go away unexpectedly. Doubtless her hope was that he would grow desperate for her companionship and her counsel, that her control over him would become more absolute. It only infuriated him. Now even Georgiana, the woman he cared most about in all the world, was trying to manipulate him, and not very subtly.

"Postpone your trip until after the ball."

Her expression was distracted. "Oh, my dear. I am afraid I cannot. I already have made my travel plans. I leave tomorrow."

He glared at her as much in anger as disappointment "Then whom, precisely, would you suggest I escort in your stead?"

"What about Mrs. Armistead?" she dared to ask. "We both know the poor dear would do anything for you. And I am certain Fox would understand if you borrowed her for the evening."

"Elizabeth Armistead is not you," he spat, infuriated by the game.

"Ah," Georgiana gave a victorious little half laugh, twirled her slim hand in the air as capriciously as a butterfly. "How true...how true."

GEORGE REMAINED AT DEVONSHIRE HOUSE only so long as he was required by propriety to do. He was angry that Georgiana was trying to manipulate him again. Even she was just like all of the rest, really—just another person, *another woman,* trying to control him.

As they crossed down Piccadilly with a fleet of other carriages and post chaises, he tapped the embroidered roof with the tip of his malacca cane. The coach lurched to a stop. George then spoke in an even, calculated tone to his valet, who sat beside him.

"Tell the driver to go to Brook's Club. I am nowhere near ready to face the opera, and I do not intend to do so in this condition."

"But you drank almost nothing at Devonshire House," Orlando Bridgeman said. "Your Highness is as sober as a Rector on Sunday."

"Precisely, my good man. Quite precisely."

When Bridgeman had imparted the Prince's instructions to the driver and returned to the cabin of the coach, they moved on down Piccadilly and turned onto St. James's Street. The wheels clicked beneath them as George pulled a small silver flask from the folds of his cloak and took a long swill of cherry brandy.

"And after you leave me at the club, you are to return to Devonshire House."

Bridgeman looked at him with widened eyes. "Your Highness?"

"Let us simply say that Fox's companion, Mrs. Armistead, and I have some...unfinished business, and this evening I find, much to my own surprise, that I am of a mind to conclude it."

No one, even Georgiana, would tell him, by God, who was suitable and who wasn't. He took a crisp white calling card from his coat and handed it to Bridgeman, then quickly returned his sights to the

41

view of St. James's Street, which passed by in a whirl of brick and stone, just beyond the glass carriage window.

"This evening, I shall be in my box at the opera until eleven. That should be enough time for the lady to see to her obligations with Fox. Tell her privately that she is to wait for me in my withdrawing room. See that she is admitted to my house without incident."

"And if she refuses?"

"She shall not refuse," George replied blandly. Then his brilliant eyes suddenly darkened to sapphire as he added in a bitter tone — no longer speaking of Elizabeth Armistead but of the scheming Duchess who mistakenly believed that she ruled him. "If it is a game she wants, by God, then it is a game she shall have!"

No one had that kind of control over his life. *No one*. And it was impossible to imagine that anyone — especially a woman, ever would.

CHAPTER TWO

MARIA GATHERED HER SKIRTS AND hurried beside Isabella up the stone stairs that led to the King's Theater. Her lips were still parted in surprise. They had passed quickly by the prostitutes in their huge, plume-feathered hats, who paraded beneath the sputtering street lamps. For propriety's sake, she could not bear to look beyond them at the well-heeled gentlemen who beckoned them from their hackney coaches or lacquered post chaises. She was too afraid of seeing someone that she might know.

"So they truly are ladies of—" She fumbled unsuccessfully for the euphemism rather than the word.

"My, you certainly have led a sheltered life at Twickenham." Isabella laughed carelessly and then added, "Of course they are. My dear girl, this is London!"

With its five tiers of boxes gilded in gold and hung with crimson velvet draperies, situated in the Haymarket, this was London's most luxurious theater. But Novosielsky's grand opera house also featured accommodations for the less grand.

Below them was a gallery and a pit upon which Isabella and her husband, Charles, could look down for entertainment before the performance began. There, the poorer classes played cards, laughed, and whispered about the ambitious middle-class ladies who had paid their ten shillings to sit among them with the hope of being noticed.

Maria spread her fan, which matched her cream satin gown, and fluttered it nervously before her face as Isabella waved across the theater to the Lord and Lady Townshend in another of the boxes.

"I believe the Duke of Bedford is going to ask our dear Jack for your hand in marriage," Isabella cooed and leaned in toward Maria, as she waved. "I watched him nearly the entire time and he was entirely besotted by you. Yes, after how splendidly things went this afternoon, I am certain of a proposal."

"I certainly hope not," Maria said sharply, then rested her fan for a moment on the tip of her nose.

Below them, the outrageously dressed fops and dandies who reveled in making a nuisance of themselves were parading up and down the pit. Some were showing off their new waistcoats and tight knee breeches while others were tapping their canes and snapping the lids of their snuffboxes to gain even more attention.

As Isabella gazed down at them she asked, "Why ever not?"

"Because I do not love him and I know that I shall never love him."

Isabella looked back at her companion. Her lower lip, pursed like a tiny bud, dropped in amazement before she broke into a shrill fit of laughter. "Oh, Maria, you are really so droll. Is she not droll, Charles?"

"I am nearly nine and twenty, Isabella, twice married already, and I do not think it too much to ask to find love with at least one of my husbands."

"Take a lover for that!" Isabella laughed again. "Everyone else does. A catch like the Duke of Bedford is far too important to waste on adolescent sentiments."

"I'll not marry him, no matter what anyone says."

"I am afraid you may have no choice in the matter. He and your brother were closeted privately for nearly a quarter of an hour after you had rather rudely gone upstairs this afternoon."

The house lamps were dimmed as low as her spirits and the curtains began slowly to part as a swell of music rose up to drown out Isabella's protestations. Maria leaned back in her velvet-covered chair and looked at the stage. But her mind could not have been further away. She could not bear the thought of a life as companion to a bore like Francis Russell.

There must be something more for her, and to find it, whatever it might be, Maria was willing to wait.

As her mind moved further and further from the evening's entertainment, it wandered strangely toward her carriage ride the day before. The sun through the windows. The glint of light through the trees. She could feel herself blush when she thought of the Prince of Wales smiling and nodding at her.

She smiled to herself in the safety of the dimly lit Opera House as she considered that everything she had heard about him was true. The mistresses. The all-night gambling. His outrageous temper. His tempestuous romances. If there were men like that in London, as Isabella Sefton claimed, she had never met one. Every man she had ever known was like the Duke of Bedford. Rich, proper—and so impossibly dull.

By the end of the first act, when the house lamps were lit once again, Maria sat up in her chair, bathed in gold lamplight, and stretched her arms. She prepared to yawn when she felt someone looking at her from the next box. The sensation was unmistakable, yet she was certain that, as the lights were dimmed, there had been no one there. It was the Royal Family's box, Lord Sefton had told her, rarely used this season by any of the family with the political tension between the King and his son at such a great height.

Maria stiffened in her chair, drawn by the sensation of someone beside her. She looked at Isabella, who, to her surprise, was slouched in her own seat, lips parted, dozing. Lord Sefton too was oblivious, holding up a silver pair of opera glasses, spying into the boxes across the way for gossip he could take to Brook's Club tomorrow.

No matter who was looking at her, it was not proper to return the gaze. Besides, any manner of things could be happening in these shadowy opera boxes. And often were!

She flicked her fan nervously and it opened with a snap. It would not be long before the second half. She waited a moment, fluttering her painted fan. It was terribly warm in the crowded theater, full of as many competing perfumes as Almack's had been. Finally, inevitably, in spite of her resolve, curiosity overwhelmed her. As cautiously as she dared, Maria turned her head until she could safely look from the corner of her eye. There beside her in the next box was that same dangerous smile as the day before, the same ice-blue eyes glittering in the freshly lit lamp glow. When he saw her turn, the Prince of Wales nodded to her again.

Quickly, she looked away, her cheeks flushing.

But few details had escaped her. George had been sitting beside his younger brother Ernest, no more than a boy. The Prince of Wales, however, looked every bit the mature and dashing royal who absolutely took her breath away.

He wore a high white cravat, dashing powder-blue tailcoat, and silver waistcoat beneath. The color made his eyes seem all the more dazzling. In the shadows the lamplight cast, he looked even more dangerous than he had in the light of day. Chestnut-colored hair tinged with red highlights and then stylishly powdered, he was the most magnificently handsome man she had ever seen. She turned away quickly.

Then, just when Maria thought she could be bold enough to return his nod, the power in his stare drew her back again. She saw him draw a hand before his mouth and lean toward his brother. The younger Prince bent forward to look at her and, to her complete horror, they both began to whisper to one another. Her pale cheeks burned with embarrassment. She was relieved when the house lamps were finally dimmed again and the audience fell to a hush. It had been foolish to imagine that the Prince of Wales had been doing anything but toying with her. For a moment she had let her imagination take control. *Silly fantasy,* she thought.

"I KNEW IT! HE MEANS to marry you! I tell you, Maria, it is a miracle that it could have happened so quickly! But apparently he is a man who knows his mind!"

Before the sun had spread fully across the pale blue canopied bed, John Smythe swept past the carved oak doors and tore unannounced directly into the alcove in his sister's bedchamber.

"He came at dawn, he was so eager to know my position! Of course I told him it would be the greatest honor to accept someone so distinguished as he as my brother-in-law..."

Maria came from sleep's dark place and began to hear the words before she felt the power to open her eyes. But marriage. That one word stung her mind like a honey-drunk bee. As her brother continued to chatter on through the haze, using phrases like, "splendid connection" and "such terribly great fortune," Maria struggled to sit up.

She pulled off her little ivory nightcap and straightened her nightgown, while Fanny, her lady's maid, pushed past John with a silver tray of hot tea and freshly buttered toast.

"Sir, Madam never does anything before tea!" she sniffed propitiously, then set the small tray onto the bedside table with a clang.

"It's all right, Fanny." Maria smiled sleepily as she covered her mouth and began to yawn.

"How can you possibly be so calm? Do you understand what I am telling you?" John growled, perching on the edge of her bed and ringing his hands nervously.

"I believe I do." Maria smiled.

"The Duke of Bedford is truly one of the best catches in London and has waited years to find the right woman! Just imagine it, my sister a duchess...Oh, it is so terribly splendid!"

Rocked from the sleepy glaze where reality had mingled with the fantasy of her two mysterious encounters with the Prince of Wales, Maria bolted upright. "The Duke of Bedford?" she gasped.

"Why, yes of course." He tipped his head to one side. "Who else?"

Maria set her blue bone China teacup back on the tray and looked up at her brother. She was not quite certain why, but it was not the name she had expected to hear.

After a moment, she swung her bare feet out from under the heavy covers and braced her hands on the corner of the mattress.

"I shall not marry him."

"Oh, Maria, really. Don't be daft. Of course you shall. You must!"

"I'll not." Maria looked back over at her brother, her full blond hair tumbling loose around her face from the movement.

"But why in blazes not? This is positively a dream match."

Maria stood. "Your dream perhaps, John. *Not* mine."

"But what more could you want? He is titled and worth more than thirty thousand pounds a year, for Lord's sake!"

Her eyes narrowed. She was angry at the need to justify her reasons at all. "He is too predictable, John. Furthermore, he is dull. And I'll not consign myself to a lifetime of that to suit your goals nor his!"

John Smythe stood and faced his sister to show his resolution. As they opposed each other in the small bedchamber, he studied her as though she were a stranger, trying to discover from her eyes, or even her slightly parted lips, what could possibly have made her so determined. She had married twice before, and substantially lesser men, without the slightest hint of disagreement.

"Dull, is it?" he finally said, his face flushed with anger. "Predictable? And what, I wonder, gives you, a woman twice widowed, the impression that you are so terribly splendid a catch yourself?" He heard the cruelty creeping into his words as she turned away, and he tried to soften them. "Please come to your senses, sister! You know you're not likely ever to hear so great a proposal again!"

"Then that is the chance I shall have to take."

As she tried to move past him, he stopped her with the force of his hand. He pinched her slim arm until it ached and she was forced to look back up at him.

"I'll not allow you to make an error like this."

"It is already made, John. You seem to have forgotten that I have already married for the sake of the family. Twice! I own this home and I have enough money to remain quite comfortable without help from you or Isabella. I need not settle again." Then her tone softened as she looked at her brother, his own ambitions worn like a placard on his blue silk shirt sleeve. "John, please. I do not want to marry a man simply because of his title or his inheritance. If I ever *do* marry again, I want it to be because we cannot bear to live without one another . . . because our love alone leads us to that commitment."

Her brother moved toward the door and placed his hand on the knob before he looked back. "I shall tell Russell that you are uncertain. That you need time."

"Do not give him false hope, John. That would be cruel."

"It would be more cruel if you came to your senses, only to find that he had withdrawn his proposal."

Maria came toward him and kissed her brother's cheek. "I love you for your concern," she said softly. ". . . but you must trust me to do what I know in my heart is best. One day, the Duke of Bedford will cease to feel regret when he meets a woman who can return his love, and he shall thank me for not giving in to the temptation of a match for his title alone."

John's dark eyes narrowed as he took her hands again. "But will you regret it, Maria? I wonder, will you be sorry one day that you went chasing rainbows instead of following convention?"

"I can never regret following my heart."

When Maria's brother had gone, her maid quietly returned through the same door to help her wash and dress. Fanny's head was lowered, as it nearly always was, and her movements were brisk.

Maria walked across the cold plank floor while Fanny filled a basin of water. As her toilette was being prepared, she stood beneath a portrait of Thomas Fitzherbert painted a month before his death. Even in the artist's flattering rendering there was evidence of the real man he had become in the end, the deep-set eyes, almost hooded, thin, wine-colored lips. Hollow cheeks.

A hard fist of revulsion grew inside of her stomach when she remembered how he had wanted her even then. The way he sent for her and waited lying naked beneath the bed linen, his doughy belly and chest both white, sagging, and hairless. The folds of skin had made actual breasts. She could still remember trying not to cringe as she walked toward his bed, knowing what lay ahead, the grotesque grunting and thrusting, the horrible sweating that followed. The memory of those last few occasions in a room smelling of camphor still made her shiver. No. She had done her duty enough for one lifetime. She would not make that mistake again. Not for John. Not for anyone. No matter what uncertainties the future held.

MARIA WAS SITTING BENEATH A window in the shadow of a blazing gold burst of afternoon sunlight when Isabella Sefton was shown into the drawing room. "Oh, I have the most delicious news!" Isabella chirped as she swept into the room and a butler closed the doors behind her.

"As long as it does not involve the Duke of Bedford I shall be glad to hear it."

"We have been invited to Carlton House tonight to hear the Prince's friend, Mr. Sheridan, read a selection from his play, *School for Scandal*."

Maria looked up from the image of a rose she had been embroidering, a single pale eyebrow lifted. *"We?"*

"Well, Charles received the invitation, of course, but as usual he shall escort us both. It is truly an exceptional honor, you know. Richard Brinsley Sheridan is *very* close to the royal family...the Prince of Wales in particular," she added, and her eyes twinkled.

"I have heard that gossip too, Isabella, and I want no part of one of those wicked evenings."

"Oh, it will not be like that," she said, her soprano voice quivering with excitement. I have already spoken this morning to Lady Cowper and the Duchess of Argyll and both of them shall be attending. With those two busybodies present, His Highness would not dare to make it anything but a most elegant affair."

Maria's head whirled as it had the night before with the thoughts and the images of the Prince of Wales. Cowper. Argyll. The names alone promised respectability. She longed to go, until she remembered the Sheridan they had seen the other night at Almack's. Drunk and dissipated, he had leaned on an equally sodden Charles James Fox as the two had crashed into dancers, furniture, and glasses, making a rather unsavory entrance.

Like it or not, she did owe it to John to consider her reputation. When word of it spread, she would already be frowned upon throughout London for having had the audacity to turn down so sought-after a prize as the Duke of Bedford. Now more than ever, she could not risk being seen at so questionable a gathering where Fox and Sheridan both were likely also to be.

"Thank you for thinking of me, Isabella, truly," Maria said, forcing the needle back through the embroidery as the sun went behind the clouds. "but I believe I shall remain in this evening."

"But you cannot!"

Maria looked up again, startled by the sudden desperation in Isabella's voice. "What I-I mean to say is that I have already told Charles you will be joining us. He has accepted for three."

Maria studied her cousin, eyes leveled. "What is *truly* behind it, Isabella?"

She stalled by smoothing out the folds in the front of her butter-yellow gown. When Maria remained undaunted, Isabella finally said, "Well...since they are such good friends, it is quite likely that we are to be presented not only to Mr. Sheridan this evening but to the Prince of Wales himself. I wondered last evening why he had not asked for an introduction." Her eyes twinkled mischievously. "Now we know."

Maria leaned back against the brocade settee and returned the embroidery to her lap. "So then. That is what is at the bottom of this, hmm?" She forced the needle through the fabric so that Isabella would not see her trembling.

"He followed us home, Maria! We both saw him. And do you not think it is just the slightest bit curious that the very next day Charles and I received an invitation to a gathering at his home?"

Isabella was positively bubbling with excitement. Her shrieking seemed nearly to bow the walls so elegantly hung with fine damask and heavily framed family portraits.

"It was Lord and Lady Sefton who were invited to Carlton House."

"Oh really, Maria. Must you be so naive? It is all over London that you have been my companion since your return for the season. What could be more certain and more proper than inviting Lord Sefton and I as a means of getting to meet *you*?"

Maria cast the embroidery aside and held her hands together in her lap in hopes of slowing her heart. The best years of her youth had been spent as a wife, now in a few short weeks, a proposal from a duke and a dangerous flirtation from the Prince of Wales. As Isabella rattled on about Maria's responsibility to join her in the evening, she heard instead the echo of her brother's words, willing her toward convention. If, for some curious reason, the Prince had indeed contrived this invitation himself and she agreed to go, what perilous rainbow might she be chasing?

George's dalliances with women older than he were common knowledge. But even the famed actress "Perdita" Robinson had managed to hold his attention for only a few short months before he was romancing another. Women were possessions to him, used and then discarded. That is what the papers said.

Since Isabella's arrival, the sky had darkened and tiny drops of rain were now beating a persistent rhythm against the windowpanes.

Maria pressed her fingers against the cold glass and looked across the street, where just last night the royal coach had waited in the shadows. Her lower lip quivered with uncertainty as she watched people scurrying past, newspapers and handbags held over their heads as protection from the sudden shower. Though it could certainly lead nowhere, she had made her decision. She would go with Isabella…just this once, to Carlton House, and at the very least indulge a curiosity.

"ARE YOU CERTAIN SHE WILL be here, Sheridan?"

"Quite certain, Your Highness. I have spoken with her relative, Lady Sefton. She assured me that she loves a good romance, and was most eager to assist us."

Dressed in a tailcoat of rich scarlet with shiny brass buttons and his signature white cravat, George stood tall and stately beside Richard Brinsley Sheridan. They were just inside the high-ceilinged entrance hall of Carlton House, which was lined with columns of porphyry marble. In the glittering candlelight, both men were dashing.

Around them, the sweeping banisters were hung with lamps and festooned with flowers. Everything glittered. The myriad sights could only be topped by the aromas. Perfume and scented oil in huge Chinese jars mingled through the richly ornate interior, which many whispered was garish and cluttered. No matter what George's father forced him to endure, the people must see the survivor in their future king. Thanks to vendors still willing to court a future king, his credit still was good and he always managed to keep just one step ahead of his creditors.

At eight o'clock, guests were ushered past the grand torch-lit portico of the Prince of Wales's London house. They were surprised to find themselves faced at once with their Royal host. The Prince of Wales preferred this position for introductions to the more pompous entrées his father the King favored, entering only after all of the guests had arrived. His secretary, Colonel Gardner, whispered to him the names and titles of each of the guests as they approached.

"How I do need a drink," George deadpanned beneath his hand when he saw the extent of the line. But tonight he intended to be stone sober.

"The Duke of Rutland, Your Highness."

George smiled smoothly as the Duke bowed to him, then moved along with the others before him toward the Gothic Conservatory.

"Lord and Lady Salisbury, Your Highness," Gardner whispered in his other ear as two more elegantly clad guests approached. While George inquired politely about their newly acquired home in Warwickshire and the health of their latest child, Gardner whispered the next name.

"Mrs. Elizabeth Armistead, Your Highness."

George broke from his polite banter and shot a glance at his secretary, certain he could not have heard correctly. "W-Who the devil invited her?" he whispered in a growl as the lady with whom he had once been involved approached on the arm of the prince's dark and clever rival.

"Fox, my friend," George said with an uneasy smile. He struggled to look politely at Elizabeth. Forcing himself to see his own weakness so glaringly beneath the lighted glass lustres was difficult this early in the evening, he still so sober. "Good of you to come. And my dear Mrs. Armistead." George took a difficult breath, weary of the pretense in his life. "You're looking lovely as ever."

He tried not to let her know that he recognized the betrayed expression that had turned the thin contours of her face to harsh edges.

"Lord and Lady Sefton together with Mrs. Fitzherbert, your Highness," Gardner whispered next, just as Elizabeth appeared to be on the verge of creating a scene.

A *woman scorned*, he thought, looking from Elizabeth back to Fox, and hoping to be blessed with the inspiration for a clever reply when, suddenly, Sheridan interceded.

"If Your Royal Highness shall excuse us, I was hoping to confer with Mr. Fox here about his speech tomorrow in the House of Commons."

Before George could utter a word, the slim, graceful Sheridan had one arm around Fox's shoulder and was leading him and an obviously indignant Elizabeth Armistead away toward the Conservatory.

"Your Royal Highness," the small and birdlike Isabella said as she moved up, then curtsied beside her husband.

"Lord and Lady Sefton," he could hear himself say. "How good of you to come." Then slowly, and as smoothly as he could manage, he turned to the more statuesque woman who stood undaunted beside them. Like Isabella, Maria curtsied, then lifted her face and looked directly up into his eyes. But she did so without being coy, without that foolish painted smile that so plagued women who were brought into his presence. Not her.

While the other women flirted and giggled behind their painted fans, the mysterious woman who had caught his attention now twice stood serene and graceful before him in a gown of hunter's green silk, her light hair worn full of curls and dotted with rose-colored ribbons. But it was her face, that lovely porcelain skin and the rich, distinctive brown eyes, that silenced him for so long that everyone else in the line behind them had begun to whisper.

"Lord Sefton, perhaps you would be good enough to introduce the lady," George managed to say without breaking his gaze from her.

Charles Sefton lifted a curious eyebrow when he saw the exchange and looked back at Maria almost as an afterthought. *The Prince of Wales and my half brother's daughter? Certainly not. It couldn't possibly be. She was too cultured for his baser tastes. Too refined—Certainly too Catholic.*

"Your Royal Highness, may I present my niece, Maria Fitzherbert."

"I am so pleased for the opportunity to finally meet you, madam," he said with as much charm as he could enlist. "Although I have had the pleasure of seeing you, the distance between us, on those occasions, certainly did little justice to your great beauty."

"I am afraid on those same occasions Your Highness's manners did not fare much better."

George saw a trace of a smile curl the corners of her mouth as those around them were shocked into silence. That she could have had the courage! *Touché,* he thought with a little half-bitten smile of his own.

How had it been, from the very first, that he had known she would be like this? Different. Daring. Yet completely without pretense. He had never believed in anything as clichéd as love at first sight. That was for romance books and fools. But now, with her dark eyes upon him, her head held high, he wasn't certain any longer what he believed.

"Maria!" Lord Sefton choked.

"It is quite all right." George chuckled. "I suppose I deserved that and quite a bit more."

"Lord and Lady Cowper, Your Highness," Colonel Garner whispered into his ear as George struggled through another interminably long silence.

"Not yet, Gardner!" he growled. But the moment was gone. He watched Maria look away, embarrassed by the time he had taken while so many others were waiting to be introduced. "Ah, well yes. To my great chagrin, madam, it would seem that I must continue. But if you should allow me, I shall very much look forward to an opportunity to speak with you more privately later this evening."

When he saw the clever expression on her face darken to what he thought was indignation, George instantly wished he could take it back. Nothing he had said seemed to have charmed her in the easy, predictable way that it had done with all of the other women he had known. But then that was precisely the point. Maria really was not like any of them.

He glanced behind her at the string of guests, now wound outside and down the stairs onto the colonnaded entry, all waiting to be introduced. When he looked back at her, she had turned away and was following her uncle, as the others before them, toward the huge Gothic Conservatory.

Watching Maria move away from him, her green silk gown shimmering in the candlelight as it swept across the floor, George felt a sense of wild elation and uncertainty that was entirely foreign. Whether it had happened at the opera, or just now, as they had stood facing one another for the first time, he knew with a strange sort of premonition that Maria Fitzherbert was about to become his obsession—the first woman for whom he had ever felt the desire to try to be worthy.

THE IMMENSELY LONG, PILLARED GOTHIC Conservatory, the room George hoped would someday symbolize his independence, was hung at intervals tonight with pale lighted Chinese lanterns. Small glass lamps were everywhere in the niches and cornices. They illuminated not only the intricate ceiling but the maze of stained-glass windows. They made it appear like a dreamworld to each guest who entered it.

"I have never seen anything like it," muttered Isabella as she gazed up at the ceiling whose intricate traceries created a sort of spiderweb effect.

"Most irregular," seconded Charles Sefton.

"Did you see the expression on his face?" Isabella whispered, turning quickly back to Maria and linking their arms. "I do believe his Royal Highness has been thoroughly enchanted. Oh! That you could have spoken to the Prince in that manner and gotten away with it! My dear, what will John say when he hears the news?"

"My brother shall not hear of it unless you tell him, Isabella, because there is nothing to tell!"

"Will you look at that," said Charles as he gazed at the head of the hall where double doors opened onto a huge garden, brightly lit with the a series of Chinese lanterns.

"I thought you both had been here before," Maria said.

"Yes, but only in the Audience Chamber. His Highness calls it the Blue Velvet Room, but I tell you, Maria, it is nothing so scandalous as this. In this one room our future King has broken every rule of proper architecture!"

It really was the most ambitious merging of the Orient with the images of a fairy tale that she could conceive. Behind them, it slowly began to fill with the Prince's guests. What sort of man would have not only the courage but the inclination to build so bold a room? What, she wondered, could the other rooms in this monumental palace be like? Maria smiled for a moment, her curiosity once again having gotten the better of her.

"So. What do you think of my Conservatory?"

They heard the Prince's deep voice, resonant in the vaulted stained-glass hall, before they turned to see him standing behind them, his gold buttons flashing like fire in the lamplight. It was the only room he had found the funds to finish. But he did not tell them that.

"Extraordinary, Your Royal Highness," said Charles, still gazing up at the grand ceiling.

"Yes. It is indeed. Not ordinary a'tall, which I shall tell you was precisely the point. And Mrs. Fitzherbert, tell me"—he turned toward Maria, smoothly moving a step nearer—"how do you find my Conservatory?"

Charles and Isabella both looked at her at the same time, willing her with their silent expressions to be complimentary. "To be completely honest, Your Highness, I find it garish."

"Maria!" Isabella gasped.

"So you do indeed," George said with a surprised smile.

He looked at her face again, warmed now by the colored light from the stained-glass windows. There was nothing there to show how monstrously he had flirted with her. No sign of disapproval. Not even in her reply. Just quiet honesty. He rarely got that from anyone—even those he considered his closest friends.

Hands linked behind his elegant red tailcoat, his hair perfumed with scented powder, George gazed around now, studying the room himself. "Perhaps you are right," he declared. "It is a bit...flamboyant. You disapprove, so I shall have it razed first thing tomorrow."

"Your Highness cannot be serious!" Isabella cried. "I am certain that Maria was only joking!"

"On the contrary, Lady Sefton. I trust that Mrs. Fitzherbert has never been more serious in her life. Nor have I."

"Maria, *please!*" whispered Isabella, her teeth clenched and her fingers plying the delicate silk of Maria's gown.

"I had no wish to offend Your Highness," she finally conceded when the weight of Isabella's distress and her uncle's disapproval became too great to bear. "Perhaps it is only that I do not understand architecture."

"I believe you understand architecture quite clearly. It is rather more simply that you do not like how it is applied here."

To his surprise, her pale unpainted lips turned up into another little half smile. Finally, when he least expected it, he had managed to be clever, and with the help of precious little palliative to encourage him.

"I would be honored, madam, if you would consent to stroll with me so that I may show you my Conservatory...as *I* see it."

Maria glanced back at Isabella, whose smile of approval was stamped boldly into the smooth contours of her face. But Maria was sobered when she looked around the crowded room at the curious stares of the other guests. Such an acceptance would only incite gossip.

"Respectfully, Your Highness, I do not think it would be proper."

"Nonsense. We shall have an entire roomful of chaperones. I shall see that you rejoin your companions in time for supper."

He took her hand and wound it through his arm before she had time to object further. Then he led her alone through his guests who parted as he and Maria moved with measured steps toward the long, crowded hall.

"If only you knew how much I had hoped for a moment alone with you like this since your arrival," he said beneath his breath as they strolled.

"But as Your Royal Highness has just pointed out, we are *not* alone."

"I was referring, madam, to Lady Sefton. Tell me, are the two of you *ever* parted?"

"Lady Sefton has graciously consented to accompany me this season here in London, as I am recently widowed."

"Yes, I'm sorry," he said, trying to sound sincere in the face of such great fortune.

They reached the double doors that led out into the expansive gardens. There, a cluster of willow trees swayed in the rhythm of a balmy evening breeze. Beyond them were two-hundred-year-old elms and a shimmering pavilion. "But for however long he had you," George added, "Mr. Fitzherbert was an exceedingly fortunate man, indeed."

They faced one another in the moonlight, her hunter-green gown whispering like tiny undulating waves around her legs. George moved a step nearer, buoyed by her kind eyes, until he was close enough to feel her quickened breath warm on his face.

"I know it is forward," he said in a deep, steady voice, "but I find that I must take the risk of telling you, I believe that I could very easily fall in love with you."

He watched her dark eyes narrow. "Your Highness is mocking me," she said, turning back toward the door.

"On the contrary, I have never uttered more sincere words in all of my life, *Maria*."

He said her name slowly, and the sound of it from his lips, his eyes still rooted on her, made her shiver. By everything she had ever been taught, it was too familiar. It was far too soon. And yet still, there was something. She felt it as well.

He still held her hand tightly in his own, trying to make her face him again. "It is curious, but I actually felt something out of the ordinary that day on the Mall when we looked at one another."

"When you were on your horse, riding so wildly through town?"

"Have you ever ridden like that? Free, the wind blowing your hair? Stinging your cheeks?"

"Certainly not."

"It is like touching heaven." He smiled. "Come, let me show you."

A small spark of something wild inside her flickered again. "Now? But it's dark outside!"

He laughed. "And what a magnificent ride that would make it!"

"You have shown me nothing of your Conservatory," she said faintly, trying to look away. "We have neglected that."

"Better to show you what *I* am about."

"But, your Highness, we have only just met."

"All I need know is there in your eyes. Let's take a chance, Maria. Take a night ride across the park with me! It frees the soul! There is little else in the world like that sensation!"

"I cannot hear this! Please, Your Highness, do not continue!" Maria looked around frantically as though she were trying to escape him. He had not expected that.

"I have no wish to frighten you. I only wish to remain in your company. I thought a bit of something unexpected would please you."

"Everything about you is unexpected."

He moved nearer until she could feel his gold buttons pressing into the tight bodice of her gown. George fascinated her. He was dangerous, wild, and totally forbidden. He was also masculine and wholly male. God help her but she desired him.

"We must go in," she said breathlessly.

"Rest assured, madam." He smiled with a regal confidence. "They shall wait for us."

Still, she wished to go. And so, he let her. She walked away from him with small hurried steps and slipped back amid the other guests, who moved slowly toward the Gothic Dining Room.

George stood at the door to the garden feeling the rush of cool air, and suddenly Sheridan was standing beside him. He was holding a glass of champagne and his thin lips were turned up with the faint beginnings of a smile.

"Your Highness is pleased?"

"No, Sheridan, it is far more than that. And perhaps to my great detriment, I do not expect from this day forward that my life shall ever be quite the same."

AFTER A MAGNIFICENT SUPPER OF salmagundi, roast chicken, pigeon pie, and salmon with fennel sauce, none of which Maria could bear to eat, the prince's guests returned to the fairy-tale Conservatory. As they strolled in, an orchestra had just begun to play behind a carved colonnade.

"Will you ever tell me what he said once the two of you were alone?" Isabella badgered from behind her fan. "I shall simply die if you do not tell me what he said."

"I told you it was only trivia. I can scarcely recall the exact words now."

Maria stood surrounded by the other guests, glad for the momentary anonymity. She had been able to touch little more than her soup, with the Prince's eyes fixed upon her from across the room. His seductive glances had been missed by no one and she quickly felt more embarrassment than fortune.

How many people were muttering about her beneath their breath, saying it was she who was next in the long line of "bed warmers" for the next King of England? She had heard that bit of gossip whispered at her very own table.

The orchestra slipped into another tune. Over near the open garden doors where it was cooler, couples began again to dance as the Chinese lanterns above them swayed softly in the warm breeze.

"Oh look, Maria. He is coming toward us again. I am certain His Highness means to dance with you! Oh, you shall be the talk of all London tomorrow!"

The fear shot through her first, then writhed like a living thing in the pit of her empty stomach. "I cannot," she muttered. "...I must not!"

As the Prince of Wales passed through his guests, parting them once again with his grand and elegant strides, Maria, like everyone else, saw him smiling at her. Was that the same rakish smile so many other women had seen and succumbed to?

He was coming toward them with Sheridan on one side and Charles James Fox on the other. What danger there was in *that* combination! She could bear no more flirtation, not tonight when he had been so forward already. The Prince was a man accustomed to getting what he wanted and he had made it quite clear that what he wanted, at least for now, was Maria.

She looked around at a blur of faces, none of whom she recognized. All of them were chatting and watching the dancers. But how could she escape the Prince without running from the room? Movement like that would only incite more gossip. If she asked her uncle Charles to dance, the romantic Isabella would be cross with her for the rest of the evening.

In desperation, she looked at a young man elegantly clad in gray and black, with a long, narrow face and permanently oval mouth, standing beside her. She had not noticed him before, but now he was her only chance.

"What would be the cost for you to aid a lady in distress?" she whispered to him as the Prince of Wales drew steadily nearer.

"Merely the request," the stranger replied, parroting her whisper. "Ask me to dance?"

As properly as if it had been his own notion, the tall stranger with dark thinning hair, turned toward her and bowed. Then loudly enough for those around her to hear, said, "Might I have the pleasure, madam?"

Maria turned to look at Isabella with feigned surprise. "Well, I don't suppose one dance would hurt."

"What about the Prince?" Isabella shrieked, seeing along with the rest of the guests that he was nearly upon them. But by the time she had spoken the words, Maria was being led past the throngs of spectators and into the safety of the other dancers.

"I am afraid I don't know how to thank you," Maria said when they were safely on the dance floor.

His smile was easy and genuine. "Perhaps you could begin by explaining my rather abrupt departure to my wife."

"Oh, I *am* sorry," Maria smiled sheepishly in return as they danced. "You looked as if you were alone."

"Lord Admiral Hugh Seymour, at your service," he said, inclining his head just slightly. "My wife had just gone to check her face when you spoke to me."

"I do apologize. I am Maria Fitzherbert."

"If I have managed to save you from a peril about to befall you, Mrs. Fitzherbert, no apology is necessary."

She looked into his long face and gentle, sleepy eyes and she felt as safe as if she had known him all of her life. "For the moment, Lord Seymour, I believe you have done just that, and for your gallant intervention I shall be eternally grateful."

"His Royal Highness is known to be petulant when he does not achieve the end he desires. You may be setting yourself up for more than which you bargained."

Her lower lips dropped. "You knew?"

"My dear woman, everyone here can see the Prince's intent. As you might imagine, you are not the first upon whom he has set his sights. Our very handsome Prince of Wales may be many things, but I am afraid subtle is not one of them."

By the time the music had ended, George had vanished. Lord Seymour led Maria back to their place, where there now stood a young woman with pale brown hair dotted with ribbons that matched her yellow gown.

"Mrs. Fitzherbert, may I present to you my wife, Lady Horatia Seymour."

Without the slightest inclination toward jealousy for the mysterious disappearance of her husband with another woman, the soft-featured, pale complexioned young woman smiled. "It is a great pleasure, madam."

"I would like to apologize for making off with your husband. I am afraid I was in a bit of a spot and he was kind enough to rescue me."

"I can imagine your desperation," she said sweetly. "I could not help but notice that His Royal Highness was positively livid when he saw you go off with Lord Seymour before he had an opportunity to speak with you."

Maria flinched. "Oh, he has already made his position quite clear, Lady Seymour."

As they stood amid a room far too crowded with guests, Maria began to look around for Isabella and Charles. "It would appear that the Prince of Wales is not the only one to have left me," she said with a sigh.

"They've gone off with the Prince. I heard him promise to show them his private apartments."

"Better it was they than I," she said beneath her breath, then felt a smile of relief turn up the corners of her mouth.

"So tell me, Mrs. Fitzherbert, do you live in London?" Horatia asked. "Lord Seymour and I have not had the pleasure of seeing you at one of these infamous Carlton House affairs before tonight."

"I live here only for the season, Your Ladyship. I prefer to live the rest of the time out at Twickenham."

"Ah, yes. It is lovely there."

"And Your Ladyship?"

"I, and the children, live here in London. Lord Seymour is an Admiral in His Majesty's Navy, which has taken him away from us far too often, I am afraid."

"You have children?" Maria asked, feeling the question catch in her throat.

"Yes. Four and another quite soon." She smiled.

Maria was tempted by envy as she looked at Lady Seymour. She had large hazel eyes and a small mouth that appeared to be fashioned into a permanently placid smile. Her hair, spilled onto her shoulders in loose beige curls. Maria had always wanted children. The idea that this frail-looking young woman could already have borne four of them while, between two husbands, she had remained barren, pulled her a little nearer toward the covetous darkness of jealousy.

"We lost a daughter last winter," Horatia added, her sweet smile paling. "So this one—" she touched her stomach gently—"means the world to us all."

"My dear, I'm certain that Mrs. Fitzherbert does not care about such things."

"Oh, but I do," Maria assured her, feeling a tug of shame for her private thoughts. "When is the child due?"

"By New Year's." Her pale eyes glittered. "We hope this time for a girl."

A daughter. How often had she wanted the very same thing for herself. Someone to teach. Someone who would have been a companion throughout these immeasurably long, lonely months of widowhood. She had thought it sad when no children had come to her and Edward, but she had been young then. There had been time. In her marriage to Thomas, all of that had changed. Maria had been plagued with sadness when, in three years of marriage, she still had not managed to have a child. It looked to her now as if she never would. That loss in itself made her want one all the more.

She looked back over to Horatia, trying to smile.

"Are little girls not just the most precious things?" asked the Admiral's wife.

"Indeed they are," Maria agreed.

THE NEXT MORNING, MARIA SAT upright in her bed and brushed the sleep from her eyes as Fanny loomed over her, giddy as a child at Christmas, and holding a small velvet-wrapped box.

"The Prince of Wales's carriage has just left, ma'am. And his footman has brought you this!"

She struggled to make her eyes focus on the clock. Quarter past seven. Maria tried never to rise before ten when she had been out the night before. She always paid the penalty the next day with swollen eyes and swollen feet. By the time she had gone to bed the night before it had been past two, and her head was splitting now in the gray haze of her unlit bedchamber.

"Oh, very well. Part the drapes, Fanny," she said with a yawn.

As her lady's maid pulled back the heavy damask draperies and tied each side with a gold cord, her pale blue bedchamber was flooded with morning sunlight. All of the miniatures of her family and the small collection of enamels on a satinwood table came to life. There were books and letters beside them on one table and a vase filled with fragrant lavender on another.

She stretched like a cat, one lazy arm after the other, and looked down at the box, wound with green velvet and tied with pink ribbons, that had been left atop her bedding. She felt her heart quicken. They were exactly the same colors and the fabrics she had worn the night before at Carlton House. Exactly.

"Are you not going to open it, ma'am?" Fanny asked anxiously as two of the other servants peered around the door frame. "Imagine it, ma'am. From the Prince of Wales!"

Maria looked back down at the elegantly wrapped little box. Slowly she pulled the pink ribbon. Beneath it was a small silver chest, carved with the image of the Three Graces. Now her heart was pounding as she carefully lifted the lid. Knowing...fearing, what she might find.

"Saints preserve us!" Fanny gasped and made the sign of the cross over her own slim, almost boyish figure.

In the box, on a bed of green velvet, lay an emerald and diamond brooch sparkling in the burst of sunlight like the fireworks at King George's coronation. She let her head drop back against the carved mahogany headboard.

"There is a note, ma'am. Would you like me to read it to you?"

"Go ahead," Maria said, then closed her eyes.

"*For the memory...of the night which has passed...and to the hope of a thousand more like it.*' It is signed, *George P*. Oh, madam!" she gasped, fingers splayed across her lips.

Maria took a breath to steady herself. "You may leave me now. Go and fetch me a strong pot of tea. I fear today I am going to need it."

When she was alone again, Maria gazed down at the extravagant heirloom, knowing how precious it was to someone, and trying to catch her breath. She could not have imagined anything like it. This jewel was as extreme and garish as the Gothic Conservatory, and with a similar theme. Diamonds and emeralds were wound in a fan of thinly spun gold. She held it up to the light and watched the brilliant color flash against the wall like a kaleidoscope, azure fusing with the light to make limpid blue...*a blue like his eyes.*

BY NOON, THE PRINCE'S YELLOW carriage had returned to Park Street. This time the footman bore an invitation on a card of ecru parchment. Another gathering would be held at Carlton House that evening. Maria shrank from the idea of another evening of dodging the ardent advances of a dashing yet dangerous suitor who just happened to be the Crown Prince of England.

Isabella, however, had other ideas.

"Are you positively out of your mind? Think of what an *interlude* with the Prince could do for your connections, not to mention the social standing of your entire family!"

"You must not breathe a word of this to John, Isabella, or I swear never to speak another word to you again!"

Isabella sat in a blue satin chair, turning the brooch around in her hand. Scattered on the table before them were two cups of tea, half drunk, and two china plates peppered with scones and honey biscuits that Maria had not managed to touch.

"He is certainly interested." Isabella smiled. "You cannot refuse a personal invitation to Carlton House now. Your reputation in London would be ruined."

"And what of my reputation if *I attend*?"

Isabella lay the brooch down on a Siena marble–topped table. She took a deep breath before she moved across the room to Maria, who stood gazing pensively out the grand, bow window. It faced onto the park, where the lilacs were already in bloom.

Her words now were softer, filled with more compassion. "You told me yourself you knew all about his reputation, Maria. It is common knowledge that he tires of women faster than he does his clothes. This interest in you shall fade before it has begun. Go to Carlton House with us tonight. Speak with him if he desires it. Flirt with him a little if you must. I promise you before this night is through, there shall be someone new to set that gleam in his eye. But mark my words, Maria. If you do find the courage to accept his challenge and attend with us tonight, your reputation in London society is certain to be set forever!"

THAT EVENING, AS THE SKY began to pale in a streak of pink and gold and blue, a welcome breeze stirred, carrying away the wretched, stifling heat of summer. Maria did not speak as the carriage bearing her, Isabella, and Charles Sefton rolled past a row of perfect Palladian houses and onto Bond Street toward Carlton House. *This one last time*, Maria told herself... *only this one time*, as she sat nervously playing with the folds in her gown.

At seven, Bond Street was still crowded with top-hatted gentlemen in their waistcoats and tight knee breeches. Fashionable ladies strolled beside them in their wide-brimmed hats, their pastel-colored parasols extended for effect. The street they passed was a mélange of shops: the tailor, the stay maker, the fan maker, the hatter, and the jeweler. A young girl selling lilacs and daisies from a wicker basket strolled among the shoppers. So did an artful and well-dressed pickpocket. Maria felt her heart quicken as the carriage turned onto Pall Mall and she could see Carlton House.

It was a long, plain brick building with an imposing Ionic screen built to hide it from the people who passed by. She had not worn the brooch, though Isabella had begged her to. Instead, she had chosen a simple ecru-colored gown, a ribbon at her throat and a matching ribbon wound through her hair. She wore no patches, very little powder, and almost no lip paint at all. She was attending this time under protest and she must not give the Prince of Wales any reason to believe otherwise.

As they pulled past the guards and into the Carlton House courtyard, the sun behind them was dying in one last shade of brilliant orange, tinging the rooftops beyond Pall Mall with its brassy flames. Maria emerged from the Seftons' black carriage, pulled by two black stallions, and nervously straightened her skirts with one hand. In her other hand, she held her small pearl-studded bag in a death grip.

"You do look delectable this evening, my dear," Charles Sefton whispered, trying to reassure his niece.

"I am afraid, Uncle," she muttered, knowing the game of cat and mouse she likely faced, "that unfortunately, tonight you just may be right."

This time the Prince was not in the grand foyer to greet his guests as he had the night before. Nor was the marble-tiled entrance hall swirling with elegantly clad nobility. There were no glowing Chinese lanterns and no orchestra music spilling out from the Gothic Conservatory. As the trio came in from the courtyard, there was only a string of footmen, liveried in wine-colored velvet, one to take Lord Sefton's cloak and another to extend to each of them a ginger cordial.

"His Royal Highness shall be greeting his guests in the Crimson Drawing Room this evening. The Conservatory is being demolished tomorrow," one of the footmen informed them and then turned to lead them up a wide flight of red-carpeted stairs.

Isabella glared at her and Maria felt the dread of responsibility. She struggled to hold her small cordial glass steady as she walked behind her uncle and his wife. Fear of what lay ahead knotted and writhed in her stomach, and as she took each step she willed herself not to turn and run. She clenched her purse tighter in her other hand.

The stairway was lined with huge portraits suspended from brass chains, all framed in heavy gold leaf. The current King George was the first to gaze down upon them in an outdated white periwig, his face powdered and lightly rouged. Beside it was a smaller portrait of Queen Charlotte as a young woman, sitting on a bench with two of her favorite dogs beside her.

Maria did not recognize the next two images that gazed down upon her from another age, but she was struck by a large portrait of the Prince of Wales up near the landing. She had heard it was painted the previous year by Gainsborough. There was something sad about it that she could not quite determine until she realized that his expression did not bare even the slightest hint of a smile.

"How lovely to see you again," said the portly Charles James Fox to Charles and Isabella.

He was swaying as he came across the intimate drawing room toward them the very moment they passed through the door. Maria had seen the well-known orator at a distance that night at Almack's. This, however, was the first time she had been close enough to see how truly offensive looking he really was. He had not shaven or applied perfume for several days. Yet strangely, she could see the famous sweetness, a kind of charm about him that caused people to overlook his shabby appearance.

"And you must be the famous Mrs. Fitzherbert. Your reputation precedes you," Fox said, taking her hand and raising it to his full, wet lips.

His hair, the color of pepper, was as unkempt as it had been that night. His eyes, large and dark, were topped by dark heavy brows. They looked like two black beetles resting over skin that was uneven and red-blotched from too much drinking.

Maria smiled politely and slowly withdrew her hand, still feeling his saliva on her fingers. Casually, she brushed her hand across the fabric of her skirts and took a step backward. "As does yours, Mr. Fox."

"I hear that you positively set the House of Commons on fire once again this morning," said Lord Sefton.

Fox smiled wickedly and then winked before he took a huge swallow of brandy. "I do my best."

As the orator bandied politics with her uncle, Maria gazed around at a huge crimson-draped drawing room that tonight was only spotted with guests. Since Fox was among them, she was surprised that the Prince's other famous companion, the Duchess of Devonshire, was once again nowhere to be seen. She had always heard that together the two were the Prince's greatest supporters. Feeling steady for the moment, Maria finally took a sip of the sweet ginger cordial and let it bathe her dry throat.

The room was elegant, what *all* of the tired and shabby Carlton House should be, she thought. It was brightened by two huge chandeliers full of lighted, dripping tapers and warmed with thick Aubusson carpets, heavy draperies, and red and gold trimmed chairs. As her uncle and Fox chattered on, Maria caught herself glancing casually around for the Prince. Perhaps he meant to make an entrance, she considered.

She took another sip of ginger cordial, which slowly began to numb her darker fears. The rest of the guests talked among themselves and mingled about the room. Several of the guests were admiring the paintings by Rubens, Poussin, Titian, and Van Dyck, as well as His Highness's priceless collection of Chinese porcelain.

Because it was a particularly warm evening, a huge window across the room had been opened. It flooded the room now with a soft breeze that caused the candles in the chandeliers to flicker great shadows on all of the silk draped walls.

As her uncle and Fox continued to speak together, Maria moved toward the open window with a view out onto the immense gardens and a sky now paled to pewter. She leaned against the fringed curtain and inhaled the summer scent of narcissus and jasmine.

"Indeed, you are a vision tonight," a voice whispered behind her, and Maria felt the press of his tailcoat against her pale gown.

Startled by his sudden nearness, she spun around and found herself facing the Prince of Wales in slim white knee breeches and a dashing purple velvet waistcoat trimmed with lace.

"You startled me," she said in a voice that was trembling slightly.

"I am glad you are here."

"Lady Sefton insisted."

"The means are unimportant."

He spoke with a voice more deeply resonant than the night before. The tone of it was almost hypnotic. His blue eyes were glowing in the shadowy light but were otherwise clear.

"We were told by one of your servants that you plan to destroy the Conservatory tomorrow," she said, struggling not to shake the empty cordial glass that she still held between two fingers.

"I do."

"But you cannot! It is part of your home! Your heritage!"

"My Conservatory does not please you, and so it no longer pleases me. It is that simple."

"I regret what I said last night. Truly I do."

"You spoke the truth. No one can fault you for that."

"It was thoughtless of me not to have considered the future generations who shall one day come to admire the uniqueness of your style."

"It shall no longer be my style if it does not please you."

Her brows narrowed and she lowered her eyes, but it was not a coquettish movement. When she spoke, it was in a fragile whisper. "Why are you doing this?"

"I thought that I had made my position quite clear last evening."

"And *I* thought last evening that perhaps you were a bit drunk."

"Stone sober, I'm afraid. Nor have I taken even the smallest cordial since." When she looked back into his eyes, he was smiling good-naturedly, dispelling the tension between them with his own easy charm. "Tell me, Maria, do you find my Crimson Drawing Room more to your taste?"

She looked around as a reflex and then met his gaze again, a little embarrassed. A flush mottled her cheeks. "It is lovely."

"I am relieved," he said quietly, with only a hint of a smile.

"But you must promise me not to tear down your grand Conservatory. I should not like the weight of that on my conscience in years to come."

He watched her mouth form the words, the soft shape of the unpainted lips that led upward to that flawless, alabaster face. It was full of a trusting innocence that absolutely rocked him.

The Conservatory was part of his most private self. It was the one room he had managed to conceive and construct entirely on his own.

In that, he considered it his greatest show of strength against his father, and he wanted Maria to see it as he did.

"I shall allow you to dissuade me, madam, only *if* you shall agree to grant me one wish this evening."

Maria looked at him with the open vulnerability of a child, completely unfettered by the pretense of flirtation, and now it was he who strained to catch his breath.

"Let me show you my Conservatory as I see it," he proposed with a coaxing timbre. "If you are still not convinced of its magnificence, then tomorrow, as planned, it shall be reduced to rubble."

They strolled together across the room and Maria felt Isabella's approving nod as they passed by her. As they moved slowly through the long double doors, he felt her hand relax, wound in his, and together they moved back down the grand staircase a step at a time.

"Well. I say, with any luck, there goes the Prince of Wales's newest mistress." Lord Sefton smiled.

"And I say, if that is true, there goes one terribly unfortunate young woman indeed," corrected Charles James Fox between voluminous swills of claret.

ARMS ACROSS HIS CHEST, GEORGE leaned against a smooth marble column in the candlelit shadows. The huge Conservatory looked different tonight without the blazing lanterns, the milling crowds. Without the mingling perfumes or the rapturous music.

Maria gazed around slowly, drinking in the fanciful, almost mystic beauty of the empty hall. She thought how now, in the silence, it resembled more the nave of a church, long and hollow, perfectly balanced, with two rows of carved columns illuminated by the magnificent fan-shaped stained-glass ceiling.

Tonight, in the moonlight through the stained glass, it was almost celestial.

George waited silently as she walked to the end of the marble floor, all the while gazing up at the ceiling, a work that had been his greatest pride. After a moment, Maria returned to him, their faces flickering in the single golden light of the oil lamp that she held for them.

"It is different from anything I have ever seen before," she said, almost out of breath.

"Precisely the point." He smiled.

"Perfectly symmetrical...and yet ornamented..."

"Like a fantasy?"

"Yes, just like." She looked back across the shadowy hall, now returned to darkness without the light of her lamp to color it. "Perhaps I haven't the knowledge of architecture to understand this room, but I believe I know enough about emotion to say that I hope you shall keep it as it is for many years to come."

He moved a step nearer and ran a hand slowly along the smooth silk of her sleeve, feeling the fabric and the warm flesh beneath it.

"Nothing, Maria, remains as it is. Everything changes, and if we are to flourish, we too must be able to change."

"It is not always quite so simple, Your Highness." She sighed, looking away from a gaze that bore through her with the same unsettling intensity as it had that night at the opera. George moved a step nearer and brought her face back in the palm of his hand.

"Oh, but it is, Maria. Like this room. You have only to allow yourself to see it."

"Why did you bring me here?"

"To see my Conservatory saved, of course." He coolly smiled.

"I mean tonight. What was the real reason you invited me once again?"

"I believe you know the answer to that," he replied deeply, then reached up to touch her cheek. But as he moved near to her lips, Maria reached up to stop his caress with her own determined grip.

"I shall not be made a fool of for Your Highness or anyone else," she said, but there was more of a tremor in her soft voice than she had intended.

"You are quite an extraordinary woman, Maria Fitzherbert," George said, still smiling. "...and I wish only to please you, just as I hoped to please you with the brooch."

Maria's thoughts, mired in the thorny implications of so intimate a moment with a notorious rogue, quickly turned. She remembered the extravagant sparkling collection of diamonds and emeralds wound in gold that lay in the small velvet-lined chest amid the scent flasks and family miniatures on her dressing table. She was embarrassed now that, for all of her suspicions, she had not at the least thanked him.

"Forgive me. It is lovely," she lied, and badly. "But still I cannot keep it."

"It is too garish?" he asked with a playful note of reproach.

"It would not be proper."

It surprised her so much when he laughed mockingly that she did not notice his hand back on her arm, threading upward toward her shoulder. She was still free to step back, but suddenly she felt strangely mesmerized, as he pressed his velvet waistcoat against the folds of her ecru silk gown.

"I have always won any woman I wished, Maria," he whispered honestly, a breath away from her softly parted lips. Her body felt swollen now. Inside she was throbbing, trying desperately to catch her breath. "It was the best way I could find to spite the King— embarrassing him with my willfulness. But since that night at the opera, none of that matters."

"I cannot risk believing you. There have been so many others."

His mouth brushed her cheek, his breath was hot and sweet. "And you shall be the last."

He was a highly physical man, she knew—magnificent and leanly muscled. George moved against her then and, as he did, the realization hit her. He meant all of this, every word. He was going to sweep her up into all of this and there was nothing she could do to stop it.

His lips moved onto hers, soft at first, then more insistent. He tasted the way he felt, purely male, slightly spicy, like cinnamon and anise. As their kiss deepened, becoming rough and passionate, his arms slipped down along the length of her back, bringing them more closely together. His body was long and taut, and the nearness of him excited her beyond belief. She kissed him back, opening her lips to him, needing more, her body remembering what ecstasy there could be between a man and a woman. It was a connection that years of loneliness in her second marriage, to a man she hadn't loved or desired, had forced her to forget about. Until now.

George treated her and touched her as if she were something precious, like no man had treated her before. As he moved against her hungrily now, a powerful hand coming around to her breasts, touching the tender swell of skin above a strip of lace, the oil lamp slipped from her weakened fingers. Instantly it ignited a furious fire amid the puddle of oil around it. Maria jerked back, gasping, and looked down at the small, contained circle of flames ablaze between them on the marble floor.

"Do not be frightened," he tried to say in a gritty whisper. "I shall simply call for—"

But before he could tell her that there were servants waiting only a breath away to extinguish such an impotent blaze, she whirled on her heels and swept past him. In an instant, she was out of the moment as she rushed back into the safety of the brightly candlelit corridor and out of his sight.

CHAPTER THREE

MARIA TOOK THE SMALL VELVET-COVERED box from her young Irish butler. Then she looked back at Isabella and Anne. Both of them sat before her on a mahogany settee with scroll armrests and scimitar legs, their tea glasses held properly.

"Another gift from the Prince of Wales?" Isabella asked.

Of all the hours of the day that he could have chosen to send something! Maria thought angrily, as she faced the curious, seeking expressions of her friends.

She looked up at Isabella's pert, witty smile, then over at the reed-slim and elegant Lady Lindsay. Anne sipped her tea nervously to keep from saying what she really thought of such scandal. Maria set the box down on the little marble-topped table beside her chair and picked up her tea again.

"Well, you are going to open it, are you not?" Anne innocently asked.

"Indeed I am," she said, taking a sip of her tea, then reaching for a piece of fresh gingerbread. "Only . . . not just now."

"Oh, but you *must*!" squealed Isabella in that same, sonorous fashion. "Lady Lindsay is your friend and, better still, *I* am your relation! You have a duty to show us what His Highness has sent!"

"Whatever it is, Isabella, rest assured that it shall be returned just like the one which came before it."

Anne looked to Isabella for verification that this was not the first demonstration of the Prince's affection.

"Can you believe it?" asked Isabella, not believing it herself. "His Highness sent her a magnificent emerald brooch and she had the impudence to send it back!"

"To do otherwise would go not only against my religion but all that I believe."

"Accepting a token from the future King of England cannot be contrary to anyone's religion," countered Anne.

Maria pursed her lips and looked back at her friends. "No, but allowing His Highness to believe that it will lead somewhere most definitely is."

Maria set down the gingerbread and tea, then rose calmly from her chair. Her face did not change or react so that either of the others could see any of the apprehension she was feeling. "I would be lying to you both if I said that His Royal Highness's attentions were not flattering," she said, and they thought it sounded a little haughty. "But you must understand. I cannot, I *shall not* submit to a position with anyone that is less than that of a proper wife."

"Perhaps he has that in mind," Anne supposed.

"Oh, let's not quarrel about this, shall we? You know as well as I about the Royal Marriage Act, which the King instituted after His Majesty's brother made a mockery out of his own poor match. If that is not enough, there is the Act of Settlement, which clearly says that if the Heir marries a Catholic he shall lose all rights to the Crown."

"Well, all right. Perhaps he is not thinking of marriage, exactly, Maria," Anne conceded. "but you do stand to gain a great deal by not spurning his affections entirely."

"Precisely what I told her."

"Please, Maria, open the gift. We are your two dearest friends in the world. If you will not share with the two of us, with whom can you share?"

Maria thought of saying that with "dear friends" like the two of them, she need look no further for a more direct line to the voracious gossip mill of London. But with patience, she reconsidered.

"Whatever it is, it is going back. So there is really no point," she said firmly. "Now that is the end of it, and I shall thank both of you not to look at me like two little lost dogs about it any longer. This charade with the Prince of Wales has gone on quite long enough."

She sat back down, fluffed her skirts, then lifted her tea glass. But now the tea tasted bitter. She looked at the two faces across from her, vivid in their disapproval. In the silence, the clock near the door tolled the hour of five. When she looked up, she saw two of her servants peering in from behind the salon doors. Quite likely, they had heard every last word

AT FIRST THE SOUND CAME from her dreams.

...Hollow and discordant. A rapping in the darkness like a branch slapping against a window. Maria stood veiled in white silk watching a faceless man nail a placard on the trunk of an elm. Its branches were bare and twisted like a skeleton. It was the only tree. As she stood straining to see, the man turned. The face belonged to the Duke of Bedford.

The sign, written in blood, said *whore*...

She woke with a start but the rapping continued. She strained to gain her bearings in the darkness. The sound was coming from downstairs. There was someone at the front door. She fumbled for the candle on her bedside table, her eyes straining to see the bronze mantel clock at the end of the room. The fire beside her bed had almost gone out but there was light enough from the moon through the window to see. It was nearly three o'clock in the morning.

Suddenly she heard footsteps in the corridor, then voices. Her servants were rushing to wake John. She bolted from her bed in her cambric nightdress and swept barefoot across the floor. Out in the corridor two of her servants stood speaking in low tones before her brother, John's, door.

"Do not wake him," Maria whispered, holding the unlit candle.

"But he sounds very insistent, ma'am. And he is, after all, the Prince of Wales."

"I don't care if Suleiman the Magnificent is outside! No one is admitted to my house in the middle of the night! If His Highness means seriously to pursue me, he shall have to learn that doing so is most definitely *not* going to be business as usual!"

"Jacko has told him that you had gone to bed long ago, but he still insists on seeing you tonight. Says he cannot rest until he knows whether or not the gift pleased you."

She looked away, embarrassed, as Jacko Payne, a tall, rugged man who looked more like a farmer than a butler, took a forward step.

"His Highness must be quite drunk, to come here like this," he said. "Everyone speaks of how reckless he is."

Like a moth to the flame, the image of George danced brilliant and wild before her now, Maria caring little what fate would befall them both if this continued.

She leaned against the cold oak door frame, her mind whirling, almost bursting with the fear and with the exhilaration of it all.

"Go to him one last time, Jacko," she finally instructed in a voice well schooled in aplomb. "Tell his gentleman that I have been awakened and that my personal instructions were specific. Tell him that I do not entertain *anyone* at this hour. And that if he does not go away, I shall be forced to submit a complaint directly to the King." *George's greatest enemy.*

When both of her servants had gone back downstairs, Maria closed the door and moved back into her dark bedchamber. It was safe here, and warm, full of familiar things, familiar smells. After she had lit the candle by the spark of the last few embers in the fire, she sat on the edge of the bed and listened through the window to the discordant strains of George's deep, cultured voice. Then Jacko's. Then George's again.

Maria held her breath until she heard the snap of the carriage door and the click of the wheels as they led him away from Park Street.

After he had gone, Maria opened her bedside table and took out the small box. It was laced with rose-colored ribbons in precisely the same way as the last. When she opened it for the second time that night, she gazed down at a small locket surrounded by diamonds. The Prince's dashing image, painted in miniature, gazed back at her from the center.

She pressed the locket to her cheek, thinking of the utterly profli-

gate Prince who had probably just awakened half the families in
Park Street with his recklessness.

VAUXHALL, THE FASHIONABLE PLEASURE GARDEN across the
Thames, was ablaze, illuminated by thousands of lamps that washed
the sky in a dazzling gold.

Before supper, guests wandered across the pale pink gravel path
amid the Canterbury bells and pink and white foxgloves. Women
wore gauzy summer gowns, their hair powdered and caught together
at the nape, then accented with huge ribboned bonnets. At every
corner of the gardens there were women dressed in lavender, olive
green, and lilac, strolling with elegant men in brown and blue and
green cutaway tailcoats over tightly fitting breeches.

In Tothill Fields and Old Westminster, just back across the river,
children were begging in the streets, running in and out of shabby
little houses and through murky alleys. Day after day the air and the
London fog was choked with coal dust. But beyond the vine-cov-
ered walls of Vauxhall, civilized society reigned supreme. Here, it
was beautiful, brilliant, and as picturesque as a Gainsborough
painting.

In a white silk gown embroidered with purple flowers, Maria
strolled between Isabella and Anne. Her pale gold hair was tightly
curled beneath a huge-brimmed hat. Behind them, Charles Sefton
and Maria's brother, John, walked side by side. Both men, one tall
and slim, the other older and more stout, were whispering and pointing out all of the pretty girls who came together to the gardens in
hopes of finding a husband.

Maria had told no one, least of all Isabella, about the disturbance
at her door the previous night, and she had no intention of doing so.
She could not bear the added complication of that delicious sort of
detail, when already they were pressuring her to submit to the most
dangerous liaison in London. And London itself would not be at all
displeasing to her, if it were not for the Prince's continued interest.
He was the one impediment in an otherwise perfectly ordered life.

She gazed down the shady avenue of rustling chestnut trees
before them as the gentle strains of Handel were played by an

orchestra in a grand pavilion at the end of the park. She could hear her brother and uncle behind them. They were arguing about a young girl who had dashed into the darker part of the park, where thick foliage and huge trees made a shady walk convenient for lovers. From what Maria could hear, the debate concerned whether or not she would come out alone.

"Will you be joining us tomorrow at Blackheath for the watercolor exhibition?" Isabella asked Anne, as she twirled her ivory and satin parasol.

"I haven't decided," Lady Lindsay replied with a sigh and gazed off toward another dark walk that led between a scatter of willow trees. Here too, several young ladies had gone giggling and were followed shortly thereafter by two eager young men. The squealing and intermittent laughter that followed was lost on none of them, especially not on Maria.

She was glad to be leaving the city tomorrow, leaving all of this, even if it was just for the day. At dawn this morning, she had received another invitation on the same ecru-colored parchment, requesting her presence at yet another ball to be held at Carlton House. The note scrawled beneath, in George's own bold hand, said that tomorrow evening she could anticipate the treatment accorded a queen.

After she had read it, Maria was more relieved than ever to be going to Blackheath with Charles and Isabella. At first, she had fancied a bit of excitement, that was true. But since their meeting less than a week ago, George had proceeded to disrupt her life entirely. She had even considered leaving London altogether rather than face further the stares and whispers that already had been cast against her. The excursion tomorrow had given her a legitimate, if temporary, reason to avoid the very persistent prince, and her own confused feelings for him.

After John and Charles insisted they wait to watch the girls run out from the trees, they all strolled back toward the small supper boxes near the orchestra pavilion. At Lord Sefton's box, amid elaborate silver dishes of roast veal, pigeon pie, leg of mutton, custard, and currant tarts everyone was surprised to see Francis Russell, the Duke of Bedford, waiting for them.

"Good to see you again, Smythe," he said, coming to his feet, a crystal glass of sherry in one hand as he extended the other.

"And you, my good man. Where have you been keeping yourself?"

"Off in Bath, to drown my sorrows, if you shall pardon the pun," he said simply, not needing to look at Maria to let her know that it was she who had broken his heart. "Lady Sefton," he said instead. "you are looking elegant as ever."

"Thank you, Your Grace."

He nodded to Lady Lindsay. Then, after an awkward moment, where everyone turned to look at one another, hoping someone would utter something pleasant, John turned to Isabella. As smoothly as if the notion had just come to him, Maria's brother said, "Well. I do believe that is my favorite tune they are playing. Would you care to dance?"

"Oh, indeed."

Charles Sefton followed his nephew's lead and turned toward Anne. "I'm afraid I'm not much good but perhaps you would like to join them, Lady Lindsay?"

Maria sank reluctantly into the empty chair beside Francis as her four companions quickly abandoned her. This sort of complication — another ardent suitor, was the very last thing she needed in the world just now.

"Well then. You might as well sit too, now that we have been left so unceremoniously on our own," she said with a huff, furious that she had been manipulated this way when she had made her feelings for the Duke more than clear to everyone.

"Yes. I'm sorry about that," Francis said, sitting back down in his chair beside her.

She looked up at him. His eyes were as plain and passionless as ever. "Was it you who arranged it then?"

"Your brother, John, called on me yesterday. He urged me to give it one more go," he said honestly and then laughed, unsettled in her presence again. He took a sip of his sherry when he could think of nothing else to say and began to look around at the people seated at all of the other tables.

"I'm really not such an awful catch, you know."

Something about the way he said it, the uncertain inflection in his

81

voice, made her instantly sorry that she had been so brusk. None of this was really his fault. He had only extended an offer. Unlike her brother, John, the Duke of Bedford was not insisting that she take it.

Maria extended her hand and placed it atop his on the white linen tablecloth. "You shall make someone a wonderful husband one day, Francis."

He looked back at her. "But just not you."

"No. Not me."

"Well, I had to try one last time anyway. You know Jack, always full of such grand hopes. Rather infectious chap."

He waited a moment, pretending to listen to the music. Then he said "So tell me, Maria, is it true? Have you cast me aside for a dalliance with the Prince of Wales?"

She felt the question sting like a needle, and jerked her hand from his. The only thing that stopped her from leaping to her feet and dashing out of the park was the vulnerable expression on his soft-featured face.

He had not meant to be crude. He had meant to try to reach her.

"I said no to your proposal, Francis, because I do not love you. Nor do I believe in so brief a time that you could have come to love me. We both deserve better than a marriage that is only socially appropriate."

"The Prince of Wales has told all of his friends that he is in love with you. He also says that you have not yet refused him. I heard it yesterday myself from Charles James Fox."

"The Prince of Wales has quite an imagination."

"If it helps him capture your heart...I envy him."

For an instant, he looked boldly at her, and she thought it was a look defying her to wound him further.

"I tell you, Francis, right now I am much more in need of a friend than a lover."

"Or a husband?"

"Or a husband." She softly smiled.

After another moment of strained silence, he reached beneath the table cover, as the ends rustled in the early-evening breeze. He took her hand from her lap and squeezed it.

"If that is what you truly want...what you need, then, my dear Maria, you may say that you have a friend for life in Francis Russell."

"Ah! There you are! Well then. Is it all settled?" John asked anxiously as he came back up and stood between them, a hand on each of their shoulders.

"It is, Jack," Francis answered him.

"Splendid! I knew she would come to her senses."

"Your sister has not altered her decision."

Isabella, Charles, and Anne settled into the vacant chairs as Maria and Francis smiled at one another.

"But, I-I don't understand. You said yourself that it was settled—"

"And it is. Your sister and I are going to be better than husband and wife, Jack. We've agreed to become the best of friends."

Maria looked up triumphantly at her brother. Then she cast a glance at Isabella. She looked over to Anne. But no one was smiling.

She had, they believed, just made the biggest mistake of her life.

"MRS. FITZHERBERT?"

Maria pivoted just as the carriage driver opened the door to their coach and directed her inside. Calling from the gate to Vauxhall was a tall young man and a much paler, a much more slightly built woman with a heart-shaped face. She recognized them at once as Lord Admiral and Lady Seymour.

"How nice to see you again," Maria said, walking toward them with a smile. "I, being in much less of a predicament than when last we met."

"We both had wondered how you'd gotten on since the other night at Carlton House after our dance," Hugh Seymour said.

"Doubtless you've heard the rumors," Maria answered, her smile fading a little.

"Believing idle gossip would be a grand mistake."

"Bless you for that," she said, clasping her hands together before her. "I really can never thank you enough for coming to my aid as you did."

"It was a gentleman's duty," Hugh said modestly, and inclined his head just as he had done that first night.

Isabella called to her from the waiting carriage. Maria bid them good night and then turned away when Horatia called after her.

"We look forward to seeing you tomorrow evening. Hopefully for your sake you shall not need my husband's aid so much then."

Maria stopped and turned back around. "Tomorrow evening, Your Ladyship?"

"At Carlton House. The party in your honor. I am told everyone is attending."

Maria turned slowly back around with a quick intake of breath as though someone had struck her. Just when she had begun to acknowledge a glimmer of feeling for the wild, impetuous prince—when she had begun to believe that perhaps all of the vicious gossip about him might be untrue, her anger overwhelmed her. Maria's face tightened and she waited long enough to mask her outrage before she spoke.

"I am afraid the Prince of Wales has been premature. I have another engagement tomorrow evening and therefore will be unable to attend his party."

She surprised herself with the control in her voice when she was so utterly appalled by George's arrogance. Maria had said she would not be available to the presumptuous prince tomorrow evening. That had been polite. In truth, she had no intention of being available to such seductive danger ever again.

No, absolutely never.

"I CANNOT BELIEVE IT!" SQUEALED Isabella. "He is actually following us!"

Maria turned around, now that she was safe inside the cabin of her uncle's leather-lined post chaise. She saw through the small glass window the same bright yellow carriage following at a discreet distance, behind a dark tandem. Maria turned back around and crossed herself. Both Lady Lindsay and Isabella gazed at her as she sat completely still on the black leather seat, looking straight ahead. Only a single soft bead of perspiration on her brow betrayed the knowledge that any emotion at all could be conjured by the Prince of Wales.

Maria was secretly thankful that her brother and uncle had chosen to go into St. James's Street with the Duke of Bedford rather than accompany them home. John was far better at seeing the truth in her eyes than anyone else, and that was a complication she did not need at the moment.

"What will you say to him?" Isabella asked breathlessly, two fingers lightly covering her lips.

"If I am called upon to do so, I do not intend to say anything at all to His Highness."

"And if he comes to your door?" Anne pressed.

"Then he shall be turned away just as he was last night."

"Maria, you *didn't?!*" gasped Isabella, still holding her fingers, spread like a fan, across her parted lips.

"I most certainly did. He clung to my door at three in the morning, frightening my servants, and that I will not have...no matter who he is!"

By Maria's instruction, with a tap of her long pearled walking cane against the roof, the carriage sped more quickly past Piccadilly and onto Park Lane.

"We shall lose him here, I am certain," Maria murmured as their carriage merged with a dozen others.

Anne and Isabella could do nothing now but look at one another in bewilderment, then turn and look out the small rear window to see if the Prince's carriage still followed. Isabella finally turned back to Maria. She had the entire world before her, and men were falling at her feet. Not because she desired it or had orchestrated it, but precisely because she had done nothing at all. There had always been something different about Maria, Isabella considered. It was something that seemed incompatible with the base sort of games played among society. A thread of uncommonness ran through her. That was certainly why the Prince of Wales was so intrigued, and the Duke of Bedford was left heartbroken. She was a challenge. She was their prey, the prize in one of the endless contests they contrived at Brook's or Boodle's or any one of the fashionable clubs along St. James's Street.

And, in that, Isabella could not help but be just the slightest bit envious.

The carriage lurched to a stop in front of her house on Park Street. Maria dashed from the cabin, past the small iron gate, and up the four stone stairs. She did not wait for Jacko to meet her and open the door. Instead, she burst through it herself, leaving the heavy black door ajar. Isabella and Anne gathered their skirts and followed more slowly.

"I suppose we did lose him, after all," said Anne, her rich voice pitched with disappointment.

"Pity," seconded Isabella.

As they stood at the top of the stairs outside the front door, Jacko now waited to see them in, Isabella glanced back down toward Park Lane, then across to Hyde Park. Couples still strolled in the shadow of the setting sun. *A pity indeed.*

When Isabella and Anne came into the drawing room, Maria was already at the pianoforte, her head lowered over the keys. Fanny was serving mint cordials in tiny crystal-stemmed goblets. As she handed one each to Isabella and Anne, the women settled together on the blue silk settee.

Even though Maria had begun to play, they did not hear the music. The click of wheels as the large yellow carriage came to a halt outside her door was too powerful to ignore. A slow squeal followed, like a screeching cat, as the carriage door was opened. Maria stopped playing, picked up her cordial, and drank it entirely. Then she set the empty glass back down and began to play again as though she had heard nothing.

As they had done all the way home from Vauxhall, Isabella and Anne exchanged another glance. There were scuffled footsteps. Muted voices. Then the click of the iron gate.

Unable to bear it a moment longer, Anne dashed to the window and peered out from behind the velvet drapery. "It *is* him!"

Isabella moved swiftly to the pianoforte and covered Maria's hands with her own. The music stopped again. The sound of the knock that followed swept like wildfire through the suddenly silent drawing room.

Jacko looked to Maria for instruction.

No one else moved.

"What are you going to do about him, Maria?" Isabella asked in a shrill, combative tone, her hands on her hips. "You cannot simply ignore the Prince of Wales!"

"I am wife to no man. I do as I please."

"Maria, for heaven's sake, be serious!"

Again the brass lion's head knocker was lifted and the metered rapping sounded firmly against the door. "Do you mean to alienate completely the future King of England?"

"I mean to make him behave like a gentleman in his dealings with me."

Isabella shook her head as the insistent rapping continued.

"Shall I answer it, ma'am?" Jacko cautiously asked, coming a little more fully into the drawing room.

"At once." Isabella waved her hand.

"No, Jacko! Let it go."

"Maria!" Anne cried, dashing toward the pianoforte beside Isabella. "You must at least answer the door! Since he has followed us, he knows that you are here!"

"I'll not have anyone, even a prince, following me around London like some voyeuristic lecher."

The rapping became more insistent. Maria studied their anxious faces. "Very well, Jacko," she finally conceded. "If you must tell him something, then tell His Royal Highness that I am not receiving this evening. Tell him I am tired and have already gone up to bed."

Isabella shook her head and turned away. "You are a fool, Maria Fitzherbert. You surprise me in that. Perhaps you do not desire his advances, and for that I cannot blame you. But by your incivility, you are cutting off your very nose to spite your face!"

Before Maria had time to reconsider, the Prince's valet, Orlando Bridgeman, had burst past Jacko and into the salon, his tall crown hat in his hands. "Madam, please. His Highness wishes only to speak with you. He is aware of your concern for your reputation and asks only that you grant him a few moments of your time."

"It is all right, Bridgeman. I am quite capable of doing my own fence mending."

Behind his servant, standing between the parted, heavy velvet drapery leading into the foyer, the Prince of Wales stood clear-eyed and steady in a dashing costume of gray satin with a starched white cravat. Anne and Isabella both dropped to deep curtsies. Maria remained seated at the pianoforte as he came down the two carpeted steps into the drawing room.

"Would you ladies be good enough to give Mrs. Fitzherbert and me a few moments alone?" he said, more as a command than a question.

Maria looked helplessly back down at the keys as her two friends followed the servants from the room. In spite of her resolve, she was afraid of being alone with him like this...again.

"This is most improper of you," she said, her voice trembling, as she tapped repeatedly at the same key in an absent way.

"I know. And I apologize. But, Maria, you have totally bewitched me and, to be plain about it, I intend to win you over."

"I am not some sort of prize to be won!"

"You are to *me*." He moved toward her swiftly and stood where Isabella had been, his square face shaded in the shadows of the street-lamp glow. But she continued to touch discordant keys in a nervous gesture to avoid his gaze. "I had no business coming here last night and you have every reason to be angry with me."

He paused a moment, careful with his words and with his tone. But he wanted to be honest with her. He wanted to make her understand that this—what he felt was different.

"Aspects of my life have been difficult lately, and I confess to having taken a bit too much to drink last evening. It is a habit I took on long ago, and one I intend to vanquish. I had arranged the evening tomorrow as a means of making amends, to show you that although they are certainly sudden, there is great depth to my feeling for you."

He touched his lips with a single finger. Waited again, careful with how he approached this very new and fragile link between them. "...But I hear now that you have refused me, and I could not help but think that my indiscretion last night had been the cause of it."

"It was your invitation that I refused."

"Yet the outcome is the same."

"I had already made other plans."

"And they could not be changed?"

"I did not desire to change them."

Surprised, George stepped back. "Well. You *do* continue to be direct."

Hearing her own harsh tone, Maria came to her feet as he gazed across the room at a collection of small, gold-framed portraits of her family beneath a sash of yellow satin.

"I shall tell you one thing, madam," he said softly, not looking back at her now. "That night at the opera, I watched you in the candlelight for a long while before you ever saw me—your eyes misted with tears at the music, and I said to myself even then, if I should let her, there is a woman who could easily break my heart. That is something, madam, which no one...*no one*, has ever done, because I have never allowed myself to feel so much."

She felt her throat constrict. "Your Highness, I—"

"I am not always a man given to wise actions, Maria. That is no secret to anyone here in London," he said, finally turning back toward her. His blue eyes upon her made her forget what she had hoped to say. "Folly, as you may know, appears to run in my family. My own dear father has blazed quite a trail in that. But I assure you that I am not entirely the man whom you see depicted in the papers. Please believe that, although they are sudden, there is not the slightest bit of folly in my feelings for you. I know, without question, what it is that I want."

They were close now, as they had been that night at Carlton House, in the stained-glass shadows of the Conservatory. His voice had been warm and coaxing then as it was now.

"There is something special, magical between us. A soul connection. I don't know how or why, but it is there. And you feel it as well."

He must not know that he had touched her this way. There was too much danger—too much uncertainty, she was trying to tell herself as he drew nearer. Only her breathing, quicker now, and the rise and fall of her breast beneath the opal-colored gown, would betray her if she just...

Suddenly she felt the same warm hand pressing her thin sleeve; the same pressure of his body against hers. This time Maria did not resist when she felt the first brush of his lips at the line of her jaw. She could feel his warm breath, his heart pounding out an impatient rhythm against the bodice of her gown.

"I...wish very much to kiss you again," George whispered, his mouth hovering above hers as he tilted back her face and overpowered her with the seductive touch of his lips.

For the moment, in his embrace, their kiss deepening, Maria could see nothing, feel nothing but a wild surge of pleasure and the power of their connection.

With her eyes tightly closed, his arms firmly around her, she felt as though she had slipped into a long, velvet tunnel where there was only darkness...and pleasure. It excited her, and terrified her at the same time, and she shuddered as his tongue swept inside her mouth, and made her melt like butter into his powerful arms.

When George pulled away, he saw that her face was flushed red and her dark eyes were wide with surprise. He touched her moist lips with a single finger. "I meant what I said. This is not folly."

"Please leave," she answered him, and again her voice trembled. She did not mean it. She did not want it. But she must convince him otherwise. *For both their sakes.*

"Very well. But allow me to return tomorrow."

"I am going to Blackheath tomorrow with Lord Sefton and his wife."

"At what time do you depart?"

"W-We leave at two."

They were still close. She could still feel his breath on her face, her own desire coursing through her veins, making it impossible to think in any way close to rational.

"Then I shall come to your garden just after eleven. If it pleases you, we will meet there."

When she did not object further, George turned victoriously from her and collected his hat, gloves, and cane. He knew the servants and Isabella had watched the entire scene, but he did not care. From a life of meaningless affairs, fostered out of loneliness, despair—and out of boredom, he was committed to finding something more pure...something true. And for the first time, this evening, he had seen in her eyes a glimmer of hope that, no matter how she spoke to the contrary, she just might want that as well.

AT BROOK'S CLUB THE GREAT, green gaming tables were full. Great-coated gentlemen played game after endless game of faro and whist and drank great volumes of brandy to steady themselves. Between their bets, tiny silver snuffboxes clicked one after the other in rhythmic syncopation. Fox and Sheridan were playing at a round table near the fireplace when John Smythe and Charles Sefton stepped into the magnificent room.

Servants were everywhere, milling around the patrons, pouring tea from silver urns, and serving brandy and cordials from the finest crystal decanters. As they played, everyone was buzzing about the pitiful state of things in France. Most were saying that it would undoubtedly lead to some great upheaval without the benefit of reform. Lord Salisbury took a pinch of snuff. He then said, in his opinion, that there was no telling where the acts of a king like Louis XVI or a queen like Marie Antoinette might lead the French people.

"Oh, Sefton, there you are," said one dour-faced gentleman in a stiff gray and white striped cravat and olive-green tailcoat, looking up from a pinch of snuff. "Do come and play. Edward here is cheating miserably and I am desperate for virtuous players."

"Then do not look in London," quipped Lord Townshend with a glass of sherry to his lips.

John moved slowly toward one of two empty chairs. Sheridan was first, before Fox, to hear the Sefton appellation and to make the connection between this young man and Mrs. Fitzherbert. He had, after all, been the one to persuade Lady Sefton to see her husband's niece brought to Carlton House that night.

He looked up, intrigued by the possibilities of so indelicate a situation.

"Please sit down gentlemen," Sheridan said, tucking his own cobalt-blue enamel snuffbox back in the pocket of his gray tailcoat. John pulled out the chair for his uncle, then one for himself.

John did his best to appear as if this was a common occurrence. But secretly he was overwhelmed to be called to gamble for the first time with so famous and celebrated a figure as Richard Brinsley Sheridan. To do the things that this man had done, see the things he had seen! John had read *School for Scandal* five times already and was midway through a sixth.

The Sheridan he now saw across the table, in the light of a heavy crystal chandelier, was a distinguished-looking man who, in his youth, had been devilishly handsome. At his temples, silver streaked the dark waves and featured a sharply angular face that still attracted the loveliest women.

"You both know Mr. Fox and Mr. Sheridan, and Lord Townshend." The aged aristocrat, Salisbury, puffed and flicked his blue-veined hand toward them in introduction.

Townshend nodded.

John smiled, then nodded in return.

"But do we know *them?*" growled Fox, looking up from his cards and frowning so that his thick dark brows merged into one.

"John Smythe, at your service, sir." Maria's brother grinned a little too eagerly for the taste of a table of London's most formidable. "This, of course, is Lord Charles Sefton, my uncle."

Fox studied him more closely. "Your wife is Lady Isabella Sefton?"

"She is, sir."

"So *she* is the one who has been squiring about that mysterious woman without whom the Prince of Wales has decided he cannot live. At least for this week," he added with a mocking, thick-lipped smile.

Everyone began to chuckle.

Fox belched and pushed himself back from the table so that the stains on his elegant silk waistcoat were visible beneath two missing buttons.

"I'm certain you are mistaken," John said, surveying the derision on each of their aging faces. "Lady Sefton's companion is my sister, Mrs. Fitzherbert, and I can assure you gentlemen that if there were a courtship involved between her and His Highness, I should be the very first to know it."

"Youth," Lord Townshend laughed into his brandy. Sheridan watched the young man's flawless face darken with anger.

"My sister, sir, is being courted by the Duke of Bedford!"

"Hush," Charles Sefton urged with a firm hand to his nephew's knee, all the while continuing to smile like the others.

"Courting, is it?" asked Fox, flippantly. "So is that what they are calling it these days?"

John pushed himself away from the table, his eyes smoldering with rage. "I bid you, say what you mean to say, sir!"

"I believe I have, boy," Fox replied, refusing to look at him again.

John stood stiff as a marble statue, his arms at his sides, his hands gnarled into fists as he loomed above the others.

"Sit down, Mr. Smythe," Sheridan said in a firm, punitive voice, as though he and Fox were schoolboys in need of reprimand.

Slowly, Fox's sardonic smile began to fade beneath the threat of youthful and untamed fury. Wisely deciding to bait the boy no further, he cleared his throat and looked back at his cards. John looked at his uncle, whose disdain mirrored Sheridan's. Slowly he sank into the vacant scarlet chair as Lord Townshend began to deal the cards.

He took his hand from the table but his mind was a torrent of emotion and shock.

Is that why she has refused Francis Russell? I should sooner strangle her myself than let her become another interlude for that spoiled, impulsive excuse for a royal heir!

He had heard all of the sordid stories. All of the women. All of the games. He could read a paper just like anyone else. No. Maria simply must not be allowed to slight the family that way.

He could feel the blood mottle his face. The vein in his neck pulsed with anger the longer he considered it. He simply could not allow it. Impossible! For her. For him. For what such scandal would do to them all.

"Are you playing, my boy?" he heard Fox ask him above the sound of his own dark rage.

John breathed deeply until he felt his reason return. Then he glanced back down at his cards. Nothing more than a spray of red, white, and black before his eyes. But he must overcome it for the moment. This was too splendid an opportunity to game with such influential minds. A privilege indeed. Anyone in London would have thought so...even if Sheridan had proven to be a little too priggish for his own taste, and the sight of the flamboyant, disheveled Charles James Fox had already begun to make his teeth ache.

THE NEXT MORNING, MARIA CLIPPED a sprig of jasmine and brought it to her nose. It was deliciously fragrant and at the height of its bloom. Lining the gray gravel path around her were primrose, geraniums, and towering white valerian. She loved summer most for the flowers.

"Am I late?"

A deep, steady voice came from behind her and she knew by the heady civet perfume shadowing the words that it was the Prince of Wales.

She had almost gone ahead of Isabella and her uncle, Charles, so that she would not be forced to face him again. But that had been a futile spark of logic in a situation that, from the beginning, defied all reason.

George had shaken her resolve yesterday as he had kissed her, and, deep inside, past the layers of denial, was some little part of her that wanted to feel the same thing again now. With him.

Maria turned around, her face shaded by a wide-brimmed straw hat, and her arms loaded with a bouquet of hollyhocks, roses, and little wisps of fragrant jasmine.

George took a step back. Her face, without its caution, was as it had been that first night at the opera, before she had seen him. Gentle. Vulnerable. Her cheeks were full of roses. Full of a zest for life he could not even begin to comprehend. His only hope was to capture it, and her, and pull her into his tumultuous, loveless world, changing it. And changing him.

"Are you all right?" she asked with a note of concern that warmed him.

"Morning light becomes you," he said softly, and then held out a bent arm so that Maria would take it.

Once she did, they began to stroll in the shade beneath a pergola-covered walk draped thickly with clinging, emerald ivy and laced with pink roses.

"I am pleased that you agreed to see me."

"I never agreed. You invited yourself," she said with half a smile.

"Ah, but you did not refuse me. That is what is important." After a moment he said, "I brought you something."

"Not more jewelry, I hope."

He stopped and turned to face her. "Not until you say that I may." George drew a small box, wrapped in orange foil, from beneath his dark blue cloak and held it out to her. She looked up at him suspiciously, the caution returned.

"Sugarplums!" He laughed when he saw her hesitation. She looked up from the box and, after a moment, she could not help but laugh, herself. "I hope that you like them," he said.

Still chuckling, she took the box and looked up again, feeling happy, light, and completely disarmed. "I do indeed. Thank you."

"Good." He smiled. "Very good."

They began to stroll again past a small clay birdbath where two putty-colored finches splashed. When George saw the small iron bench beneath a painted arbor, he took her hand and led Maria toward it. For a few moments they made idle conversation beneath the shade of the arbor as the bees droned in the flowers around them. George was the first to change it.

"Do you know that there has never been a woman before you who has had the courage to refuse me?"

"They do say there is a first time for everything."

"You really are the most curious, and yet fascinating, woman I have ever met, Maria," he said in a voice so commanding that her skin turned quickly to gooseflesh.

"Your Highness, please—"

Maria sprang to her feet, but George caught her hand and pulled her back beside him. Powerful. Commanding. A streak of danger. All the things she had wished to know in the men who had loved her, and yet never had.

He bent his head to take in the fragrance of the bouquet of roses and jasmine she held between them like a shield. His action was a nuance to make her relax. "The last thing in the world I want is to offend you, and yet I seem to do nothing but."

She actually felt the sincerity in his words this time, as if they had a power of their own, and the knowledge of that suddenly made her want to be kinder.

"It is simply that you are always rushing at me, pressing me to accept you, as if this were some sort of contest. But never before have you spoken sincerely about yourself so that I might come to know something more of the man than the image."

George paused a moment, then looked up at her with surprise. "I don't suppose anyone has actually ever asked that of me."

She touched his hand. "*I* am asking you."

The spark of hope had become a flame. His voice went lower as he chose his words carefully. "I suspect that what all of the others were interested in was precisely that image, not the man. I merely grew accustomed to giving women what I *believed* they wanted."

"I don't wish to be like other women," she said, and her hand flexed over his.

There was the faint glimmer of a smile between them. A true bond beginning.

"To consider you like anyone else would be impossible."

"Tell me," she whispered.

He looked away from her, out across the garden. He had never been entirely honest with a woman in his life and he was uncertain if he could be now. The risk was so great. But for the first time, for Maria, he wanted to try.

"I suppose you could say that my life has been a facsimile." He waited to hear how that had sounded, to decide if he could bear to continue a confession. The sensation that hit him in the echo of his own first words was strange, and yet somehow comforting at the same time.

He went on. "Yes I have lived quite grandly, most would believe. I have, at different times, and at the King's pleasure, possessed the trappings of royalty. And yet, even during the periods when I was in possession of those things, I know I have not really *lived* a'tall." George turned his hand over and clutched hers with a kind of measured desperation. "I wonder, can you understand that?"

"I'm not certain."

"No, I don't suppose you could, really. After all, why should you? You had a family who looked upon you as something more than the mere continuation of a dynasty, a commodity to cultivate and keep in line."

"But surely your life has been about more than that."

"I am not certain that it has."

"There must have been someone, along the way, who truly cared for you."

The image of Belle Pigot came to his mind. But he didn't say it. "One day, the Lord willing, I shall be King of all this," he said, extending his hand. Then he looked back at her with the saddest expression she had ever seen in her life. The way his eyes leveled upon hers just then took her breath away.

"But I want more. What I *want*, Maria, is to feel loved as a man is loved, not as a prince is desired for what his position affords. And the saddest thing of all, I think, is that I did not even know how lonely I was until that first time I looked into your eyes."

When he moved to kiss her, Maria backed away. "Your Highness really must stop this."

"Because you still do not believe me?"

"Because I do not feel the same."

"But how do you know that when you have spent all of your energy resisting the possibility?"

"You are the Prince of Wales and I am simply another conquest."

"Great God above, woman! I have lain open my heart to you simply because you have asked me, and then you have the courage to wound me with indifference like that! I do not understand you at all!"

She let the silence between them stand a moment as she fingered the white ribbon on the unopened box of confections. "You frighten me."

"Because I have the courage to be truthful?"

"Your passion frightens me."

He took her chin gently in the palm of his hand, only spurred by her sudden honesty. "You must not fear any part of me, beautiful Maria. I want only to bring you happiness and contentment. And I can, if you will give me the chance."

This time when he moved toward her, Maria did not resist him. Dangerous as it was, she craved the feel of his warm lips on hers. She longed to have him pull her body toward his, to feel the full weight of his desire again.

She was possessed by overwhelming contradictions—craving, lurching, leaning, and yet still a small urge to push him away for the danger of it all. Kissing, breathless and urgent, his tongue wrapped with hers, Maria felt euphoric and, at the same time, on the brink of tears. His grip on her arm tightened and she gasped for breath, feeling as if she would drown.

"I want you," he was whispering into her pale golden hair as they parted. "I want all of you. I am desperate to feel your body beneath mine, to give you the rest of me just as completely as I have given you my heart."

Maria jerked away from him. The flowers and the box of sugarplums tumbled to the ground. "So you do want me to be your . . . *mistress?*"

"I wish for you to be the only woman in my world. Whatever that comes to mean between the two of us."

He tried to pull her to him again but she resisted, sobered when she realized fully what he was proposing. It should not matter. She should not be entertaining *any* sort of bonding with this entirely untouchable man-prince. Good Lord, what had she been thinking? Feeling?...*Fantasizing?* This was insanity.

Yes, she wanted to be in love. Yes, she wanted to feel what an incredibly handsome and dangerous Prince was making her feel. Adored. Swept away. But not at that price.

Honor. Reputation. If that was lost, what was there left to her?

How different she was from this man beside her. How different their pasts. Even so, it seemed, how different their dreams for the future. One's reputation was impeccable. The other's could not have been worse. He was the reckless, profligate Heir depicted in caricatures all over London. Every moment with him like this was a risk.

As he sat silent and surprised, her own face quickly transformed into a protective mask of reproach, her dark eyes blazing.

"This may come as a shock to a man like you..."

He shook his head. "Everything you do surprises me, Maria."

"I am a devout Catholic, Your Highness," she tossed her head, trying desperately to sound more firm than she felt. "I cannot be anyone's mistress. No matter what I feel, not even for you."

"I had no idea at all that you would take my feelings for you as an insult."

"Well now you know."

He took her hand again, tightly. "Come with me."

"I could not possibly."

"Your honor will not be challenged. You have my word."

She paused a moment, studying his face. There was only sincerity there. "But where is it you wish to go?"

"Not far from here. Just around the corner, really. I should like to pay a visit to the tenants of a little house on Canterbury Road. There is someone very special there I should like you to meet. I shall see you returned long before your departure time to Blackhealth."

He could see her surprise. Canterbury Road was a modest area housing London's working poor. In the silence, George drew her to her feet. They faced one another. "Just out your garden gate. It is only a short walk. Please, Maria. It is important to me."

"But your driver, your guard? Is that safe?"

"We shall go unnoticed, appearing like any other London couple out for a stroll. That, in itself," he smiled, "shall be worth the deception."

THE WOMAN WHO ANSWERED the door after two clicks of the half-rusted knocker was small and plain. She wore an unadorned, ivory linen gown with a white fichu and bonnet. Her dark eyes grew wide with surprise to see the Prince of Wales at her door.

"What in Heaven's name — What are you doing here, sir?"

George smiled. "Do invite us in Belle, would you, before your neighbors are asking the same thing?"

The half-timber house, belonging to Belle Pigot's ailing brother, was small. But what it lacked in size it more than made up for in warmth and charm. There was a huge inglenook fireplace dominating one entire wall of the low-beamed sitting room, stuffed chairs, and a trestle table with a vase of daisies on top of a slip of white lace. Maria felt herself relax with her first step past the threshold. This was a world away from the pomp and grandeur of Carlton House and George's *other* friends.

"How is he, Belle?"

She curtsied properly. "My brother is much improved at the notion of our going to Madeira. That all is your doing, sir, and we so kindly thank you."

George chuckled and kissed her cheek. "Sir, is it now, when once you wiped my tears and tucked me into my bed? Not with me you don't, dear heart!"

Belle glanced at Maria, surprised at the circumstance and Maria knew instinctively that a woman's being brought here was not a common occurrence. "Mrs. Fitzherbert," he said. "May I present my dear and most precious friend — as dear to me as a mother ever could be, Belle Pigot."

"It is an honor Mrs. Pigot." Maria smiled, and extended her hand.

"When I was a child," he said, showing Maria to one of the chairs, Belle to the other, and sitting down himself only afterward, in a most unprincely order of things, "Belle saved me, quite literally, not only from the King, but from myself. I was a miserable lad back then, lonely, afraid, lashing out at the world. And she alone made me believe there was something out there beyond the bleakness that would be worth waiting for."

"I only helped you see the things you already knew yourself."

"Oh, no. You were my savior then." He smiled again. "And you are my dearest heart, forever. Which leaves a little less for me to give to the woman I one day marry. But I trust"—he glanced at Maria—"the right woman shall understand."

He was such an enigma, Maria thought, watching him relax, watching as he became, here in this room, a man just like any other man. Full of feeling and honesty and dimension. Just when she was ready to believe the rumors about him, he did the most extraordinary things to destroy them all.

Belle made tea after that with delightful little sandwiches and cake and then George helped her ailing brother into the sitting room and covered his knees over with a knitted quilt, settling him in a chair nearest the fire. Charles Pigot was pale and gaunt but he smiled at the idea of unexpected company, especially that the future King of England had taken the time to come to his modest little house to check on his health once again.

After they talked and laughed and had their tea, and George insisted on being the one to help Charles back to his bed, Maria helped Belle clear the tea things. "He's a very different man here with you, isn't he?" Maria asked carefully.

"The only thing different this time, child, is that he's brought you. This is quite extraordinary for my brother and I, this lovely visit."

Maria settled the dishes on the kitchen table. "You mean he has never brought a woman here to meet you before?"

"Never. I've known about them, of course, heard about many of them. But until today, he has always come here alone."

Maria was struck. "You're very dear to him."

"I was just going to say that very thing to you." Belle settled her dark eyes on Maria. "Do you care for him then?"

"I don't know."

"He clearly cares a great deal for you."

"I haven't wanted to believe that."

"George is a very complex man, my dear. He has been hurt a great deal in his young life. If he has brought you here, I believe that means he finds you worth the risk of loving. I bid you, take great care with the knowledge of that."

"Do you know that I am a Catholic?"

"Love is love, child. It knows few bounds. To this day, I am still in awe of a Prince's affection for a simple woman from the country such as myself. But I take him as I find him, *not* as the gossip says he is. In your heart, you find him different as well, or you wouldn't be here with him today."

"I do not intend to become his mistress."

"Then become his friend." Belle's smile was warm and rich, and full of kindness. "He has precious few true of those at places like Brook's Club, or lurking around that old mausoleum he has tried so desperately to make into a home, and I will be gone from London with my brother for a while. So many others here in the city want a piece of the Prince of Wales. How refreshing it must be for him to have met a woman whose self-respect means more to her than power. If I may say so, it is little wonder that he is enchanted."

WHEN THEY CAME INTO THE drawing room that night, it was nearly midnight. Most of the lamps had been extinguished and the fire was only sputtering. Maria sank exhausted into one of the stuffed chairs without even removing her hat and gloves. She felt as heavy as a stone. It had been a long trip out to Blackheath and back, the roads being much worse than any of them had remembered from last summer.

John poured himself a sherry as Jacko took his greatcoat, hat, and gloves and Fanny added another small log to the waning fire. As she pushed it with the long, slender poker, the red cinders flared and Maria felt a new glow of warmth. She closed her eyes for a moment until she sensed John before her holding out a second glass of sherry. She took it with a nod and slowly sipped the warm liquid.

For the first time this season, Isabella and Charles had chosen to leave them off at the little iron gate and return home to their own brick house in Piccadilly without joining them in a nightcap. Maria had been relieved. The nights cooled everything, and the peace, when one was left to enjoy it, was so lovely.

"May I take your hat now, ma'am," her maid asked in a voice almost as soft and unassuming as Maria's.

"Thank you, Fanny," she said wearily.

She did not even have the strength to look up or acknowledge her lady's maid who stood over her, hands clasped gently at her waist. It had been a long day and yet, even now, Maria could not force the Prince from her mind.

No sooner had John settled into a chair beside his sister with a copy of the day's newspaper than it began again...a rapping at the front door.

"Jacko!" John called out absently from behind his paper. He looked up and smiled over at his sister but she was already lunging at him.

"Do not!"

Jacko came back into the drawing room, coats still in hand. The expression on his rugged face was as full of concern as Maria's. He stood beside Fanny, whose own face had gone pale. She stepped a little nearer to Maria. "What are we to do ma'am? It is the third time tonight already."

Again there was the rapping.

John looked over at his sister, his lips parted and his eyes wide with surprise.

"Who, in the name of Heaven, is that?"

Jacko looked to Maria, not daring to speak without her approval. But she only looked away. Fanny was ringing her hands nervously and glanced back at the door.

After a moment's pause, it changed to the same persistent clacking against the lion's head knocker that had been heard two nights before. There wasn't a house all the way to Park Lane that could not have heard it.

When no one answered his question, John raced to the window and peered out from behind the damask draperies, as Isabella had done. There, beside a bright yellow carriage, with a lowered crimson shade, stood two coachmen costumed in royal livery. They were whispering to one another as the Prince of Wales, clothed in dashing red and white, stood tall and commandingly at the door, as if it were the middle of the afternoon.

John spun around, his eyes blazing and his slim nose pinched white with anger. "How *dare* you not tell me that something was going on between the two of you? I even risked my own standing last night defending you to Charles James Fox himself!"

Maria looked at her brother and her expression was grave. "I thought it was only harmless flirtation, in the beginning. Isabella and Anne even encouraged it."

"So this has happened before?"

"Yes."

"Good God above! That profligate will make us all the laughing stock of London, Prince or no Prince!"

"His reputation is far worse than the reality, brother."

"Well, what else on earth is there *but* reputation?"

Thinking of George, what he had shown her today, of himself and his world, she felt her heart soften. "I am beginning to believe a fair sight more."

"In one night he is proceeding to undo all that I have tried to do for this family!"

"Will you speak to him then, sir," Jacko carefully asked as the cook and a chambermaid peered in from the kitchen, both already dressed in their nightclothes.

John looked back at his sister's tall, rugged butler as though, in the midst of his surprise, he had forgotten there was anyone else in the room. He saw the look of expectation on the servants' faces.

After all, he was the head of this household now. It was up to him to act. But as angry and shocked as he was, he could not risk insulting the Crown Prince. That would do far more damage to his social standing than any commotion His Royal Highness might cause outside his sister's door.

"Wait until my sister and I are safely upstairs," John finally instructed, "then tell the Prince firmly that we have retired for the evening. He shall have no choice but to go away."

Jacko opened his mouth to speak. Then, thinking better of it, he decided to remain silent. He glanced over at Maria one more time, seeking her approval. But she was too confused, by what she continued to tell herself she did not feel, to say anything at all.

"Very well, sir." Jacko finally nodded into the silence, and then turned back toward the door.

"What on earth could have possessed you to tolerate this flirtation?" John charged.

Maria looked at her brother. So proper, so dignified. Could she ever make him understand when she wasn't certain she understood it all herself? Maria drew in a breath and saw George's eyes, his handsome face, his smile. "Very well," she said evenly. "You truly wish to know? The truth, dear brother, is that, after two forced marriages that left me cold, rich, and alone, everything suddenly now seems changed. He makes me feel like someone entirely different!"

Fanny blushed and lowered her eyes. John moaned. "Good God, it is worse than I thought."

Her eyes suddenly blazed. "I am attracted to him, dear God yes, that. He's handsome, he makes me laugh, and, for the first time in my life, he makes me want to see what lies ahead in my life, not dread it! I cannot imagine any longer being the predictable and lonely woman I was before I met him!"

"Sheer lunacy, Maria! I cannot believe what I am hearing!"

"Nor can I, frankly believe what I am saying. But that changes nothing." Maria slowly stood, her eyes still locked with her brother's astounded gaze. "May God save me for putting a voice to these most intimate of thoughts, but like no man before him the Prince of Wales has found a way to confound, excite, and to entirely amaze me."

Fanny followed Maria up the mahogany stairs then, and into her bedroom, holding one white taper in a silver holder. She lit two others and then a third from the single wick until the entire room flickered a warming gold. She closed the door and Maria sat on the edge of her bed, but a moment later John pushed it open so hard that it hit the wall behind it with a great thud.

"Leave us," he said in a harsh monotone.

Finally, Fanny set down the candle on a small, cluttered table, curtsied, and withdrew.

A moment later, they heard the front door close downstairs. The firm rapping against her door had ceased. There were no other sounds outside her open window but the now familiar sound of the Prince's carriage as it rolled steadily into the night.

"If I mean to keep a modicum of my self-respect I have no choice, do I, John?"

"None that I can see."

Maria pressed her face in her hands, as if some part of a spell had slowly begun to fade with the absence of the powerful man who conjured it within her. The reality, not the emotion of it, returned. She had everything to lose by allowing this dangerous attraction to continue on to where it next would surely go. He was England's heir, she must remind herself no matter what he made her feel—and she was a Catholic. Period.

Part Two

I TOLD MY LOVE,

I TOLD HER ALL MY HEART,

TREMBLING, COLD, IN GHASTLY FEARS—

AH, SHE DOTH DEPART.

—WILLIAM BLAKE

CHAPTER FOUR

AUTUMN LEAVES BLEW AIMLESSLY ACROSS the cobble-paved courtyard, whirling a tangle of red, gold, bronze and brown. France early in October of 1784, two months after she had fled England, was a bonfire of color. Chestnuts and oaks with their gnarled branches dropped multicolored leaves like tears against a blood-red sky.

Down in the valley, the little market stalls were still bursting with fresh harvest. Potatoes, bright orange carrots, and beautiful waxy green beans. Old women cried a litany of French commands from withered lips, their worn aprons and their wooden sabots caked with mud. Carts pulled by donkeys, some by men, crowded the roughly cobbled streets. Wealthy ladies from England hiked up their elegant skirts and walked among them beside their husbands for the sake of the town's curative springs. But at the top of the gentle sloping hill, framed by forest, simplicity blocked out the rest of the world.

Maria sat alone at twilight on the tile veranda, sipping sugary tea from blue china as the aroma of roasting foul and herbs filled the air like a heavy veil. It was a different world than the tumultuous one she had left behind.

The house in Plombières to which she had escaped was really a group of low-gabled buildings surrounded by an open courtyard. All of the buildings were timbered and bearded with pale green moss. When it was cool like this, Madame Mouchard, her wide-hipped housekeeper, urged her in a guttural, punitive French to come indoors. But since leaving England, Maria had come to favor dusk more than any other time of day. The cold wind against her face, bronze leaves whirling past her. It was the feeling of freedom, freedom from everything and everyone who had bound her in England.

When Madame Mouchard was unsuccessful in her bid to make her mistress come inside, she slammed the small green door against the wooden frame and sent out reinforcements.

Lady Lindsay was tall and thin, almost gaunt, which was not at all fashionable. But her beauty was in her face, a smooth oval with wide violet eyes and full, voluptuous painted lips. She stood looming over Maria now, her face curiously troubled.

"You had better come in," Anne said.

"Is supper ready then?"

"Not yet. But perhaps you would like to come in a bit early just the same." She looked down, her violet eyes intense. "You have a visitor."

Maria looked up and set her empty teacup down on the little wicker table beside her. How could George have found her here? Her itinerary had been so swift and well thought out, so changing.

Her heart began to beat so loudly now that she could not hear her own thoughts. In these past weeks she had only begun again to feel what it was like to live without fear, without the devastating whirlwind that had robbed her of her peace. She was not ready to see him. Not yet.

Maria stood slowly, letting the loosely knit shawl fall to the tile. With a defeated sigh, she followed Anne back inside the house. She moved into a room that was spartan but elegantly furnished by three chairs with sunken brown leather upholstery and two matching tables with ebony veneer. Four small botanical prints, framed in oak, were the only decoration for the white plaster walls.

"Madame Mouchard and I shall be just outside if you need anything at all," said Anne in her distinctively haughty voice, then closed the door behind herself.

Maria held her breath and curled her hands into two small fists.

She was not ready to see him again. Not nearly ready, she thought as she slowly turned around.

"You?" she cried.

"But of course." The amiable Duke of Bedford smiled.

Maria swept across the room, which was shadowed red and blue and green from the stained-glass windows, as he held out his slim elegant hands to her.

"But what are you doing here, Francis?"

"As I recall, you told me at Vauxhall one afternoon that you needed a friend far more than you needed a husband. I simply took you at your word."

They stood facing one another holding outstretched hands, Maria's fearful expression having been melted by surprise.

"But how did you find me?"

"Your brother told me where you were. I hope you're not angry."

"Of course not. I am just so glad to see someone from England!"

"Yes. He also told me that Anne had come over to keep you company for the month."

"She has been a dear friend through all of this. Please." She motioned with a twist of her hand. "Let's sit down." She waited a moment, then said, gripping the top of her head. "I am just so terribly surprised to see you."

"Surprised, I should imagine, that I was not the Prince of Wales."

Francis saw the smile on her face fall by degrees. "My brother, John, has been quite thorough, I see."

"He's been terribly worried about you so far away, Maria. And to be honest, so have I."

The sincere expression on his slim, soft-featured face and the tone in his voice reassured her that speaking the truth was for him as important as breathing. She came and sat beside him.

"If it at all puts your mind at ease, Jack told me very little actually. But nevertheless, the scandal is all over London. They are even whispering that you secretly married the Prince before you left."

"Gossip mongers."

"Are they?" Bedford looked at her with such bone-chilling sincerity that she was forced to look away.

"Oh really, Francis. Don't be absurd. How could I marry the

Prince of Wales? You know as well as I that I am a Catholic; a blight on England as far as the King is concerned."

"What I *know* is that you are a beautiful, kind, and sympathetic young woman who could easily fall victim to the more circuitous means a man might take toward his ultimate desire."

Maria leaned back into the dark leather chair and studied his face. Its smooth surface was all planes and angles in the evening shadows. But it was a kind face, still possessed of an interest in her that surpassed the boundaries of friendship. No, it was not safe to tell him the truth of her feelings. At least not now. Not while things were so uncertain.

Roasting chicken and herbs, fresh currant buns and tarts loaded with fat, ripe strawberries wrapped the house in a thick, smokey aroma. Through the stained-glass window, the sunset's brassy bonfire began to pale.

"Will you stay for supper?"

"I would be honored." He smiled, his face not in the least affected by the censure of his questioning. *There will be enough time for that,* he thought. *Better not to press. She is like a skittish young colt; press too hard and I may push her away entirely.*

"I've taken a room in town, just down the hill, at a little place near the Hotel de Ville."

They both heard the heavy brass dinner bell that the old French cook still insisted upon ringing. A black crow squawked in the cobbled yard just beyond a set of long carved doors, which muted the sound. Francis smiled at the earthy peace of the place. *Perhaps this is precisely what she needs until I have a chance to win her from him,* he was thinking.

"Then you plan to stay in Plombières?" Maria asked.

"I plan to stay in France, madam," he finally replied, rising to escort her in to dinner. "So long as you have need of me."

THE NEXT MORNING, BEFORE SHE had even finished her tea and toast, the Duke of Bedford's shiny black tandem turned down a lane of rustling poplars and clicked up the hill toward the courtyard of Maria's rented house. The single horse, a sleek black and white gelding, whinnied and snorted as Francis pulled the reins to stop him.

Anne, who sat beside Maria at the table that had been set out on the veranda, looked up from a week-old copy of the *Morning Herald* and a half-filled cup of coffee and milk.

"My, how you do have them eating out of your hand."

Maria blinked hard. It was not the sort of comment she had expected to hear. Throughout all of this, she had come to think of Anne as a dear friend. Before she could protest, however, Francis had stepped, lean and graceful, from his carriage.

Dressed in an elegant maroon velvet tailcoat, double-breasted and cut long in the back, smoke-gray breeches and matching leather boots to the knee, he stood in the courtyard and held up a hand in greeting. Then he gave the reins over to Monsieur Mouchard and came bounding up the four stone steps that led to the veranda.

"Good morning, ladies," he said, rocking back on the heels of his dark leather boots. "Sleep well, I trust?"

"You're here awfully early this morning," Anne sniffed with a circumspect expression.

"It must be the fresh air. I slept like a baby last night, and woke at dawn." He smiled and gripped the back of an empty cane chair. "May I?"

"Please." Maria nodded as Madame Mouchard stepped out from the kitchen holding a tarnished brass teapot that was steaming from the spout.

"*Bonjour, Monsieur,*'" she huffed in a tone not unlike Anne's in its reserve. "*Du café?*"

"Might I have tea instead?"

Madame Mouchard, a coarse, heavy woman with dark, beady eyes, and full, ruddy cheeks, glared down at him, her English better than she preferred to admit. She was not at all pleased that what the young Duke desired made more work for her. The furrowed, heavy brows directed at him made that quickly apparent.

"Ah. Well. Perhaps I shall have coffee then."

"Madame Mouchard, please bring His Grace some tea and some fresh toast. This is already cold," Maria said firmly.

"You know there really is no good tea to be had but in England," Anne sniffed and raised her copy of the *Morning Herald* back before her face.

As Madame Mouchard lumbered away from the table she muttered something indistinguishable in French that seemed to mirror Anne's comment, and disappeared back into the aromatic kitchen.

"I am sorry about that," Maria said, and tried to smile. "The Mouchards have worked for the owner of this house for nearly twenty years and when he leases it out in the autumn and winter I'm afraid she's rather come to think of it as her own."

"Yes. I see what you mean."

A cool breeze stirred the dry leaves in the courtyard and a pillow of clouds scudded across the morning sun, darkening the horizon.

"Perhaps we won't have so beautiful a day as I had hoped," Francis said to Maria.

"By noon it shall be clear again. The weather is simply lovely here. It has been like summer every day," Maria said.

"Splendid." Francis smiled, looking back at her. "Splendid indeed."

He had come to take her exploring with him to some of the old churches and villages that dotted the expansive forest around Plombières. After he had finished his toast and tea, and she had gathered her wide straw hat and blue velvet cape, he settled her on the red leather seat beside him. He pulled twice on the reins and turned back with a sly smile for the benefit of Lady Lindsay, before the horse lurched forward and the tiny black tandem clicked ahead over the stone and down the tree-lined hill.

"How glorious!" he said, smiling over at Maria, his tight blond curls rustling in the breeze as they rode through the forest. "So you really have explored none of these lovely sights since you've been here?"

"I'm afraid not."

"But with all of this beauty and adventure at your doorstep—"

Maria touched his hand softly, as a friend might do. "Since I have been here, Francis, I have had a few other things on my mind."

Francis stopped the carriage near a little town with the ruins of a stone abbey on its outskirts. He tied the horse to a tree. "Shall we explore it together then?" he asked, pointing toward the ruins.

Maria nodded, then pulled the cape over her shoulders. They walked through a neglected garden and in through a little open side door. Ivy was climbing through the space where there once was a glass window. A streak of sunshine glittered through cobwebs. More clouds passed over the sun and a sudden gust of wind stirred. Francis saw her shiver beneath the velvet.

"But perhaps first we should find a place to warm you?" he reconsidered as they walked back outside and headed into the village.

Bains-les-Bains was a cluster of little timber-framed cottages. From those nearest came the voices of children. Broad-hipped, big-busted women in coarse gowns and worsted kerchiefs crossed the narrow streets ahead of them. Some were carrying full milk jugs, others were carrying their smallest children. All around was the subtle, delicious scent of brisk country air.

"Perhaps we could even find a glass of sherry to put the roses back in those cheeks." Francis laughed and took Maria's icy hand.

"That would be lovely," she conceded, still shivering.

He looked back over at her and, at that moment, he had the most overwhelming urge to kiss her. Still the time was not right, he told himself. But one day...

AS MARIA AND FRANCIS TOURED the stone ruins of a thirteenth-century abbey, Anne came down from her room and met Madame Mouchard at the bottom of the stairs.

"I have another errand for you," she said distinctly and handed forth a sealed letter. "I want you to have this sent to England by tonight."

"*Oui, madame. Je vous empris.*"

The housekeeper wiped her sweaty palms on the front of her plain black gown and took the letter between two stubby fingers. She recognized immediately the name of the man to whom it was being sent. It was the same as last time. And the time before that. He was a very famous man indeed. Royalty. Almost as notorious as their own King Louis.

"As before, Madame, neither you nor Monsieur Mouchard shall speak of this to Mrs. Fitzherbert, I trust."

"*Mais absoluement, non, madame.*" She shook her head earnestly.

"Good. Then the price shall be the same."

The old woman's smile revealed rotted teeth and she quickly covered her mouth with an awkward hand. "Oh, and Madame Mouchard," she said, stopping her as the servant took a few steps back toward the kitchen. "Do see that it is sent this morning, would you? As you might imagine, it should not be at all agreeable if Mrs. Fitzherbert were to discover it was *I* who was informing the Prince of her whereabouts."

Anne felt the guilt at deceiving Maria this way only for a moment. Then it passed. The potential for gain was too great. It had been Isabella's idea to feed the Prince with information. She had done it herself the night His Highness had first met Maria. Along with Richard Brinsley Sheridan, she had arranged their encounter. Both Maria and Anne stood to gain a great deal with the Prince of Wales if he was happy. And after all, who could it really hurt? The fickle prince would tire of the chase soon enough and no one would be the wiser. Maria would recover... Of course she would recover. It was clear to everyone involved that the Duke of Bedford meant to see to that.

THREE MONTHS IN FRANCE STRETCHED into six, then a full year more, but Maria's feelings for George did not pale the way she had hoped they would. She heard from Anne that news all over London was rife with the King's barring of the Heir from going abroad. His Majesty was afraid, it was reported, that George would elope with his newest dalliance.

Anne also wrote to her that everyone in England now knew about the situation, and all were in favor of her becoming his official mistress. Better that, they said, than to risk the Prince's place in the line of succession. But it was George's long and beautiful letters to her that began to change everything, sentiments that made a difference.

Apart, they had both had time to reflect and consider the consequences of their feelings. In firm and beautiful lines, written in sloping black ink, George filled his letters to her with commitment and love. He talked about news from Belle Pigot, his struggle with the restoration of Carlton House, and he told her that he considered daily what it was they were heading for. It was not the dalliance she had first believed. Her absence had changed nothing in his heart or her own. He was coming to France, he told her, illegally if need be. But she was far too precious to let go.

In his final letter, one she carried in a pocket of her gown, George had proposed a morganatic union, according to the laws of Hanover, and a quiet life together in France. He was fully prepared, he told her, to give over the succession to his brother, Frederick, and for the Crown of England to descend to his children. The end was always the same. He assured her over and over again that he would not give her up.

"Another letter, is it?" asked the Duke of Bedford as he came out to her in the garden.

Maria quickly folded the missive and looked up. For a moment she wavered between anger, for the horrible choice to which George was subjecting her—and tears for what the newly instituted laws of England would see they were never allowed to become.

Francis was furious at the Prince and envious at the power he possessed over Maria, both at the same moment. "Oh, how I do hate to see you so tormented by all of this. Why can he not simply leave you alone?"

Maria folded her arms across her breasts and they began to walk together along the flagstone path. "He says that he loves me, Francis."

"Ach! What does a man like that know of love? Women are acquisitions to him! It is the thrill of the chase which intrigues him."

"When I first met him I would have agreed with you."

"And now your conviction has abandoned you."

She shook her head yes. The long-standing tension had thinned her voice. "He says he is preparing to come abroad, to meet me in Hanover, and to marry me there in a morganatic ceremony."

"Oh, I tell you, the man has no conscience at all where his desires are concerned. Listen to me, Maria. Could you actually live with yourself if you allowed him to give up the Throne of England for what he believes, at the moment, is love? Dear Lord, you would change the entire course of history!"

Maria's sigh was a heavy one. "It was why I came away to France in the first place. But I don't honestly know anymore. It has all gotten so very complicated."

Francis took her arms and held them tightly until she twisted around to face him. "Then marry me, Maria. Let me make it all simple for you again. You know that I adore you and that we would make a good match. Let me help you stop this madness. *Please*. Let me protect you."

Maria reached up to touch him, her hand a gentle pressure along his smooth-skinned face. She did her best to smile. "Dear, Francis. What a special man you are."

"Then say you will marry me."

"I am in love with him, Francis."

The words, unexpected, clawed at his heart and he released his hold on her. Maria saw the hurt and turned away from him. She could not bear to see his pain just now while she was so enslaved by her own. She reached out to touch the tip of one long red rose, whose fragrant petals fluttered like tiny crimson sails in the breeze.

Yes, I am still and all in love with him. God save me, she thought, from what surely lies ahead.

"I have resisted him for so long...and yet his love has gone unchanged," she went on quietly. "You must know *that* has surprised me more than anyone. He is willing to risk everything for me, Francis. How can I turn away from him?"

"You cannot possibly intend to *marry* him! Good God, Maria, you're a Roman Catholic! You know it would be completely illegal! The King would never give his blessing to such a union for his heir, even if he had not instituted laws against it! Mother Mary," he moaned. "Maria, please! Think about what you are heading for!"

"You know that I have done nothing but that for nearly a year here in France. If I want to stop him from leaving England and risking his future, then I *must* return. And it is not only that. I want to go home, Francis. I want to see my family again, my friends."

"And the prince."

She looked at him but she did not reply because it had been more a statement than a question. Her expression was guarded now, closed off to him. She had shared with him all that she meant to.

"Then I expect there is nothing I can do to stop you."

"I shall always love you for wanting to try."

"But not enough to cease this madness."

There was a little pause before she answered. She turned her face away, but her voice, when she spoke again, was rich with a kind of conviction he had never heard before. It was a tone, framed by words that, when he looked back on the entire affair, would haunt the kind and well-meaning Duke of Bedford for the rest of his life.

"Once things were so different for me, Francis," she said, finally answering him. "But I no longer believe that there are any among us powerful enough to stem the tide of our own destiny. Mine, I have come to believe, is to be caught up...and will forever be, somehow, with that of the Prince of Wales."

CHAPTER FIVE

"SO TELL ME THE TRUTH, Duchess. What do you *truly* know about it?"

Charles James Fox posed the question in a clever bit of verbal jousting with the Duchess of Devonshire as they danced together in December, in the stifling and impossibly crowded assembly rooms once again at Almack's.

"Charles, dear." Georgiana smiled in response. "What lady of quality do you know who gives away all of her secrets?"

"A wise lady does what she must to prevent disaster," he corrected her. "You are His Highness's dearest confidante. If he meant secretly to marry *that woman*, surely he would have confided in you."

They were not two people to break easily from traditions long established. As they danced together, Fox's probing was as clever as ever, but he was quite drunk. As usual, his finely embroidered waistcoat was stained with his supper.

For her part, Georgiana's repartee remained viciously witty. Tonight, as every night, she was heavily powdered, patched, and painted—a barrier to the real woman beneath.

"Well, at least you can admit that she is back in London," Fox pressed.

"I have heard the same rumors, yes."

"Dear lady, you know as well as I that such a state of affairs can lead to no good for our mutual friend. The lady in question has been away so long and resisted His Highness so forcefully that she certainly would not have returned to England unless some legitimate way had been found for them to be together."

"Why not ask the Prince of Wales yourself if you have such great concern about his private affairs?" Georgiana asked as the two friends whirled together beneath the bandbox.

Fox lowered his thick beetle-brows in a formidable scowl. "I have tried to do precisely that, madam. But of late, His Highness has done everything in his power to avoid me. That in itself has made me fear the worst."

To Charles James Fox, it meant more than the implications of the illegal marriage of a close friend. To the entire Whig Party, who were struggling now once again to gain supremacy over the Tories, it meant risking the power of their most potent supporter. George must do nothing to endanger his future succession to the Throne. If he married this commoner illegally, he risked everything, not only for himself but for the entire party.

The Duchess of Devonshire could not be blind to that. She had struggled too long and too hard alongside of him to see it all cast away now for the sake of a dalliance. They both knew better than anyone else how quickly George forgot his mistresses...even the ones he believed, for a time, that he truly cared for.

George only wanted this chit so badly because she had refused him. Of course that was it. What else could have blinded him to the pleading of his friends to all manner of reason?

"Perhaps, then, you should simply let it alone," Georgiana proposed. "Let nature, and the nature of the man, run its course."

"I cannot do that! You know I cannot! We have come too far with him! Invested too much!"

Georgiana felt him miss the step as he became more agitated. More desperate. He was right. The Prince of Wales's marriage to a widowed Papist would mean disaster, not only to the Whig Party but to her own long-developed influence over him. Georgiana had a duty to side with Fox in this.

"If he will not see you, then you should write him a letter. Voice your concerns that way."

He looked back at her, his dark brows arched with surprise. "Of course that is the answer! A letter! Why the devil did I not think of that?"

Georgiana tipped her head back, flashing a white-toothed smile, her hazel eyes glittering in the candlelight. "As I said before, Charles, what lady of quality do you know who would give away *all* of her secrets?"

A HARSH DECEMBER WIND SLAPPED bare branches against the window, rattling the glass like dry bones. A delicate gold clock on the marble mantel ticked like a metronome. George stood tall and silent beside a blue velvet armchair. He looked dashing in his bright red waistcoat, tight white breeches, black boots, and tall white cravat. He had chosen his garments carefully. There would never be an encounter more important than this one, and he knew it.

Finally, the silence was broken by soft tapping footsteps and the mahogany stairs creaking beneath them. He could smell the soft aroma of Maria's lavender perfume before he looked up and saw her coming toward him. The swift movement made peach ripples at the bottom of her gown.

He was surprised to see that the time apart—a year and half in total, had not changed her. Her hair was still the same mass of soft blond curls. Her eyes were still dark and fathomless. But what had changed was the expression in them. It was a new kind of calm. The uncertainty that had driven her from London was gone.

He wanted to rush at her, take her into his arms, and never let her go. But he didn't. He took one step forward and then stopped. He must take great care. She had endured a great deal to get to this place between them.

"That will be all for now, Jacko. Thank you," Maria said simply as they faced one another for the first time in so long. Neither George nor she moved until they heard the click of the door against the frame and could be certain that he was gone.

"You have not changed at all," he murmured.

"Nor have you."

"I don't know what I expected, but I am surprised."

"Pleasantly, I hope."

He moved forward and took her hands. It was like holding wrapped velvet. "Words can never tell you what joy I feel just now."

Maria had forgotten what a handsome, intelligent face he had, and those lips curved in a perpetual, enigmatic smile that made her feel the optimism he had for them. In some ways it was as if she was seeing him for the first time. But the eyes she had not forgotten, brilliant and crystalline in those dreams that had so haunted her since their meeting. They were clear now and resolute.

There was another silence. He waited.

She felt the reticence.

"I had to return," she said.

"If you had not, I would have come for you."

"I actually believe that you would have."

Things they had said, words he had written to her, moved in and out of her mind, blurring it. There was joy, desire, lust, and love, all slashed still with overwhelming fear. And with it there was anticipation of a connection that seemed only to have grown stronger during their separation.

"I told myself that somehow I must make you believe."

"And I do," she said in her soft, steady voice. "But I am still afraid. It all seems so uncertain."

"It does not matter. Nothing does, but that you love me."

"I cannot forsake my religion. Even for you."

"Then I shall not ask you to."

They stood very close, gazing at one another, their hands still linked, both of them trembling.

"I want to give you everything."

"I want only what is yours to give."

"I *will* marry you," he declared deeply. "For now, whatever way I am able to do that."

"Then I will accept."

His eyes were rooted on her. "Even if it means that, for a short time, at least until I become King, we shall be forced to live a deception?"

"As long as you do not openly deny our marriage, neither then shall I bid you publicly to admit it."

"We will be breaking the law," he warned. "There will be danger every day."

"But we will be together."

George closed his arms around her tightly and held her, neither of them speaking, neither of them wanting to lose what it had taken so long to finally acknowledge and capture.

Waves of fear for the future crashed against the calm of Maria's mind, but she closed her eyes to it, willing it all away. There was peace now; the feel of his powerful arms around her made it more intense. She was glad to have come home.

Glad to have finally surrendered.

When she let him finally, he kissed her deeply, passionately, and she felt a wild surge of pleasure as his mouth opened over hers. Finally, the thoughts and the fears were overcome by the crush of his strength and the softness of his warm, full lips. Held like this, for better or for worse, Maria knew now that she would love this man — *Yes, love him forever.*

The rest of the house seemed very far away now. Around them it was quiet, peaceful, but for the wind rattling the long, paned windows behind thin gauzy curtains.

Maria stood with George, knowing, *seeing*, how much more he wanted than their kiss. How much more he deserved, after the time he had waited. After the unbelievable commitment he was making. She drew in a breath, trying to steady herself — trying to remind herself how much her religion and her honor meant to her. *Let him want to wait a while longer,* she was thinking. *Until we both know that the moment is right.*

As if he heard and understood her thoughts, George dropped to one knee before her, taking her hands and pressing them to his lips. "I worship you," he declared in that soft, steady baritone that, itself, could wound her with its sincerity. "... Every part of you, Maria. And I shall prove that to you for the rest of my life."

She looked down. His gaze lingered on her face, a face he had given up hope ever seeing in this light. The light of a new and powerful intimacy.

Anticipation shot through her as he reached up then and pushed away the lace of her gown, touching very tenderly the full, soft part of her breasts. She heard him draw in a ragged breath, knowing how much more of her he ached to touch. Yet he did not rush at her. They both knew how long they had waited to come even this far. After a moment, George came to his feet again and pressed a moist, lingering kiss onto the curve of her throat.

Maria looked at him and swallowed thickly as his fingertips grazed her flesh where his lips had been. First her neck, then that small tempting portion of her breasts that her gown revealed.

George took them both in his hands, through the fabric, kissed each swell that burst forward above the cool bit of silk, then gently, erotically, pressed them together, his lips nestling for a moment between them.

For the first time in her life, Maria felt the totality of her own self-control begin slowly to spiral away. He moved back, looked at her again, and the flames of desire shot through her with a force that overwhelmed her completely.

As he bent down, she reached up, meeting his new kiss halfway. Their mouths formed together as his hands braced hers at her sides. "God, you are exquisite," he whispered onto her lips just before their kiss deepened and became demanding.

His chest against her breasts was hard and hot, slightly sweaty through the fabric, and she clung to him desperately, trying to pull him as close to her as any man had ever been—yet knowing in her heart that it was not yet time to let him make love to her completely.

Still, George kissed her again and again, until she thought she would go entirely mad for the dizzying desire that was pressing her down, hard and fast. Until she wanted more than anything in the world to give in completely. To have what they had waited for, what they both so desperately desired.

She moaned breathlessly as, finally, he pressed her onto the settee behind them. Tears pricked the back of her eyes as he buried his face in her hair, lying long and golden, splayed out on her shoulders.

His powerful hands reached beneath her then, clutching her buttocks through her gown, pulling her up and pressing himself against her, deeper, higher, harder, kissing her, seducing her. All the while, their clothing separated them from the last most intimate act, but that did nothing to hold back his arousal. As George moved against her in a rhythm that was rough and instinctual, caring not for their clothing or for propriety, her name slipped across his lips again and again like a mantra. He was touching her breasts in a way that set her on fire, and wounding her mouth with such wildly sexual kisses that she heard nothing beyond the thrumming beat pounding in her ears.

After it was over, they sat bound together for a long time, intimate, yet not fully, both of them trembling in the afterglow of a prelude that had been almost more erotic than the act ahead.

"Forgive me," he murmured raggedly.

As he pulled back to look at her, Maria was rocked by a new and overwhelming wave of love, knowing that nothing in this world had ever felt so exquisite, nor so right, in spite of how boldly wanton it had been. As he brushed the tears from her cheek she realized the reason he had apologized was not only because of what they had done, but because she was crying.

She had tested him in this. She had allowed him to have her in the way that he had. If an intimate conquest of a forbidden Catholic was all that the reckless prince desired—as the gossip mongers inferred, then she had given him at least in part, just now, his wish. But he was still here, still holding her tightly, his eyes still full of love and commitment.

"My darling, believe me," she managed to say. "There is nothing to forgive. The truth is, I am simply happier than I have ever been in my life."

George leaned over and kissed her, softly, gently again, sated.

"When I was a boy," he began again after a silent moment, though this time tentatively. "...I learned very swiftly to be afraid of loving anyone. I could not let anyone get this close to my heart. I spent so many years satisfying every other part of myself after that in defense. Every part, that is, but that one special place you alone have touched."

He looked back at her. Their eyes locked, and she felt a lump of emotion swell her throat because she knew he was telling her something he had never shared with another living soul.

"Promise me that we shall always have this intensity."

"My heart, my body, and my soul, now belong entirely to you, George. For better or for worse."

In the first place, you are aware that a marriage throws the Prince contracting such a marriage out of the succession of the Crown. Now what change may have happened in Mrs. Fitzherbert's sentiments upon reli-

gious matters I know not; but I do not understand that any public profession of change has been made; and surely Sir, this is not a matter to be trifled with; and Your Highness must excuse the extreme freedom with which I write. If there should be a doubt about her previous conversion consider the circumstances in which you stand...

Your Royal Highness knows, too, that I have not in my mind the same objection to inter-marriages, but under the circumstances a marriage at present appears to me to be the most desperate measure for all concerned...

George did not finish reading Fox's solicitous letter. "Feckless meddler!" he brayed. "If he ruins this for me after everything I have—"

Behind him in his withdrawing room, new alabaster draperies were being installed. Long, silk strips of fabric from floor to ceiling were tied back with gold fringed cord. A new settee had been installed as four footmen around him were busy polishing the Limoges vases, the tall gold-leaf picture frames and the marble table-tops. Everything must be like new. Everything must be perfect, for Maria.

"The Reverend Johnes Knight has arrived, Your Royal Highness," Lord Onslow announced with a grave nod after he had come alone into the withdrawing room.

George looked up from his writing table. The response to Fox would have to wait. He placed the blank slip of paper back in the drawer along with the letter and locked it. Reverend Knight was the second clergyman his secretary had been entrusted to find. It had not been a simple task. Due to the illegal nature of George's request, he had already been forced to approach only the most unscrupulous among the clergy. But marriage—some sort of marriage, was the only way to keep her his completely. So bargain he must.

After their reunion in Park Street, Maria told him that she knew that their marriage could not be a public one. At least for now. But within the confines of whatever sort of secret ceremony by which George felt able to abide, she hoped to be joined by God.

It would not only satisfy her own soul through the trying days ahead, but it had been the argument she had used with her brother and Uncle Errington when they finally had to be told. The King was continually ill. The deception would need not last long. There was great comfort to be taken in that.

Before George could see to the details, he discovered that it was illegal for a Catholic priest to celebrate a wedding between a member of his faith and one of the Church of England. George was also made to understand, by the members of his staff who knew of his intention, that he could not dare risk granting her even the one thing she desired.

If this ceremony he was now so eager to solemnize ever became known, he risked it being regarded as an act of communion by the Heir Apparent with the Church of Rome.

An unforgivable offense.

Finally, he was forced to dissuade Maria from her single request and to assure her that an Anglican ceremony was valid in the eyes of Rome and all of the Christian world. A clergyman from the Church of England was the only way. But even at that, finding one who would agree to break the law, even for him—perhaps because it was him—was another matter.

"Very well. Show him in."

George came to his feet and moved across the blue and green Exeter carpet to the center of the room. He was still wearing his blue silk dressing gown and Turkish slippers. With the snap of his fingers, he ordered all of his other servants out into the hall. Lord Onslow held the door as the cleric was shown in, then closed it behind him.

"Thank you for coming, Reverend Knight."

In his presence, Knight bowed. "One would not be likely to refuse a private audience with the Prince of Wales, Your Highness."

"No, I suppose not," George conceded, then indicated that they should sit in two chairs opposing one another.

Knight sat nervously on the edge of an ebony chair wringing his blue-veined hands. This small, elderly clergyman with great waves of snow-colored hair tamed with fragrant oil, suspected the reason he had been summoned. Everyone in London was whispering that the Prince was seeking a way to marry his mistress. Knight had, in fact, just that morning come from the Mount Coffee House, where that had been the single topic of conversation.

He had agreed with his friends that even if His Highness did desire to marry the woman, no respectable clergyman would be found in all of England to perform such a dangerous and clandestine ceremony.

"May I offer you a brandy, Reverend?"

"No thank you, Your Highness."

"Tea, perhaps?"

"I have just had a spot of coffee. But I do thank Your Highness just the same."

He shifted nervously on the edge of his seat. The Prince was grand, more regal in person than he had been led to believe. But in his blue eyes was that spark of desperation that made him believe that the gossip might actually be true.

George drew in a breath. "Very well then. I shall come straight to the point. It is no secret that my heart has been captured by a particular lady of a rather great reputation. In fact in the past year we have endured a great deal to be together."

"Your Royal Highness speaks of Mrs. Fitzherbert."

"It has been a difficult trial for us both, Reverend Knight. I must impress that upon you above all else," George said, not particularly surprised that the clergyman knew her name.

"Now, I am well aware that there are some who might say that I am not capable of distinguishing love from lust. That is gossip I have allowed to stand unchallenged. There are others who may say that I am too young to know what or who it is that I want for the rest of my life. But I cannot disagree with those sentiments more strongly."

Knight's gray frog-eyes widened as he realized what the Prince of Wales was about to say. But it surprised him in what an eloquent, levelheaded speech it was being presented.

"It is my wish, and now my Maria's desire as well, that she become my wife."

Knight sank back against the chair, seemingly breathless. His pale lips were parted by the surprise. "But the Royal Marriage Act, Your Highness?"

"I will repeal it of course, the instant I ascend the Throne. You know of the King's health. That cannot be far off."

George let the words settle like dust in the strained air between them. He stroked his chin with his thumb and forefinger, studying the little man, trying to gauge his response. "As you might imagine, this is not a particularly simple thing for me to risk discussing."

"Nor is it, in the least, a simple thing to hear, Your Highness."

"I am a desperate man, Reverend. I will have her whether it is you, or someone else, who performs the marriage."

"I do believe you will, at that."

George moved forward to the edge of his seat, his hands steepled together. "Then tell me you shall agree to marry us."

He gazed intensely at the Prince. "It is not such a simple matter. Your Royal Highness must certainly realize that. Not only do I risk the penalty for performing an illegal act, but further penalties of praemunire, if I agree." An offense against the English Crown, which that would be, was the gravest offense, and could lead the curate to a penalty of death.

"I am fully prepared to make the risk worth your while."

"And what of Your Highness's future Crown? Will the risk to that be worth *your* while?" There was another long silence. Neither man seemed to breathe. "Very well then. If you are certain that is what you truly desire, then I shall perform the ceremony."

George bolted from his chair and charged at the little man, taking his hand. "Thank you, Reverend Knight. Truly, thank you. And it will not be the clandestine sort of ceremony you anticipate," his voice accelerated slightly. "The Duke and Duchess of Devonshire shall be present, as will my own uncle, the Duke of Cumberland and his wife. Once again, thank you."

Knight's face was grave. "No gratitude yet, Your Highness. I agree to perform the marriage ceremony *only* if someone does not bring you to your senses in the meantime. Or if they do not stop you altogether. I shall not give up hope of that until the very end."

George looked down on the old man who sat before him all in black, his face blanched to the color of bed linen. His own expression now in light of that was, once again, equally sober.

"Ah, yes. To that end, I am certain I need not tell you that you must swear fidelity to your future king in this. You must not breathe a word of my plans to anyone...for *both* our sakes."

"I would not dare."

"Good." George smiled, but it was a weak smile. His head was too full of details. "Now you must listen to me very clearly, for you cannot risk committing these details to paper."

Knight's wide eyes grew wider still.

"On Saturday evening, next, you shall feel desirous of a breath of air. Between the hour of seven and eight o'clock you shall find yourself at the upper end of Park Lane near Oxford Street. Someone will meet you there to lead you onward."

"Onward where?"

"That does not concern you now. But be there at the end of Park Lane between the hours of seven and eight."

When George sat back down, Johnes Knight slowly rose, betraying nothing of the apprehension he felt. If it was not him to do it then it would be someone else. The Prince had made that clear. A lesser man would surely use this opportunity to bribe the future King by taking the information of an illegal wedding to the Tories.

As a man of God, he must aid the Prince of Wales in this. It was his duty to save England's heir from a worse fate than the one to which his impetuousness and his lust had already committed him by seeking so absurd a marriage in the first place.

AFTER THE REVEREND KNIGHT WAS shown to his waiting post chaise, Onslow returned.

"He's agreed to do it." George smiled broadly.

"Congratulations, Your Highness."

"I want you to go personally to Mrs. Fitzherbert, Onslow. I cannot risk another messenger in this. Tell her that it has all been arranged. Tell her for me that I love her more than life itself, and that by this time next Saturday...at last, she and I shall truly be man and wife."

"Should Your Highness not go in person for a communication so intimate as this?"

"I would like nothing more. But I cannot afford to incite more suspicion than there already is, being seen at her house, before we manage this. Besides..." His eyes, those blue chips of ice, sparkled with satisfaction that, finally, finally things were about to go his way. Having remembered the possible complication Fox might well create, he added "...just now I have an urgent letter to write."

My dear Charles,

Your letter afforded me more satisfaction than I can find words to express as it is additional proof to me of your having that true regard and affection for me which it is not only the wish but the ambition of my life to merit.

Make yourself easy, my dear friend. Believe me, the world will soon be convinced that there not only is not, but never was, any ground for these reports, which of late have been so malevolently circulated. I have not time to add more, except to say that I shall meet you at dinner on Tuesday; and to desire you to believe me at all times, my dear Charles, most affectionately yours,

George P.
Carlton House
Sunday, 2 o'clock
December 11, 1785

"Who is it from, Charles? Oh, do let me see," Elizabeth Armistead coaxed in a seductive tone she had once tried to great success with the Prince of Wales.

She tried to tear the letter from Fox's meaty hand as they lay naked together beneath a salmon-colored coverlet on his grand poster bed, the drawn bed curtains sealing them in as though it were a cave.

"Infernal woman! Leave it be!" he growled and turned onto his side away from her.

The silk sheets slipped away. His fleshy body was still wet. The aroma of their lovemaking hung like bitter perfume in the air between them. Elizabeth sighed and stroked the back of his matted, pepper-gray hair while he read the reassuring words once again.

When Fox finally turned back onto the other elbow, he saw her lip turned out in a pout, her green eyes wide with disinterest. Her ginger-colored hair was fanned out on the pillow. He touched a strand, then ran a teasing finger across her bare breast and watched as the large pink nipple hardened. But when he moved to kiss her, she turned away.

"Now, Bess, don't be cross with me. It is only business."

"Business from the Prince of Wales, I'd wager."

"And if it is?"

"You promised to keep nothing from me, Charles, just as I promised to keep nothing from you. You know about His Highness and me—why is it not my right to know about His Highness and *you?*"

He sighed, leaning back on his elbows and exhaling a puff of air. "Our connections to the man are entirely different."

"Not so different really. One, his whore by night—"

Without thinking, Charles James Fox sprang up and struck her hard across the mouth. The sound was like the crack of a whip in a room where the only sound was the movement of the servants' hurried steps beyond the carved mahogany doors. Elizabeth looked back at him, her cheek burned but her face glowed more with desire than revenge.

"Bastard!" she growled.

Her defiance excited him again and he kissed her roughly. She struggled to resist but he pinned her arms against the bedsheets. "Now who is the whore?"

"Swine!" she cried.

"Bitch!" he countered.

He had managed it. He had brought the prince to his senses about that woman, and averted disaster. His head whirled with triumph as he entered Elizabeth again, this time with a vengeance. There would be no marriage. Poor Maria Fitzherbert was destined to follow all of the other pretty little melodies that had danced in and out of the Prince of Wales's life. The Whig Party was safe. *He was safe,* and he had the Duchess of Devonshire to thank for it.

He felt the heat building, felt his body pulse as she arched beneath him. Charles groaned as her nails tore the skin in his back. Triumph and no one to stop us, he thought just as he felt the blood on his back mix with sweat the moment before he fell into the dark abyss of rapture.

"IT'S ALL OVER ENGLAND, MARIA. Really." Her brother John smiled. "Not that we mind, of course," seconded her uncle Henry Errington who had come from Shropshire as soon as he had heard, to give the bride away to the man who would be King. "Your father

133

would have been so proud. His daughter, one day Queen of England!"

In the excitement of the moment, the two men had wisely chosen to omit the fact that, in her absence, their relation had actually become more infamous than famous.

In all of the elegant clubs and coffeehouses along St. James's Street, as well as the great drawing rooms of London, John had personally heard nothing but whispers about the terms of her return from abroad. Even her friends from Almack's supposed, behind their elegant fans, that it was the twice-widowed Maria Fitzherbert who was leading the Heir Apparent steadily toward his own destruction.

"It is imperative that you hear this," Maria said, turning back around to face the two of them, both grinning like eager children. "I do want you to give me away, Uncle, but not in quite the ceremony you expect." She watched her brother and uncle exchange a glance and then look back at her as she tried calmly to sip her tea. "The King has not been advised of our intent to marry...and he shall not be."

"But that is illegal!"

"Entirely."

"Then your marriage shall never be valid!" Henry Errington gasped, the shock paling his red patchy cheeks.

"His Highness has found an Anglican parson to perform the ceremony. He has assured us that our union shall stand valid in the eyes of Rome. It can only be said, because of the newly instituted and controversial Royal Marriage Act, that we are not wed so far as English law, and you know, as Catholics, we have always answered to a higher authority than that."

"But I do not understand—"

"We do not ask you to understand, Uncle, something which even we do not conceive fully. What we must ask is something far greater. It is a test, I believe, of your love for me, for I have no one else in the world upon whom I can depend to ask but you and John."

"Dear saints preserve us," Errington muttered in disbelief. "I have heard the whispers too that it was to be something as foolhardy as this, but I believed it was all just gossip!"

"The Prince and I need you and John to stand as our witnesses. The Devonshires...and even the Cumberlands have changed their minds suddenly. They have sent letters to George, at the last moment, saying they shall not be in London this Saturday. I suspect fear of the unknown has gotten the better of them all."

"Perhaps it was wisdom more than fear," Henry Errington mouthed, and washed a hand across his drawn face. He then looked back at his niece who sat as poised and elegant before him on the edge of her chair as if they were discussing the time of day or the weather. He did not see the fear or the apprehension for the great crime she was about to commit.

Maria hid that far too well.

"Will you not be admitted as his wife then?" John asked from his place beside the hearth.

"Not at first, no. But the King, God save him, is frequently unwell and George has promised to repeal both the Royal Marriage Act, as well as the Act of Settlement, the moment he is in a position to do so."

"But to deny a *wife!*" Errington said with a hard voice.

"He shall not deny me, Uncle. Please, you mustn't ever think that he would do that. He has sworn to me by his honor that he shall never deny me. He shall only not admit outright to anyone in the beginning that we are actually married."

"But your children...they would be bastards!"

Her response was measured. "If we are blessed with children, Uncle, they would be illegal only so far as the law. They would not be illegitimate. Really, both of you, please...don't look at me like that. There really is no other way in this."

"This is madness!" moaned her uncle, slapping a hand across his forehead.

"There was another way and you know it." Her brother scowled. "With the Duke of Bedford."

"I do not love him, John."

"Love, love, love! Like a silly mindless chit that is all I hear from you! For that fleeting and fickle emotion you are willing to risk, not only your social standing, but your entire future?"

"Without love I do not believe I have a future," Maria said stubbornly, leveling her dark eyes on her brother. "I am going to marry him, John, whatever that means for me. And may I remind you that you could do worse for a brother-in-law than the Prince of Wales."

"She's right, Uncle," John finally conceded when the air between them grew too heavy, and the resolve on his sister's face had grown too difficult to bear. He moved across the room to sit beside her on the small embroidered sofa. "If this is what you truly want, Maria."

She smiled softly and kissed his cheek. "Then will you both act as witnesses?" She heard her uncle gasp. "I know well that I ask you to risk a great deal and I am sorry for that. But I really have no one left that I can trust."

In the silence that followed, Maria looked over at her brother, hope and ambition piquing his long, handsome face and lighting his dark eyes. When she glanced back across the room at her uncle Errington, he was shaking his head. Finally then, when the realization hit him, the enormity and the grandeur of it all, he too began to grin.

"WHAT DO YOU MEAN, HE has changed his mind?"

"Reverend Knight has sent a letter just this morning saying that he had been forced to reconsider a previous promise with regard to breaking the law."

"I cannot believe he would dare to do this, and to *me!*" George raged.

Orlando Bridgeman continued with great caution. He understood what this news would do to the Prince. "The Reverend said that, after much prayer and reflection, Your Highness, he feels unable to perform the ceremony you desire, and begs you to release him from the commitment."

George tossed a huge scent holder, shaped like a Chinese Buddha, across the room, smashing it against a satinwood table. The table, ornamented with a collection of enamels and a miniature of his mother, went crashing onto the carpet.

"Damn him! Damn them all! First Georgiana's refusal, then my own uncles, men who should understand this all better than anyone else...and now this! *Out of town!* they write. *Not available,* she says. Indeed! They all think they are wise to betray me! Well they are not! I will not allow this to disappoint Maria! She has asked for so little and given me everything in return....She is counting on this ceremony and, by God in his Heaven, a legitimate ceremony she shall have!"

The minister's change of heart alone had been enough of a disap-

pointment to ignite a pyre of anger in the volatile prince. The Devonshires' all-too convenient trip out of London had only fanned the
flames of that rage. But his greatest disappointment had come from
his uncle Henry, a man who understood firsthand what it was to
want to marry for love.

George had pleaded with Henry, Duke of Cumberland, to witness
the ceremony to legitimize his marriage to Maria. Along with his
other sympathetic uncle, the Duke of Gloucester, they, above all others, could understand his devotion to a woman not approved of by
the King. It was, after all, William's marriage to the widow of the
King's great enemy, and Henry's subsequent marriage to a coarse
and spirited widow named Anne Horton, that had so angered the
King it prompted the institution of the Royal Marriage Act in the
first place. The act required the sovereign's consent to the marriage
of any of his descendants. But no matter what affection or sympathy
they held for their nephew, in the end, neither uncle could so obviously support such a flagrant a violation of the law—even a new one,
by England's future King.

Bridgeman loomed over the Prince as he sank onto the edge of his
bed. "If I might suggest, perhaps Your Royal Highness should consider
the delicate nature of these circumstances before you are moved to act."

"What are you saying?"

"Better to find another parson than push this and risk angering
Reverend Knight to the point where he may indeed betray your
intentions to your enemies or, worse yet, to the King."

"But it is already Thursday, Bridgeman! Where can you find
another? You have tried everyone you dare. Sweet Jesus, what am I
to do? Tell me that! You know that I *must* make this happen for
Maria. That's all there is to it!"

The Prince's valet stared down at him as he trembled with pent-up
anger and frustration, those huge hands now covering his face.
Accomplishing now what His Highness thought he wanted most in
the world, when he could turn nowhere else, would not quickly be
forgotten.

Bridgeman felt the beginnings of a smile stretch his thin, pale lips.
There was one last thing he could try. His Highness cared not from
where the cleric came. After all, he was desperate. At this critical
juncture, the Prince of Wales cared only that someone was there and

137

that in the eyes of God he had the power to unite them. Beyond that, the concern...and possibly the glory, belonged only to the one man ambitious and reckless enough to make certain the Prince's desire became reality.

"What is his name?"

"Reverend John Burt, sir."

ORLANDO BRIDGEMAN LOOKED around the shabby windowless office in the Fleet Prison, at walls grayed by grease and stained black from the constantly burning lamp oil. The room was airless and smelled of human sweat and stale food. Plates of half-eaten veal and juice-soaked bread littered the tables and chairs, all but the one on which he sat.

Bridgeman had detested coming here but it had been the only way.

"Would one hundred pounds be enough to liquidate the young curate's debts?" he asked, taking out a wide leather envelope stuffed with money.

"Indeed it would," the jailer grunted, gazing down greedily as the Prince's valet began to rifle through the notes.

"But 'e ain't willin' to leave here without a promise of 'is own."

Bridgeman glanced up.

"He's a rash and ambitious young curate, John Burt, 'e is. Likely what brung 'im 'ere with them kind o' debts in the first place."

"Indeed," said Bridgeman, lifting a single suspicious brow.

"'E'll be wantin' a post, 'e says."

"What sort of post has he in mind?"

"As one of 'is Highness's chaplains," the bald, greasy little man said directly.

Bridgeman took a breath and set the envelope down on the marred oak table. "And what else does the *Reverend Burt* require for his services, Mister Hawkes?"

"'E wants a promise...a written promise, that when the good Prince is made King of England, that 'e shall be made a bishop."

"A bishop, is it?"

"I'tis, sir."

"And you, no doubt, shall receive a stipend for negotiating the affair."

"Business is business, ain't it?" He smiled past a row of brown, rotting teeth. "Appears that way we all win."

"It would appear so."

"So, what say ye, Mister Bridgeman? Will ye be takin' young Burt for what purposes you will, or no?"

Orlando gazed back down at the money. A hundred pounds, a post as royal chaplain, and a promise of a bishopric. He knew what the Prince would say. There was no obstacle too great to surmount in the quest to make Maria his wife. Not a felony. Not bribery.

Not what was even likely to lead to extortion.

Orlando pushed away his hesitation like an unwanted lover, and dipped into the leather envelope again. As he counted the money, he could feel the odd little man behind him, breathing hotly onto his bare neck.

IT HAD JUST BEGUN TO snow when George's brightly painted yellow carriage came to a halt at the corner near Park Street. Lamps lit early against the dark winter sky glowed from the windows of the neat brick houses, and only an occasional trader's wagon clicked past them on its way back from the Billingsgate market.

"Well, I shall leave you all here," George said, his voice pitched low. "Wish me good fortune in this."

"I am going with you," Bridgeman said.

George reached across the carriage with a gloved hand and touched his valet's knee. "I cannot allow it, good friend. You've endangered yourself too much already with what you've done for me."

"I am Your Highness's humble servant," he said with a note of indignation.

"And I shall never forget what only you were able to do for me, Bridgeman. But I will not allow you to risk anything further."

Lord Onslow and Lord Southampton sat silently on the opposite cushion watching the exchange, neither anxious to join Orlando Bridgeman in the dangerous liaison about to take place.

Onslow looked outside and watched the small white flakes whisper past the glass, still unable to believe that the Prince really meant to go through with it.

"Let me be a witness for you," Bridgeman pushed, and his tone became pleading.

"Maria's relations have consented to act as witnesses for us."

139

"Be that as it may, I cannot allow you to go alone. It is a distance to her house from here. It would not be safe."

"I have a better chance of passing undetected if I go on foot and alone, Orlando."

Everything had been organized to the most minute detail. They had waited until just before dusk when the streets around would be bare, all of society having returned home to prepare for the theater and parties in store for the evening. Then George would turn up the collar on his cape, lower his head, and walk alone down Oxford Street to the corner, as any commoner would.

Once he was certain he had not been followed, he would turn onto Park Street and advance quickly to the little pink brick house where Maria, and his future, awaited.

"Then at least let me act as a sentry outside her door. I shall follow you only at a discreet distance."

"Perhaps Orlando is right," Lord Onslow braved an intercession. "If His Majesty or any of your enemies has managed to discover your intentions, the ceremony could be prevented."

"Having him posted outside the door would at least give Your Highness ample warning if there was to be trouble," Southampton agreed.

George looked at each of his aides, their faces touched with concern. The snow was coming down more heavily now. He squeezed the top of his malacca cane. Of course they were right. Despite the fact that he had been painfully discreet with all of the wedding plans, there was no telling what morsel of gossip could have reached the King's ears. Now that he was this close, there must be no one and nothing to stop him.

George exhaled deeply. "Very well then, Bridgeman, my good man. I would be honored if you would consent to act as guard during the course of my marriage ceremony."

THE YELLOW DRAPERIES IN THE drawing room of Maria's house had been pulled. They kept away the danger, and drowned the sound of the occasional carriage wheels clicking on the frosty pavement, just beyond the grand bow window.

Inside, white candles and brass lamps glowed with fire. The furniture and the silver had been polished. A full crystal decanter of sherry and five glasses stood ready on a little tea cart near the fireplace. But beyond that, there was no evidence at all of the monumental event that was about to take place. Even Jacko Payne and Fanny Davies had been dismissed for the evening, along with the rest of the staff. They had, all of them, come too far to take any more chances than necessary now.

Maria and her uncle were already standing in the center of the room speaking in hushed tones with Reverend Burt when John opened the door to the Prince of Wales.

Maria watched breathlessly as George removed his own dark cloak, hat, and gray kid gloves and tossed them on a chair beside the fire. He moved into the room smiling radiant confidence at her.

"So then. We are all here," said the young clergyman as he stood in his surplice.

"Indeed we are." George smiled, his cheeks and nose red from the cold. He rubbed his hands together as he moved, tall and magnificent, to Maria's side.

Maria could never have looked more beautiful than she did at that moment, George thought. Perhaps it was because today she was finally about to become his, completely.

She stood in simple traveling clothes, a gray velvet *redingcote* with a white lace-edged scarf at the tip of her shoulders. A simple pink ribbon ornamented her throat and her hair was curled tightly into side ringlets.

In her hands she held a small prayer book that her father had given her as a child. It was the only evidence of her Catholic religion that she had allowed herself on the day she betrayed England.

"Are we ready then to begin?"

Maria and George both looked up at the young clergyman whom Orlando Bridgeman had mysteriously found only the day before. His honey-colored hair was full of too much powder, his eyes were shot with red, and he smelled of gin. But they had been assured that he was legitimate enough for their purpose, and beyond that they dared not question.

He began the service according to the Form of Solemnization of

Matrimony in the Book of Common Prayer. As George took Maria's hand, the wind softly slapped the bare tree branches against the windowpanes.

It felt good to have him touch her again, she was thinking as her heart thumped wildly beneath her gown, good to be this close. Yet, even now she longed for so much more. Far more than the unbelievably erotic interlude they had shared in her private salon. Her cheeks stained crimson as she remembered what they had done, and not quite done, together.

What she had held fast to that day, and since their meeting, was that test of sorts. Maria had wanted, needed, to challenge his devotion. And yet, here he was. Even so, it was still difficult to believe that George meant to go through with a risk that was this great. *For her*.

John watched his sister, her hand linked with the Prince of Wales, and he too thought of the future as the young clergyman mouthed the words to the ceremony. He had been willing to settle for a duke when just beyond lay a king.

Well, nearly a king.

The Prince of Wales may have a dreadful reputation for constancy, but of one thing he was certain. For now, this strange, enigmatic man, this prince, worshiped his sister, and that just might be enough one day to see her made a queen of England.

"I, George Augustus Frederick, take thee, Maria Anne Fitzherbert..."

John watched the Prince's blue eyes rim with tears as he spoke his vows. What had she done exactly, he wondered, to garner this extraordinary sort of devotion? It was positively puzzling. George was risking everything in the world at this very moment by speaking these words.

"...for better for worse, for richer for poorer..."

All of her life, Maria had been the fortunate one. As smart as she was beautiful. First with Edward Weld. Then Thomas Fitzherbert. Now this. More to the point, perhaps it was what she had *not* done that had led her here. That was certainly what had been chuckled about in all of the clubs in London. They said that the Prince of Wales had never refused a challenge, and by withholding her body, Maria Fitzherbert had given him a challenge with which to reckon.

John thought about how many women there had been in his own life who had refused to bed with him. Yet the thought of marrying any one of them for it had never even crossed his mind. Perhaps he would never know, never understand. After all, he had never been in love. Not really.

"...in sickness and in health, to love and to cherish till death do us part, according to God's holy ordinance."

After Maria had spoken her vows, George took her hands and softly kissed her. John watched their lips barely touching in the chaste way that children kiss, and he felt a shiver blossom at the base of his spine. *God Bless you both,* he thought. *For you both shall so sorely need it.*

Suddenly there was a low-pitched, squealing sound as someone opened the front door. Aware of the danger, everyone turned with a start. John heard his sister stifle a little gasp. Orlando Bridgeman came in and stood on the black and white marble just inside the door, his face crimson and his body rigid as he rubbed the cold from his hands.

"Come in, Bridgeman. It is finally done," George called out with a welcoming smile as everyone moved forward solemnly to sign the official and very illegal certificate of marriage. "Do have a cup of wine to warm yourself and then you alone may have the honor of being the first to congratulate me and my bride!"

THE ROAD TO ORMELEY LODGE near Twickenham was thick with snow. They had taken Maria's post chaise and no staff but a driver for the short honeymoon. There would be fewer questions that way. But neither George nor Maria had bargained on the dreadful weather conditions outside of London. It was dark by the time they left and staining the snow were pools of thick mud in ruts deep enough to strand them.

Maria lay her head back against the cold leather seat. The strain of the marriage ceremony and an empty stomach was made worse by the fact that she was exhausted. The days past, so shrouded in secrecy, had taken their toll and she had managed no more than a few hours' sleep in the hours closest to morning. Without warning, she was jerked forward as the carriage sloped to one side, then stopped.

"What is it?" she asked.

"I think we've broken down."

Maria glanced around. There was nothing around them but dark, endless fields and bare twisted trees. George knocked on the door so that the driver would open it for him.

"Where are you going?"

"I'd better try to help," he said with a tired smile. "Unless you want to spend your wedding night on a cold and deserted country road where Heaven knows what might befall us."

George held the lamp on the roadside as he and Maria stood watching the driver make the repairs to a broken axle. The snow had finally stopped, so had the wind, and the winter air was cool and crisp and still. It helped to invigorate them and also helped to remind them both of how hungry they were.

As the driver repaired the damage, George looked over at his bride. Her skin, bronzed in the lamplight, was like whipped gold, her beauty more rich, more radiant than he had ever seen it. He had not thought in all of his life that it was possible to feel such joy.

Sensing his gaze, Maria turned into the lamp glow, smiling a luminous smile, and George wanted to reach out and touch her, take her into his arms there beneath the stars. But he knew that if he touched her now he would not be able to let her go. They had waited so long, *he* had waited so long, and, as a man not previously given to self control, these months without intimate companionship had been a torture.

After the carriage axle had been repaired, they moved another mile down the road to Hammersmith, where the light from a little inn and the aroma of boiled leg of mutton and fresh coffee drew them.

George sat alone with Maria at a table in a paneled alcove near the fire, holding her hand beneath the table. They had eaten bread and cheese and mutton and between them they had drunk a bottle of port. Now, with the scattered plates and cups around them, Maria took a small package wrapped in blue velvet from her handbag and set it in the center of the table.

"What is that?"

"It is a wedding gift." Maria smiled.

George looked back at her, his tired eyes full of surprise. Slowly he set down his empty cup. "But...I have nothing for you. In all of the rushing, I entirely forgot."

She put her warm hand on top of his and squeezed it. "Darling, you have given me your love. Today, amid great danger, you have made me your wife. Surely you must know that there is no greater gift than that."

He did not look away from her dark eyes as he peeled away the velvet. When he finally did look down, he saw a small, diamond-studded locket identical to the one he had once given her. This one, however, bore a painted miniature of Maria, and it too was suspended from a black velvet cord.

George's full lips parted in surprise. "Oh, my darling, it is exquisite."

"You like it then?"

"Like it? I adore it!" He looked down at the image again, then back at Maria. "The artist has captured you exactly."

"Do you really believe so?"

"I do indeed." He slipped the cord over his head and pressed the locket to his chest. "I shall wear it here, always. Next to my heart. That way you shall always be with me...no matter what life has in store now for the two of us."

He wrapped her hand in both of his on top of the table and squeezed it tightly. But now he was anxious to do more than simply touch her. The feel of her warm skin was almost unbearable to him now that all his other senses had been satisfied. Now that she had given him this gift of love.

It had been a long day for them both. He had waited so long to make love to this woman he would forever call his wife. But he must wait a little longer still...yes, until everything was perfect.

BY THE TIME THEY REACHED Twickenham, it was after midnight. It had not been safe to travel after dark, but George had insisted. No matter what he had felt as they sat so close together at the little inn, he had not wanted to spend their first night as man and wife among strangers.

As their carriage pulled into the circular courtyard, candles flickered pale gold in the windows to light the way, and Maria's servants stood at the door to welcome them. A footman from her own staff helped Maria from the carriage and onto the gravel. They then walked together up the pale yellow stone steps.

"Will ye be wantin' supper, ma'am?" her housekeeper, an old, weathered-looking woman, asked as she lumbered beside them.

"No, thank you, Mrs. Bennet," Maria replied as they walked through the doorway and into a foyer that was painted green and white and gold. "We stopped for supper in Hammersmith. I believe we are ready to retire for the evening."

The old woman nodded. "Yes, ma'am."

They stood alone near the staircase as the driver went back out to fetch the rest of their luggage. "Are you all right?" George asked in a whisper as he faced his new wife.

Maria tried to smile but with each moment she was becoming more and more overcome with the need for sleep. "I am fine," she said wearily, and let him take her hand as they walked together up the carved mahogany staircase.

The large bedroom, with the high, coved ceiling, into which they were shown by Mrs. Bennet, was hung with beautiful, soft blue damask. The bed, canopied in the same fabric, sat in a small recess.

"Will you be wantin' me to show the master to his own bedchamber, ma'am?" the housekeeper asked as delicately as possible.

"That will not be necessary, Martha. I shall show him."

After the last of their bags were brought up, George kissed her cheek. "I shall leave you for a few moments. Give you time with your lady to change," he said simply, then followed the driver who had borne their bags, from the room.

He went alone back downstairs and found the drawing room. It was lit only by the glow of the moon through the windows, but it was bright enough to see that there was a full bottle of brandy and a ring of glasses set out on a little table near a case of books. George poured himself a full glass of the amber liquid and eased into a large embroidered chair.

He was grateful for the dark. Time to calm his mind, to still his heart. He had wanted Maria for so long, imagined how it would be, and now that it was here, he actually found himself disarmed by the prospect.

He had been with dozens of women. Duchesses, Ladies...whores, but for the first time in his life, this, their first coming together, actu-

146

ally mattered. Maria had been married before. She knew what to expect. Her experienced past added to his apprehension. His hand shook slightly as he held the glass to his lips.

"May I light the fire for you, sir?" a thick, man's baritone called into the darkness.

"No, thank you. And please tell everyone that they may retire now."

"Very well, sir."

He was glad to hear the servant's heels click across the plank floor and fade into silence, then a door close. No one had addressed him as His *Highness*. Was it that they did not know, or that propriety had stilled them?

Whatever had caused it, tonight he was simply George, In Maria's arms, he would be just a man, like any other man. He looked up over the fireplace. In the shadow of the moon he could see a portrait. It was Maria as a young girl, in a pale pink gown, her expression warmed with a curious little half smile. She had really changed very little since then.

He moved across the room and poured himself another brandy. This one did not burn his throat quite so much as the first. He felt himself relax and the apprehension begin to fade. He closed his eyes for a moment and saw her in his mind.

The lines of her body were full of soft curves. Even beneath all of the deceptive layers of petticoats, the rest of her must be as beautiful as her face. He reached up and pulled the locket she had given him out from beneath his embroidered waistcoat. He held it tightly in his hand. Finally, he felt the first stirring of desire since supper at the inn. He finished the brandy and set the empty glass on the small satinwood table beside the chair and went upstairs.

Two candles beside the bed were still burning when George opened the door. He crept nearer until he saw that Maria was asleep atop the bedcovers in a long, white gauze nightgown edged with French lace. Her long hair had been brushed out of the curls and now lay shimmering against the thick pillows like gold flames.

Despite her overwhelming beauty, and the wild desire she made him feel, he could not still the apprehension gnawing relentlessly at him. George moved nearer until he was standing over her. He looked at the milky-white skin of her neck and her arms lain softly across her chest; lace whispering at her elbows.

She looked so like an angel. But even for all of the desire that burned inside his body, he could not bear to wake her. He moved across the room, softly taking a quilt from the back of a brocade chair. As gently as if he were covering a china doll, he lay it over her. Then he moved back across the room to remove his own clothes.

He lay his shoes, waistcoat, cravat, breeches, and stockings in a little pile on the same chair, then moved naked back to the bed. With a hand around the flame, he softly extinguished the candles, then sank in the darkness onto the edge of the bed beside her.

After a moment, he felt her stir beneath the quilt, and as though their bodies were connected, he felt his own violent shudder follow. It was several minutes more before he could bring himself to draw back the quilt and lay beside her.

The touch of her skin was a like a potent narcotic and he was powerless to stop his fingers from trailing downward to one of her breasts, so full and warm, just beneath the thin layer of fabric. He could feel the nipple respond to his gentle touch, then spring into a hard little peak.

Slowly, he unlaced the pink ribbons at the top of her gown and folded back the fabric. George ran his tongue across each rose-colored nipple, then looked up at her face, but Maria still did not stir. His hands trembled with passion as he touched one breast and then the other.

Driven by something primal and overpowering, he reached down and began to lift her gown past the smooth length of warm flesh. He brushed the soft downy hair on her thighs; pressed his hands, his fingers into the milky flesh of her abdomen. Feverishly, he kissed her throat, then her mouth, his hardness pressing against her thigh. He moaned and she stirred again.

George turned away, unable to catch his breath, his body raging now with unmet desire. This was not proper. He could not do it this way no matter how much he wanted her. Suddenly he felt her turn, her breasts full against his back. "Darling," she whispered in the darkness.

A shaft of desire thundered through him. He lay frozen, unable to move, as her warm hand moved seductively across his back, up to the curve of his shoulder. George was stopped by the delicate sound of her voice, the gentleness of her touch, and by a desire he was afraid, if he moved even the slightest muscle, he would no longer be able to control.

"Do not turn away from me," she whispered into his hair, and he gasped as her fingers trailed down the curve of his bare, broad back.

He dared not move, dared not respond for fear of crushing her with the weight of his longing. But her fingers, long, nimble, and warm, were a more powerful temptress than his conscience could resist.

Coaxed by her delicacy, he fell onto his back, his heart beating so wildly that he could not breathe. He watched her slowly unlace the remaining ribbons that bound her nightgown. Then she pulled the fabric away and lay back down, her own bare body pressed against his.

"I warn you now, my love, you've a long night in store if you mean to continue that."

"I shall consider myself warned."

"And I cannot promise to be gentle."

"I was hoping you would say that."

Need and desire raged through him then in a hot, delicious wave. His muscular body arched for only a moment before he cast off what was left of his restraint, held her arms, and pushed himself urgently inside her.

George groaned as the little grinding, rhythmic movements took control of his body, paling his mind to black. Whirling, beating, crashing. Blinding heat and lust...and power. Again and again he thrust into her, hard and long, the perspiration dripping from his chest and hands. He could feel her clinging to him like English ivy, feel her lips moist on the pulsing vein in his neck. He heard himself cry out but it was someone else's voice.

At the end of a long, dark tunnel there was light and heat. Blinding heat. He moved faster and faster toward it. Thrusting. Straining. His heart crashing against his ribs.

When it was over, and he could finally breathe again, he pulled away from her and lay back against the blue damask bedcovers.

"I haven't hurt you, have I?" he asked when the silence between them held too much agony to leave it untouched.

"No, my love, you haven't hurt me," she whispered in return and ran a single finger through the chestnut hair that fell in a wet tangle near his cheek. "I am your wife, *truly* your wife, now and forever. And nothing in the world has ever felt more right."

He looked back at her in the moonlight, her dark eyes glinting and her face still flushed with passion.

"I have never been — never wanted to be, vulnerable with anyone in my life. The risk was always too great. I come to you tonight, defenses down." He inhaled a breath, wanting to tell her the words no other living soul had ever heard him utter. "My beautiful Maria, you alone have the power to destroy me...I bid you please, take care with the knowledge of that."

"I love you," she softly said.

George turned back toward Maria and kissed her fully, their mouths warm and open to one another, for the first time that night. He touched her in the moist hollow of her throat and she met him willingly.

"You shall never be sorry, my darling, for what became of us today..." he whispered back. "You will see, now that we have each other, as man and wife, everything is going to be perfect."

"THEY'RE MARRIED, I TELL YOU!" sniffed Isabella Sefton, "And I simply cannot fathom why she would not have confided in me about it. I knew about it all from the beginning."

"Perhaps because she knew you would not approve," Anne Lindsay countered as they sat together with a larger group of guests in the rose damask music room at Devonshire House.

"Well, she is right about that. I advised her over and over again to become his mistress. I certainly gave her no counsel to marry him!"

"From Maria's perspective, I suppose it was better to break the law than one of the Commandments."

"Wretched Catholics!" Isabella sniped, then put her fingers to her lips and looked around herself once she realized how loudly she had spoken. "Sure as the devil, the Duchess knew about the marriage."

They both looked to the head of the room, where Georgiana, the Duchess of Devonshire, stood speaking with her favorite violinist, a little black boy in neat blue breeches and a matching brocade tailcoat, who was about to entertain them.

"I cannot believe she would have supported it any more than you or I," Anne whispered more carefully in reply. "It is common knowledge how close she and the prince are."

"Well, His Highness denied it completely to Charles James Fox. Wrote him a letter that a marriage between them was out of the question. Fox has been boasting about that all over town."

"Then perhaps it is only gossip."

"If that is true, then where are they? Every time I call on her, Maria's housekeeper will say only that she has gone out of town. And have you not noticed that, coincidentally, the Prince of Wales seems to have disappeared from the London scene as mysteriously as she?"

Isabella and Anne were not the only two stymied by the question. As Christmas neared, the air across London was as thick with rumor of an illegal marriage as it was with fog.

"Pardon me. Are you not Lady Sefton?"

It was a wispy voice that tore them from their dangerous conversation. Isabella and Anne turned around to see a small, thin, and very pale young woman standing beside them.

"I am."

"I see that you do not remember me. I am Lady Seymour. I met you last spring at Vauxhall with your relation, Mrs. Fitzherbert. We were all waiting for our carriages."

Isabella sized the woman with her eyes. Lady Seymour waited confidently, her small mouth turned up in a gracious little rosebud of a smile.

"Ah, yes. Now I remember. And Maria stole away with your husband at Carlton House to avoid a dance with the Prince of Wales."

"Precisely." Horatia Seymour smiled eagerly.

"Pity she did not continue on in her good sense."

"I only thought I should come and say hello. I haven't seen Mrs. Fitzherbert about in such a long time. Might I inquire where she has been keeping herself?"

"Would that we knew," Isabella replied derisively, but she did so beneath her breath enough so that only Anne could hear it. "...And speaking of disappearances, Lady Seymour, where are you keeping that handsome husband of yours?"

"I am afraid the Captain is at sea once again. He's gone a great deal and does love it so. But I confess that it does make long work of my days alone with the children."

"Well, then you simply must consent to come to tea at Sefton House this Thursday."

151

"It would be a pleasure." She smiled, but suddenly it was a pale smile, full of more effort.

Although she was gowned beautifully in violet silk, and her face was impeccably powdered and rouged, decoration was not an entirely successful veil. It was clear that Lady Seymour was unwell. Her pale brown hair was brittle and was receding from her forehead. Her slim face was drawn and it seemed an effort for her just to maintain the rhythm of breathing.

"Come at half past two, so that we have time to chat a bit before my other guests arrive, why don't you?" said Isabella.

"I would be delighted. Thank you, Lady Sefton."

"Was that not carrying pleasantry just a bit too far?" Anne whispered as they both watched Horatia Seymour sift through the other guests, back to her chair on the other side of the music room. "She is not at all your type."

"Now Anne, dear. Where is your sense of charity? The girl is a bit simple, I shall grant you. But after all, she *is* rather newly acquainted with Mrs. Fitzherbert."

Isabella watched surprise distort Lady Lindsay's very proper expression. "You didn't know? I shall tell you this much. When it comes to connections like that, simple or not, a wise lady can never have enough *friends*."

A spark of recognition passed through the shock and lit Anne's wide blue eyes. "So that is it! You are hoping for a few morsels of information to be tossed your way!"

"After all, there is more than one way for a clever woman of means to discover what she wishes to know, and I tell you, Anne, when it comes to Maria, I mean to discover the truth!"

TWO DAYS LATER, NEWLY BACK from her honeymoon and anxious to see her dearest friend, Maria took a chance of calling on Isabella unannounced as she had done many times before. As the sun paled and a hint of rain moistened the air, she stood at the front entrance and faced a formidable footman. Beyond the door there was laughter and the clink of glasses.

Her face blanched. "But there must be some mistake."

"No, madam," he said cooly but respectfully. "I assure you there has been no mistake. Lady Sefton is not receiving this afternoon."

"But I can hear them in the drawing room. I can—" Her words fell away with the realization. Isabella did not want to receive her.

God help them all. Clever. Ever resourceful, Isabella had discovered the truth.

"I am sorry, madam," the footman added after a moment. "but I have my orders."

She took a breath to steady herself. "Yes. Well." Maria straightened her back slightly, tipped up her chin, feeling the sting of her first rejection. "Certainly not half so sorry as I."

As she turned back around to her waiting carriage she could still hear the women's laughter and the clinking of cordial glasses, her faith in long-standing friendship completely shaken. "These days I might have believed betrayal of anyone," she muttered as slow measured steps brought her away from Sefton House toward the street. "But, Isabella, not of you."

Strangely, it made her understand her husband better, the many betrayals he had endured in his life. But she could not help wondering if she would ever become accustomed to this sort of pain.

GEORGE CRUMPLED YET ANOTHER LETTER into a ball and leaned across Maria's bare breasts to toss it into the last embers of a waning fire.

"From the Queen again?" she carefully asked. "Perhaps you should just have done with it and see her."

"No."

"But she *is* your mother."

"If I go to her at Windsor now it shall be disagreeable all round. The queen is clever and bound to force me to confess what I do not yet wish her to hear."

In the early hours of morning, they lay together beneath the heavy damask bedding in the little blue bedchamber on Park Street. For George and Maria both, this time, before the sun had fully risen, when the house was still silent, had quickly become the most precious time of the day.

Unlike before their marriage, George now woke clearheaded and early, wanting time to talk and plan privately with her before he was forced, for propriety's sake, to make the solitary ride home across town to Carlton House.

It was just before Christmas, two weeks since their clandestine wedding, and they had returned to London, fearing more gossip if they were away for the holidays. Though Carlton House was still the place in which he worked and received guests, *home* was here with Maria.

George lay back against the pillows and looked at his wife, detesting the thoughts of discontent that his mother's letter had stirred within him. Even now, before the fresh morning fires were lit, or the servants could be heard dashing one way and the other out in the corridor beyond the sealed doors, the entire house was warmed by the fragrant holiday smell of rosemary and holly.

It was calming. Peaceful. Beyond the windows, a filigree of leafless trees pressed against the dark sky and a powdery new snow had quilted everything in softness. Made it fresh again. A symbol of beginnings. Now that he finally had Maria, the pain and disappointments of the past mattered little.

Until he heard from the Queen.

"Perhaps if you tried to explain to her—"

"I cannot explain this, Maria. Not to anyone. You know that."

She lowered her head. "I only meant..."

When he saw her surprise, he tried to soften the harshness of his tone. He ran a finger beneath her chin and drew her lips onto his. "I know what you meant, darling, and I love you for it. But you must understand that in this, I know what is best."

Maria looked away, helpless tears moistening her eyes. "Would that there was another person in all of London happy for our circumstances."

George turned her face back with his fingers. "I do believe that your brother, John, is ecstatic," he said with a generous smile, hoping to make her laugh.

He knew what his marriage to Maria could quite likely cost him. He also knew what following her heart to become his illegal wife was likely to cost her, and that dark reality was there with them, always.

This delicate flower to whom he had irrevocably joined himself before God, who had been the pillar of society, had already been reduced with him to the butt of scandalous gossip. She was also being avoided by the majority of her London friends, who suspected in this, that the irreverent Prince of Wales may just have gone too far.

When Maria did not laugh at the joke about her brother, George took her in his arms and held her to his chest until the tears stopped. "I'm sorry." She wept. "I don't know what has gotten into me already this morning."

"Perhaps you haven't had enough sleep. I know *I* haven't." He chuckled, then kissed her hair, which fell in a pale, unruly tangle around her face.

"I suppose I just didn't know what to expect from all of this."

"Nor did I, my love," he said softly. Honestly. "But we are together, and is that not what is most important in the world?"

His sentiment touched her, and with a faint smile she wiped away the tears with the backs of her hands. She did not often forget what he had risked by making her his wife, but yesterday had been unusually difficult. She could not yet press what had happened at the door of Sefton House from her mind in the determined, disconnected way she had done with everything else before.

The simple truth was that Isabella, and their friendship, had mattered.

As if that had not been enough for one day, on the way home, her carriage passed the first of several windows on St. James's Street where the reality of what she and George had done stared back at her with glaring cruelty. The celebrated cartoonist, Gillray, who so often satirized the royal family in his cheap color prints, now took Maria on as his latest target.

She had looked in helpless horror at "The Marriage of Figaro," which showed the Prince of Wales placing a ring on her finger. Not two doors away another print was posted called "The Royal Toast: Fat, Fair and Forty," which also satirized them both.

She was forced to stop the carriage to be sick in the street.

But even for the cruel jolt that spun her back to reality, Maria did not tell George. He would find out about the cartoons soon enough. But she would not be the one to burden him. Just now there were too many other demons with which they both must contend if their love had even a chance of surviving the onslaught against them.

"But if you do not see the Queen, what will you use as your excuse?" Maria continued on, forcing the thoughts of Isabella's betrayal and the cruel caricatures from her mind.

"I shall tell her that I cannot come to a place where I am not accepted fully. It is that simple."

"But it is the King who has refused you, not the Queen."

"She is my father's wife, Maria. She is bound to side with him in something so great as this. To see her now would be far too great a risk to us both."

LATER THAT MORNING, GEORGE WALKED through the corridors of Carlton House toward his private apartments. Keate and Onslow, who waited every morning near the door for his return, now followed dutifully behind him.

Seeing his frown and remembering the expression well, Orlando Bridgeman prepared a full glass of brandy as soon as the Prince came into his bedchamber.

"I don't want that," he growled, tossing his cloak and gloves at a waiting groom. "It is eleven o'clock in the morning! Take it away."

Bridgeman looked up at the other two members of the Prince's private staff. All of their faces were piqued with discreet surprise at his refusal as George sank hard into a chair and flung a single leg over the padded arm. He propped his head in his hand, deep in thought.

"The Queen has sent another messenger from Windsor, Your Highness," Bridgeman was first to volunteer.

George looked up. "When?"

"At half past the hour. The messenger was very insistent about seeing you, himself. He said that he had been instructed by Her Majesty not to leave here without your personal reply. I'm afraid we were forced to tell him that Your Highness had taken too much laudanum in an effort to sleep last night and that we were unable to wake you."

"Clever." George smiled. He brushed his hair away from his face with both hands and sighed with a huge rush of air.

"But what do we say when the next one comes?" asked the thick-faced Lord Onslow.

"By then I shall be out for the afternoon. Then you may tell him the truth."

The three men exchanged another glance, then looked back at the Prince. "Any word yet from the Duchess of Devonshire?" George asked.

"I'm afraid not, Your Highness," replied Keate.

"Is she thought to be in town?"

"I saw the Duke last evening at White's Club," Onslow carefully offered.

"Damn her," George muttered to himself. "Betraying me now, as well. Have my costume readied, Bridgeman. I think it is about time I pay the good Duchess a little unexpected visit."

"But Your Highness has already committed to a game of whist at Lord Townshend's house at three," reminded his valet.

"Has he extended the invitation to myself and Maria?"

The Prince's bedchamber was silent. Heads fell. Bridgeman's voice, when he finally replied, was high and on edge. "No, Your Highness."

George looked up, his crystal-blue eyes narrowed with anger. "Then how could I be committed to a game of whist at his house?"

"Your Highness accepted the invitation...before...well, before your trip to Twickenham, sir."

There was little George could do in these first few weeks to win for Maria the respect he believed that she deserved. But what he could do, he did with a vengeance.

Among his friends, he immediately made it a condition of all gatherings that he attended that Maria should be thusly included. If she was not asked, then neither of them would be present.

George looked up, studying their tenuous faces, tired from too little sleep and too much joy, and the letdown that always followed when he had returned here to Carlton House without her.

"Ah. Well, then," he finally said. "See the good Duke this morning, Onslow. Clear up the little misunderstanding, and make certain that my position is entirely clear. Tell him, any way you desire, that it is quite simple: If he does not wish to entertain Maria, then he does not wish to entertain me. To that rule there shall be no exceptions."

"I AM SORRY, YOUR HIGHNESS, the Duchess is dressing at present."

Later that afternoon, George pushed his way carelessly past the slim, liveried footman who had answered Georgiana's door and moved into the marble foyer of Devonshire House. "No matter," he said. "I shall wait."

"I must be totally truthful, Your Royal Highness. Her Grace does not wish to see you."

"And are you going to be the one foolish enough to try to stop me?"

He turned back around after the words had been spoken and looked at the footman, who lowered his dark eyes. "No. I thought not." George moved a few steps toward the carved staircase beyond the entrance hall. When the footman moved with him, he stopped, and with a flick of his wrist, he added, "Don't bother, my good man. I shall show myself up. I know the way."

He knew about the slight at Lady Sefton's door and about the other ladies who had stopped calling on her since their return from Twickenham. Although Maria had not admitted it, for a few guineas, her coachman had.

Now the influential friendship of the Duchess of Devonshire was more crucial than ever in gaining respect back for his new wife. Georgiana would lead the way. He would see to that.

When he opened the door to her private withdrawing room, she was surrounded by ladies; two of them curling the last rings of her pale blond hair. A third was preparing the powder. Georgiana did not need to turn around. When she saw her servants all fall into deep curtsies she knew who had forced his way into her home.

It was more than she could have hoped for.

"That will be all," she said wisely.

But to George's surprise, she did not turn around even after her ladies had left the room. Instead, she calmly took a small pink scent flask from her marble-topped dressing table and began liberally to apply the noxious Essence of Bergamot perfume for which she was famous.

"Not even so much as a civil greeting after the pains I have taken to see you?"

"We have nothing to say to one another. Now, why do you not show yourself out the same rude way you showed yourself in."

"Not until we have spoken."

"What is it Your Highness desires of me?" she asked coldly, gazing at his reflection behind her in the mirror.

"So, after such a long and distinct friendship, we return to formality, do we?"

Georgiana set the flask back down on the dressing table and slowly pivoted around on the small velvet stool. She spread her fingers out on both of her knees and looked up. Then she said with a look of cold irritation, "Very well then, George. What is it that you want?"

"I want the friendship that we are supposed—that I know we have had, to continue."

"Friendship requires honesty. Lose one, lose the other."

"Is it really so simple?"

"For me it is."

"Then be good enough to tell me to my face, at least, how you feel I have been less than honest."

"Oh, George, is such pretense truly necessary?"

"I believe it is, yes. I need you, Georgiana. So does Maria."

The sting of her latest rival's name between them pricked her. Georgiana stood and walked across the room to the daybed, her gown trailing a path of powder-blue satin along the French carpet. "The truth is, I had hoped that my saying I would not support such madness between you, refusing to be present at a ceremony, would have stopped you from making so grave an error."

"How can you be certain that it did not do precisely that?"

She turned back around, her oval face alight with a glitter of hope. "Then tell me that I helped to bring you to your senses."

"Neither your protestations nor my uncle's could ever stop me from what I feel for Maria. Surely you must know that by now."

Georgiana's voice was brittle. "That is *not* what I asked you."

"Better to ask only what you wish to hear."

"I asked if you married her."

"I did nothing which I shall ever regret."

"Damn your verbal jousting, George!"

"It is against the laws of England for me to marry anyone of whom my illustrious father has not approved." When she still glared at him angrily, he added, "Georgiana, you know as well as I, if I am to be King after my father, I may marry no one without his approval. And, as you are well aware, I did *not* have his approval."

"Then you did not marry her," she pushed.

"Even if I had wanted to break the law, where would I have been able to find a parson here in London who would be willing to go so boldly against the Crown?"

"Stop equivocating and tell me you did not marry her!"

He saw the hopeless desperation; the need to believe that she was still foremost in his life. He turned away, pretending to finger a small clay bust of the Duke of Devonshire. Her face was too full of hurt. They had meant too much to one another.

Away from her gaze, he found his voice again. His next sentence was constructed as carefully as a house of cards.

"There were many along with you who disapproved of my intentions. You knew that. I suppose I finally realized that, in the eyes of the law, it was not within my power to see Maria made my true wife."

"But it was within your power to make her *believe* that she had been made your wife."

"I suppose that it was."

The conversation was taking a turn George had not expected, but he must continue in it…to protect Maria, and keep safe what they were building, which no one, not even those precious few well-meaning friends, must be allowed to destroy.

If he could convince Georgiana that he had lied to Maria and not to her—if that was what she required to keep Maria's reputation, then he would do it.

"You may take comfort in knowing that Mrs. Fitzherbert has been to Mass at her own Roman Catholic Church on Warwick Street every morning this week. Now I ask you, dear friend, if we were living a life of sin, or had broken any great law, how do you suppose she could manage to reconcile that with her conscience?"

As Georgiana moved toward him her voice softened. So had the tension between them. "You say you love her and yet you mislead her so boldly?"

"As you might imagine, this is a difficult situation. I cannot be entirely honest with everyone." The Duchess smiled for the first time in over a week and moved close enough to George so that he could embrace her. "I need for you to be kind to her, Georgiana," he whispered when he knew that he had stemmed the tide of her anger.

As they stood together, he spoke in a tone so low and desperate that she felt, just for a moment, as if they really were the lovers she had always hoped they would one day become. Once again she was ready to give him anything just for the asking.

"Maria needs your kindness just now, and if the other ladies see your gracious support, then I know that they will follow suit."

"As always, my dearest, if it means that much to you," Georgiana murmured into his smokey gray lapel. "Then you know that I shall do it."

AS HE RODE BACK DOWN Piccadilly, hidden away in his lacquered yellow carriage, the guilt seeped into his mind, feeling like poison. George was not happy to have deceived an old friend, especially one who had been so dedicated to him through the years.

He lay his head back against the crimson cushion, lulled by the click of the carriage wheels, and felt the return of the guilt he had begun to feel for lying to his friends. But there had been no other choice. He must protect his love, his wife.

This afternoon, he had acted the only way that he could.

For the most part he had been honest with Georgiana, and he comforted himself with the knowledge that omission was not necessarily deception. Maria had indeed been to Mass and accepted Communion at her church, but not for the reasons he had led Georgiana to believe.

According to the laws of the Roman Catholic Church, he and Maria had been joined in a legitimate ceremony. And now, in the eyes of God, Maria Fitzherbert was every bit his wife. The Catholic Church accepted their marriage and accepted her. It was, as he had said, only by laws of England, that their marriage was not valid.

When he returned to Maria's house across from Hyde Park it was already past seven. She was dressed for the opera in a new lilac silk gown and waiting for him in the drawing room when he came in.

"I'm sorry that I'm late."

"You're not dressed," she said, rising to her feet and tossing down a blue leatherbound volume of poetry by Blake.

George stood before her in the same costume that he had left her in that morning. His hair was tousled and he was still unshaven. Without noticing or caring that Fanny was in the room, dusting the base of a brass lamp, he went to Maria and took her powerfully into his arms.

Fanny saw the Prince's desperate face, watched them embrace, then silently took up her polishing cloth and left them alone.

"What's happened?"

"Just let me hold you like this a while," he whispered as he kissed the velvety softness of her neck and felt a vein pulse beneath his lips.

But even now, back in the safety of her arms, his mouth moving urgently over hers, he could not make the ugliness of the deceit disappear. He took her wrist to his mouth, kissed the inside where the faint scent of lavender remained. Then he looked at her, his eyes shimmering with a desire she now recognized easily.

"But we shall be late for the opera."

"Damn the opera," he breathed and led her slowly backward to an embroidered settee where she went limp beneath him.

"Great God, not *here*, George!" she whispered in fear as he kissed her neck, her chin, and her face hungrily. "What of the servants?"

"To hell with the servants!"

"George, I cannot! They could enter at any time!"

"Ah, but we've done it before, have we not?" He smiled. "I shall lock the door."

He had the insolent grace of an animal as he moved across the floor, almost soundlessly, and saw to the lock. Maria watched him, feeling the same amalgam of passion and fear that he always ignited inside her.

The closest they had ever come to anything so wanton was that time before their marriage, here in this very room, when they had very nearly become lovers.

She remembered the wild intensity of that afternoon, their first back together after her trip to France, and her heart began to pound with anticipation.

When George turned back around, she was leaning on her elbows gazing up at him, exactly as he had left her. She had not tried to change his mind again, nor rushed back to her feet. And in that she could see she had surprised him.

Maria watched the desire deepen and build in those blue, luminescent eyes. He strode quickly back and moved on top of her, all silk and velvet, muscle and skin. Shuddering as he kissed her with an open mouth, she felt the slow surge of fire, felt the pulsing of his body through her heavy winter gown.

Maria helped him with his fitted breeches first and when they were at his knees he flung them, along with his stockings and shoes, to the carpet. But her gown was too full of ties and laces to easily free her. George kissed her lips, her cheeks, and her eyelids in the shadow of the setting sun, then pulled away desperately, his breathing fierce and quickened by frustration.

As the last bit of crimson sun fell, the drawing room paling further and further to gray, Maria slowly lifted her heavy skirts, removing the final barrier between them.

When her stockings and petticoats joined his on the carpet, George pressed her back into the settee and pushed inside of her. It was a sudden, almost violent movement, but she was soft and welcoming as their bodies twined like fine silk braid.

Maria moaned and buried her face against his throat as she felt him push deep and then withdraw again and again, taunting her with his every sensual movement.

Finally she opened her eyes and watched with an infinite sense of pleasure, his face glistening with perspiration, his powerful body tensed and straining.

She loved it like this, when every muscle in his taut young body belonged to her, when he was as vulnerable with her as she was with him.

He was moving his tongue over hers with rough thrusts. His hands burned a path from her breasts to her hips. Feeling the feverish rise of passion in her own body, Maria arched with a little cry. She did not know how long it was before they shuddered and fell exhausted against one another.

"What we have, this wild kind of passion, it means everything to me," George said a few moments later, both of them still breathless.

"And to me."

He was surprised by her admission and she could see it on his face. "It is true. Before we met," she continued in a whisper, "I could not have imagined making love this way, so wantonly and free. Now I could not imagine it any other way."

"Shall we go on to the opera?"

"We would be late if we did."

"No matter." He smiled. "Remember, madam, you have your own box with the Prince of Wales now."

"Would you mind terribly if we didn't go?

Her expression was so sincere, her face in the shadows so lovely, that just then he could have denied her nothing. He would have liked to go to the opera, to show her off. Everyone would be there tonight, and this was the second time this week she had asked not to go.

He was well aware of the gossip that was circulating, but they must meet it all head-on. Running from it would only make matters worse. They must hold their heads high. They must appear together and often. Gossip would not be silenced by retreat, and his father, who was more frequently ill all the time, could not live forever. So long the inveterate gambler, George had banked everything on this small bit of time amid a deception, to one day make her a queen.

"What would you like to do instead?" he asked, running a gentle hand across her cheek.

"I believe I should like to stay with you as we are for a while."

"Much longer alone in here and your servants really will begin to talk." He chuckled.

"Just now I don't care at all what *anyone* thinks," she replied, her soft face gleaming with the exultant pleasure.

George leaned down and kissed her again, trying to stem the fresh tide of guilt he felt for the clandestine sort of life to which he had seen his precious wife committed.

She may say that she does not care, he thought. *Now here with me for the moment, she may even believe it. But she does care. She cares a great deal, and we cannot hide forever.*

He looked back down at her smiling, hungry eyes. Maria laughed a little winsome laugh, then pulled him into another kiss, drawing his tongue into her mouth. *God, how she does surprise me!*

Already he felt his body begin again to stir. Yes, there was a cruel, unforgiving world beyond those walls, one sooner or later they both must face. But the rest of the world would have to wait for now... now that the Prince of Wales had so much to be contented with right here in his own arms.

CHAPTER SIX

"IT IS REALLY SO KIND of you to call on me. Your visit is quite a surprise."

"Yes, I should rather imagine that it is."

Maria sat back in the heavy, saffron-colored armchair at her new house in fashionable St. James's Square as Fanny first poured tea for the guest and then for her mistress. The steam from the two china cups spiraled upward from the tea cart and disappeared into the perfume-scented air as the old woman studied Maria with intense gray eyes.

"Such a lovely home," Lady Clermont casually observed in a raspy, age-tempered voice as she looked around at the well-appointed drawing room.

"Thank you, Your Ladyship. But I can take little of the credit, since I have only rented it from Lord Uxbridge."

Her wrinkled smile was genuine. "Yes, I had heard that."

What she also had heard, along with the rest of London, but now kindly omitted, was that the expenses for renovations at Maria's house in Twickenham, together with those going on at Carlton House, were staggering, taking nearly all of the unbelievably small stipend the Prince of Wales was accorded.

What Lady Clermont guessed, after only a few moments in her company, was that Maria was a woman of great pride. No matter what anyone else was saying, clearly, it was the Prince, not Maria, who had insisted she give up her own house in Mayfair to be nearer to his official residence.

Fanny offered Lady Clermont a selection from a plate of confections. "Ooh, I shouldn't," she smiled. "But then at my age, one has so few great pleasures left to indulge!"

She laughed an infectious, throaty laugh, then took a butter biscuit and a berry tart and put them side by side on her little blue china plate.

Maria took only a small biscuit, with no intention of consuming it. She had been much too surprised by the unexpected arrival of her influential guest.

Frances Fortescue, wife of Baron Clermont, the tiny, white-haired doyenne, was the pillar of London society. She was rumored to be a great friend of Marie Antoinette in France as well as England's own Queen Charlotte. Their house in Berkeley Square was the site of some of the most sought-after parties in London. Yet, until today, when she called unexpectedly, their paths had never crossed.

Lady Clermont bit into the tart and rolled it around in her mouth with a tremendous smile. "Delicious, my dear."

"Thank you, Your Ladyship." Maria lifted her tea slowly as her guest wiped her fingers daintily on a small lace-edged napkin, then lay it back in her lap. "Well, now then. Since we've gotten the pleasantries out of the way, perhaps we should come straight to the point."

"As you wish," Maria nodded, feeling a tiny jolt of apprehension.

"Oh, I do so prefer it. I find it such a waste otherwise. And to look at me perhaps you've noticed that I haven't a great deal of time left to waste!"

She laughed again and the little lines around her eyes and at the corners of her mouth deepened. But the way she spoke, the sheer delight in her voice, transcended age. It made Maria smile back, and after a moment she felt the apprehension begin to fade.

"As you might imagine, I have heard quite a lot about you these past few months," said Lady Clermont. "Truthfully, it seems that no one speaks about much of anything else since your name has been linked with the Prince of Wales. Rather tedious to be so myopic, to my way of thinking. And then of course there are those awful caricatures that seem to be cropping up simply everywhere."

Maria lowered her eyes a degree, the pain of the latest image, one called " 'Twas Nobody Saw the Lovers Leap," burst through the edges of her memory, stinging her.

"I understand that since these inconvenient rumors about you and His Highness commenced, you have been having trouble with some of the ladies."

"It is really very nice of you to be so charitable in your concern, however—"

"Oh, my dear," she finished Maria's thought with a wave of her bony hand, "this is not charity entirely. Believe me. I am, above all things, a prudent old woman. Rather dull to admit, I'm afraid, but true all the same. The reality is this: If you are a friend of the Prince of Wales, then you are a friend of mine. It is that simple."

"Then you do not believe the rumors?"

Lady Clermont was a wise woman. Her slim face, all lines and sagging flesh, covered with white ceruse and colored with blush, was as full of character as her voice. She studied Maria's face intensely, pure and innocent by comparison to her own, before she replied.

"My dear, what is between you and the Prince is none of my affair. That is not why I have come. I would imagine that the two of you have enough difficulties without trying to convince an old woman of whether or not you are secretly married."

"Thank you for that," Maria said softly and looked back into old, tired eyes that had not lost their warmth nor their compassion.

"I would like you to come to Clermont House this afternoon at four. I am having a small gathering of ladies and I, for one, think it is high time to see you among them once again."

Maria's heart swelled with a sudden rush of wonder. "You came all the way across town to personally extend an invitation to me?"

"Well, my dear, why not, precisely? Considering your circumstances of late, and since we had not yet met, I was not at all certain you would come if I simply sent an invitation with my coachman."

"You are very kind."

She leaned across the tea cart, which sat between them holding the little delicate china teapot and the plate of scones and cakes. She put her spotted hand atop Maria's and gently squeezed.

"You musn't take any of this too much to heart, my dear. Truly. It will not last. The whims of society are as changing as the tides. If you do not shrink from it, next week it will be another of the King's sons who has garnered their attention. And to that end, with seven robust sons to plague him, our good King shall likely know little peace anytime soon."

Maria's lips parted in a broader smile as she set her tea back down on the cart.

"So then you will come?"

In the two months since their marriage, Maria had not seen Isabella Sefton, Anne Lindsay, or even the Duke of Bedford, who had so generously professed his devotion to her in France. With the Prince, she had been a guest several times of the Duke and Duchess of Devonshire. But as it was today with Lady Clermont, Maria knew the gatherings had been arranged.

George had put the poor woman up to this, she thought. But Maria liked her. Her Ladyship was direct and honest, and that was more than she could say about her treatment from the rest of London.

Apparently, it had been one thing to have been pursued as a potential mistress by the Prince of Wales. It had been clearly another to have broken the law to marry him.

"I would be honored to come to Clermont House," Maria finally consented. "Thank you, Your Ladyship."

"Ah. Enough of that. Let's just see things here set back to a normal course for you both, and that will certainly be thanks enough for me."

LADY CLERMONT HAD A LOVELY tea set out on white silk cloth in the drawing room. It was a grand room, hung with melon-colored chintz. The chairs and settees were covered with the same plush fabric. There were huge dark oil paintings framed in gold. The carpets, like most of the furniture, were priceless French. Against one wall in front of the glass doors that faced the garden, musicians played a light concerto.

Maria moved into the room with Jacko but, as her butler, he

could press no further. He stopped just inside the doorway. He must leave her there alone. When this grand hulk of a man moved to turn away, she took his arm and squeezed it, not wanting to let go.

She had wanted to come and was relieved to have been invited, finally, by someone who had the courage—and the power—to go against society. But now that she was here, knowing the looks she was certain to face, Maria was not so certain anymore.

"It'll be all right, ma'am," Jacko said in a whisper. "But I shall be waiting for you just outside, just in case you need me."

Then he was gone.

Maria looked back into the huge, vaulted room. Her heart was beating like a drum. Before her now were a dozen ladies whom she knew—another dozen that she had never seen before. But among them were all of those who had so boldly snubbed her when rumor of her marriage to the Prince of Wales had first begun.

She made little fists with her hands and then released them, but she could not still the rapid beating of her heart. She glanced quickly around the room. Lady Townshend, Lady Lindsay, and, against her private wishes to the contrary, even Georgiana, the Duchess of Devonshire.

Maria could tell that they were talking about her. It was subtle at first, with their hands held before their lips, fans held to the tips of their noses. Then it grew more bold. It quickly became clear that not only was she the guest of honor, but Maria was also the leading topic of conversation. An afternoon's curiosity.

"Mrs. Fitzherbert, how good of you to come," said Lady Clermont, coming slowly toward her, the small, frail body depending heavily on a black onyx walking stick. Then she took Maria's hand in such a dramatic gesture that there was no one in the room who could have been permitted to miss it.

"Your home is lovely," Maria said, managing to force the words from a miserably dry throat.

"Thank you, my dear."

Her Ladyship fingered the string of pearls, wound first near her throat, then draping down past her sagging breasts, as she gazed across the room. "Please, now. Do come in and have a glass of lemonade with the others. I've had it spiked just enough to make the afternoon interesting!"

Lady Clermont leaned on her cane with one hand, and with the other, she took Maria by the elbow and set the pace slow enough for the two of them to make a grand entrance across the long chasm of her drawing room. Maria was shocked to hear the hushed whispers cease in a quick snap and the sweet ring of pleasantries commence in their place.

"Nice to see you again, Mrs. Fitzherbert," Lady Townshend said as they passed.

"You're looking lovely, Mrs. Fitzherbert." The Duchess of Argyll nodded.

"How are you faring?" she heard the old woman whisper through an elegant smile. Maria glanced over at her, the white curls held high with pride, her eyes crinkling in the corners. At the end of what seemed like an endless procession, she stood with Lady Clermont at a table full of tall pale yellow glasses of lemonade.

Before she could reply to her hostess's kind inquiry she sensed someone behind her. She recognized the shrill voice before she turned around. The sound of it turned the blood cold in her veins.

"My dear Maria. It is so good to see you out without His Highness like this," Georgiana said with a hint of mocking that she could not see her way clear to suppressing. "I was just saying to Abigail that it was high time. There are so many places besides the opera that one really must be seen."

"Thank you." She forced herself to smile.

Solicitous words aside, Maria knew only too well what the Duchess of Devonshire's true feelings were toward her. Still, these women were all catering to her, quite suddenly, as if she were important, as if they truly wanted to draw her into their circle, make her one of them. And for that small miracle, she knew, there was only one person in the world responsible...

"Mrs. Fitzherbert, I believe you know Lady Horatia Seymour," the Duchess then said.

Maria looked at the slightly built, frail young woman who stood beside Georgiana. Although she could not place her, she knew the face, the turn of her almost gaunt, pallid cheeks, the wide, sincere hazel eyes. Suddenly then, she remembered.

"Of course. We met at Carlton House last year."

"I'm honored that you recall it, Mrs. Fitzherbert," Horatia replied in a voice as mild and vulnerable as the rest of her.

171

"And how is your husband?"

"Away at sea once again, I am afraid. We've not seen one another since Christmas." Her pale smile fell. "I thank God for the constancy of my children. Without their company I believe I should go absolutely mad in his absence...and of course, without Lady Sefton. We have been her guest several times these past months," she explained, never having realized Elsabella Sefton's true motive had been to press the well-connected Lady Seymour for information. "We've actually become rather good friends."

"How surprising," Maria cautiously remarked.

"I'm sorry for what has been happening to you here in London," Horatia said, sincerely. "It has all been so terribly unfair to you, and so unflattering."

Maria tried to smile, still finding it difficult to be a party to this grand deceit into which love and passion had led her. "Thank you, Your Ladyship."

"Lord Seymour and I spoke of it at Christmas when he was home, and I can assure you that there are at least two people here in London who do not believe a single word of that vicious gossip. Imagine, *you* actually marrying the Prince of Wales!"

Maria held her head high and she turned her face back into the crowd of ladies. "Your faith, Lady Seymour, is much too kind."

THE MUSCLES IN GEORGE'S FACE tensed.

"In spite of what his advisers tell him, the King continues in his refusal to take off the restrictions on my income," he tried to say offhandedly. The Prince of Wales sat between Fox and Sheridan at a private gaming table at Brook's Club as Lady Clermont was having tea with Maria. "It is the only way that he has left to force my hand, and he is using it to the hilt."

"But Your Highness has sent the further documentation he requested, did you not?" asked Richard Sheridan, looking up from his fanned selection of cards.

"We did. And yet his people tell me that he is incensed at my refusal to deny all of the rumors going around about a marriage."

"Perhaps it is true, that all he wants is your personal denial of something illegal," Fox observed just before he took a long swallow of brandy.

"Nonsense. It is his way of making me agree to an alliance with some foreign princess or other! He has boxed me into a corner by using money, and it has worked splendidly, as he knew it would. Remember, I am a property to be married off to align two countries, not for anything having to do with love. I have told him I shall never marry, and on that I stand firm. We may even be forced to go and live abroad for Maria's sake if this cruel gossip, so much of it against her now, continues."

"But, Your Highness, if that is your goal, your influence shall be greatly reduced, and what then shall become of the party?" asked Fox, his resonant voice full of alarm.

George looked up at his two closest friends. Fox's dark bushy eyebrows were peaked like a steeple and his pale mouth was a thin, hard line of apprehension.

"The momentum of the Whig Party could never survive without your assistance," Sheridan carefully seconded.

"I will never abandon you entirely. You know that, both of you. But right now things are not good. I am worried about Maria. The King is using my affiliation with the Whigs as one of the many reasons he remains my adversary. We all know, however, that his treatment of me stems from another issue altogether. To that end, I may be well served to bear a somewhat lower profile in political matters... at least until all of this is resolved."

He took a cherry brandy, the first in days, and drank it in one swallow. "I truly am at a loss with how to win the war against him."

"Perhaps if you just denied the marriage to His Majesty outright, it would be enough," Sheridan bravely cut to the heart of the matter. "Then he would not be so terribly anxious to see you married to someone else, just to keep you safe from your Catholic."

"He's right, you know," Fox agreed, his voice quick now, and filled with hope. "After all, Your Highness denied your intentions to me."

George conceded the point with a solemn nod. "So I did."

"Then doing it a second time would be such a simple thing."

He let out a heavy sigh. "My letter to you seems a long time ago, Charles. A great many things are different now."

"Would it really be so different to set the King's mind at ease the same way you did mine?"

"I will not dignify that sort of gossip with a reply, Fox!" George spat, angered by the prodding.

"But admission is such a little thing," Fox unwisely pushed.

"Do not ask me to explain something you could never begin to understand!" George charged. "I shall *not* deny Maria to him, and that is the end of it!"

Sheridan waited silently as Fox laid down his cards and stood. "Perhaps I should take that as my cue to join the others for a game. If Your Royal Highness would be good enough to excuse me." He nodded politely, then lumbered off across the room.

Sheridan looked back at the Prince once they were alone. "Charles means well enough."

"I know he does," George said, drinking a second brandy in a single swallow to hide the note of regret he knew would take over if he let it.

"He's a good man," Sheridan said, then added cautiously, "but he does not really understand all that is at stake, does he?"

George looked up at his friend, rocked by what he was implying.

He studied the slim, elegant face, the eyes focused with the intensity of a Bengal tiger. Richard Sheridan was not asking for a confession. No words of admission needed to be spoken between them to know that somehow he had discovered the truth, or at least, he believed that he had. George drew in a breath, then leaned back in his chair and wiped a hand across his face.

"No one understands the position I am in. It would be impossible."

"If you will permit me, I believe I do, Your Highness."

George looked up, his passion for Maria and the despair of his circumstances a bright flame between them. "Then tell me, Sheridan, can you understand loving a woman so much that there is nothing... *nothing* you would not do, nothing you would not promise, to have her?"

"I believe I can."

He shook his head. "To love someone with such desperation that deception, coercion... even murder would not be out of the question?"

"I believe I can understand that kind of desperation, yes."

174

George looked back at his old friend, his tight jaw softening. Finally, in a low, resolute tone he said, "Then you must also understand that there is nothing I would not do to keep Maria safe. I will go to any lengths, Sheridan—*any* lengths. Even to my own peril."

"Then would you not speak a few meaningless words, publicly, in order to buy time for the two of you? To keep the King from forcing you into a political marriage with someone else?"

His sigh was heavy. "I promised her that I never would deny it."

"Your father is not a well man. You know that. You are near to being able to repeal the Royal Marriage Act yourself and make Maria your queen."

George raked a hand through his hair. "But the truth is everything to her."

"There are times when the end justifies the means. I believe, sir, that this may well be one of those occasions."

"Before I take that risk," he said, and sighed, "there is one last thing I can try. One person I can go to who has the power to stop all of this before it gets dangerously out of hand."

GEORGE CLOSED HIS EYES FOR a moment as the carriage pulled into the gravel courtyard at Windsor Castle. He had not wanted to come. He had promised himself, after his last run-in with the King, that he was finished. But there was still a small shred of hope the Queen would see that he was happy, stop all of this madness by siding with him, and make any dangerous declaration against Maria unnecessary. And they had been close once. It was nothing like what he had shared with Belle Pigot, but she was still, after all, his mother.

The March sky only now had any spark of color as the blood-red sun began to set behind the sprawling gray stone castle. The horses pawed at the gravel and shook their lustrous, dark manes when the driver pulled the reins to steady them.

"Whoa!"

George raised the crimson shade and looked out at the magnificent palace silhouetted against a palette of colors in the early-evening sky. Memories of childhood summers spent here whirled in his mind. He saw himself. His brother, Frederick. He could almost smell his mother's delicate perfume. He remembered the collection of Chinese Mandarin figurines she had kept here. ("Be careful, George. Only look at them. Stand here beside me. Do not touch them. *Never* touch them.") Fragments of the past, for a moment, paled the hatred he now bore for the two who occupied this house.

Two liveried footmen, wearing crisp white gloves, moved quickly down the front steps and opened the door to his carriage. *The prodigal son returneth*, he thought bitterly as a flash of icy winter wind pushed through the open door, sobering him for what lay ahead.

They walked together, George and the footmen, into the entrance hall, three sets of heels clicking out a rhythm on the pale salmon marble.

Queen Charlotte sat, hands linked in her lap, in a private sitting room. The room was still ornamented like the rest of the house, in the Elizabethan style, with dark, heavy paneling and a huge stone fireplace that dominated an entire wall.

She was surrounded by paintings of her children. They cluttered the other walls now from floor to ceiling. Amelia, as a baby, framed in gold near the window that looked out onto the garden. Frederick at fourteen, his cheeks full of rosy innocence, hung from a brass chain beside a small gold-framed painting of Ernest.

His own portrait, painted when he turned twenty, had the place of most honor, above the blazing hearth. George gazed up at his own image. That had been their best year, she always said. Before he became a man. Before he had left her for Carlton House to get away from his increasingly mad father.

The Queen was sitting with one of her youngest daughters, the Princess Sophia, and two of her ladies-in-waiting, listening to the child's recitation from Homer's *Iliad*.

She had not changed, George thought when he first saw his mother sitting in the glow of the firelight. Her gray hair, like polished silver, crowned a face that had not lost all of its youthful prettiness but she still had that same regal way of carrying herself that had frightened him when he had grown old enough to see it.

Her back was as straight as a board and her hands were clasped neatly in her lap as Sophia read. The young princess spoke in a perfectly fluid voice until she saw her brother. Like everyone else in

England, even Sophia had heard rumors about George and the Papist.

After a brief pause, she glared up evilly at the mysterious and destitute-looking heir and then began her recitation again.

George listened to his sister and watched their mother as he lingered just inside the door. The act of reciting for his mother took him to another time, another place, when he was once young and was looked upon with favor by her. He felt a twinge of jealousy at that.

Charlotte was a good woman and she had been a good mother. In her own way. But she was not capable of dealing with the grayer areas that life presented. For England's Queen, it was either black or white. There was room for nothing in between. Even when it concerned the happiness of her own son.

George had never been a child definitive enough to suit either of his parents. He was too willful. Too reckless. Too wild. As the little Princess Sophia read the last words, the Queen finally sensed him standing there and looked up at the door.

"George!" she cried out his name, more with surprise than with pleasure. The two ladies-in-waiting sprung to their feet and then fell into deep curtsies. "I'd all but given up hope that you'd come."

"Well, here I am."

"Does His Majesty know that you are here?"

He looked back and then moved toward his mother. "No, and I prefer it remain that way. May we speak privately?"

The Queen came slowly to her feet, azure taffeta folding out from her lap like ripples in a stream. She smoothed her skirts, then looked back at her son, a long room and a great distance of tension between them.

She dressed in the old school. She still wore a powdered wig, her skin heavily powdered and two small patches near her chin, but there was still enough evidence of what she once had been to charm even the most ruthless diplomat. When she nodded, his sister, a child he barely knew, was issued from the room by the two women servants.

As he stood before her, Charlotte's mind whirled with an intricate contradiction of thoughts. Her son looked calmer and happier now than she had ever seen him. The desperation and the anger were gone.

She had met Maria Fitzherbert and remembered her as appealing, but several years older. That was, no doubt, the primary reason her son had been so taken with her. Maria certainly was not the first mature beauty to have turned his head. But to have married her! To have behaved so brazenly against the Crown! Going against his duty! Could he actually have done it?

She drew in a steadying breath as they faced one another. Perhaps she had worried needlessly. Perhaps he had come to deny the rumors… finally. She was, after all, the first woman in his life. He could still come to her, even now. One at least could hope.

When the servants and Sophia had gone out of the room, the Queen moved across the floor and embraced him. It had been so long since she had held this child, her first child. But she felt him quickly stiffen beneath her grasp and so, slowly, she moved away.

"I wrote to you several times, you know," she said, her tone like her posture, finding its formality again. "I even sent my messenger to your house. The King and I had hoped to see you at Christmas."

"I know, and I'm sorry about that. But things have been rather complicated lately."

"You are referring to Mrs. Fitzherbert, I presume."

George looked up at her, unable to mask his surprise. "You know about Maria then?"

"My son, I doubt there is a soul in all of England who does not know about you and the lady by now."

"I love her, mother, and for the first time in my life I am happy. *Truly* happy." He smiled, his wide eyes shimmering as they had when he was a boy, and Charlotte felt an instant stab of guilt. To have to deny one of her children the look of happiness she saw on his face just now—the knowledge that this was far more than the dalliance she had made herself believe for what lay ahead was almost painful.

"Maria is wonderful. God has blessed me this time. I want so much for you to meet her, for you to receive her at Court. I know that would help heal so many things."

"I doubt very much whether that will be possible," Charlotte forced herself dryly to say.

"She's been presented before, Mother, I know that she has."

"Things were different then."

Her rebuke silenced his fantasy and jerked him back to the moment. "Because of the King?"

178

"Because you have gone against him too many times, George. I am certain it comes as no surprise that he is exceedingly angry with you."

"Yes, I know."

She was cool now. Completely in control. "You've been quite extravagant with your restorations and improvements at Carlton House. Which seems curious to me, since, when my messenger comes to call, you are almost never there." She put a hand on his shoulder and gently squeezed it. Her fingers were bony, like those of a skeleton, and there was no warmth there.

She had gently, yet persuasively, as mothers do, turned the tide of conversation away from the unimportant and directed it to what she most desired to know.

"Tell me, George," she said softly, caressingly, but as adroitly as a politician, "what have you done?"

They both knew she was *not* speaking about Carlton House.

"Nothing which I shall ever regret."

"I wonder, my son, can you be so certain of that? Life is long. Sentiments change. Yours certainly have changed in the past where women are concerned."

"I shall not change, not where it concerns Maria. Mother, please." He turned to face her again, his voice edged to desperation, wounding her now more than she would ever have thought possible. "If you would accept her, then the King would be bound to accept her also. I would not face the impossible choice I do now. Please." He loathed pleading. But there were so few options left. "Just receive her at Court. Just once. For my sake."

"I cannot."

"You mean you *will not* do it."

"I mean I cannot. In over thirty years of marriage, I have never gone against my husband, and I do not intend to begin such a course of action now. You know as well as I that those episodes of madness from which he suffers have worsened, and I shall not bring any more turmoil into his life because of you than need be."

"Not even to see to my happiness?"

"I cannot do it to him, George."

He hesitated a moment before turning around one last time. Her face was set tightly, and in the firelight he could see all too clearly that her mind would not be changed. Finally, when there was nothing left to be said, when the last pleasant recollections of his youth that he had forced himself to conjure had vanished like the mist, George leaned forward and placed a chilly kiss on her cheek.

"It was good to see you again, Mother," he said dryly, then turned away and walked out of the room.

THE NEXT MORNING, GEORGE CAME into the breakfast room just as Jacko Payne was laying out clove tea, freshly made biscuits, and a tray of toast. With a single expression, he dismissed the butler, and when they were alone he sank into the seat beside Maria and took up her hand.

His eyes were shot with crimson and his mouth was as dry as desert sand. His body ached for sleep that, for several nights, he had been unable to find for the way things felt as if they were closing in upon him.

"I'm sorry about last night," he said softly, smelling proper now of cold water and costly civet perfume. But his head was still a reminder, pounding out rhythms like a drum. "...For coming home so late."

"I cannot say I like your friend Mr. Fox very much," Maria said, stabbing at a piece of bacon on her plate.

After his disastrous meeting at Windsor Castle, Charles Fox had seen George home from Brook's Club, to which he had returned.

They had not made a good impression.

"Let Jacko make you some tea, George," she had urged as she'd come to the front door.

"Tea!" Fox had growled at her. "He doesn't need tea, woman! The man needs a brandy!"

"I think he's had quite enough of that."

Fox had glared at her as possessive as a rival lover. "Well, I think not, and I have known what's been good for him a far sight longer than you have, Mrs —" Then he had purposely let the pause ring before he added in a perfunctory tone, "It still is Mrs. Fitzherbert...isn't it?"

"I want to leave London," George announced now, taking up her hand more tightly and squeezing it. "Right now, today."

Maria looked at him curiously. "Where on earth would we go?"

"There is a little village along the coast. It's a place I went to clear my mind when you left me and went to France."

She put down her fork. It clanked against the china plate as she looked up at him. "Brighton."

"Yes, Brighton."

"But there is nothing there except beach."

"Precisely! Miles of beach, and cool crisp wind." He brought her hand to his lips and kissed it. "And freedom...glorious freedom from all of this, from the indecent gaze and the questions of our friends, from the King...from Fox."

She looked away but he still held her hand tightly. *And can we run from fate as well?* she wondered. "I don't know, George."

"It's beautiful there. I promise you will love it. Oh, the sky and the water are both so blue. I tell you, darling, you cannot tell where one ends and the other begins." He moved closer to her, placing her hand across his heart, his eyes dancing with excitement. "I've leased a small farmhouse there. It's nothing terribly elegant, mind you, but it has the most glorious view of the sea. And at night the gulls screech out a rhythm more hypnotic than any lullaby."

He kissed the little vein on the inside of her hand just below the wrist, then held it up between them as he leveled his eyes on hers. "The truth is, I've got to get away from here, Maria. I think we need to be free of all of the mayhem for a while."

"But what of Carlton House and all of the restoration going on there? You're right in the midst of so much, and you've worked so hard to make it something of which you can be proud."

He sat back in his chair, still looking at her. Her pale flawless face held such innocence. Such devotion. She would never really understand what demons possessed him, drove him. How much he needed to escape them for as long as he could.

"I'm going to close the house for a while. I've already spoken to Onslow about letting most of the staff go."

"But why?"

He paused a moment, then told her the truth. "I cannot afford to keep them on."

She gazed around at the cheery lemon-yellow breakfast room that only recently had been papered with expensive hand-painted cloth.

The new Wedgewood china. The embroidered ecru table cover. All of which he had insisted on buying for her so that she would be surrounded with beautiful things.

"It is this place that's the problem," Maria said, shaking her head.

"No! I don't want you even thinking that! I want you surrounded by beauty and the things that make you smile. You deserve more than I can ever give you. Besides, this was something between the King and I long before I met you. It is certainly about more than money. A battle of wills—now to become a game to the death, apparently."

"But if I'd only known. If you had only said something—"

His lips curved into a gentle smile and he ran a finger beneath her chin. For a moment he was silent. "What would you have done? Hmm? I know that your husband left you secure, darling, but not even your jointure could rescue me now from the mammoth predicament I created in my youth, by stubbornly continuing to defy the King of England."

She moved to the edge of her chair. "But I don't need all of these things, George. Honestly I don't! I never wanted this house in the first place, or these expensive gowns," she said, pulling at her silk sleeve.

"Then come with me to Brighton, to the farm." He pressed her hand to his heart again. We will leave it all behind. We shall live a simple life, like simple English people. Just the two of us. Please, Maria. Say you'll come."

She gazed into his eyes and saw more than a need to outrun his creditors or even the outrageous swell of gossip that had now taken over London. But what truly plagued him he would not let her see.

No matter how close their love had bound them, there was a part of George still closed to her, that was closed to everyone who tried to love him. It was a restless, tortured side, something in his soul that he was trying to escape by this move, and it frightened her.

She ran her fingers softly against his unshaven jaw. "I am your wife, George Augustus," she whispered, pushing away the doubt. "And I shall go wherever you go for as long as you want me."

"Oh, my darling..." he whispered into her fingertips. "That shall be forever."

THE BELLS OF BRIGHTON RANG out their greeting, and the guns of the battery fired a royal salute for the arrival of the Prince of Wales and Mrs. Fitzherbert. A week after George and Maria settled into the modest "farmhouse" that faced the shore, the streets of the little seaside town were illuminated with a colorful display of fireworks. In the Castle Tavern and the Old Ship Inn, townspeople eagerly toasted their newest and most famous resident.

"Look at that, will you!" George said as they stood together before the long, open window, the summer sky bathed in a vibrant explosion of color and light. "Those are for us!"

"Those are for *you*, my darling. They adore you here."

"Not half so much as I adore *you*."

She turned to him and for the first time in several days she watched a serene smile turn up the corners of his mouth as he looked out at the sandy beach and the sea beyond. No cruel Gillray caricatures. No Cruikshank jibes. No angry creditors. No dark temptations from Fox or anyone else.

"Can you tell me now that you do not think it is beautiful here?"

"But I do," she whispered in reply and lay her head on his shoulder.

The change in George had been immediate. They had been in Brighton less than a week but the reemerged temptation to numb himself with the palliatives of brandy or with gambling had faded with the problems and turmoil they had left behind in London.

Since their arrival at the shore, he and Maria had walked freely about the town, George bowing and smiling openly to the townspeople who passed them. He reveled in their greetings of friendly respect. But he marveled that here, for the first time in his life, he was free simply just to *be*. Like any other man, with a wife who was the world to him.

Maria turned from the window and moved back into their cozy, ivory-colored bedchamber, which glowed like melting honey with candles, oil lamps, and a warm fire.

George watched her face, lit with blue, then red, then gold as the fireworks continued to explode in the sky. Her hair was long tonight, brushed onto her shoulders in soft gilt waves, and her face was free of cosmetics. She had worn none at all since they had come away, preferring the freedom.

He watched her blow out one candle and then another. Finally the oil lamps too were extinguished until the room was filled with rich shadows. But there was still light from the sporadic burst of fireworks and heat from the fire that blazed beneath an old beige stone hearth.

Maria watched the flames dance. She felt the heat warm her face. She breathed deep and felt a new wave of calm. It had been so long, this tumultuous whirlwind of a year, that she had forgotten what peace had felt like. But this was it, here in Brighton with George, in this simple little farmhouse by the sea.

"And are you happy?"

"I am happy because *you* are happy, darling." She smiled serenely into the burst of colored light.

He kissed the top of her head, then pulled her closer to him as the fresh salt air came on a cold breeze in through the window. "It will be all right now," he whispered. "Everything will be all right. You shall see."

THE NEXT DAY THEY CHOSE a small adjacent house for Maria to formally occupy, for appearances. It was a modest brick house but it was close enough to the more grand farmhouse to serve their purposes. Even this far from London she could not risk living openly with the Prince of Wales.

Not until he was finally free to acknowledge her as his wife.

After their afternoon stroll along the beach, they browsed in the tiny shops along North Street. Both of them were forced, like everyone else, to step over fishermen's nets and duck beneath the low-roofed sailors' cottages to make their way. But it all only added to the charm. Maria bought a quilt made by a fisherman's wife for their simple poster bed and George bought her a copy of Shakespeare's plays, which she had never read entirely.

They passed by Raggett's, a subscription house, with gaming tables in imitation of Brook's Club in London. But clinging fast to Maria's arm, invigorated by the air and loaded down with their treasures, for the first time he could recall, George felt no compunction whatsoever to join the gamblers.

She gave him that, she gave him strength—his Maria.

As they passed, the townspeople who had gathered there waved and smiled through one of the great bow windows. They watched the famous resident walk with his lady back onto the crowded North Street.

It had taken no more than a few days for the people of Brighton to accept the royalty who now resided in their midst. They treated George and Maria as they wished they were—any other man and wife. No one questioned whether or not they were married. No one seemed to care. They were poor and in debt because he still had not yet denied their marriage to the King. Their future could not have been more uncertain.

And it really was the very best time of their lives.

BY LATE SUMMER, MARIA SAT rapt in the little garden behind the farmhouse that faced the sea as George recited a passage from *Hamlet* that she found strangely fitting. Her thick, lilac skirts and large straw hat with long pink ribbons rustled in the breeze as she watched him pore over the words.

The Shakespeare play had been his favorite as a young boy; the theme, betrayal of a son by his mother. The book he had bought for her in the village, and which he read from now, had been his way of trying to share with her a childhood and a past he had never been able to disclose, outright, to anyone.

When he reached the passage spoken by Laertes to Ophelia, George's voice wavered and he felt the words at his core.

...Perhaps he loves you now
And now no soil nor cautel doth besmirch
The virtue of his will. But you must fear,
His greatness weighed, his will is not his own,
For he himself is subject to his birth...

She watched his square jaw as he formed the strangely appropriate words, his eyes narrowing when something touched him most deeply. The cool breeze tossed his chestnut curls around his face and filled his cheeks with pale roses.

Maria reached up and touched his hand when he finished the recitation. He looked at her and saw her eyes rimmed with tears.

"It wasn't meant to make you sad," he said.

"It is just such a tragic story."

"But, you know, I believe I really understand Hamlet, what drove him, the betrayal and the disappointment that seemed to define his life and to foreshadow his tragic end. What he was is all so brilliantly summed, I think, in those few lines."

"It is a beautiful passage."

"You know, I always thought of myself like Hamlet. Like him, I certainly never believed that I could be so fulfilled."

Maria looked out at the sea that shimmered like liquid jewels beneath a sun-kissed sky. "Nor did I."

"Sometimes, when you are not beside me, when the past grows inside my memories and I am forced to remember it, I begin to fear that what is between us cannot last."

"You must not even think such things," she said tenderly.

"There is just so much darkness around us, so many people who would be glad to see us fail." After a moment's reflection, he smiled and kissed her cheeks, one after the other. "But then you, my darling woman, you are my light, brilliant and shining enough to illuminate any darkness that others try to cast upon us. With love, we can battle anything. I do believe that."

"Love was not enough for Hamlet."

George smiled and chucked her gently beneath the chin. "Ah. But then Hamlet didn't have you!"

Maria watched his eyes, so full of sincerity, so full of love. Tears shined in her own. Reassured, he pulled her to him and kissed her cheeks as she whispered, "Nothing can ever part us that we do not allow. That is what we must believe."

CHAPTER SEVEN

"OF COURSE, WELTJE, SHOW HIM in!"

In the summer of 1786, the piggish looking man who had func-
tioned in London as the Prince's cook became his majordomo in
Brighton. Later that afternoon, he stood before George, a fat little
man balanced on very short legs, having announced the arrival of
Richard Brinsley Sheridan.

Maria looked up from her embroidery and saw the fires of old
friendship burning brightly in her husband's blue eyes. She felt her
heart sink, remembering how Fox had so vulgarly insinuated himself
into her house and back into the Prince's life that night before they
had first left London. Sheridan was as much a friend to George as
Fox, and the effect of his presence was bound to be the same. She bit
her lower lip as George stood and moved toward the door.

"Richard, you old hound!" He beamed as the tall and noble-
looking Sheridan rounded the corner past the door. He wore an elegant camel-colored tailcoat and black hat, his arm loaded with a
bouquet of lavender. His hair was still the same shade of brown, but
now it bore little touches of silver at the temples. Maria had not
noticed that night at Almack's what a striking man he actually was.

"Your Highness." He bowed properly, until George slapped his back, never forgetting his loyalty—how Sheridan had helped him out that first night with Maria at Carlton House when Elizabeth Armistead meant to make a scene.

"Forget about that here, my friend. Here in my farmhouse by the sea, I am only George."

Maria watched the two men embrace and chuckle together like brothers. She felt a twinge of envy as George held him tightly, as if it had been several years, not simply a month, since they last were together.

"Oh, it is good to see you!"

"As it is to see you."

"Blasted, Richard. Why did you not tell me you were coming?" George grinned and draped his arm around Sheridan's square shoulder. Please come in and meet my..." He stopped himself. "Meet Maria."

"I've heard a great deal about you, Mr. Sheridan," she managed to say in an even tone as she extended her hand.

"If but a word of it was flattering I should consider myself fortunate for it to have reached your ears, madam."

He handed her the bouquet of lavender, the fragrance of which had already filled the room. The apparent coincidence seemed to please her. She was certain that he could not have known they were her favorite flower or that she always wore their scent to sweeten her skin. "It is the very least I can offer for having descended upon you so unannounced like this," he said smoothly.

Maria took the flowers and brought them to her nose. She felt the corners of her mouth twitch in a reluctant smile. "It was lovely of you, Mr. Sheridan. Thank you. Now, if you will both excuse me, I shall go and see if Weltje has a vase."

When she reached the door, she stopped and turned back around. "You will be staying for supper, Mr. Sheridan, won't you?"

"I shouldn't wish to impose, dear lady."

She glanced back at her husband, who was still beaming with the surprise. "No, Mr. Sheridan. No imposition at all."

When they were alone, George showed Richard to the chair where Maria had been, the embroidery hoop cast casually onto one of the chair arms. He sat down and the two men faced one another.

"So. What news do you bring with you from London?"

"Things in the city remain unchanged. Dark, dirty, and rather dismal, I'm afraid."

"And how is Georgiana?"

"Piquant as ever." He smiled. "I suspect she misses you. London may still be London, but it really isn't the same since you took your leave."

"I expect not. Now there is no one quite so delicious to gossip about."

Sheridan let the remark go unanswered.

But it was true. For so long, he and Maria had been the principal topic everywhere. Society chattered about them. The newspapers hinted at the nature of their liaison. The caricaturists were less kind in their suppositions.

"And you, sir," he wisely changed the subject and fingered the embroidery. "How are things here at the seashore? I must say, you are positively glowing."

"I've left that other world completely behind, Sheridan. I simply stopped fighting to change the things that were beyond my control, and I can tell you, I've never been happier. It may sound impossible, but it is as if, before I met Maria, I wasn't living, a'tall. Looking back now, I believe I was only marking time."

"She *is* lovely," Sheridan agreed.

"But her beauty is not the thing I treasure most," he said, coming forward on his chair. "Maria's greatest gift is that she is more than beautiful *inside*. I tell you, thanks to her patience, and her love for me, I have begun to discover things about myself that I never even knew were there. I think now I might actually make a rather acceptable king one day."

"I am pleased for you."

"And I haven't had a brandy since we've been here. Do you know that? Haven't felt the slightest inclination to bet anyone for anything either."

"Now that *is* a surprise," Sheridan said, and then smiled slyly, knowing the darker side of George that the seemingly virtuous Maria was not likely ever to discover.

George sat back in the chair again and his smile began to fall by degrees. "If only the King would stop threatening to force me into a political marriage to see me safely away from Maria, my life would be close to perfection."

"Yes, that does continue to be a problem. I heard last week he's actually close to selecting your bride. It is said that she is from Hanover."

"I refuse to deny Maria, so he threatens me with that."

"Perhaps someone else of note could deny your marriage. Someone in Parliament. That may be enough for His Majesty, without it needing to be you."

This was a dangerous line and Sheridan well knew it.

People in London already believed Maria to be the Prince's secret wife. Belief was one thing, but the Protestant sentiment was so strong in England that it would be completely ruinous to the Whigs if they were the ones to stand up in Parliament. Publicly supporting a man who it may well turn out had gone against the law, and against public sentiment, to marry a Roman Catholic could be the death knell for the party.

"Perhaps if I were able to locate an independent member who would be willing to speak on your behalf."

"Speak publicly?" George laughed bitterly. "Like looking for a needle in a stack of hay!"

"Oh, I don't know. You trusted me once before to make certain your Maria was presented to you at Carlton House when she at first wanted nothing to do with you. Did I not earn your respect in that?"

"But who could you get, for Lord's sake? You know as well as I that there are precious few in London who have not chosen to side with either the Whigs or the Tories."

"We only need find one."

He stood beside the Prince, their voices low now, passing between them in a whisper.

"I suppose that much is true."

"Then trust me in this."

George stroked his chin as his forehead wrinkled in a frown. "If I agree, you must promise me that Maria will know nothing of my involvement," he implored, squeezing Sheridan's arm to punctuate his point. "She has been through enough already with all of that gossip and those horrible caricatures. I do not want her worrying over something else."

"Of course not."

"It could well get ugly," George warned his old friend. "Things could be said about you."

"I understand that. But it is a risk I shall gladly take for the sake of my future King."

"I have your word then?"

"Sir." Sheridan inclined his head respectfully. "You need not even ask."

THE NEXT AFTERNOON, THE THREE of them went out to the Downs. Surrounded by miles of velvety turf and cooled by the sea, it was the perfect place to spend an afternoon. Brighton was famous for its beaches, which every summer drew Londoners as well as the French across the channel to bathe in its curative salt water. But the little town also took pride in one sparkling, special weekend.

Carriages held the gentry who had come down from London to watch the races on the horseshoe field while the townspeople stood or sat on the mossy ground around them. French patricians who had heard about the event mingled freely among their English counterparts and sat around the track in new expensive "randems."

Ladies in their huge straw hats all decorated with pastel ribbons and bows, like a Gainsborough painting, strolled across the grass twirling their parasols and waiting for the race to begin. The Duc de Chartres was rumored to be among the spectators and everyone strained to get a glimpse of him.

He was not however the only gem to sparkle beneath the Brighton sky. Since the King's brother, the Duke of Cumberland, had a house here, Brighton was already considered a royal residence. Several military regiments were based nearby.

Maria sat between George and Richard in the prince's open black barouche, surveying the crowd. She saw the spangle of military uniforms catching the sun as the officers moved proudly among the civilians.

"Oh, isn't this exciting." Sheridan smiled. "I haven't been to the races in ages. Shall we bet something with the others?"

The words were out of his mouth before he realized he had said them. His slim face blanched. "Oh, I *am* sorry, Your Highness."

George only smiled contentedly, his hand resting on Maria's apricot satin–covered knee. It had been a difficult habit to break in the beginning. No reason Sheridan should find it any easier. "Thank you, no, Richard," he said kindly. But you go ahead. Please."

Maria looked back and saw her husband's easy smile, a soft blush painting his cheeks from the salt air. From happiness. It calmed her to see that, almost like an evil spirit, the desire to gamble had left him.

"Well, perhaps just something small," Sheridan relented. "Mrs. Fitzherbert?"

"Certainly, darling," George encouraged. "Go right ahead, both of you. Perhaps you would like to stretch your legs a bit."

"If you're certain you shall be all right alone," Maria said, looking back at him.

"As long as you are not gone long." He smiled and brushed his fingers lightly over her thigh.

They were married!

They *must* be married. The change in him was too dramatic to have been cast by a mere mistress. But Sheridan said nothing. He helped Maria down the two carriage steps and onto the soft emerald grass. He watched the breeze ruffle the folds of her gown. Then she held up her parasol to shield her face from the sun as they moved together into the crowd.

"You know, madam," Sheridan began as they passed a group of townspeople who were having a picnic on the spongy grass. "You've made him an extraordinarily happy man."

"It is no more than what he has done for me."

"I've known His Highness a very long time, and I simply wished an opportunity to say privately that I am glad he has you in his life."

Maria tipped her head to one side and studied him, then said, "You are really very different than the Prince's other friends, Mr. Sheridan."

"You mean Fox?" he asked, his voice curled thickly with Scottish. "Not really so unlike. The packaging is different perhaps, but the essence is closer than you might imagine."

"I have met Mr. Fox and I have met you," she countered firmly, "and I can say without hesitation that you are not a'tall alike."

As the breeze moved across them, up from the sea, he caught the scent of lavender from her skin. It had been a mark of brilliance to have brought the flowers yesterday. A gesture to be sure, but it had made a difference with her. A wise man, he stored knowledge away like a squirrel storing nuts. One never knew when a need might arise. He held her arm above the elbow as they moved past a group of gentry, all speaking rapidly in silky-tongued French. Sheridan smiled.

"I do so often wish I had mastered that damnable language," he lamented. "I should love to know what they're betting."

Maria paused beside them a moment, then looked back at Sheridan, her smooth lips curled into a smile. "They all think the horse ridden by Sir John Lade is going to win the first race."

He looked back at her, a slow smile turning up the corners of his mouth. "Mrs. Fitzherbert, you are a marvel!"

After they had placed their bets, they returned across the crowded Down to the Prince's carriage. They could see from some distance the back of a woman in pale rose-colored silk standing beside a man, and all of them were laughing.

"There you are!" George called out to them with a wave. "It seems I've found some old friends of yours. Lord and Lady Seymour, this is my dear friend, Mr. Sheridan." Then he looked down at her, his lips turned up with wicked delight. "And I believe you already know Maria."

They both turned around at the same moment, and Maria was faced with the man who had saved her from dancing with George that strange first evening at Carlton House. The blush rose from her neck and blossomed on her face like wine spilled on a tablecloth. It all seemed so long ago now but his face and his kindness she had not forgotten.

"It has been a long time, Captain," she said, letting him take her hand. "I, however, have had the good fortune of seeing your lovely wife on a number of occasions."

"At Lady Sefton's and at Devonshire House, as well," Horatia seconded with an eager smile.

"She has told me repeatedly." Lord Seymour smiled adoringly at his wife.

"Your Ladyship is looking much improved," Maria observed.

"Thanks to the sea air," Horatia replied. "We're staying here the rest of the month."

"You, and of course Lady Sefton, have helped my wife through a rather difficult time while I was away Mrs. Fitzherbert, and for that I shall never be able to thank you enough," Lord Seymour charmingly said.

George loomed over them from his new barouche, his lips stretched into a delicious sneer. "I was just telling cousin Horatia here what humor I find in the curious friendship between you and the two people, that night so long ago, who rescued you from what was to become your destiny."

Maria paled. "Your *cousin?*"

"Surprise." George smiled broadly, his blue eyes twinkling.

"In addition to being my wife," Hugh interceded, "Horatia is also cousin by marriage to the Prince of Wales. The former Horatia Waldegrave."

Maria gasped and put her fingers to her lips. "I had no idea. Why did Your Ladyship not tell me that first night? I clearly put you both in a very awkward situation."

"It would have made no difference how either Lord Seymour or I acted on your behalf." She smiled kindly and then tossed a remonstrating little glance at George.

Maria had heard socially of Horatia Waldegrave in years gone by. Horatia and her sisters had been raised in the turmoil surrounding their mother's second marriage to the King's brother, the Duke of Gloucester. A marriage widely known to be disapproved of by His Majesty and one of the primary reasons for the Royal Marriage Act.

All of this time Maria had sought to keep her distance from Horatia. She had feared that someone so simple as this pale little flower could not possibly understand what had driven her to commit a crime when she became George's wife. She saw the truth now. Horatia had endured a very similar sort of turmoil on behalf of her own mother. Horatia Seymour could understand better than anyone but the Duchess of Gloucester herself, all of Maria's thoughts and her fears.

"Oh, splendid, the races are beginning." George smiled broadly.

Then he glanced back down at all of them gathered around his carriage. "Lord and Lady Seymour, any friends of Mrs. Fitzherbert's are friends of mine," he mused. "We haven't anything terribly elegant to offer, I'm afraid, but if you'd care to join us tonight for supper, we would be delighted to have you."

They looked at one another, both of them beaming. Everyone knew that since the Prince of Wales had come away from London with his lady, they rarely entertained and only then were they in the company of their most intimate friends.

This was a far greater honor than an invitation George was more likely to extend to Carlton House. Having made agreement with their eyes alone, Hugh and Horatia both looked eagerly up at the Prince, who loomed over them like a statue. "At the farmhouse then, Your Highness?"

"Ah. So then you know where it is?"

"Oh, Your Highness." Lord Seymour smiled. "It took us only an afternoon to discover that everyone in Brighton knows where *the* farmhouse is!"

When the Seymours had gone back to their own phaeton and Maria was sitting beside him once again, George lifted her hand to his lips and softly kissed it. "You needn't be embarrassed about something that happened between you and me and Hugh so long ago, darling."

Lord Seymour was very kind to me that night," she said in a whisper. "But it does all seems rather foolish now, to have actually been afraid of you."

"Yes, well, you're right about that." He beamed. "Considering the way things turned out."

THE SUPPER TABLE WAS SCATTERED with empty dessert plates and half-full glasses of burgundy wine. "What more may I offer you, Lord Seymour?" Maria asked.

"Oh, I couldn't eat another morsel," he answered, patting his flat abdomen and smiling like a well-fed cat.

"Everything was splendid," Horatia added in her weak, slightly kittenish voice.

"Indeed," seconded Sheridan. "Even better than last night."

"I would love your cook's recipe for the lamb dish," said Horatia.

"Oh, I'm afraid Weltje never divulges the contents of his concoctions. He considers each of them as precious as if they were his own children," said George. Then he added in a whisper as he leaned forward. "I'm afraid he's a bit of an eccentric."

"Speaking of children, how many is it you have now, Admiral?" Maria asked, and the question caught in her throat in a way she had not expected.

"Five, madam." He smiled with pride. "All of them sons."

"Such great fortune," Maria tried to say but her face was sad.

"Yes." He nodded gravely. "But I suppose all great fortune has its price, does it not? It has been difficult for my wife. Her health has never been quite the same since the birth of our second."

Horatia lowered her head, stifling a rheumy cough. Maria looked over at each of them. She, with the pale brown hair and pallid skin but the luminescent eyes of an angel. He, robust and full of health. Her protector. Each was more in love with the other, and blessed with a house full with the laughter of children.

The envy in Maria tonight was like a mild poison.

"If you will excuse me," she said, rising gracefully from the table, needing desperately to catch her breath. Maria went alone out onto a balcony that faced the sea. Almost immediately she felt the spray of the ocean and the cool night air. It washed across her face and through her hair and slowly began to revive her. Almost as quickly she felt foolish for the less than Christian thoughts.

"I don't like them sometimes, you know, my little ones." Horatia's weak voice tangled in the rush of damp air behind her. Maria turned around. "God help me but there are times when I do not..." Horatia moved closer to Maria. They looked together out at the unending blackness of the sea. "I was so healthy once," Horatia said. "I know it is difficult to believe, looking at me now, but when I first met Hugh I was not unlike you. He said that he fell in love with my smile... which is not so fetching any longer."

Maria tried to avoid the compulsion to stare at the hollow cheeks and thin-lipped line of her joyless smile. But she had seen that face painted in another time. Another era. Horatia was one of the beautiful Waldegrave sisters whom Sir Joshua Reynolds had painted in the prime of their beauty.

"I imagine the thing you want most in the world is to have what I have. And yet I feel as if I would give anything to, once again, have the beauty and health that you enjoy."

Maria lowered her eyes. "I am so sorry."

"Don't be. I made my choices. We all do. And they are such good children, really. Each of them with such different personalities, such different goals." She turned away from Maria and let the breeze blow her hair back like a pale, brown sail. "My dearest regret is that I shall not live to see them become the fine people I know they will."

"You mustn't say such a thing!" Maria gasped.

"It's all right. Really. I've known it for a long time. Oh, I'm not going to die just yet, mind you. But I'll not live a long life. Hugh brings me to the sea like this, or sometimes to France, to the springs, trying always to find a new cure for what it is that ails me."

"He is a good man," Maria cautiously conceded.

"That he is, Mrs. —" Horatia let the appellation drop and turned to look at the beautiful Catholic who had stolen the heart of a Protestant Prince.

"George has told you," Maria said with a note of surprise.

"My mother, who was invited to the ceremony, did. George could not deny it to me now in the face of that."

"I'm sorry, I —"

"You needn't be. He is very proud of the fact that, against overwhelming opposition, he has had the courage of his convictions to marry you. I suspect he has told precious few other people, even that Mr. Sheridan, when all the while he has wanted to shout it from the rooftops all over England."

Maria looked up at her again, trying to gauge the expression. "And you do not approve?"

"Only God has the right to do that."

"It really was an impossible situation we found ourselves in."

"As I said before, we all make our own choices. You have chosen to spend your life with my cousin, whatever that may bring you both. I will tell you this, Mrs. Fitzherbert. In all of his life, I have never seen him happier."

"Please," Maria whispered, reaching out to take her hand. "After tonight, you must call me Maria."

"Then you must agree to call me Horatia."

"I would like that."

When everything that could be said had been spoken, they turned back together toward the sea, their hands still linked atop the black iron railing.

THAT NIGHT, WHEN THE GUESTS had gone, Maria lay in George's arms, close against his bare chest. She was fingering the black velvet cord from which the locket containing her miniature still hung around his neck. The moon that came in through the undraped window cast the room in silver and shadows. She looked up and on a simple satinwood table by the bed she saw the book of Shakespeare he had bought for her, two of George's enamel snuffboxes, and a stack of unopened letters from Isabella. That was still a wound that bled. But it was not thoughts of Isabella, or the rejection at her door, that had so completely disheartened her.

"What is it, darling? Was it something Horatia said?"

Maria looked up at him, her mind filled with images of Isabella that she wished to forget, and memories of her conversation with Horatia that she could not help but recall.

"You would like a child, wouldn't you?"

"I think I should like nothing so much in all the world," she answered him, her voice breaking slightly.

"But we both know that it is impossible."

"Nothing is impossible for us."

"The child would have no future, George. Remember, in the eyes of England, we are not husband and wife."

"But you know that is only a temporary state of affairs."

She looked at him with a somber gaze. "Until you are King."

"Yes. Until I am King."

"It would be too great a risk until then."

"But what if you get with child before that?" he asked, a little slyly, sharing his hope, for the first time, that she might accidentally become pregnant.

198

"I don't want to talk about it anymore, all right?" she said, and he could hear the pain in her voice. "I am feeling rather tired just now."

He kissed her hair and pulled her closer. "Hush then, my darling girl. And in the morning when you wake, I shall be, as always, right here beside you. We shall speak of it then."

She needed a child, and he wanted to give her one. He had never seen her look so sad as she had tonight faced with Horatia and the thought of all of her bright and beautiful children.

It was a desire so deeply routed in the core of her womanhood that he could never fully comprehend it. But she needed a child, of that much George was certain. As they lay together against the cambric pillows, he found himself wondering what sort of being their union would create. The question excited him. To have a child with Maria... *Yes, it must be a girl,* he fantasized. That much seemed as fated as they had been.

She would look just like Maria. The same fair hair. The same eyes that were deep and filled with such sincerity. A symbol of the love they shared. Maria was the key to his happiness—a child was the key to hers.

He gazed down at her and touched the skin of her shoulder. Soft. So soft. Like a child's...Sometimes it frightened him how much he needed her, how even in the having her, it was never enough.

Gently, George moved his fingers across her breast to the rose-colored nipple. It hardened beneath his touch, and he watched the gooseflesh spread the length of her magnificent body. His mind began to whirl. Lust. Fear. Lust. Then fear again. He touched her thighs beneath the bedcovers, then parted them as if it were the first time. He looked back at her and she opened her eyes. His mind and heart flooded with feeling, flooded with fear. Pulling her into his arms, he kissed her lips and tore at her sheer, mint-green nightgown.

"Love me," he whispered over and over again into the luxuriant tangle of her golden hair. "Just love me, and I know together we can face anything."

"That," she whispered back, "I shall forever do."

CHAPTER EIGHT

THE BRASSY COLORS OF AUTUMN, and the blood-red sky that marked the dawn, came and went twice in their safe little haven of Brighton. And as they prepared for their second inevitable return to the city for the winter, Maria's flux did not come. There was, as well, a difference, a physical sensation, that she was finally about to be blessed with the one thing she had long desired most in the world.

A child...she thought excitedly, *their child*.

But in a brutal twist of fate that kept Maria silent about what she suspected, the King was now insisting, through their representatives, that George make a political marriage if he would not deny a secret marriage to Maria. He had, in fact, chosen a wife for him already. The bride was to be George's own first cousin, Caroline of Brunswick. And the King would force the union by sword and guard, unless George agreed, once and for all, to deny to him personally the rumor of a secret marriage.

In a race against time that George was swiftly losing, Sheridan still had not found a member of Parliament to speak with authority on the Prince's behalf. The Whigs urged him to find another avenue. The Protestant sentiment in England was too strong, they said, to risk it being discovered that their most famous supporter, the Prince of Wales, was indeed secretly married to a Catholic, after all. It could mean ruin to the party, not to mention the brutal prosecution of Maria for having broken the law if he did not make some sort of declaration soon.

So George lost either way.

If he made a declaration in order to save her, he lost the precious trust of his wife. If he remained silent, Maria might one day well be jailed for having broken the law.

They left Brighton late in November, when most of the little honey-colored houses with their bow windows were closed up for the winter, and the fog blanketed the little sea village like a shroud from morning until night.

Reluctantly, they returned to London. George reopened a portion of Carlton House. Maria returned to the clandestine life in the manor he had leased for her in St. James's Square, still not able to tell him what she suspected until she was absolutely certain.

It was a return to hiding, lying, and deception. All of London saw it as nothing more than a return to business as usual. Maria saw it as the beginning of a very precious dream. And the timing could not have been worse.

"NATHANIEL NEWNHAM."

In Maria's breakfast room, George looked up from the morning paper at Sheridan, who stood tall, elegant, and out of breath at the breakfast room door.

"Nathaniel Newnham is an independent and he has finally agreed to raise the subject of your situation in Parliament, this afternoon."

"Shhh! Maria may hear you!" George whispered and motioned for Sheridan to close the whitewashed door behind him. "How on earth did you get him to change his mind after so long?"

"Oh, who knows why people do the things they do? All I can say is that he called on me at home yesterday and said that now he is prepared to do it."

"Today?"

"Today." Sheridan smiled and buffed his nails against his embroidered black waistcoat, obviously pleased with himself.

George tossed down his paper. In the silence, he ran a hand through his hair, feeling the weight of temptation. If this one calculated act could bring an end to his father's pressure to marry someone else, if it could help him bide his time until he could make Maria his Queen, and protect her from any sort of prosecution, then it would be worth the risk.

"Sweet Jesus...Even if I am not actually the one to mouth the words—if it comes to that for Newnham, if he is pressed, the effect on Maria will still be the same."

"In time, she will come to understand, and forgive you. For however it began between the two of you, whatever was said, if I may say, sir, you are left with little choice any longer."

George washed a hand across his face. "I must break a promise I swore I would never break."

"But if it works, if the King is satisfied, and stops this madness, will the end not have justified the means, as I have said once before?"

"Will *you* be there?"

"Oh, sir," Sheridan said, with a wry look of self-satisfaction, "I can assure you this is one event I would not miss."

"I shall want a full report immediately."

"I shall return the moment I am able."

George raked a hand through his hair again and glanced over at the door. "You had better come to me at Carlton House. There is too much risk of Maria discovering this if you come back here."

GEORGE WAS ALONE IN THE Crimson Drawing Room when Sheridan arrived at Carlton House at half past eight that evening. The Prince's confidant was not nearly so full of the smug self-assurance that had possessed him earlier. He was late now because he had stopped at Brook's Club for a brandy to bolster his courage and to mend his frayed nerves.

It had, in fact, been one devil of an afternoon.

"Come in, Sheridan." George sprang to his feet the moment he saw him and motioned impatiently for the footman to close the door and leave them alone.

He was burning ginger-scented wood and the entire room was

filled with it. Sheridan began to feel a little sick from the aroma and from the apprehension.

"Well? How did it go? Tell me everything!"

George took his friend by the shoulder and led him to an armed chair facing his own. They both sat on the edges of the crimson velvet cushions. He had hoped to be offered a brandy, one final palliative to soften the sharp edges. But the Prince was too excited to remember the courtesy.

"I am afraid it is not good, sir."

George's face fell by degrees. "What happened?"

Sheridan took a breath. "Well. As we agreed he should, Newnham did speak up on your behalf."

"And?"

"He was really rather grand at first. He called your situation, *an embarrassment someone of your stature should not be forced to endure.*"

"So then what is the problem?"

"It was not so much what as who, sir. The Prime Minister."

"Pitt?"

"Pitt, sir, yes. He rather boldly demanded to know what proof Newnham had that the gossip spurring the King on was untrue. When backed against a wall, Newnham was forced to admit that he was not well enough acquainted with Your Highness to produce proof. He was, I am afraid, pitiably silent from then on."

"Damn it to hell! The effort was then totally negated!" George sank against the chair. "Is that all?"

"Would that it were, sir."

"Let's have it then, Sheridan."

"Prime Minister Pitt suggested what we have feared most—taking legal action against Maria and her family for breaking the law."

"Bastard!"

"I fear, Your Highness, now that the fat is in the fire, so to speak, Pitt and his supporters shall not let the matter rest until it is resolved entirely. We gambled today and now have, I believe, passed the point of no return."

George stood and went to the window, where wind and rain rattled the long panes of glass. "I just never thought that it would come to this. I thought Maria and I could outfox them all for that brief time until I was King," he said quietly as he gazed across the rain-soaked garden that extended all the way to Marlborough House. "I gambled my soul that no one would ever truly believe the Prince of Wales would break the law so boldly as I have done. For a time, I had incredulity as my best defense."

"Now that it is out in the open, some action will need to be taken to keep you and Maria out of danger," Sheridan braved, standing but not moving from his chair. "The issue is at an impasse. Your wife and her family shall never be free from the danger of prosecution—and even imprisonment, if this marriage is not denied categorically. You, sir, must deny her."

"I will not! Maria and I will go to Brighton and stay there, out of the fray, until it is my turn to reign." There was an edge of panic now to his voice. "Then she will become Queen, just as we have always planned!"

"You could do that," Sheridan responded carefully. "But when that day comes, perhaps you should consider what your people might say of you. They would have a new King who had not faced trouble—but ran from it."

"Well, I certainly cannot stand and deny the very existence of the person who has given me back my life! I would sooner cut out my tongue than do that to her!"

"There is one last thing. One thing a friend can do on good authority...a thing *I* can and will do. Unlike Newnham, *I* will be believed."

George understood and was deeply touched. "I will not ask you to lie for me."

"I would do it gladly, if it would help you keep your conscience clear with your Maria, and keep her from danger. Our friendship is widely known and my declaration, unlike Newnham's, *will* be believed. Besides, they have no tangeable proof of such a union with her to use against any of us."

George turned back around and leaned into one of the long red draperies rippling beneath the press of his body. His face in the gray light of the window was composed.

"Newnham was one thing. But, old friend, even in a matter so desperate as this, I cannot allow you to do it because, at the heart of it, you *know* the truth. That would be too much deception, even for me."

"Then another friend, someone respected, who knows you well, but does not know the truth?"

"Would that there existed such a creature."

Sheridan scratched his chin. "...What about Fox?"

The room fell silent for a moment. His mind swam back to Fox and the profligate past they had shared, the bond that was created. "But how?"

"There was a letter once, in Your Highness's own hand, denying it all. I know that he still believes it."

George took a breath. "I'd entirely forgotten the letter."

"Well then, it's that simple. He can go before the members, the Prime Minister especially, and speak with confidence, as your friend, about what he believes is the truth. That may well be enough to appease them, and you will not have to break your promise directly."

All he could think of, all he could see in his mind, was Maria. The only person in the entire world who mattered. Visions of her being shamed, prosecuted...Good Lord, possibly even imprisoned for illegally marrying him!

Desperation clung to him like a heavy cloak. "Do you suppose he would do it?"

"I suspect he would take great pleasure in denying your marriage to Maria in the House of Commons."

George cringed at the sound of her name. The honesty and truth it evoked. He was getting himself in more deeply by the moment. If he allowed this to happen—this denial, how could he ever change his story with the English people later, once he was king?

How could he ever hope to make her queen?

He closed his eyes but her face remained. Loving. Trusting. The woman who had changed him so completely. Who had given him a future. George opened them again and saw Sheridan still before his chair, his expression tentative and expectant.

"If I had any choice...any choice at all. But if I do not stop this somehow, the King shall see me made a bigamist."

"Do you want me to go to her, Your Highness, while you see Fox? I can caution her, since I was there today, that things might well get ugly now that the debate has reached this level. My going to her might seem more natural and keep you uninvolved."

George heaved a heavy sigh as he moved back toward the collection of chairs and little satinwood tables beside the fire. "She really has become terribly fond of you, Richard. You have her trust. Damn, how I despise the need to do this!" he groaned, raking fingers through his tangled hair and looking, at once, as frightened and as fierce as a hunted lion. "All that is left now is for me to protect her, in spite of the price I will likely have to pay with her."

"Yes, sir."

"Go to her in the morning. Tell her what happened today, about Pitt's call."

Sheridan shifted on his feet. "I shall, Your Highness."

"Warn her. But tell her nothing else about our plan for Fox, and all of that. God willing, an outright denial may not be necessary. Something yet may happen."

"I shall use the utmost discretion."

"I wanted to protect her forever, you know." He sighed again, his heart aching. "Now I must protect her for as long as I can."

SO, IT HAD COME TO this.

Maria walked in her garden, all bare brambles and rain puddles in sunken brick paths, long after Sheridan had gone. Her mind was as raw and cold as the slate-colored sky.

Poor Richard, forced to soften the blow. He had come to her on George's behalf, with his hat in his hands. Somewhere in the back of her mind, she had known that the issue of her true relationship to the Heir Apparent would one day be made public. And still Maria had harbored a secret hope that it would come one day when he had already publicly acknowledged her as the future Queen. But that notion was quickly fading to fantasy. What Sheridan had come to warn her about was the reality.

The reality of the deception she and George both had knowingly created.

Sheridan had told her, as stoically as he could manage, that some response would likely be necessary today in the House of Commons concerning her connection to the Prince of Wales. But the tone in his voice had foretold something far more grave.

She walked a few more steps and let the cold wind sting her face. Maria had vowed long ago that she would say nothing to risk the future to which George had been born. No matter what happened, she would remain silent as to their true connection. He would do the same. She knew he would not deny her. She must trust that no matter what happened, the one true love of her life would keep his honor and his word on that.

"Fanny said I would find you out here."

Maria had been too lost in her thoughts to have heard anyone come up behind her. She whirled around and saw Isabella standing on the flagstone path in almond-colored velvet, her hands hidden in a fur muff. Her face was flushed from the cold but her eyes were as clear as they were resolute.

"I hoped if I came here that you would be far too gracious to ask me to leave," she said softly.

"Hello, Isabella," she replied, her own voice thin and removed.

"I am so glad for an opportunity, finally, to speak with you."

Maria looked at her, her own soft face tight with anger. "And what makes you believe you have one now?"

"The grace you have always borne makes me think you shall not turn away from a friend."

Better to leave that reply unclaimed, Maria considered, than to say that it was Isabella who had first turned away so cruelly and severed the tie between them when she had needed their friendship most.

"Oh, Maria please. I acted in haste on that afternoon, and I shall regret it for the rest of my life. I swear it..." She moved a step nearer, beseechingly. "And we had such fun that first season, did we not? I felt such a part of your life then and you were so great a part of mine. I was there through all of the Prince's impetuous ministrations. I felt I had helped you through it all, in my small way. Then suddenly you shut me out. I didn't know what to do, what to believe. When I finally discovered the truth, I am afraid that I panicked."

"There are some things, Isabella, no matter how compelling, that are simply not discussed," Maria replied, her voice tight now and low. "Not even among the dearest of friends."

"No, I suppose not," she conceded, unable to look up as her tone went suddenly lower. "The truth, I expect, is that I envied what was happening to you, I truly did. You were caught up in the most romantic whirlwind then, and I wanted to be in its midst with you. It hurt that I couldn't be."

All of the pain, betrayal, and isolation she had felt came rushing back now with redoubled force and Maria looked at a woman she had once trusted as her friend. "The *truth*, Isabella, is that you also disapproved, and that more than anything else is why you could not face me when I first returned from Twickenham. It is why you barred me at your door."

They stood in silence for a while, Isabella nervously toying with her muffler. "Your life is your own, Maria," she finally said as her eyes filled with tears. "It is not for me to disapprove. If you have actually married him, one way or another as they say, and you are happy, then I am glad for you. Truly glad."

Maria stifled a smile. It really was good to see her again, faults and all. And she needed a friend just now. These months with George had been the best months of her life, but she had missed the easy familiarity of female companionship. In spite of everything that had passed between them, she had missed Isabella. Maria held out her arms and Isabella fell into them with the abandon of a little child who had once again found favor.

"Oh, I am so sorry for excluding you that day..."

"Hush," Maria admonished, clutching her as close as if they were sisters.

"But I have behaved so badly."

"It was a difficult time of decision for us all."

"That was no excuse. I was your friend and I was not there for you when you needed me. It began as a great game and I was just so shocked that you had actually—" Isabella bit her tongue.

"Perhaps we have all learned something," Maria said kindly. She felt the sting of tears in her own eyes as she sensed the bond between them slowly begin to rekindle. "Let's speak of it no more, hmm?"

Isabella's friendship and her support could not have come at a better time. She had been frightened by Sheridan's visit and his veiled warning. He had not told her everything. She was certain of that. But what was going to happen in the House of Commons today? What would the Members be moved to do now that an illegal marriage had been hinted at?

For that, she must wait.

"I have not come alone," Isabella finally said as they stood facing one another, their warm breath visible in the cold damp air between them. "I hope my surprise will please you."

Maria tipped her head to one side, her teary eyes filling with question. But Isabella only smiled, linked their arms together, as good friends do, and led her back down the path toward the house.

Maria saw three feminine figures in the drawing room as she and Isabella came in from the garden. Lady Lindsay and the Duchess of Devonshire stood flanking a pale blue elbow chair where Lady Clermont sat like a grand dame in amber silk, her hair wound with pearls.

Maria stopped just before the door and watched them. Anne and Georgiana spoke to one another in low tones as Lady Clermont sat as motionless and regal as a queen. She looked back at Isabella.

"They do so want to be your friends, Maria, but if it does not please you to have them here," Isabella whispered. "I will ask them to leave."

"No. It was kind of you to bring them. As it happens, their support means a great deal to me just now. Thank you." Maria squeezed her arm and they moved united into the drawing room.

"Ah, there you are, child." Lady Clermont smiled and held up an age-spotted hand.

"It was so good of Your Ladyship to come, as well," Maria countered and took her hand. "Thank you."

"I've missed you since you've been away, my dear."

"As have we all," said Anne, who smiled and held open her arms. Maria moved toward her and they embraced.

"I know that we've had our differences," said Georgiana, who moved a little nearer, taking her turn. "I suspect I was quite unpleasant. But I must admit that you have completely changed the Prince. Everyone is saying so. We all think now that we've had time to see the change, that you have made him a wonderful wife."

Maria turned away from the Duchess, stricken by what was really a very cleverly veiled accusation, a way to get her to admit the truth. Considering what was at stake right now, what was happening in Parliament, her face blanched with fear.

"Oh really. Don't look so surprised. We all know about it," said Anne, as casually as if they had been talking about something that had not been illegal or vastly unpopular. "It is not something one can easily keep secret in a society so intimate and so closed as ours."

"What we are trying to say," Isabella interjected, "is that we are honored to be among the friends of Her Royal Highness, the Princess of Wales."

"You *musn't* call me that!"

"But you are the wife of the Prince of Wales. We know that you are," badgered Georgiana.

"There is danger in your words—danger for George as well as for me!"

"That is why we are here. We heard about what happened yesterday in the House of Commons," said Isabella. "News like that does travel with the speed of lightning. But the issue was probably bound to come up sooner or later. Hopefully one day soon, with our support as a beginning, you shall gain the favor of the King and you both can put this dreadful mess behind you."

"I think that is quite enough, ladies," Lady Clermont interceded with an upheld hand.

As though she were a safe harbor, Maria sank into the chair beside the old woman, her face gone ashen. She thought again of Sheridan's warning. He had urged her to consider the extreme danger in George's position just now.

The least hint of a marriage could ruin them both.

"You must promise me, all of you, if you truly are my friends as you say you are, that you will never, *never*, refer to me that way again. Promise me!"

Isabella and Anne looked at one another, then down at Lady Clermont. Maria had neither denied nor admitted the rumor. But Horatia Seymour had already all but confirmed it.

And if it were true, then one day when he was finally crowned king, the Prince of Wales might well find a way to make her his queen. In that case, they might only hope to stay in her favor by acting as she wished now.

Now when things were so uncertain.

CHAPTER NINE

IT HAD GONE EXCEEDINGLY WELL.

Or so Charles James Fox thought as he sipped his cognac in the dim candlelight of Brook's Club. Although the Prince had denied it, he knew he had fallen out of royal favor since she had come on the scene. Or rather since Maria Fitzherbert had erupted onto the scene, like Vesuvius, scattering debris of changed lives behind her as she went.

His speech in the House of Commons, designed to defend the Prince of Wales, had been the perfect opportunity to redeem himself. When he had been called late last night to Carlton House, he had volunteered his assistance before it had even been asked of him.

Then, this afternoon, armed with the letter he had received some time ago from His Highness, to give him courage, Fox had been bold. Brilliant. Decisive. As an intimate of the Prince of Wales, he had proof positive that there never was any marriage. But he would have done it for less just to deny that self-righteous Papist in such a splendidly public way.

Married indeed! How did such baseless rumors begin?

Ah, glory was so divine. He laughed, a look of smug satisfaction sharpening his dark beetle brows into a hard peak. Quite likely it would go down in history that he single-handedly had saved the Prince of Wales from destitution and marriage to a royal cow like Caroline of Brunswick. Yes...quite likely.

Now he intended to get drunk. Very drunk. A celebration. A renewal of his power. When the chips were down, who had been called upon? *Once Fox. Always Fox.* That woman could lure the heir off to Brighton or whatever hideaway she chose, but she would always bring him back the same hungry animal he remembered.

Fox's love for passion and excitement was a tonic to George that Maria Fitzherbert's female companionship could never provide. He would stake his life on that now that he had been so suddenly and admirably called into service once again.

"Mind if I join you?"

Fox looked up at the unexpected face of Orlando Bridgeman, the Prince's valet, as he swayed bleary-eyed in the shadows between the fireplace hearth and the three filled gaming tables. Clearly he had preceded Fox to the state of intoxication that, tonight, the Whig orator had hoped to attain. Fox did not like the fellow. Never really had. He was too solicitous. Too ambitious....Too much like himself.

"If you must." He smiled insincerely, and lifted a hand for another cognac as Bridgeman settled into the leather chair beside him.

"I heard what you did in the House of Commons today." Bridgeman continued to sway as the firelight shimmered across the angular features of his face.

"Did you now?"

"They say you were splendid."

"Hmm," Fox sounded, as he took the new cognac and lay his head back against the deep red leather.

"Pity you were misinformed."

It was like a slap of icy water. First the words, then their implication. Fox lifted his head as quickly as he had rested it and looked over at his unwelcome companion. His eyes played across a grave face, not unlike his own in its severity or in the accent of its dark, arched brows.

"I imagine you mean something in particular by that," Fox huffed.

"Only that you needlessly defended the Prince."

Fox rolled his eyes. "Oh? And why precisely is that, Mr. Bridgeman?"

"Because, you don't know your old friend so well as you profess. There are others who know him just a bit better." Bridgeman whispered then, cupping his hand around his mouth to hide a silly drunken grin. "They truly *are* married after all!"

"Your jest is really in rather poor taste," he said, turning back to face the fire.

"It is no jest, sir, I assure you."

"And under what authority do you deign to make such a claim?" Fox asked with suspicious gray eyes turned quickly back upon the ambitious young valet.

"Under direct authority, sir. I was there."

Hmm. Direct authority indeed. Precisely what I said in the House of Commons, Fox thought, appraising the younger man silently and fingering his glass of cognac.

"So, why tell me this now?"

"I respect you a great deal, actually admire you."

"Spare me the duplicity," Fox groaned. "I've heard you swear your allegiance to His Highness a dozen times myself."

"But in this, His Highness is not the one who was asked to play the fool."

Touché. Fox looked down and wiped absently at crumbs on the front of his velvet waistcoat. The sensation had been quick and fierce, like a knife wound. Now he bled. He bled loyalty. Trust. Even love. They flowed freely from the long blue vein that pulsed in his thick neck. Was it possible that the Catholic really was his wife, after all? That they had broken the law and then called on him to do their bidding so that he might save George's standing with the rest of England?

Fox tried not to let the wound show but the shock had made it impossible.

"I trust I have not made things worse for you, Mr. Fox," Bridgeman now spoke as insincerely as the famous Whig.

"I don't suppose such a thing is possible."

As the first wave of shock receded, the reality crashed full of force against the corners of his mind. Knowledge of this had landed him in a very dangerous position. He had lied to the House of Commons! He had unwittingly helped the Prince of Wales deceive the Crown! And yet if he attempted to recant what he had so boldly claimed just

213

this afternoon, it would not only ruin George's reputation, but it would dash his own hopes of rising to power politically ever again.

He would never find that power without the Whigs.

And the Whigs were nothing without the Prince of Wales.

Rising to his feet with difficulty, from the cognac and from the trauma, Charles James Fox stood for a moment hovering over Orlando Bridgeman. This sycophant had done him a favor really. Painful though it was, he knew now without a doubt where he stood with England's Heir.

"I should like to thank you for your honesty," Fox said curtly.

"Oh, that is hardly necess—"

Fox held up his hand. "I said I should *like* to thank you. But I find in this deplorable instance of subversion, Mr. Bridgeman, that good taste and good judgment simply preclude it."

He tapped his walking stick on the floor like a punctuation mark, but he said nothing else. The elder statesman, famous for never being at a loss for words, at this moment, had nothing at all left to say.

With his political future at risk, and his loyalties completely shaken, he turned away. His short, brisk footsteps carried him across the carpeted floors of Brook's Club and out into the crisp night air to his waiting carriage. But they could not take him from the haunting sound of Orlando Bridgeman's eager confession that the Prince of Wales had deceived an old and devoted friend...and that he had done it intentionally.

"I WILL NOT SEE HIM," Maria said flatly, as if the life had gone out of her.

"But His Highness is outside, threatening to break down the door if we do not admit him," Isabella urged, looking over with a worried expression at Jacko Payne, who stood ready in the entry hall.

It had taken precisely an hour for her to hear what had passed that afternoon in the House of Commons. It had taken little more than an instant for her marriage, and her faith in George, her husband, to be shaken to the core.

A zealous young reporter from the *Morning Herald* had come to her door to ask if she wished to comment on the Prince's dear friend Mr.

Fox's public and very authoritative denial of her marriage to the Heir Apparent.

That was how she had heard of it, from a stranger.

Maria knew exactly what this public repudiation meant to her reputation and what it meant to their future. She also knew who was behind it.

"MARIA!" George raged as he pounded against the painted front door. It reminded her of an earlier time. Of ardent pleading. Of forbidden desires. Before she had given in. *Before she had risked everything in loving him.*

"Do not answer it."

"Maria, really!" Isabella cried in horror. "The man is your husband, for Lord's sake! Do you wish to air your soiled linen to the entire neighborhood?"

Tears rained down her face faster than she was able to wipe them away. *"My husband* has betrayed me."

"How do you know that? You have not even given him a chance to explain!"

Her voice quivered as she brushed the tears with the back of her hand. "Explain what, Isabella? You know as well as every one else here in London that Fox is entirely his puppet! He would not have dared make a move so bold without George's sanction."

"Do you not at least owe it to him to hear him out?"

"Hear him explain away the truth? I could not bear that."

"MARIA! Open this door!"

"If you do not let him in, I will!" Isabella shouted.

"Betray me again, Isabella Sefton, and this time our friendship truly will be over!"

George's violent pounding shook the entire house. The huge gold-framed paintings around the door swayed on their chains with each thrust. The enamels and family miniatures in the foyer rattled on two opposing mahogany tables. Maria put her hands to her ears as he cried her name again and again.

Suddenly, and unexpectedly the room fell to a hush. Maria looked up. The click of the lock sounded in the drawing room. The grand, painted door opened with a squeal. Isabella froze as John Smythe followed the Prince of Wales inside.

"Good God, Maria, what on earth were you thinking, keeping

His Highness locked outside?" her brother asked with an incredulous gasp.

No one responded. Everyone seemed to hold their breath. George looked at Maria but she turned away. Slow, measured steps brought him to her side.

"I should like to speak privately with you," he said, his chest still heaving.

"I do not wish to speak privately with *you*."

"Maria!" John gasped. "Forgive her, Your Highness. Perhaps she has taken ill."

"That much is true. I do not recall ever feeling worse in my life," she said, toying idly with the little gold wedding band that the world believed belonged to Thomas Fitzherbert.

The pungent scent of burning wood from the fireplace, of Isabella's jasmine and Maria's lavender perfume, wafted in the silence between them.

"Perhaps I should speak to her for a moment, Your Highness," John suggested. "See if I can improve her spirits...if not her manners."

"There is nothing you could possibly say," she said back to her brother in a thin, barely audible response.

John looked over at Isabella, who only shook her head.

"What on earth has happened here?" he asked. But no one in the tension-filled drawing room made any attempt at reply.

"I appreciate your concern," George finally said beneath his breath. He put a friendly hand on John's back. "I fear there has been somewhat of a misunderstanding. But if you all would be good enough to leave us, I am certain we would be able to clear it up." When Maria looked at him now, her face was angry and accusing but she said nothing further.

"Please," George repeated until John, Isabella, and Jacko left the room through the two open dining room doors.

George sat beside her on the blue and green brocade settee and gently took her hand. He watched her as he brought it to his lips and kissed the finger that wore his ring.

She did not pull away from him, but neither did she encourage him. He felt her indifference more powerfully than he would ever have felt her resistance. Her face, when he looked up at her, was cold, bearing no expression at all.

"I know it was a shock," he said slowly, struggling to find words she would believe. "God in His Heaven, if I could have spared you that...But in the end, I had no other choice in order to keep you safe."

"There is always a choice, George."

"Maria, you must understand, the political climate is very dangerous now," he said after a moment, forcing his voice to remain steady.

"You promised. And I believed you."

"God help me, don't you think I know that?" he whispered gripping his forehead with the palm of his hand.

Finally she looked over at him, searching desperately for sincerity in his eyes. If she could only believe him, trust that he had not willingly betrayed her. Maria's mind was a blurred, red haze of fear. She was afraid again of the power of what they had found together. Afraid of what she believed that, by this betrayal, George had caused them to lose forever.

How could she ever believe him again, let alone trust him?

There was no way now for her ever to become his rightful Queen. And the child she carried, still a secret from this man, would forever be a bastard, a jest, with no more legitimate place in the world than she.

As Maria's eyes played over his face in silhouette, she bled a little more with each heartbeat. After a few more moments of strangled silence, when he could not bring himself to look back at her, Maria had her answer. She had put all of her love and trust in this man and, whatever the reason, he had betrayed her.

"I cannot go on with this. It must be over."

"You're not serious."

"I am."

"You are my wife. It can *never* be over between us!"

"You swore to me that you would never deny our marriage."

"And I did not! You know it was Fox who stood up before the House of Commons! I intentionally did not speak myself so that I would not be forced to go against that promise!"

"Still, you played your part," she said with bitter resolve, fighting the sting of angry tears. "...as I played mine."

"No! I will not permit this to be the end of us!"

"George, I cannot live like this any longer! All of England thinking I am no better than a backstreet whore you have merely deceived for your own well-known purpose! The greatest dupe of them all!" She sprang to her feet and moved away from his touch and from the foul vapor of his deceptions. "Jacko!"

After a moment her brawny Irish butler, with the tousle of auburn hair, returned alone to the drawing room. "Yes, ma'am."

"Jacko, be good enough to show His Highness to the door."

"Maria, this is not over between us!"

"Please, George...let it go...Let me go."

"But you are my wife! My wife, for God's sake!"

Anger and betrayal burned like an onyx fire in her dark eyes. "After today, in the eyes of England, I am nothing but your concubine, and I told you long ago that I could be a whore for no man. Not even for you."

As Jacko opened the door, John and Isabella came slowly back out of the dining room, having heard every bitter word spoken between the Prince and Maria. A cold winter wind rushed in at them as they stood in the foyer watching England's future King linger at the door, hoping for one last chance to change her mind.

Maria met his eyes squarely, the pain on her face hidden by a thick layer of resolve. She must not let him see that her heart was breaking. "The damage is done, George. I can never be your rightful wife, your Queen. Not after today. Let us simply leave it at that."

"Never!" he declared, and his voice now was bitter. "What we have will never be over! You were born to be my wife, Maria, and by God Almighty, you alone shall die my wife!"

After he had gone and the house fell back into a strained silence, John bounded down the two mahogany steps and back into the drawing room toward his sister.

"What, in the name of God, were you thinking just now?" he asked incredulously. But his sister did not answer.

"Perhaps now is not the best time—"

"Stay out of this, Isabella!" John snarled, his face set in anger. "Maria, I asked you a question!" When she still did not reply, he clutched her shoulders and spun her around so that she was facing him. They were nearly the same height and he faced her squarely. "How could you speak to your husband like that? You are endangering everything we are building!"

"He is *not* my husband."

"What are you talking about? I stood right beside you when you took your vows!"

"Empty vows."

"They were as binding as Isabella's vows to Charles!"

Maria looked angrily at John. "They were illegal and you know it! But it doesn't matter anyway, now that everyone in England has been told publicly by one of the Prince's dearest friend that we were never married at all."

"You cannot actually blame George for that, can you?" John asked, his desperate fingers piercing her skin. "You know Fox is the one who spoke!"

"Perhaps Charles Fox mouthed the words, and for that I shall never forgive him. But someone else put the notion inside of his head."

"Don't ruin this, for us, Maria, I warn you!" he said, shaking her. "Not when the current King is ill and you are so nearly Queen!"

Maria's mouth was a hard line. "That is all that matters to you, isn't it? No matter what the cost, it is only important that one day, despite it all, I become Queen of England!"

"And what, precisely, is so wrong with that?" he asked as she jerked free of his grasp. "Tell me, did Edward Weld or Thomas Fitzherbert ever offer you a future so divine as that?" He let the words fall away. When he continued, the sound of his voice was more pleading. "Think of it, Maria, please! One day, Queen of England!"

"And you the consort's brother! Isn't that it, John? Isn't that what this is *really* all about?"

He waited a moment, considering whether or not to try to deny it. "All right, yes. I would like it if my sister would one day renounce her Catholic faith and become Queen. But where is the harm in that? Good God, Maria, the man is wild about you. Surely you know that better than anyone! Look at the lengths to which he went, the laws he broke, to marry you!"

"And in the blink of an eye to see that marriage denied."

"You know that our very mad King has made an issue of this and that George's back was pressed against the wall! My God, you really want to see him made a bigamist now, forced to marry again, in addition to everything else, just to save your precious honor?"

Maria stood there silently, her back turned toward her brother as she gazed vapidly into the blazing fireplace hearth, trying desperately to calm her heart. She saw their life together in little flashes, moments frozen in time, as though from a painting. Her first sight of him on the Mall, smiling at her so unsettlingly from his carriage window. The rose he had left on her doorstep. The fire from the candle she had held between them in the Conservatory that night. The one that had sent her running from Carlton House...and from him.

But the strongest image was of him lying beside her in their bed, and the words that had captured and reassured her for all of these difficult months. They were the words that had given her the strength to endure all that she faced as his secret wife.

Perhaps I cannot make you Princess of Wales just yet, he had said. *But neither will I ever deny that you and I are man and wife. That much, I do promise you.*

She shivered and closed her eyes. Love was so impetuous. So dangerous. *If only he had come to me first.*

The thoughts, all of them, hummed in her head. She tried to blink them away again but they would not be vanquished. She had loved him. Trusted him. She would soon bear his child. He had betrayed her. Simple. Direct, and as painful as death.

"Maria. Sister...please. Think about what a mistake you would be making in this. Think about what it would mean for us all."

Finally she turned and looked at her brother again, her face set tightly with resolve. "John, I could not sell my soul for the Prince of Wales. What makes you think I could do it for you?"

BELLE PIGOT WAS STANDING IN the doorway as George came in. He had been such a captive of his thoughts since Sheridan left late the night before, that he did not see her until they were facing one another. It was just past dawn, and he had not yet slept.

"I've had a letter from Madeira." She smiled, having left her brother there some months ago to convalesce.

"From your Charles?"

"The doctors tell him he is nearly well enough to come home. Thanks to you."

The two old friends embraced and George felt her joy. For a

moment it made him forget his own pain. There was no one who deserved happiness more than Belle.

"How can I ever repay you?" she softly asked.

He chucked her beneath the chin. "That look on your face just now is payment enough."

They walked hand in hand into the shadowy Conservatory. It was the same grand room in which the ball had begun that night when he had first met Maria. The night his life had changed forever.

Belle was aging. In the first light of day he could see that. The skin around her neck had begun to sag, and when she smiled there was a whole network of new wrinkles around her eyes. Wretched mortality, he thought. It was upon them both. But this happiness, this thing that she had hoped for and prayed for, her brother's recovery, had happened and George found himself believing for the first time since he had met Maria in the possibility of miracles.

Now if only the Lord would grant him one of his own.

Belle reached up and ran her hand tenderly along George's jaw. "What troubles you, dear heart?"

"Only the world, Belle." He sighed.

"I heard about what happened in the House of Commons yesterday."

"You and all of London."

"Ah. Then she, a woman of great honor, is angry to have been publicly denied."

"Would you not be?"

She smiled a sad smile. "I don't know precisely how I would feel. I don't expect anyone but your Maria could know a thing like that. What I do know, one woman to the next, is that this all cannot have been easy on her."

He curled his fists and held them up helplessly. "And I cannot bear it that she is unhappy."

"This I know, child."

"Then why does *she* not know it, Belle? Why does she not trust in the love we have for one another? That I will do anything to keep her safe. And keep us together. That the rest will all work out when the time is right?"

She looked up at George, her dark eyes full of devotion. "I suspect the two of you are doing the best that you can with a very difficult situation. I will say this: You have made me terribly proud of the way you stood up to the King's manipulations for her sake."

George took the old woman into his arms, but unlike the way it had been in his boyhood, now it was *he* who held her. Still, what comfort there was in her arms. It was as if all of the cares in the world were cast away for that single moment. The way it should have been with his own mother.

In the pale rosy sunshine of early morning, they stood together at the windows, he and Belle, looking out onto Pall Mall.

"You're going to make it, you know," she said softly. "Your love *will* survive this test."

He looked at her with pain in his eyes, wanting to believe what she said. "How is it that you sound so certain?"

"Because the love you share is once in a lifetime. It is the sort of thing of which fairy tales are made. Mark my words, child. They shall write volumes about the two of you and wonder about you, long after all of us are gone."

Beyond the screen that hid Carlton House from Pall Mall, George watched the wagons on their way to market and the early-morning passersby as he held Belle's reassuring hand. But as it always was, his mind was filled with Maria. He prayed a silent prayer for the day ahead. For another chance to put things right.

And he dreaded it all, without her.

"THE BLOODY BASTARD HAS USED me!" Fox moaned in despair.

Elizabeth Armistead did not need to ask to whom he had fallen victim. It was bound to happen sooner or later. She had known the same pain herself, inflicted by the Prince of Wales more times than she cared to count, when he thought himself in love with her...and then after.

"You might as well join the club," she said unsympathetically. At first it was the best she could manage to say. Her only show of sensitivity was that she dotted his glistening brow with a lace-edged handkerchief while he moaned.

Elizabeth's face was still pretty. Thick, red hair, only partially streaked with silver, fell in tangles now around her chin. The hair softened a long nose and thin red lips.

The circles beneath her eyes could still be covered with ceruse and her more ample flaws still corseted. Next to Fox's porcine face, red veined cheeks and flapping jowls, she actually appeared rather youthful.

"I tell you, it is sheer lunacy!" Fox puffed into a glass of port that he held with three fingers. "Not only have I heard tonight from his puppet, Bridgeman, that the Prince of Wales is actually married to that harridan, after all. Oh! That would be awful enough! But now, after he had as much as asked me to deny her publicly, it appears the lady is incensed by what I have done! And can you imagine? Now he actually expects me to go back and soften the blow of it tomorrow in the House so that she will take him back to her bed! Well I refuse, I tell you! I categorically refuse!"

Elizabeth sat back in the gold and amber firelit shadows of her bedchamber as Charles muttered his angry, half-audible rebukes. How ruthless was the Prince of Wales, she thought. How self-absorbed! It would serve him right if his latest paramour...wife... whatever—that Fitzherbert woman—had left him. How glorious it now was to see the tables finally turned on him! But these days George was only partially in her thoughts.

Elizabeth Armistead was surprised that she had come to care for Charles as quickly as she had. Her affair with the Prince of Wales, and his rejection of her, had taken its toll, and shaded her with cynicism. She had gone into this latest encounter initially as a way to aggravate the Prince. Bed his dearest friend. That was how it had started. His royal face, that night for her presentation at Carlton House, had been a potent elixir toward revenge.

She looked back at Charles now, his head slightly inclined, his short fingers, nails half bitten, nervously toying with the crimson braid ornamenting the edge of his striped jacket.

He was a dark, heavily built man but he possessed a strange sweetness that had steadily won her affection. She knew about his gambling, about his drinking. And about the other women. But she cared for him anyway. After all, she was no longer a young woman, and she could spend her last remaining years of relative youth on a far less worthy object than London's greatest living orator.

She lay her head against his shoulder, covered in red silk, knowing what would calm him. He reached up without looking at her. Her unbound hair was a coarse tangle between his fingers. The connection encouraged her. In her best attempt to soothe him, she reached down and slowly unfastened the two buttons on each side of his breeches. He tried to push her hand away. Too much had happened today. But she persisted. He gasped as he felt her delicate fingers wrap around his limp flesh.

"Not now, Bess," he whispered, not really meaning it, as his head rocked back and his eyes fluttered to a close.

Her hold on him grew tighter. She could feel the pulsing beneath her fingertips. She closed her eyes and saw instead George naked with her, as he once had been, so young and magnificent. The memory was hauntingly real. The scent of civet in his darkly draped bedchamber at Carlton House. The feel of his solid hands pressed against her back. His lips molding into the curve of her neck . . . What he had shown her. What he had forever taken from her life. *Damn you! Damn you to hell, George Augustus! Now you too will know this pain!*

Charles panted as he slumped against her moments later, his anger and his passion drained. When his heart began to slow, he reached up to touch her hair again. "I cannot see him," he muttered into her luxuriant blue-velvet bosom as reality jabbed at him again. "If I now recant what I have claimed, my honor would be lost forever."

"But what about your overall connection to His Highness if you refuse his entreaties for help in this?"

"We have no connection," he breathed. "Orlando Bridgeman has shown me that . . . the vile little bastard."

THE LATEST GILLRAY CARTOON PORTRAYED MARIA sitting abandoned on a rock, holding a crucifix. As they sailed away in a boat, called *Honour*, George was saying to Charles James Fox, "*I never saw her in my life!*"

George tore the paper after no more than glancing at it and hurled the fragments into the air so that the room rained white parchment. "So help me God, I could kill that man with my bare hands for what this must be doing to her on top of everything else!"

Orlando Bridgeman stood helplessly beside the Prince, who had spent the day riding to try to quell the frustration that burned and whirled inside him. And when that did no good, he drank, giving in to the great vice he had once willingly eschewed for the love of his wife.

It had been three days, and still he felt the helplessness like a flame. He looked up again at the largest portrait he owned of Maria. It was one he had watched her sit for in Brighton. Her image stabbed at his heart from its heavy gold frame. Her serene smile could have killed him if he had looked at it a moment longer.

Bridgeman had no idea. No one could understand what she meant to his life, how in betraying Maria he had really betrayed himself. "It's not over," he murmured, with a hand over his eyes. "It can never be!"

MARIA SAT ALONE ON TOP of her bed watching the single gold flame flicker from a glass lamp on the ebony bureau across the room. She looked beyond and saw the rain pelting the long, draperied windows. It had been raining all day. Fitting, she thought, for the dark gray gloom that had taken control of her spirit and did not seem to want to let her go.

She had not been able to do anything or think of anything else since the Prince's messenger had come at eight from the House of Commons.

In a long and conciliatory speech, Richard Brinsley Sheridan had spoken that afternoon about the Prince of Wales and *another person*. In this veiled reference to Maria, dear Sheridan had declared that, contrary to anything that might have previously been inferred, the widow of Thomas Fitzherbert was entitled to the truest respect.

That it was Sheridan who had leaped to her defense pleased her. After the time they had all spent together in Brighton, she knew that he was a kind man. But it still did not change the betrayal that George had brought, like a dark and dangerous mistress, between them.

Maria looked over at her bedside table at the copy of Shakespeare's plays that George had bought for her. To Maria, that book had symbolized so much between them. It lay beside the companion miniature of George on a black velvet cord.

She turned the image over and looked away. Her tangled thoughts were stopped by a knock at the door.

"Thank you, Fanny, but I am not hungry," she called out. The knock came again. "Fanny, I said—"

It was George who opened the door. "May I come in?" he asked, moving into the light.

Her heart leaped, seeing him. As it always did. As it always would. She felt a wave of nausea then. *The child again.* God, how badly she wanted to tell him.

"I am very tired," she said instead.

He came toward her in a gray, rain-soaked cloak that he had not bothered to leave at the door. "I can think of nothing else but about what has passed between us."

"It is good to know I have company in that."

He sat on the edge of the bed and took her hand, but she turned away. "Look at me, Maria." His voice was deep, pleading. "I bid you, look at me!"

Reluctantly, she turned toward him. She was surprised that his elegant face was gray and tired, and that he had not shaven. "Did you hear what happened in the House of Commons today?"

When she tried to look away again, his finger played at her chin, forcing her back, to look at him. "Please do not turn from me."

Their faces, near to one another, were rich with shadows.

"If I could take back what happened, you know that I would. But I had to protect you from danger. Please see that!"

When his entreaty had no effect, he let go of her hand and stood rigidly beside her at the edge of the bed. "You cannot continue this, you know. We are man and wife before God."

"And before the King of England what are we, George?"

He stepped back. "I honestly don't believe you realize what sort of peril we are headed for Maria. This is not some sort of game. I am fighting for *both* our lives against the King of England, and with Parliament! We have broken the law!"

"As we knew we were doing so the day we married."

"I honestly thought he would die before now. I banked everything on it! I thought I would have the power to change things. Everyone believed it, with the lunacy that has nearly taken him over."

She moved from the bed but he caught her. Suddenly she was trapped, pressed between the heavy bed frame and his forceful body, his fingers pinching into her arms.

"Don't walk away from me!" he commanded, roughly kissing her lips and then her burning cheek.

He bit her neck, then kissed it over and over, trying to make her submit in the only way he knew how. It was suddenly a battle between them. She struggled against it but it only made him more determined. His eyes glinted like cut sapphires as the sheer force of his weight pressed her back into the unmade bed.

"No, George—" Maria tried to cry out but he stifled her words with his tongue.

"You are my wife, by God!" he growled hungrily as he tore the bodice of her nightgown away from her breasts.

The delicately woven cotton ripped easily beneath his inflamed hand. Then, just when instinct prepared her to struggle again, she looked up and saw the fear on his face mixed with a raw kind of desperation. It shocked her into passivity. He felt it and stopped moving against her. The air between them was thick with anger and passion, and with candle smoke when the door opened again.

"I know you said you weren't hungry, ma'am, but I've brought you some tea and toast anyw—" Fanny's words trailed off as she stood in the open doorway, a silver tray held rigid in her hands. "Oh, forgive me, ma'am! Sir!" she gasped. "I had no idea Your Highness was in the house!"

Maria's maid was out of the room as fast as she had come in, muttering as she ran down the hall. The fierce contest between them was over.

Slowly, George backed himself onto his feet. Maria did not move. She lay in the same place where he had held her captive, her gown torn away from her breasts, and her splendid white face scratched red from his two-day beard.

He looked at her in horror. Shame strangled any words of apology he might have tried to utter as she doubled over suddenly, her face contorted with pain. "What is it? What has happened? Maria! You must tell me!"

"No." She wept, not hearing him, the wrenching pain completely taking her over. It was a violent pulling sensation, deep and low in her belly that blotted out everything else. "Not that!" she cried as George held her, helplessly watching the wave of bright red blood stain her nightdress. "Please, oh God! You cannot mean to take that from me, as well!"

CHAPTER TEN

HE WALKED ALONE BACK INTO the dimly lit bedchamber, all pleated with shadows. Candles glowed beside her bed on a little rosewood table. Maria was asleep again, and had been most of the time for the past two days, on a blue satin bolster and a dozen silk-covered pillows. She wore beautiful ivory bedclothes now, the trauma of her miscarriage cleaned away by Fanny and the doctor who had at first sedated her.

Yet, in spite of the laudanum, she had known he was there, sensed his presence, felt his touch, felt his tears. With a determination that was regal and surprising to everyone, he sent them all downstairs, her doctors and staff, while he alone saw to her care, changed her dressings, fluffed her pillows, gave her water, and cooled her brow.

Now once again, George sank onto the chair beside her and drew up her hand. He had left her side for no more than a few moments since that first night, with coffee and love alone sustaining him.

"I am *so, so* sorry," he whispered again, as he had so many times, running a finger over the vein on the back of her hand. This time, finally, Maria opened her eyes.

George lurched forward. "I didn't know about the child...I swear I didn't know."

"I was being petty and foolish," she said weakly in reply.

"You weren't," he assured her, and held her hand more tightly, then drew it up to his cheek, where there were tears. "We both so dearly wanted a child. Why did you not tell me?" he asked brokenly.

"At first I was uncertain that it was actually true. I'd waited so many years...Then things with the King escalated. The time just never seemed to be right."

"When we married, we vowed for better or for worse. And I do not suppose it could get much worse." He tried to laugh but the intensity returned quickly between them. He gazed at her directly and with such sincerity that she believed she actually felt his torment. "You *are* my life," he said deeply.

"As you are mine." She reached up and cupped a hand at his jaw, and he turned his face gently into it. "I just so desperately wanted our child."

"And we shall have another...My God, Maria...I never meant to hurt you."

"I know."

He took her hand and brought it to his lips, his face shining with renewed hope. "Say you will go away to Brighton with me," he said tenderly. "I want for us to go the moment you are well enough to travel. You know that is where we were the happiest. We can begin again, together, and the devil with what the people think of me! The devil with the King's tainted money or his threats!"

"It will not be so simple to turn away from what is rightfully yours."

"Simple, no. But together we can do it. With your love, I know that we can."

"You are my husband," Maria softly said, and her rich brown eyes shimmered with devotion. "And whither thou goest..."

"I do worship you," he murmured, pressing a single soft kiss onto her forehead. "It will be so wonderful there. You shall see. There have been so many changes. Weltje has been overseeing the expansion of the farmhouse, at least what we can afford, while we've been away. He says, under the circumstances, what they've done so far is nothing short of spectacular."

"With your, shall we say, *innovative* sense of architecture, darling," she said, and smiled a crooked smile, remembering her first sight of the Conservatory at Carlton House, "I'm quite certain it will be dazzling."

CHAPTER ELEVEN

THE FARMHOUSE IN BRIGHTON HAD been completely transformed. It was now being called the Marine Pavilion by a proud
Weltje, who had orchestrated the renovations. Gone forever was the
cozy purple brick dwelling that had been their haven that first summer
after their marriage. In its place, Henry Holland, the famous architect
of the Drury Lane Theater, had created an imposing Greco-Roman
structure encircled by six Ionic columns bearing classical statues.

The alterations in the farmhouse mirrored changes in George and
Maria's lives. At long last, the Prince of Wales's patient waiting had
brought him a victory he had given up counting on in the stalemate
with the King. He had actually won the war over finances with the
scrupulously stingy and vindictive sovereign.

In July, George was shocked finally to be granted £161,000 from
Parliament with which to pay his outstanding debts and another
£60,000 to be put toward the completion of Carlton House.
Appeased by the public denial of his alleged illegal marriage to a
Catholic from one of the Prince's closest known friends, the King
had also surprised his eldest son by granting him £10,000 more a
year from the Civil List on which to live. It was still not the £100,000
that had been granted to previous Princes of Wales back into the

231

seventeenth century, but the father had finally made a concession to the son who had refused to surrender. Although the King had increased the pressure on George toward a legal marriage, here in Brighton the Prince could ignore it. And George was free to be the man with whom Maria had fallen in love.

Here, by the sea, he was more devoted than ever, and they were seldom apart. Even in the early hours of morning when Old Smoker helped him take his daily dip in the sea, Maria waited for him on the shore with a ready towel. "How do ye fare today, Mrs. Prince?" Old Smoker always called out to Maria, his face as dark and tanned as leather, his smile pearly white. "Life is glorious!" she would answer back and wave to him across the sand.

Then she and George would spend the afternoons amid a devoted circle of friends—dominant among them, Hugh and Horatia Seymour, who had followed them down from London. They whiled away the hours playing whist or endless games of cricket in the expansive, moss-green gardens that faced the sea. Maria was relieved that they saw less of the Duchess of Devonshire. She was not so glad that they saw less of Richard Sheridan, whom she liked a great deal. But, thank the good Lord, they did not see Charles James Fox at all.

Here in Brighton, it was another world. Safe. Kind. Insulated from the gossip up in London, Maria continued to be greeted with respect and admiration. Here, there was only happiness—and dreams. *Their dreams*. Especially, God willing, another child.

By the late summer, George felt as if he had the next best thing. His brother Frederick, the dearest friend and confidant of his youth, had been allowed to return to England.

In explaining his upbringing to Maria, George had often used the story of his younger brother's exile to illustrate their father's cruelty. For six years, Prince Frederick had been banished to Hanover and France because the King did not like the influence George was having on him.

"Now that the *eldest son* seems to have gotten his life in order," George had mocked to her with surprising bitterness as he prepared to go to Windsor to bring him down to the beach, "perhaps His Majesty has decided that the risk to the *favorite son* has passed."

"Oh, George, really. I cannot believe His Majesty would be so—"

But Horatia had gently concurred. Cruelly, the King had never hidden the fact that he preferred Frederick to all of his other sons. Keeping him from George, who, as his Heir, it would have been dangerous to exile, was the only way the sovereign believed he had of protecting him. But now Frederick was returned and he wished to come, straightaway, to Brighton. Only the child Maria so desperately wanted could have made their life more perfect.

TWO DAYS LATER, AS THE fog, thick as clouds, rolled over the little brick houses, the two eldest sons of King George III rode together into Brighton inside the Prince of Wales's elegant black barouche. Even within the safe confines of the luxurious carriage, the mist managed to dampen their clothes and crust their faces and hands with sticky brine. But it was the part of this little sea village George had come to like the best. It had the gritty smell of freedom.

"So then, tell me the truth. Did you really marry her or not?" Frederick asked when they could finally see the dome of the Marine Pavilion in the distance.

George crooked an eyebrow and looked across the seat at his brother, a younger version of himself. He had the same square jaw and ruddy cheeks; the same tousle of curly hair, but a tone lighter. The innocence he remembered, however, was gone. It was replaced by the same recklessness and yearning for adventure that had nearly ruined his own early years.

"So when did you begin believing gossip, Freddie? Is that what those Frenchwomen taught you?" George laughed, leaning over and lightly cuffing the side of his brother's head.

"I had reason to believe it was not gossip."

"Oh? And what reason was that?"

"Mother believes you are married."

George stiffened back against the leather seat. The easy smile fell away. "Did she tell you that?"

"She did not have to. I could see it in her eyes when she spoke about your situation."

George gazed out at the stormy sea beyond the carriage window. "You've been gone a long time, Freddie boy. A great many things have changed."

"Then what is so wrong with telling me the truth?"

"You know she is a Catholic."

"So? If I were a Tory, would you deny me?"

"It's not the same thing, and you know it."

They were at an impasse. The carriage clicked past a little row of red brick houses where fishermen sat cleaning their day's catch. Bronzed faces were bent over coarsely meshed fishing nets and everything was permeated with the smell of salt air, fish, and damp earth.

"Well, if you're not married, of course you could certainly put an end to all of this scandal. Do as father bids you, why don't you. Marry our cousin, Caroline, and keep the lovely Maria as your mistress."

"I told you in my letter, I shall not marry Caroline or anyone else."

"You mean you cannot?"

"Take it as you will."

Frederick waited a moment, then turned to look at George. "If you truly love this Maria, then perhaps there is a way, some maneuvering that can make your connection legal."

"I don't know, Freddie. It all seemed so simple once. But now..." George did not finish his sentence. Instead he pulled out a little silver flask from a compartment before the seat and passed it to his brother. "Something to warm you before the introductions."

"Brandy?"

George smiled mischievously. "Cognac, of course."

Frederick took a long swill and handed the flask back to George. The aroma circled around him and filled his nostrils with the comfort of an old friend. He had not expected that. He had not taken a drink since his reconciliation with Maria over the incident in the House of Commons.

Without drinking himself, he replaced the top.

"Are you not going to join me?"

George glanced back at the flask, the pungent aroma and the warming effects only a cap away. "I think not."

"Oh, come. Just a taste. I do hate to drink alone."

"And I hate more the man I am when I drink."

"You really have changed, haven't you?" Frederick smiled. "So tell me about her so I shall know what to expect."

It had been so long since he'd had a someone—a brother, to whom he could *truly* talk. Having Freddie home was nicer than he would ever know. George settled back against the seat and, after a moment, began to smile.

"Well, first of all, with Maria you can never be certain of what to expect."

"Mystery is always nice." Frederick chuckled and took another swill of the brandy.

"Do not misunderstand me, Freddie. There is no finer woman in all of England. In all the world, for that matter. But she is not like anyone I've ever known..." He heaved a little sigh, missing her. "...or ever will again. She is the first woman who has ever made me want to change."

He lay his head back against the cushion as the carriage turned up the private road to his pavilion.

"That special?"

"That special."

"Then you have married her," Frederick smiled slyly. "Because you're much too self-absorbed to have let someone like that get away, no matter what the odds were against it."

"You think so, do you?" George asked with a clever smile.

Maria was supervising the hanging of the green and white checkered silk over the bed in the Prince's bedchamber, when the two brothers came in. As George moved toward her, Frederick put an arm up to bar him. She had not heard them come in, and he wanted to watch her for a moment, at a distance. Before the introductions, he wanted to see the woman for whom his impulsive brother had dared to risk a country and a Crown.

They were too far away to know what she was saying to the workmen, but Maria looked up over the bed at two of them on ladders who suspended, like a billowing tent, the brightly colored fabric that she and George had personally chosen.

They both watched her as she moved with the easy grace of a swan. Two steps forward, then one back. Hands on her hips, then one long arm in motion to direct their movements. Her hair was not as curled as she usually wore it when she went out in public. Instead now, it lay in honey-colored waves across her shoulders. From the corner of his eye, Frederick looked at George. He saw the anticipation on his face.

"And you still maintain that she is not your wife?" Frederick whispered as he watched his brother's eyes lit like sparkling jewels.

"A little decorating, that is all. It is nothing Georgiana did not do for me at Carlton House."

"I was not speaking about decorating your bedchamber, George." He chuckled silently. "I was referring to that silly devoted expression on your face just now."

George lost his smile. "Leave it alone, Freddie boy. And be happy for me that I have found some bit of peace."

Suddenly, as one of them shifted a floorboard creaked and Maria looked back toward the door. "George!" she called out and waved a hand before she saw that there was someone standing beside him.

After that, she moved toward them more cautiously than she would have. There was more propriety in her stride, and her hands were clasped lightly before her so she would be certain not to touch her husband in the presence of a stranger.

But Frederick had seen all that he needed to see. He knew that by watching them as he had, for even that brief moment, he had seen the real relationship that existed between them. Never again would there be any doubt in his mind that his brother had lied...that he had indeed risked his future Crown, and his life, for this woman.

"Welcome home, Your Highness," she said, and dipped into a deep-kneed curtsy, her gown rippling into waves of amber damask.

"Maria Fitzherbert, may I present my brother Frederick," George said with as much formality as she.

"Well, it is a pleasure to meet the woman who has finally managed to capture my brother's heart in earnest," he said with George's same thick-lipped and dangerous smile.

As she curtseyed again, she let George's brother take her hand. He kissed the pale skin above her fingers. "It is an honor to meet Your Highness," she managed to say in a voice as smooth as cream.

"Well now. I certainly hope we will not be standing on that sort of formality in private, will we, George?" He cast a glance at his elder brother while he still held Maria's delicate hand.

"Here at Brighton, Freddie, we do as we please."

"Splendid. Then, Mrs. Fitzherbert, you must call me Frederick."

"Oh, I could not possibly."

But when she looked up, George nodded his approval. It was

almost like looking at twins. Prince Frederick was not so tall, and his face was free of the lines that now encroached on George's once smooth skin. But otherwise they were startlingly alike. "Well, all right then," she conceded when she could see that, like George, he meant to have his way. "I am honored...Frederick. But then you must call me Maria."

With the introductions out of the way, and newly kindled friendships begun, Frederick stretched like a cat and began to yawn. "Perhaps, brother dear, now you would be good enough to have one of your servants show me to my accommodations. I would like to take a little nap before supper."

"Of course," George said and waved his hand for one of the footmen who lingered behind them, just outside the door. "Take His Grace to the Blue Room," he said, then patted his brother on the back. "It is a lovely room, Freddie. Maria decorated it herself. It has a view of the sea just like this one, and I guarantee with the sound of the waves to lull you, you shall sleep like a baby."

Frederick turned and stopped when he reached the door, his blue eyes glittering the same blue as George's. "Oh, I don't know about that, brother dear." He smiled. "Now that I have met her myself, I don't know that anyone in Brighton sleeps quite so well as you!"

SUPPER WAS IN HONOR OF Frederick.

The long, mahogany table, polished to a mirror sheen with thick beeswax, was set in the center of the yellow and maroon painted dining room. It was crowded with Hugh and Horatia Seymour, Richard Sheridan, and Lord and Lady Abergavenny. Lord and Lady Clermont had just ridden down from London. The Princesse de Lamballe had only recently come to England from France for her health, at the suggestion of her mistress, Queen Marie Antoinette.

Lord and Lady Jersey who sat near George at the center of the table, were the only two people among them whom Maria had not yet met.

It was to be the most grand evening the Prince of Wales could fashion for his brother. Crystal decanters full of the best French wine. Almond cream soup. Silver dishes piled high with sliced veal and lemon sauce. Beef. Lamb. Pear tarts wrapped in marzipan. Brightly lit chandeliers. Silk draperies the color of a fresh apple. Wedgwood china. Chinese carpets. The best of everything. For his brother Frederick, only the best.

In spite of the extraordinary opulence and festive atmosphere, all anyone seemed to be able to speak about as they lifted their wine-glasses was the tumultuous situation in France. Disorder in the streets, in the government and, most dramatically, in the public mind was threatening total political disintegration. As they sat around the table, George and Maria's guests were trying to guess what form such a dissolution might take.

"Well. All that I can say is that I think it is in very poor taste of those French indeed," sniffed Lady Abergavenny, a barrel-chested woman with a deep, throaty voice not unlike her husband's. "I tell you, I simply do not see how something so terribly barbaric as beheading one another like a collection of savages is going to put more food on the table!"

"I quite agree. But the French do operate by different principles you know," said Hugh Seymour, a spoonful of soup poised near his mouth.

The very French Princesse de Lamballe, a dignified woman with fair hair and blue penetrating eyes set in a small pale face, set down her glass so hard that red wine splashed onto the white silk table cover. "Not really so different, Lord Seymour. At the moment, per-haps only more desperate."

It was quite by accident that, in the center of all of this, Maria noticed the first surreptitious tossing of glances to her husband from the very flirtatious Lady Jersey.

Frances was not a woman of great beauty, nor was she particu-larly young. Her children were already grown. But the memory of the loveliness of youth still clung to her dark hair, coal-black eyes, and pale olive skin like a haunting shadow.

After several attempts, she caught the Prince's glance, then looked away. A moment later, she looked at him again, this time with a bla-tantly saucy smile.

Maria shifted stiffly against the back of her tall chair, seeing everything before she turned away. She understood flirtation and the power George had always had over women. But what made it worse this time, somehow, was that since he had been back in Brighton with Frederick, they'd had not five minutes alone together with all of the preparations for tonight. Maria had not had a moment with him to tell him of the strange and ominous fear cloying at her now for several days, and to know the reassurance his tone and his touch always would bring.

"How many of their own have they killed now in this frenzy?" asked Lord Abergavenny as blithely as if he were asking the price of tea.

The Princesse de Lamballe glared at him. "I would not suspect they are counting, sir."

Lady Jersey fingered the string of black velvet around her throat as she flirted with George more boldly now. Finally Maria rose, a ripple of anger coursing through her. The conversation stopped. "Excuse me," she said crisply. "I should like some air."

"I will go with you," Frederick said, springing up from his chair. He walked out of the dining room behind her.

They strolled side by side for a long time, slowly winding among the hollyhock and the fragrant jasmine, waves crashing in the black distance. Neither of them spoke. In her mind, Maria saw Lady Jersey's face, her eager red lips, the seductive glances from marble black eyes. She shivered. They could run from reality, here to Brighton. But it was always there, waiting at any moment, to take them back in—the real world, and something that could destroy them.

Frederick had seen what upset her but, knowing well his brother's past, he could not bear to confront it. He already liked her too much.

"Have you a chill, madam? Would you like to go inside?"

"No!"

He saw her eyes moist in the night shadows. "I am not quite ready to return," she softened. "Thank you, Frederick."

He shrugged his gray velvet shoulders and continued to walk beside her. "It is all right with me," he said. "I have seen enough of France these last years to remain with me a lifetime. I need not hear about that bloody awful mess as well."

They walked down a narrow path that edged the sand. It was a gravel path guarded with a sentinel row of pink and white foxglove. Beside it was a vine-clad wall with another maze of blossoms. Maria kicked off her shoes and walked onto the beach in her stockings. The full moon shone down on them like a huge lemon flame.

"You know, I have wanted to tell you"—he took her hand and squeezed it in a gesture of friendship—"that I am so very glad to know that it is you who is my brother's wife."

Maria paused, feeling her heart stop. Then she gathered her composure enough to continue strolling along the thick, moist sand. "You mustn't believe everything you hear, Frederick," she said without flinching.

"Oh, you needn't deny it to me, Maria. After my own lengthy banishment, I understand better than anyone how difficult relations with this family can be, the lengths to which one can be driven. Especially someone like George. But be assured, there is at least one royal who is thrilled that my brother has found the good sense to take such a thoroughly charming wife. I only hope that one day he shall find the courage and the opportunity to confess you to the rest of the world."

Maria smiled feebly, then stopped again to look up at the moon. She took a deep breath, holding it in as though it might be her last. Frederick held out his hand to her. Finally she took it. When they went back inside, George and his guests had all gone into the library for brandy. Everyone was sitting near the fire, still discussing French politics. Everyone except George and Lady Jersey.

They were on the other side of the room, she leaning against one of the silk draped walls, her arms at her sides. She was gazing up at him as George stood speaking with her.

So is it possible it is to begin again? That his old ways are returning? A small sick thread worked its way up Maria's throat when she saw them together. Perhaps this was what the fear was about, the feeling she had been having for days that something dark and awful was about to happen.

"Oh, Maria, you're back." Horatia smiled and held up her hand. Maria looked at her and had a moment's softening. What a dear friend she had become here in Brighton, to her and George both. "Come, sit beside me," Horatia called, but Maria could see only her husband and the wife of the fourth Earl of Jersey still rapt in whispered conversation.

"I'm afraid I'm not feeling very well. I believe I shall say good night."

Horatia followed her eyes and saw what Maria saw. "Let me come with you. We can talk a bit before you go to sleep."

Horatia reached up and put a hand on Maria's shoulder. Very quietly she said, "Do not make too much of this. It means nothing, his speaking with her. It is a game, nothing more. Lady Jersey simply wishes to say that, for a moment one enchanted evening, she was able to captivate the attentions of the dashing Prince of Wales."

"The married Prince of Wales."

"He worships you, Maria." Horatia whispered intensely. "You are his wife. Think of what he has risked for you already. You are his one true source of strength, the woman who has changed everything for him. Anyone who cannot see that is a fool. No matter where life leads the two of you, you are the one to whom he will always return."

This show of conviction from someone so gentle and unassuming as Horatia surprised her. Maria reached out and tucked a strand of loose brown hair behind Horatia's ear; a friendly gesture. There was always that one strand, no matter how much she curled it, that would fall flat and escape the tight ringlets. Maria remembered how it had been like that every evening they had spent together since last summer. A ripple of tenderness spread through her to realize that at least some things never changed. Maria embraced her, kissed each of her cheeks tenderly, and then bid the woman who had become like a sister good night.

The candles were still lit and a fire blazed in the little stone hearth in Maria's house across the garden from the Pavilion. She tossed her cape on the peg near the door. She could hear Belle Pigot, assigned now as Maria's new companion, her warbled strains rolling through the modest house as she sang in the kitchen. Such a dear old woman, one Maria had come to depend upon more every day, just as George had done in his youth.

Shortly after the fiasco in the House of Commons, Belle had agreed to accompany Maria everywhere in public and in general to make life a bit easier. George knew, from a lifetime of experience, that there was no one in the world who could bring his precious wife more comfort and strength than his own dear Belle.

Maria sank into a chair beside the fire when the door leading into them swung open and the short, little figure tottered into the light. "You're home early, ma'am. How was the party for Prince Frederick?"

"It was lovely, Belle. Thank you."

"Will you be wanting anything from the kitchen? Some tea perhaps?"

"No, thank you. I am just going to sit here awhile and catch my breath. The solitude just now will do me good."

"Then I shall bid you a good night."

"Good night, Belle," Maria called after her. When she was back in the kitchen, the odd singing began again.

After a moment, Maria turned toward the fire as tears shimmered on her pale cheeks.

Foolish woman! You know you are the only woman George desires! No matter what the rest of the world might believe. He has changed with you. For you... Because of you.

Still, like everyone in England, she knew his reputation with women, and it frightened her beyond reckoning to think that her George, the man she had come so to adore and hold up as the light of her life, could ever be reduced to that again. And as she sat near the fire a slip of crumpled paper caught her eye. Thrown into the hearth to be destroyed, it had not yet burned. Maria picked it up and opened it. Realizing that it was a printed verse like the ones she'd been subjected to in London, her heart skipped a beat.

'Tis at Brighton, the mirror of watering places,
Assemble their Honors, their Lordships and Graces,
But nay, it is England's first Prince — and the infamous
Dame Fitz...

It was all she could bear to read before Maria reached for the bell pull and yanked it, her face white as alabaster. A moment later, Belle returned to her drawing room. "I'm sorry, ma'am. I thought you'd gone up to bed."

Maria held out the crumpled slip of paper containing the moralist's crude poem. She felt entirely broadsided. Here in Brighton, where she had always been safe, she had not even seen this coming. Here now too she was to become a ribald jest? Whore to a prince?

"Have you seen this?"

In an instant, Belle's eyes were downcast. "I am sorry to say that I have, ma'am."

"How did it find its way into my house?"

"Surely not by my hand. But when I did find it I sought to burn it straightaway. I'm sorry I did not do a better job."

"Are there other copies?"

Her voice was tight. "Posted in town, yes, ma'am."

"But I do not understand." Maria breathed, a slim hand pressed to her forehead as her mouth began to go very dry from the surprise. "George and I have always been safe from persecution here...The people of Brighton have so openly embraced us."

"If you'll pardon me for saying so, ma'am, it is really not so bad as what is up in London. Perhaps you should think on it like that."

"These words are meant to be cruel, Belle." She pointed the poem at her, feeling her head begin to whirl with a virulent mixture of disappointment, shock, and betrayal. "Reminding one and all that I am of no nobility a'tall. Surely you can see that. I had no idea, truly, that the people of Brighton, as well —"

"No doubt it is the work of but one disgruntled man."

"But I am still the object of derision. Even here..."

"People fear what they do not understand. I am certain it is nothing more than a reaction to that."

"But I have never given anyone here a reason to despise me, have I? I live a quiet life, only in the shadows. Please, Belle. You must tell me why."

"Respectfully, ma'am, they believe that you've married their Prince and then been bold enough not only to lie about it yourself but to lure people to do it on your behalf in Parliament."

Maria sank back into a silk-covered chair, stunned. For a time, coming to Brighton had been like finding a safe harbor. But now here, as well, in the one place she had thought they were accepted, respected, she was thought no less a concubine than back in London.

"So all of this time I have been fooling myself. Even here, in our haven, we are no longer safe."

"The verses are the words of a fool."

Maria closed her eyes. "They are the words of the people."

"What can I do to help? I care deeply for both you and George."

Maria took a deep, labored breath, trying to push away the tears she felt stinging the back of her eyes.

Finally, she extended her hand and Belle took it. "Thank you for that. But there is nothing anyone can do. They say that the truth can wound. I suspect, coming down out of the clouds, I am just finding out how terribly true that is." It felt like the final straw.

FRANCES HAD KNOWN THAT HE would be there.

All of Brighton knew the Prince of Wales went sea bathing in the morning. But only Lady Jersey had been bold enough to follow him. He stood on the sand, dripping water, as Old Smoker dried his legs and Orlando Bridgeman helped him on with a heavy blue robe.

"Lady Jersey." George smiled, a little surprised to see her unescorted like this.

She looked elegant and fresh in apricot silk, her ebony hair pulled away from her face and topped with a matching ribbon-trimmed hat. "What brings you out here so early in the morning?"

"I always rise early when we come to the seashore," she lied. "I suspect it is this splendid air."

Bridgeman knotted the robe and scowled suspiciously.

"Yes. It is rather splendid at that."

"I wanted to thank you for last night," she said seductively, lowering her dark eyes as if she was referring to more than the supper he and Maria had hosted. "I had a marvelous time."

"Yes." He looked at her. "So did Maria and I."

"Walk with me?"

George glanced at Maria's cottage, then back at Orlando Bridgeman, who took no pains to hide the fact that he disapproved. He should not accompany her. It might well incite even more gossip, since he knew that Lady Jersey was flirting with him. She was dangerous. That much had been obvious even last night.

"I don't think that would be a very good idea."

"Simply a stroll, Your Highness. What harm could there possibly be in that?"

"I have made a career of underestimating harm to myself and others, madam."

"Just one little stroll?"

"Very well," he conceded. "Until Maria finishes her correspondence and is free to join us, I shall be your escort."

The beach was still coated with fog as they strolled together into the thick white pillow and disappeared quickly from Orlando Bridgeman's protective view.

"You will forgive me, I hope, for saying so," Frances said, clinging fast to his arm. "But Your Highness is not a'tall as I expected when I came here to Brighton."

His lips twisted into a little sneer. "And how precisely is that, Lady Jersey?"

He saw her blush and struggle for a reply. The nuance was coquettish. She had no idea how unappealing such blatant flirtation was to him. Now that he had Maria.

"Perhaps you mean that I am not quite as the caricatures portray me, a worthless, spoiled wreck of an heir."

"You are far more charming. Certainly more handsome."

George stopped and turned to face her. "Why, Lady Jersey, I do believe you're flirting with me again."

She tossed him her most beguiling smile. "And if I were?"

"If you were." He exhaled a breath, remembering how it felt to be so skillfully baited into a trap like this by a beautiful woman who wanted his power and his connections. Not his heart.

God, it was wonderful to be a million miles away from all of that. To have Maria's love, here by the sea.

"If you were, of course I would be terribly flattered. But, as you might imagine, I would have to decline."

She ran a slim hand seductively along the gold-braided edge of his robe and then gently touched his lips with her own. It was a chaste kiss, but with the promise of much more. "No one would have to know. It could be our little secret."

George stepped back, still tasting her ruby lip paint. "There was a time in my life when I might well have taken you up on that."

"That certainly was the rumor."

"But, alas, *I* would know, my dear Lady Jersey...I would know."

Frances moved close to him again, pressing her apricot silk gown against his firm, muscular body as the waves crashed against the shore. But she only left him cold.

"Well. If you should ever change your mind—" She sighed and kissed him again, this time openmouthed and hard, before she turned and walked alone, back toward the shore.

245

MARIA WAS ON HER KNEES, weeping, when George found her.

He stood frozen at the door to her bedroom as she knelt on the floor, her hands clasped together and her head bowed in prayer. A shaft of pale sunlight came through the windows and made golden her tangled blond hair as the soft sound of her weeping filled the early-morning air.

Damn them all to hell! Those criminals have managed to get to her, even here!

George had foolishly slept alone in the Pavilion last night, too tired when the last guest left, to come across the garden. He had no idea that Maria had spent the morning, not at her correspondence, but in prayer and meditation—nor that she had barely slept at all.

Belle had gone to him the moment he came back from the seashore with Lady Jersey. She had warned George about the cruelly trifling verse and its effect on Maria. But nothing could have prepared him for seeing the woman he loved like this. Weeping. Praying and weeping. She had waited so long to be acknowledged, to receive the respect she deserved, and yet that seemed only to be slipping further away.

"Give me strength, dear Lord, to face this," Maria whispered through her tears, not hearing him at her door. "I am a laughingstock to the world. Even here now, *here,* I cannot escape it…Oh, how I despise this!…despise what I have become. A joke. An object of derision…The whore I swore I could never be!"

She dropped her face into her hands. "It should not matter to me, I know, but it does…God help me, but it does!…"

George stepped back from the door, shattered.

In this single excruciating moment, he realized there was no way to save her from this torture any longer, nowhere he could keep her safe until he became King. He had believed with his whole heart that by marrying her one day he would be able to make her a Queen, and this all would be healed.

Instead, because of him, she had no child, no family…and no longer even her honor. He had been unbearably selfish. He had no idea, until this moment, all that his love had cost her.

Before she could look up and discover him, George turned and went back downstairs, his mind as muddy and rutted as the Brighton streets in winter. Again he saw the caricatures in his mind. Heard the relentless gossip about her. The memory of Isabella Sefton's cruel rebuff early on up in London...and the whispers of so many others.

"I am a fool," he mouthed, staggering out into the garden between her cottage and the Pavilion.

George stood on the slim brick path that wound between their two houses and stared up at the sky. A cool morning breeze blew across is face. "I am the blight on her life...and all that she holds dear. Yet, God forgive me, she is *my* life. Am I man enough to turn away from that?"

GEORGE GAZED BLANKLY ACROSS THE dark and cozy seaside tavern, the charm of the place lost on him even as he sat across from Frederick at a scarred oak table that smelled of ale.

"It would well do you good to talk about it," Frederick said.

"There is nothing to tell." George looked away into the roaring fire beside their table.

"Oh, I believe I know you a little bit better than that."

A group of old men beside them played cards as the air in the low-ceilinged tavern curled with stale and thickly clotted smoke. Local fishermen were telling salty tales. Barmaids were laughing. Frederick ordered himself another drink with a wave of his hand and then looked back at George, who still refused even a taste of brandy.

"It is Maria, isn't it?"

George looked up, his eyes half glazed. "Why do you ask?"

"Is there anyone else in the world who could have you looking so glum?"

George was silent. His frown deepened. Then finally he said, "I want to do what's right for her, Freddie. God, I want her to be happy."

"And you do not believe she is any longer, with you?"

"I know that she loves me. That's not it."

"But there is something."

George continued to gaze only at the fire, its tall golden flames shooting up into the blackness of the hearth.

"Please," Frederick pressed. "You were always there for me, all those lonely years when I was abroad, always writing to me, helping to keep my spirits up. Let me return the favor."

When George looked back, he studied Frederick through tired eyes. So young. Naive. And so eager to help. Just as he had been when they were children. But it was late. Too late for confessions. No one could help him now.

"It's nothing, really. I am just tired. That's all."

"Go home," Frederick tenderly bid him. "Talk to her, George."

"I cannot go home. Not yet."

What he did not add was that he could not bear to return to the searing pain he had seen in Maria's eyes that morning as she knelt praying, weeping. Not when he knew that, even without meaning to, his love, and his single-minded desire to have her, was the cause of such unhappiness.

No, facing Maria now would only push him toward the one solution he could not yet bear to consider. And anything, at the moment, was preferable to facing that.

IN A BLUE SATIN CHAIR, she waited.

Maria looked up at the clock, bright in the glow of the moon through the window, still smarting from the cruel verses she had discovered last night. Half past two. Just after midnight, Weltje had come to her cottage with a letter for George from the queen. Before he returned to Windsor, Her Majesty's messenger had indicated that His Highness was to read it at once. George, however, had been off with Frederick since the early hours of afternoon.

Maria had not allowed Weltje to light any of the candles or to stoke the fire. It was better like this. Easier not to face the truth, at least for a little while.

That verse here in Brighton, where she believed herself safe, had weakened her and she had needed to be alone with her thoughts. She would not have come now if not for the need to deliver the letter.

As she waited, Maria surveyed the room, one of many she had helped to create. The embroidered ottoman, the satinwood cabinet... the paintings; all of it they had chosen together. So much love, she thought. She drummed her fingers impatiently against the arm of the stiff walnut chair. The waves crashed over and over onto the sand just beyond the windows, and yet she did not hear them. Nor did she hear the door latch click when the two brothers finally returned.

"Why are you here at this late hour?" George asked as he came into the darkness, seeing Maria.

He had loitered at the tavern as long as he was able—avoiding her, and still here she was before he was ready to face her with the great painful task that lay before him. That disappointment came through now in his tone.

"Really, George. No need to be rude," Frederick said with a firm hand of restraint on his shoulder.

Maria moved to stand, her body shimmering before him half in silhouette, half in moonlight. "You've had a message from the Queen."

"Oh, splendid," George shot caustically into the air.

"I think I shall say good night," Frederick said.

"Perhaps you should stay," Maria countered as she shifted and George lit a brass lamp. "The King is very ill."

"Oh, nonsense. He's too bloody vile to be ill!"

"George, the Queen says he may be dying."

He looked at her, the lamp held up between them.

"Has he had another of his fits?" Frederick asked.

"Her Majesty says that his mind is disordered and that he is at present unable to function as King."

"That certainly does not make him near death," George shot back.

"He is feverish and Her Majesty says in great pain. The doctors have no idea how to help him this time."

"What does she want from me?"

"She has asked you to come to Kew Palace at once. They can no longer put off naming a Regent to act in His Majesty's stead."

His father had suffered from periodic bouts of madness for years but he had always managed to recover before any intervention was required. George glanced at his brother, then back at Maria, daring to consider once again that the end to all their problems could be so near.

"We must go to Kew Palace," said Frederick.

"I suppose you're right," George answered but in a discordant voice that mirrored his complete surprise. "Tell Weltje that we will leave at dawn, and have him rally Hugh Seymour to join us, will you Freddie?"

"Of course," he replied before he left the room.

Once they were alone, George moved swiftly to Maria and took her into his arms. Sobered by the implications of this turn of events, he forgot completely the circumstances that had brought him home so late in the first place. George held her quietly in the darkness, plying a long strand of hair near her face with his fingers.

"Sweet Jesus, do you believe it could finally be happening?" he whispered. But she did not reply. "If he should die, that would change everything for me — for *us*. God, finally."

Maria pulled away, the harshness in his earlier tone still lingering there — the unexplained way he had left her all day and all evening still a wound that was raw. "Perhaps you should try to get a few hours of sleep before morning," she said in a voice that was cool. One it had been years since he had heard. "You have a long ride to London ahead of you."

GEORGE'S EYES FLASHED ANGER.

"How can you actually do this?" he charged into the Queen's Music Room at Kew Palace, which was overflowing with guests.

They were listening to a recital of the King's favorite works of Handel in hopes that it might rouse him from his malaise as he lay infirm across the hall. Queen Charlotte came to her feet, dressed in pale green satin. Her contented smile fell at the sight of her contentious son. The music stopped. George lingered in the doorway, his body ramrod straight and his face flushed crimson with anger.

"Play on!" the Queen ordered as she left the room, George following behind her. "Do not ever dare to embarrass me like that again or, I swear by all that is holy, you shall live to regret it!"

"Tit for tat, is it, Mother?"

Charlotte closed the library doors behind them when she could see that his anger was not fading in the least. She could see that her eldest son had been advised of the terms of his Regency since her message as to the King's illness had come.

Knowing full well that the Heir Apparent had married a Catholic widow and then denied it, the Queen and the Tory Prime Minister, William Pitt, were terrified by the danger the power as Regent would now give him. There would be no telling what title he might bestow upon Mrs. Fitzherbert, nor what Act he might repeal, to make their marriage legal.

Thus, the Queen had been counseled by Pitt that she had no choice. Her eldest son should be given no power to touch the property of the King, no power to grant offices or pensions, and no power to create peers. If he chose to agree to those terms, then and only then would George be named Regent for his ailing father.

"This is not a game, George. This is England!"

"The full authority of the Regency is my right!"

"In my lifetime, by God, there will be no Papist as Queen of England!

"How dare you side with that bastard Pitt against your own son? You have made me your puppet! Tied my hands with the people!"

"I am first the Queen of England, George, and only then am I free to be your mother!"

The words hung between them gnarling and writhing in his belly like a poison. But it was an old poison, an old pain. A memory came to him then, one long forgotten but no less powerful as it surfaced again in his mind, gaining dimension and depth.

He was a boy again of no more than six, sweet-faced, wide-eyed, a boy who had known in private moments the tenderness of his mother's embrace, she always smelling like musk roses, often coming into his bedchamber to sing him to sleep, and the sweetness of her laughter when she was free to be herself, his mother. And yet he still struggled to accept the primacy of her duty overall—the long absences from her children to accompany the King wherever obligation or their pastimes took them. This time, they had been away for three months.

He could still remember standing beside Frederick on the shore at Dover; the salt air, the sound of the gulls, as they waited formally for their parents to come ashore. They had been waiting an eternity, he had thought, beneath the sun, in the view of a great crowd of people. Suddenly he'd caught the scent of her perfume and, for that moment, there was nothing else but a little boy's longing to be near his mother again, to feel the shelter of her arms, to know her kisses upon his face. He broke away from the rigid phalanx formed by his staff and ran to her as she came down the gangplank. Somewhere on the breeze, he heard the sudden hush of the crowd. But it did not matter just then. She was his mother and he had missed her. Now she was home.

"Not here, George," she stopped him at arm's length. "Not before I have greeted the Prime Minister."

He looked up into his mother's eyes as she pressed him away, but they were not the beautiful, cool blue eyes he remembered. Her gaze now was vacant, her smile to the crowd polite. George felt his cheeks burn and tears sting his eyes as someone near them dared to chuckle at a child's public rebuff. His mother did not belong to him, he realized then, but to this crowd of strangers—and primarily to the stone-faced man beside her who ruled all of England...and him.

Later that evening, he remembered her saying, "You must understand, George. I have my duty, and you shall have yours."

Yes, he did have his duty now as plain and clear as the summer sky—a duty his childhood and his parents had cultivated in him from that bitter early age. It was to Maria, the one person who loved him unconditionally, and only her. He looked at the Queen, old and unbending. It was difficult now to remember ever having cared for her that much.

"You have no right to attach conditions to the Regency!" he said as the bitter memory slipped away and the moment returned full force.

"I have every right in the world to protect England from your Whig friends, not to mention your mistress!" she shouted back at him. "I do not understand you anymore, George, truly I do not! You behave as if this is all a game, first allying yourself with the King's opposition just to spite him! Then not only do you break the law, but you risk your succession with your blatantly illegal marriage to a whore!"

There. It was out between them.

In the silence that followed, her accusing words flowed into the rest of the vile poison that had spewed from her mouth at him. Frederick had been right. She did know, or at least she believed that she did. Her eyes were a storm of contempt as she stood, hands on pale green hips, a breath away from him.

"Why are you trying to do this to me? Why are you trying to take away this one bit of happiness from me?"

"George, please. Quit this dangerous game you're playing, only to defy us."

His eyes narrowed as the image of his sweet Maria filled his mind. "If that is what you believe I am doing, mother, then you never really knew me at all."

"All the King and I want for you is to marry someone, legally. Maria may remain your mistress forever if you wish. All will be forgiven, I assure you of that. Make Caroline of Brunswick your wife and you shall have the kind of Regency you crave, and more money than you can spend!"

"I have told you, I shall *never* marry!"

Her blue eyes glittered with anger. "You mean legally."

"You cannot force me to do anything, Mother! Not even accept a conditional Regency!"

"That is true. You can refuse. But then you know *I* will take the Regency myself and then your tart will never have a chance at any position of respectability! And consider what will be left to you! More gossip! More scandal!...And I promise you, by God, more poverty!"

He would not be free of his father's manipulations after all. Nor would he have the power to make Maria his legitimate wife. George could not save her image from the gossipmongers and cartoonists who had reduced their relationship to nothing more than a petty joke. This had been his last chance...*their last chance.* The blow had been a heavy one as he stood facing his mother—a woman and a Queen he did not like, or understand.

"Take great care, madam," he seethed, turning away from her anger and from her accusations and bolting for the door, "for I believe that you are as much deranged as the King. And sanity, unlike loyalty, is one commodity you cannot buy from William Pitt!"

CHAPTER TWELVE

FREDERICK TOLD HER WHAT HAD transpired at Kew Palace, so she had been warned. Maria was waiting for George in his bedchamber at the Pavilion when he finally arrived. It was not her custom to come here, especially at night, but after a disappointment so grand, she was certain he would need her. And in spite of the mounting tension between them, George was her first concern. When she heard the door slam shut with a loud thud, her heart stopped.

Across the chasm of his darkened room, she heard the slice of steel as he drew one of his swords from the glass display case near the door. Then, dashing about the dark room, George slashed at tapestries and draperies. "Damn! Damn! Damn it to hell!"

Maria came forward, shimmering silver in the glow of the moon as she held her arms around her waist as though trying to hold herself up. Her hair was uncurled, long honey-colored streamers rushing over her shoulders. She sat on the little embroidered stool before George froze, seeing her. Neither of them said anything for a very long time.

"Perhaps I should not have come here. I know we agreed you would always come to my home instead," she finally said in a voice barely above a whisper. When he did not answer, she added, "I understand your disappointment. But I don't know what to do to help you, George, when you will not even come to me with your pain."

Even in the shadows, he could see the concern etched into her face, as well as the disappointment. "It's not you," he finally said. "The Queen and I quarreled."

"I am frightened."

"Of me?"

"Of the distance that is steadily growing between us."

"You're imagining things."

"Am I? There was a time when you would have come to me before anything."

"It was late, Maria. I was tired."

She took his hands in hers. "Please don't shut me out, George. Let me be a part of your pain and your disappointments as well as your glory...Let me help you." Slowly, he looked up and found her eyes again. The pain of her devotion to him, in those eyes just then, was excruciating. And he wondered, in that silent moment between them, how he could ever tell her that the only way out of this quagmire, the only way to give her the happiness she so dearly deserved, was to betray her—yet again. The only way in the world was to set her free.

"You cannot change this," he breathed. "No one can."

He looked up at her and parted his lips as though he meant to say something more, but all he saw was her kneeling, in tears, trying to be stoic, all he felt was the decimation he had brought to her life. He reached out and touched a strand of hair near her face as though he was touching a precious jewel. Then, without saying a word, he turned and very slowly went out of the room.

MARIA WATCHED FROM HER WINDOW in dawn's first light as George's yellow carriage pulled away from the Pavilion beneath a thick cloud of fog. He had not come to her. The light of day had not changed his mind. He meant to keep her at a distance now. To close her out of his life at least as confidante.

She had wanted to tell him that she needed to get away from here for a while. That she needed the safety and sanity of her house at

Twickenham, and time to grow strong again in her resolve. But apparently it did not matter. He had somewhere of his own to go.

"Yes, ma'am?"

Maria looked up with glazed eyes at Fanny, having forgotten that she had called for her. Slowly she came away from the window and spoke quietly, trying to bridle her emotions. "I would like you to begin packing our things. We shall be leaving for Twickenham this morning."

"Yes, ma'am." Fanny turned halfway to the door and then looked back at Maria. "And will His Highness be accompanying us, ma'am? I shall need to know which carriages to have readied."

"No, Fanny," she said, and her voice was full of a heavy grief. She had made the only decision she could. "This time we shall be leaving alone."

CHAPTER THIRTEEN

"SAY IT'S NOT TRUE, SIR!" Orlando Bridgeman stood in shock, certain he could not have heard what he thought he had. "You are actually going to marry Caroline of Brunswick?"

"It may as well be her as any of the other candidates. Who it is matters not at all."

"Pray, consider this more dearly, sir!"

"I risked everything on the hope that I would be King by now... that Maria would be my Queen..." George's words were hollow, his face ghostly pale as he drained yet another brandy, then tossed the glass into the fireplace hearth. He pressed his hands together like a steeple and touched his lips; The pain deep within him was like a small death. "The *only* way to save her now is to set her free. Completely free."

"But, sir," Bridgeman lunged forward. "You cannot do this! You love her! She is your wife, your heart...your life! I know, I've seen you! Sir, please, she does not deserve this!"

"Of course she is my heart, you fool! My heart and my life!" Through tears that came suddenly now at the very thought, tears he had not cried since he was a child, George lunged to his feet, stalking across his bedchamber. "I shall *never* love another! Maria will be in my heart until I die! She is everything to me! *Everything*!" he shouted. "But it is *because* I love her that I must do this—for *her!* Don't you see? Good God, man! The very thought of another woman sickens me!"

"But to cut out your own heart like this, sir!"

"I *must* do this! I must do it for her! She deserves a life, one of respect I thought I would have been able to give her long before now! And the only way to do that is to make her so angry that she despises the very thought of me!...Maria, the love of my life, my heart, my very soul, must have a chance at a real life, perhaps even with someone else!" he brayed, grabbing a vase and smashing it violently onto the floor. "Great God Almighty..." He sank onto his heels. "She must entertain no hope of a reconciliation. And there is but one way to see to that."

"There must be some other way but something so horribly drastic!"

"Do you not think I have considered everything? Do you not know that this has plagued every breath I have taken since I realized fully how she felt—how this life was destroying her? No, Bridgeman, there is no other choice on this earth!"

"Will she not believe you were forced by the King?"

He drew in a breath and let it out on a heavy sigh. "Not if she hears that I have fallen back to the ways of my youth. She must believe that I have taken a mistress."

"Oh, no, sir," Bridgeman shook his head. "Not that unsavory Lady Jersey."

Commitment rang in George's voice as a gray afternoon shadow stretched across his tear-wetted face. "Do you not understand? I *must* spare Maria any more of the ridicule that shows no sign of ending, the making of her a caricature, a jest to all of England! It seems now that bloody bastard, my father, may well live on forever!"

After a moment, Bridgeman sank slowly onto the floor beside the Prince.

"God help me, Maria must believe I am mad for Lady Jersey! That foolish woman is just eager enough to be my unwitting accomplice in this." George shot him a sudden glance. "I trust you can incite the proper gossip."

"Oh, Your Highness, I bid you, do not ask me that."

"I will not be denied! You found your lips loose enough with Charles James Fox! You owe me, Bridgeman!"

His slim face blanched. "Your Highness, I am so terribly sorry about that. I had drunk too much. It was a dreadful error in judgment and I—"

"Do not explain what cannot be changed!" George charged wildly again now, vaulting back to his feet. "That is in the past. And I need your help now, as I have never needed anything before!"

"But, listen to reason, sir! Your public standing will slip even further!"

"I could not give a farthing for any of that! What I do care about, the only thing I care about in this world, or ever will, is Maria!" His hands were clenched in determination, his face painted with dry tears. "Asking her to live as we have for this long has been wretched. I have thought only of how I needed her in my life. But from this final deception something good can come *for* her! It must!"

CHAPTER FOURTEEN

MARIA SAT LIKE A STONE before the sputtering fire in her drawing room at Twickenham.

"Will you not at least do something to fight for him?" John asked incredulously.

"I cannot."

"You mean you *will* not! Good Lord, sister, are you willing to simply hand your husband over to that woman on a silver tray?"

"George has made his choice without my help, John," she said stubbornly, hoping to keep the pain from her voice. "I came away for a few days...He decided that he preferred to make it much more of an estrangement."

"Lady Jersey is a dalliance to him, nothing more. You alone are his wife. Unless of course you give him reason to believe you no longer desire to be."

"Perhaps I don't."

Maria had heard the gossip about George and Lady Jersey. And, try as she might not to believe it, a part of her knew that on some level it must be true. She had, after all, been an unwilling observer to its inception that evening at Brighton. But despite John and Isabella's encouragement to go to London to fight for her husband, she had steadfastly refused. She would say no more. Her grief was heavy, a very private thing, something she could not share. The images and the betrayal were still so vivid, so raw.

She sat alone for hours in the same blue bedchamber in which they had begun their marriage, listening to the monotonous tick of the tall ebony clock and the shrill scratching of the crickets outside of her window. No candles or lamps burned. There, sitting rigidly, and wrapped in the memories of his early tenderness, praying to God she would hear from him. Sometimes, she even slipped on his crimson tailcoat and sat in its heavy folds just because it smelled so much like him. The faint traces of civet, the scent of a coat well worn.

John thumped a fist against the fireplace mantel. "How can you be so apathetic? You know what they're saying, don't you? The Jersey woman is trying to persuade him to marry that homely German princess, Caroline of Brunswick, to advance her own standing with the Court and with him! She is working against you as we speak!"

"Then bigamy shall be his choice, John." Maria tossed her head bitterly, conviction lighting her eyes. "Not mine."

TWO DAYS LATER, AT SUNSET, Maria and John welcomed Richard Sheridan, his wife Elizabeth, and Horatia and Hugh Seymour to the country for a supper party. Frederick, the Duke of York, had come willingly out to Twickenham in spite of the absence of his elder brother. Having heard all over London of the Prince's conspicuous dalliance with Lady Jersey, the group had come as much to show their support for Maria as to show their condemnation of George's curiously cruel behavior.

After dinner, Belle Pigot supervised the serving of raspberry tarts, apricot cake, and spicy gingerbread out on the marble terrace overlooking the banks of the Thames so that everyone could watch the sunset. There were still little rowboats on the water filled with Englishmen and their ladies, most of them rowing slowly now toward shore beneath the dazzling play of light and color.

"My, the sunsets are brilliant out here, aren't they?" said Elizabeth Sheridan, taking a slice of the apricot cake from the white-gloved servant who held them on a long, handled china tray. The corners of the French blue table cover rustled in the breeze.

Maria glanced over at Frederick and saw his elder brother in him once again. Now that George was absent from her life, the likeness haunted her. They had the same nose and the same smile. Their eyes twinkled that same incandescent sky blue.

"Pardon me, ma'am," Jacko Payne said and bowed to her with one hand behind his back. In the other hand he held a letter. She could see at a glance that it was George's stationery.

Everyone looked at her. They recognized it too. She saw Sheridan lower his head. She looked at Hugh Seymour but he was quick to look away. It was as if they knew something or that they sensed it.

"Are you not going to open it?" John asked, full of an anticipation that he was not so successful as the others at masking.

Maria ran a thumbnail tentatively along the edge of the paper, then stopped. "Perhaps later."

Frederick glanced up again, hoping his brother had come to his senses, knowing what this was costing him—what this was costing them both. "It may well be important, my dear."

She longed to say that George had not had anything important to say to her for some time. Instead she opened the parchment. Everyone was gazing at her again. There was a rush of wind off the water and the shiver that shook her body was almost painful. The sun was fading quickly now, the last orange burst slipping behind the bristling bank of willows near the shore. Maria had trouble reading the words at first and she squinted to make out his hand. Suddenly her face changed. Her skin followed and went white as powder.

"What is it, my dear?"

She heard Elizabeth Sheridan's question. Or perhaps it had been the voice of Horatia Seymour. She could not entirely tell. Someone else asked her if the news was bad but the voice was distorted, unrecognizable.

"What on earth is in that note?" asked Hugh Seymour, gazing down incredulously at Maria, who still was not fully conscious.

John washed a hand across his face and looked down at his sister along with everyone else. "It is from the Prince of Wales. He says..." The words caught in his throat. Unable to explain, he handed the note to Lord Seymour.

Hugh read the Prince's words first to himself, then looked back up at the other guests, who stood around Maria in stunned silence.

"Bloody bastard!"

"What is it?" Horatia asked, her face and voice full of alarm.

"That Jersey whore has finally gotten what she wanted all along. He says,... God help him, the fool says that he has no wish ever to see Maria again."

LONG AFTER THE OTHERS HAD all gone, Maria sat alone in her dark bedchamber as thoughts swirled in her mind, blending together. Colors. Memories. Images of the day they had married. Of her and George so much in love. So impenetrable. Once he had sworn that nothing would ever part them. Another empty promise. Another deception.

There were little gouges in the palms of her hands that were throbbing now and dried with blood, places where she had dug her own fingers to try to quell the pain in her heart.

Suddenly, she saw a man clothed in midnight shadows standing in the doorway. His image flickered like a candle flame. She squinted, trying to make out the face, then ran a hand over her sleep-glazed eyes.

"Who is it?" she called out hollowly. "Who is there?"

The image moved, then swayed. Finally a voice called back. "It is I, Maria. Frederick."

She had fallen into his arms and the weeping had begun again. He held her and comforted her, stroking her hair saying nothing until, once again, the tears had ceased.

"It will never be the same again, Freddie."

"No. I don't suppose anything ever shall."

Then she let him kiss her. But it was a kiss that passes between friends. First one cheek and then the other. Softly, like a caress. Her eyes filled again with tears. Tenderness. It had been so many weeks, and he looked so much like George.

Maria sank back against his chest, loving the feel of him. The musky smell of his man's body. It was safe here. Warm. In his arms, safe and protected as she had ever been, Maria closed her eyes and Frederick, more like a brother than her own brother, held her like that, barely moving, until she finally fell asleep.

Part Three

AND WHEN THEY DO REPLY, STRAIGHT,

GIVE THEM BOTH THE LIE.

—RALEIGH

CHAPTER FIFTEEN

MARIA AND FRANCIS RUSSELL WALKED hand in hand down near the river's edge just behind the bank of willows that nestled against the shore. The breeze was as warm and soft as a caress and the long velvety leaves made sweet summer music with their bristling. It was still early morning, the Duke's favorite time of day, before the heat and the heavy perfume of the jasmine and the roses stole away the freshness.

By August of 1794, it had been six weeks since Maria had received the letter from George. Six weeks without living, without eating or sleeping. Finally now she was empty. Of tears. Anger. She was empty even of the love. Or, she believed, most of it.

To add to the void created by the loss of George, war had been raging for a year already with a revolutionary France under an upstart General named Napoleon Bonaparte. Both Hugh Seymour and Frederick had left England to answer their country's call. She prayed every night that God would keep them safe so that these two men who had come to mean the world to her might be able to return... That she was not destined now to lose them too.

Three white geese cut across the silvery surface of the river and Francis reached out with crumbs of toast from breakfast and tossed them across the surface of the water. He and Maria watched the birds' graceful movements quickly transformed into a greedy frenzy as they plunged their long necks into the water over and over again until all of the little white specks disappeared and the water was calm once again.

Francis had waited a long time for Maria to need him like this. But through the years, he had found strength in the belief that one day it would happen.

It had been simple enough to gauge when one considered who she had the appallingly bad judgment to have illegally married. But none of that mattered, because he loved her. Finally, Maria had called for him and, seized with a bittersweet joy, the Duke of Bedford had come willingly to Twickenham asking no questions and offering the friendship he once had promised at Vauxhall.

There would never be another woman for him like Maria, no matter what the future held, and there were no conditions upon which he gave himself to her. Whatever she wanted, needed, for however long, if it was in his power to give it, it was hers.

"I've actually begun to like these early mornings," said Maria, leaning on Francis's blue satin-draped arm.

She looked back across the sloping, emerald lawn and up to her house, the beautiful gardens, the mossy willow trees, all of which evoked the reassuring memories of earlier years.

They strolled back up the hill and past the garden where the roses were in bloom, and Francis took her hand. God did have a grand heart for some things, Maria thought as she glanced at a brilliant red blossom that a greedy bee was draining of its nectar. Even if, at the moment, He was heartily testing her by what seemed like indifference, He had long ago granted her a little miracle with a friend like Francis Russell.

He squeezed her hand and she looked up at him. The years were changing the mild young Duke. His blond hair was tinged now with early shafts of gray. On Francis, it had begun to add a depth of character, making him far more handsome and confident than he had been in the bloom of his youth.

It was curious, Maria thought as they strolled, that she should find him attractive now when once the sight of his simple grace had left her cold. But so much had happened since those carefree early days. Since the opera and the garden parties out at Vauxhall, the dances at Almack's.

The changes in Maria may not have been visible but they had been profound.

In their brief and tumultuous marriage, she had forgiven George so much. Finally, his deceptions had stripped away a layer of naïveté that now was gone forever. She was no longer eager or idealistic. She was no longer the young woman who had come to London believing that the only path for her life was love.

The great folly of innocence! she thought bitterly, holding tighter on to Francis Russell's hand.

MARIA CAST THE LETTER TO the floor. "I do not want his wretched money!"

"Well, he is going to marry her, sister, that much has been settled. So you might as well have something for your trouble, if not for the embarrassment of it."

John Smythe and Henry Ernington, the two men who had been witness to her marriage, stood before her now in the Great Room of her house in Twickenham, a room ornamented with the three views of Rome by Panini, that George had admired.

Maria's uncle Henry had, that morning, received a communication from lawyers for the Prince of Wales. They had explained that, despite his intention of marrying Caroline of Brunswick, His Royal Highness wished to continue the £3,000 a year income that he had bestowed upon Maria at the time of their union.

To this he had added a further element to muddy the fine line she felt between anger and pain. The lawyers explained that, in the event of his death before that of his father, the Prince of Wales had asked His Majesty to continue Maria's pension. In a move that surprised everyone who knew about it, the King had actually agreed without contest.

Mother Mary! Maria's head spun with anger as her uncle Errington spoke the words. Was it possible? The King of England had enough of a belief that she was truly his heir's wife, after all, to agree to care for her for the rest of her life —yet they were about to let him commit bigamy to be rid of her!

She left the chair she had been sitting in and stalked the hall like an injured lioness. The Duke of Bedford saw how distraught she had become. "Do you want them to leave?" he asked protectively, as he stood tentatively beneath the door frame.

Maria glanced up at him, unsure of anything but her anger and surprise.

"Stay out of this, Bedford!" John growled and moved a step closer to his sister.

"Really, my dear," Errington said to Maria. "At least this public action is a grand gesture, considering the circumstances. I am convinced after speaking with His Royal Highness's lawyers this morning that the Prince has no wish to see you hurt any further."

"Yes, gracious of His Majesty to agree to continue supporting his son's concubine!"

The room was stilled by her words. For a moment, no one seemed to breathe. But it was more than compassion that pressed Henry Errington to silence. He and his nephew had participated in a crime against the country themselves by agreeing to witness her illegal marriage to England's Crown Prince. They must never forget that, as long as things remained as they were now, not only Maria, but they too were in the greatest danger.

GEORGE FROWNED AS HE HUNCHED over a rosewood writing table and an unfinished letter he had been writing to her, a letter like the drawerful of others that he would never send. There were times when the exercise gave him peace. Today it had done nothing but stir bitter memories. There were no words to make her understand what he had done for love of her.

To give her back the life she had lost by loving him.

"Bring me another brandy!" he barked at a new young servant whose name he had not cared to learn. He then rose up from his desk without bothering to lock away the unfinished letter.

It had seemed like the right thing to do at the time, that day, months ago now, when he had sent that cruelly blunt letter to her—when he had declared boldly that he had no wish to see Maria ever again. He had regretted it that very night, alone in his bed, exhausted and besotted by brandy. But it had been the only way to turn her against him completely, to put a finish on the act that would save her life and her honor—to give her back the one thing she held most dear.

Since then, futility had seen him agree to marry his cousin, Caroline of Brunswick, sight unseen. Come what may, he meant to keep to his word. An act so drastic, like his dalliance with Lady Jersey, was the only way he had of assuring himself he would not weaken and try to return to Maria. The servant, liveried in crimson and gold, handed him the brandy and George drank it in one swallow.

"Another!" he summoned as he sank into the rich folds of a brocade settee, one leg slung over the carved mahogany arm.

It was raining again and the sky was as gray as his heart. Maria had always liked the rain. She said it washed away all of the ugliness. Hurting, missing her still, *always*, he looked beyond the windows as it splashed from the roof and streaked the windowpanes.

"I beg Your Highness's pardon," said a tall, ruddy-skinned servant just as George was falling into despair.

"What is it?" he growled, his blue eyes downcast and glazed with the memories.

"I'm sorry, Your Highness, but there is a woman here to see you. A Miss Pigot."

George was off of the settee in an instant. "Belle is here? Well, good God man, send her in at once!"

"Belle!" He smiled and held open his arms to her, refusing to allow any formality between them.

"How is she?" he asked as they embraced, and the words hurt as they passed across his lips.

"Honestly, as well as can be expected," The old woman said without reproach, then added in the same sweet voice. "I might say that Your Highness is not looking so well yourself."

"These past few months have been difficult, old friend. Here, come and sit beside me. I'll certainly not lie to *you*."

They sat together on the same settee that faced a painting by Poussin. George ordered tea for her and another brandy for himself.

"So, how is she really, Belle? Is she getting on all right?"

The small, old woman studied him for a moment to determine for certain why he had asked. His eyes quickly gave him away. Even after all he had done to chase her from his life, the bridges he had burned, what she had always believed was true—this poor man was still in love with her.

"Well, she doesn't go out a great deal anymore, George," she said

271

cautiously. "She keeps to herself. But the Duke of Bedford has taken a house nearby in Twickenham and he is there with her a great deal of time. I think he has been some comfort to her throughout all of this."

"Bastard!" he spat, not feeling so charitable as he would have liked. "I knew the moment I was gone he would be there trying to fill my shoes!"

"He is a good man, who has been in love with her for a very long time."

"I know." George added more softly, letting the words and the anger fall away. "Perhaps it is for the best."

She wanted to ask if he meant what he said—why he continued to look as if he hadn't a single friend left in the world. But that was not why she had come. Both of them were plainly miserable without each other and she must act more subtly if there was ever any hope at all of helping them to reconcile.

"Madam received word from your lawyers last week."

He moved to the edge of the settee, his eyes lighting with hope. "And did she understand that, no matter what, I do not mean to abandon my commitment to her?"

"She was told by her brother and her uncle that you and the King shall continue her pension," she said, correcting the subtle difference.

He took her hand and squeezed it for strength. "Oh, Belle. I have made a dreadful mess of things," he said into his hands, free to be himself with her. "I can scarcely believe I ever found the courage to let her go."

"It is not too late." She gently stroked his back. "Go to her, child. Talk with her."

After a moment, George sighed heavily and looked back at her. He lay his head back against the blue and green brocade. He must be strong. For Maria. And he had said too much already.

"It is too late, my old friend. And now all that is left to me is to somehow find the strength to marry Caroline."

"Then it is a pity," said Belle Pigot, not understanding, as two footmen brought her tea. The china cups, delicate rose and white Wedgwood, clanked against the tray as the servants crossed the room. "Had you both been able to stay your course, I shall always believe Maria would have made a splendid queen."

CHAPTER SIXTEEN

HE HAD BEEN INFORMED ABOUT his prospective bride by the ambitious Lady Jersey, who, owing to the gossip about herself and the Prince of Wales, had managed an appointment as Lady of the Bedchamber to the future Princess of Wales. She had been there when she came ashore and flirted openly with the sailors on the docks at Gravesend. At Greenwich, she had also been beside the short, stout German Princess who reeked of unwashed flesh and soiled clothing, as she was greeted by staff and patients of the pensioners hospital. There she had loudly asked, in a grating soprano, "Is every Englishman without an arm or a leg?"

But knowledge of these unsettling incidents, as well as reports about her homely appearance, did not deter George.

"Disgust for my German wife," he confided in Richard Sheridan the eve before their meeting, "shall be part of my penance for what I have done to Maria."

Now, properly bathed and attired, in jadegreen waistcoat and breeches, he sat alone in a small withdrawing room at Windsor Castle, preparing himself to be pleasant when they met, to inquire about her sea crossing, made hazardous now in wartime, and the health of her parents.

Outside the long window the sky was blue and the air was bitter cold. Fitting he thought for the frost upon his heart. "Are you ready, sir?" Orlando Bridgeman asked from behind him.

George stood slowly and with great effort. He drew in a breath and vanquished the image of Maria that had been clouding his mind all morning. *I must do this for her. I must.*

He walked boldly into the adjoining drawing room then, head held high, to greet the Princess and her escort, Lord Malmesbury. They stood together before the grand, marble fireplace hearth. The woman he neared was smiling, but in the shaft of sunlight in through the long window, he could not see her fully.

She was much shorter than himself, he noted, but full chested and wide hipped, wearing a pale blue gown and matching head-piece. Her dark hair was tightly curled into ringlets. Good, he thought, how vastly different she was from the statuesque beauty of Maria.

As he neared, Caroline tried to kneel, which Malmesbury had instructed her to do, but George swiftly drew her up and embraced her in welcome. But the moment of his graciousness was short-lived when the sour odor of unwashed flesh and dirty stockings came at him full force. She smiled. Dark teeth met him. His stomach turned.

Without speaking, George pivoted and walked back to Bridge-man, who had remained beside the door. "Pray, get me a glass of brandy," he said.

"Sir, had you better not have a glass of water?"

George glanced back at the woman whose manner, he had been told, was as indelicate as her appearance, and the full force of his commitment to marry someone whom he could never love or desire settled on him like a sudden, heavy weight.

"Make my apologies to her, Bridgeman, and tell her that we shall speak at supper. Right now I must go as I am about to be sick."

FRANCES JERSEY REARRANGED THE PLACE cards at dinner. Her place was conspicuously made beside the Prince of Wales. Caroline sat on his other side, belching when she sipped her wine, and still George noted with disgust she had not bathed. The King and

Queen were seated at the opposite heads of the long, white-draped table, unaware of the Princess's strictly gauche behavior, as the Court musicians played in the recess above them,

As the second course was served, George turned away when she began to slump in her chair, her legs spreading apart in a relaxed manner he had never witnessed, even among his servants. Slovenly, he thought with disgust. Lord, she was horrid!

Yes, she was precisely what he deserved.

He listened with half an ear as she chattered nervously—endlessly, to Malmesbury, who nodded and smiled politely at his future queen. But it was Frederick to whom she suddenly and boldly turned her attention when he joined them late, and took the place between her and Lord Malmesbury.

"Well now, are you not simply the most intriguing thing on two legs! Or is that three I see?" she cackled gratingly, leaning across the dignified man who had chaperoned her from Brunswick, and batted her pale eye lashes at the married Duke of York. "I cannot say that I would mind keeping a bit of company with *you!*"

Good God, thought George, she was vulgar, as well. He closed his eyes and called for another glass of wine. Yes, precisely what he deserved.

MARIA HELD UP THE SKIRT of her saffron taffeta gown and lowered her head as Francis helped her into his waiting carriage. It was a lovely day, as lovely a spring day as she could ever remember. The sky was a cloudless china blue, and a cool breeze ruffled their clothes and hair as it swept up full of butterflies sparkling from the silvery Thames.

It had been her choice, three years after her separation from George, finally to go up to London. They were going to Tattersall's, the auctioneer at Hyde Park Corner, to look at thoroughbreds. That had been her ostensible reason. But more important, there was a Royal wedding finally taking place at St. James's Palace.

"Are you certain you are up to this?" Francis asked, settling into the worn leather seat beside her.

Since he had taken a house out in Twickenham to be near her, he had little used the larger carriage. The aroma that came from the seats and the quilted door panels as the driver sealed them inside was miserably musty. Maria took out her fan and opened it, moving the air between them with delicate little flicks. "As ready as I shall ever be," she said in reply and did her best to give him a convincing smile.

What Maria did not have the courage to tell him was that she *must* be in London today. It had been eight months since she and George had spoken a word. But even with their estrangement, beneath the sight of God, they were still bound as man and wife. The wounds may have begun to heal on the surface, but at their depth, they would never heal. She would never be able to convince herself he had found the courage to marry another woman, unless she was there in London nearby.

The auction house would be close enough.

"This isn't the way to Hyde Park Corner," Francis said late that afternoon as his carriage circled around Charing Cross and headed down Pall Mall. He glanced out the window and then over at Maria but she was staring straight ahead, her face unmoving. "Did you speak to my driver without telling me?"

"I requested that he cross by St. James's Street."

"You mean you asked him to cross by St. James's Palace!" He turned and took her shoulder, squeezing it until she felt the blood begin to pulse beneath the skin. "Good Lord, Maria, what good can come of it?"

When she did finally look at him, her face was tinged with an inexpressible sadness, one that took his breath away. *Bloody fool,* he thought angrily of the self-indulgent Prince. *Even now after all you have done to her, she loves you still. And this is how you repay her trust? Her fidelity? A public marriage, and bigamy for all the world to see?*

"I don't know what can come of it, Francis," Maria said softly. "I know only that it is something I must do."

"But it has been years. It is over between you. He has seen to that. Can we not try to put all of this behind us, finally?"

"Perhaps after today we can."

When they settled back against the carriage seat, Maria looked once again from her window. She had asked the driver to take a small detour through St. James's Square because she once had especially liked it. The square had not changed, but even here her feeling for the city that had so maligned her definitely had.

The buildings were still elegant and orderly, and in the center was a grand splashing fountain, past which groups of well-dressed ladies and gentlemen strolled, their arms laden with packages.

As they moved back onto Pall Mall, their carriage tangled with the afternoon crush of other phaetons, tilburies, and tandems. Coachmen yelled "Whoa!" as carriage wheels clicked and horse hooves clopped across the pavement.

She heard the shiver of the chestnut trees in the waning sun and the warbled strains of the vendors calling, "Gingerbread!" from the crowded street corners. Yet another was singing for shillings and holding up ripe, red apples as their carriage passed by. Maria felt herself smile until she remembered the real reason for which she had finally, grudgingly returned to London.

"We don't have to do this, you know," Francis murmured.

Maria stared straight ahead. Resolute. Unmoving. "But *I* do."

St. James's Palace was crowded with the carriages of wedding guests all of the way down St. James's Street to Piccadilly. She signaled for their driver to stop at the corner facing the palace, a Renaissance structure made of dark red brick.

"It is nearly seven o'clock. They must be taking their vows just now."

He looked over at her. "How do you know that?"

Maria's unmarred, ivory face was silhouetted against the burning orange sunset. Quickly the sky darkened to violet, then paled to gray as the sun dipped below the London skyline. "I just know," she answered, her head held high, hands clasped delicately in her lap.

But when the bells of the Chapel Royal rang out at half past seven, Maria gripped his arm suddenly. Her heart stopped beating. Now it was really over. He had actually done it. The Prince of Wales was now a man with two wives; *one in the eyes of God ... the other in the eyes of England.*

He watched the tears glisten in her brown eyes, darkening them to coal, but they did not fall. "I want to go home, Francis. Please, take me home."

He felt her shudder against him and heard a small, strangled sound, but still she would not cry. It startled him to see how quickly she could change, in a heartbeat how her defenses could be completely torn away; how vulnerable she truly was beneath that proud, brave exterior. He kissed her cheek softly, wanting to do so much

277

more to comfort her. "Your house has been opened and your staff shall be waiting for us."

"No! I don't want to go there! Not ever again. It is his house, not mine! Take me to *your* house, Francis, please!" She looked up at him with the desperate need of a child and his heart leaped with a mixture of grief and complete devotion. The house she could not bear to see was one that George had leased and decorated for her so grandly. It would be filled with the prying eyes of servants who knew as well as she precisely just what had occurred that day at St. James's Palace.

Francis leveled his gaze to hers. "But my house has been closed since winter. There are no servants there. There is no food, probably nothing to heat the place."

She shifted closer to him and reached up with her fingers to touch his face. The tears, glistening in her eyes, still did not fall. "I don't care. I don't care about any of it! Just take me away from here, Francis. Please! Take me away now!"

She was too close for him to think, her soft fingers touching his face and the other hand still pressed into his arm. Her perfume and her nearness made him drunk with lust. He kissed her forehead and felt his groin surge. At that moment George, and the reality of what Maria felt for him, seemed very far away.

"As you wish," he said gravely, kissing her forehead again.

The elegant white house on Curzon Street opposite the Mayfair Chapel stood back from the street behind a well-tended lawn and was shaded by plane trees. Inside, the darkness made it seem less grand. The furniture was covered with white cloths and it was as cold and dark as a funeral chamber.

Maria stood behind Francis in the entrance hall, dotted with recesses that were filled with marble busts. She held up a single glowing candle.

"Just as I told you," he turned back to her. "Positively dreadful. Are you certain you want to stay?" When she nodded he said, "Very well, then. Let me go and tell the driver to bring in our things. I shall tell him to come back for us in the morning."

When he disappeared, out into the courtyard, Maria walked slowly into the drawing room. The moon's glow lit the blue damask-colored room as though it were storm gray. It was a room very much like the Duke of Bedford. Everything was ordered, tables and chairs beside one another, all perfectly matched.

The carpet beneath her feet was one of the key elements of the room. It echoed the pattern of the high ceiling above them. There was a huge fireplace with a painting of a dour, aged-looking man over the mantel. Beside it was a dusty pianoforte only half covered with a white sheet. She moved to it, sat on the little needlepoint bench, and the sheet fell away. It had been nearly a year since she had played.

In a veil of memories, of things they had done, and things they had never found time to do, Maria thought now how she had so rarely played for George. She touched the a key with one slim finger and the sound echoed through the hollow, vacant house. *Stupid, gullible woman!* she thought achingly as she tapped the same key again and again and the house was filled with the discordant sound.

Francis came into the drawing room and saw her slumped over the pianoforte, sobbing into her folded arms. Finally, as he knew they must, the tears had come. He motioned for the driver to leave them and waited until they were alone to go to her.

"Oh, Francis! I am such a foolish woman!" she cried as he swept her up into his arms. "In spite of everything, I wanted him."

"Shh, my angel," he said, caressing her hair. "You are a trusting, wonderful woman who believed in the sanctity of her vows."

"Vows! Ah, what a laugh that is!" she cried out bitterly and her tears spilled like rain onto his dark blue tailcoat. "Dear God, I have had enough torment to last a lifetime! I don't want any more!"

"Then there shall be no more. Not with me. I promise you."

His words were a balm on the tattered shreds of her emotions and she melted against his body. It would have been so easy to over-power her now like this. But he loved her too much. Instead, he stood patiently in the darkness, held her and let her cry for every-thing that loving George had cost her. She had borne it with such dignity for so long that the tears, when they came now, were accom-panied by almost convulsive sobs.

Her dark green cloak had fallen halfway down her shoulders as her body was racked with emotion. Instinctively he reached down to catch it. Slowly he pulled it back up, inadvertently touching her bare neck. It was every bit as soft and luxuriant as his fantasy.

"Why, Francis? Why did it have to come to this when I loved him so much?" she was saying in little spasms between the sobs.

When he looked at her face, that beautiful visage that had ruined him for any other, he saw that it was swollen with tears. Her slim nose and unpainted face were mottled red. He kissed her cheek softly and tasted the salty tears.

"Hush now, my angel. Hush." He kissed her other cheek as tenderly as the first and she reached up and fingered a lock of his hair.

He felt a shiver of excitement at her touch and hated himself a little for it. She was so vulnerable, but he could not stop himself from softly touching the tip of her nose with his lips, then her cheeks again and again. It was as sweet and velvety as he had always known it would be.

Francis paused a moment, their faces close, nearly touching. He felt Maria's arms twine around him, suggesting that if he would but touch her lips with his own there would be more. He pulled away quickly.

"Come. It has been a long day," he said. "I shall show you to your room."

Maria followed him silently into the hall and up the sweeping, mahogany staircase without protest. He heard her footfalls come more slowly behind his. It was a strain, after so much emotion, poor darling, for her even to walk. He carried her bag in one arm and a sputtering candle in the other.

Like a wilted flower, she clung to the door frame as Francis set her bag down and lit two glass lamps with the single flame. The room deepened to bronze. It was a small room with salmon-colored draperies covering the window and a matching coverlet on the heavy poster bed. Two large pastoral landscapes done in muted greens, browns, and blues ornamented the walls on both sides of the unlit fireplace.

"It is far from grand now," he said as he closed the curtains and turned back the bedcovers for her. "But I thought you would be more comfortable here than in one of the larger rooms, since we have nothing with which to light a fire."

She tried to smile. "I will be fine."

She waited in the same place as though the door frame alone was bearing her weight while he went back down and brought a full pitcher of water and some towels. "I thought after the long ride today you might like to freshen up a little before you retire."

"Thank you, Francis," she replied softly, gazing up at him with the wide eyes of a child. "Thank you for everything."

"Sleep well." He smiled and moved past her swiftly, afraid to pause a moment longer.

"Must you leave?"

Francis stopped once he was safely out in the dim hallway. He turned back around and his heart swelled when he looked at her, so beaten and fragile, lit like a white dove, golden in the glow of the candlelight. "I think it would be best."

But she held out her graceful hand to him and the lace spilled back from her wrist. "Please stay with me...only for a little while."

She took his hand and led him across the room to the painted beechwood stand where the pitcher of water and the collection of towels lay beside the second lamp. Slowly, she began to unfasten the breast buttons of her forest green redingote. She peeled it away to the white shirt beneath.

Francis watched her, his eyes fixed on the rise of her breasts, unable to speak up in protest. A button at a time, she unfastened the shirt and tossed it to the carpet as she had the other pieces of clothing. He stood mesmerized before her, unable to move.

She removed the pins from her hair and the golden tendrils spilled in a cascading mane onto her back and shoulders. Slowly, she moistened a small cloth and looked back at him.

Now the tears were gone and the swollen features of her face had softened. She did not speak as she held out the cloth to him, meeting his gaze completely, but he knew that she wanted him to touch her. His blood burned with desire, searing his skin and blotting out his reason. He should not. It was not right to take advantage of her this way.

When she insisted, he took the moist cloth from her hand, his fingers trembling, and ran it across her pale shoulder. He watched her eyes flutter to a close. The rich lines of her body were bare to him now as she stood in her camisole and heavy green skirts.

He was thankful that she could not see him. That way he was free from guilt to explore the elegant curves of her breasts. He moved his fingers slowly across her neck and then downward to the swell beneath the layer of cotton and lace. Her head fell back and he heard a little moan come from the back of her throat. They were close again. He could feel her breath on his face.

Then she opened her eyes to him, eyes as deep and rich as melting chocolate. "Do you want me?" she whispered, and ran her hand again through his tangled gold-gray hair.

"I—"

She put a finger to his lips to silence the objections she sensed, then replaced it with her own lips. She moved closer and wrapped her arms around him. "Please say that you want me, Francis. Please, I need to hear that I am desirable."

"More than anything I want you, my angel. More than anything, I do want you..." he finally whispered back into her hair.

It had been years since he had been with anyone but one of the prostitutes in Covent Garden, and when his passion overwhelmed him he forgot how to be gentle. Francis pressed her forcefully back into the bed and sprawled over her, straining to undo his slim breeches.

He was kissing her mouth, forcing his tongue so deeply into her throat that she could barely breathe. But Maria did not struggle against him. The more frenzied it became the more she wanted him—the more she wanted anyone who wanted her. She knew that Francis was still in love with her but giving herself to him this way made the disappointment and the pain she had borne today a weight she could almost bear.

He lifted her skirts and the layers of petticoats as he whispered her name over and over again into the luxuriant tangles of her honey-blond hair. He pushed inside of her in a single swift movement, knowing he could never be close enough. She was everything that was good and desirable to him. She was the only woman he wanted in the world. Yet she was the one woman he knew, even now, he would never have completely.

Only a moment later, overwhelmed by this, by her body, by the precious jewel he held in his arms at last, he shivered and fell limp against her and the bunches of fabric around them.

As Francis still lay on top of her, his heart beating wildly against her chest, Maria felt a strange indifference. But it was not regret. She was not sorry this had happened. Nor would she ever be. It had been a matter of survival.

I may never love another man but you, George Augustus, she was thinking as Francis Russell slowly pulled himself from her body. *But so help me God, I will not let you destroy my heart entirely!* It was also the last thought she had before she fell asleep in someone else's safe, gentle, and very protective arms.

SHE DID NOT KNOW HOW long she had been asleep, but when Maria awoke, a warm fire sputtered and cracked in the hearth beside the bed and she was alone. On the pillow beside her was a single pale pink rose. The sweet fragrance and the fire helped to warm the dampness out of the long-sealed room.

Maria stretched as gracefully as a swan and then smiled. She was still glad it had happened. The pain was not so dark, so unbearable, by the light of this new day. There was not the same passion there was with George, nor was his body so robust or appealing, but Francis was a good and kind man. It had been right between them. Just as she tried to sit up the door squealed and then opened.

"Good morning," he said smiling as he moved across the room toward her.

He was dressed only in a loose, white shirt and tight black breeches. In his arms, he held a tray laden with food. She could smell the welcome aroma of freshly made tea.

"What have you found? I thought you said there was nothing to be had here."

He sat down beside her on the edge of the bed and ran a hand across her face to brush the unruly hair from her eyes. She yawned as he set the tray between them. "So I did, but I've found tea, some biscuits, jam, and even some candied plums."

"A feast!" She smiled.

He poured the tea and handed her a cup. As she sipped the warm liquid, something made her think of the first time she had watched him drink tea in her drawing room, those years ago. But when she looked at him now, lifting his own cup to his lips, all she saw was a gentle man full of infinite kindness. Impulsively she reached over and kissed his cheek.

He smiled and set the cup back down on the tray. "What was that for?"

"For you. For being the man I finally see that you are."

"No regrets?"

"None."

He touched the back of her hand. "Are you warm enough?"

"The fire is lovely. But where did you find the —" Her voice trailed off as she glanced over at the hearth and saw what remained of a an expensive Hepplewhite chair. "Oh, Francis, you didn't!"

"Well I couldn't very well let you freeze to death, now could I? It may be spring but the nights in an old house like this are still cold. And besides, I was thinking of replacing it anyway."

His impulsiveness surprised her and made her smile. It was a side of him she had never seen before. "Oh you were, were you?" she laughed and kissed the tip of his nose.

"Yes, I was indeed," he said and playfully kissed her nose in return.

This time when he reached out to touch her, he found her bare breasts with more patient hands than he had the night before. He moved his finger gently across the nipples and looked back at her. Maria set the tray carefully onto the night table and let him press his mouth onto hers.

After they made love a second time, she lay bound by his arms, feeling as if she never wanted to be set free. It had been a long time, this peace.

"Are you hungry?" he asked.

"Famished."

Francis sat up and took the tray back onto the bed with them. "I'm afraid the tea's gone cold."

"A small price to pay," she said, snuggling against his chest.

They ate all of the biscuits and most of the candied plums as they sat cross-legged on the bed beside the fire. They laughed together and, as they ate, both of them recounted stories about the awkwardness of their childhood and the years before they had met. Francis wanted to know everything about her and Maria freely confided in him. The sun had long since risen but they had kept the room dark with drawn draperies, savoring the last moments of intimacy between them.

Finally Francis drew her to him and kissed her as if it would be their last. Then he moved from the bed and began to dress.

"Our driver will be here soon," he said.

"Oh, can we not stay a little while longer?"

"You know that people would talk."

She laughed an unexpected bitter sweet laugh and brushed the crumbs from the bedcovers. "That is certainly something to which I have grown accustomed."

He looked back at her from the foot of the bed, as though he too would like to have stayed. Then he turned away and walked toward the door. "I shall give you time to dress."

"You don't trust yourself with me?" she asked with a clever smile.

Francis turned the handle and opened the door but he would not, could not, look back at her lying naked, as beautiful as a goddess, in the bed they had shared. "Nor, I fear, shall I ever be able to again" was all he managed to say before he smiled at her and then went out of the room.

THE YEAR THAT FOLLOWED HIS marriage to Caroline of Brunswick was a tumultuous one for the Prince of Wales. Within weeks of the ceremony at St. James's Palace, it was reported that Her Royal Highness was with child—a child George did not want, created with a coarse, slothful woman he had quickly come to despise. His new wife still seldom bothered to wash, nor even change her underclothes, he soon discovered. But even more unforgivable than her lack of personal hygiene was that the new Princess of Wales was *not* Maria.

As salt on a wound that he had inflicted upon himself, Frances Jersey (of whom he had long ago regretted ever knowing) remained on as the Princess of Wales's principal lady-in-waiting. Not only had his supposed mistress been present at the wedding, but she had been honored with this most desirable post as a reward for her efforts in separating the Heir Apparent from a Catholic.

In January, exactly nine months after his second marriage, the bells of London rang out from the high and gilded steeples of London, proclaiming the birth of a daughter to the Prince and Princess of Wales. The child was named Charlotte, in honor of her grandmother, the reigning Queen of England.

"Oh, I am sorry. I don't know why it should bother me any longer." Maria wept unexpectedly as Lady Clermont kindly held her in a motherly embrace.

"There, there, child," she said softly as she stroked her silky hair in the drawing room of Maria's newly purchased house on Tilney Street in Mayfair. "You mustn't be so hard on yourself about it all. You really have been dealt a rather nasty blow."

"But it has been almost a year since they married, and more than three since I have even seen him."

"And you know what they say about absence and the heart, child."

Maria sniffled and wiped away the unwelcome tears with a white handkerchief. "But I do not love him any longer! How can I? He is another woman's husband!"

"But he belonged to you first, did he not?" the old woman knowingly asked, and smiled with a kindness that brought another onslaught of tears.

"It is just all so wretched." Maria wept. "And whether I am out at Twickenham, or here in London, it never seems to end. Have you seen the latest caricature by that vermin, Gillray? He has outdone himself with his cruelty this time. He has drawn the Princess of Wales and I fighting one another for the three feathers of the Wales. And, as usual, has seen that it is plastered all over town!"

"My dear child," Lady Clermont said tenderly, patting Maria's hands as Belle Pigot brought tea and blackberry scones. "Have you not yet learned that you cannot battle this sort of thing yourself, and win? Your only recourse, if you are to survive, is to rise above it."

Maria looked into the eyes of a woman who had seen far more of the world than she. They were kind sky-blue eyes, shaded by an overhanging brow and surrounded by a deeply etched pattern of wrinkles. "But how can I?"

"First of all, my dear, you can accomplish it by not keeping so much to this new house of yours, lovely as it is. You have a devoted circle of friends here in London whose admiration for you in all of this has only deepened. Get out. Put yourself among us. Let those of us who admire you for what you have endured give you the strength you need just now."

"If you will pardon the observation, ma'am," said Belle Pigot as she set down the tray, "I quite agree with Her Ladyship."

Lady Clermont tapped her own bony knee. "There. You see?"

Maria looked at each of them in turn. Perhaps they were right at that. Since she had returned to London last spring, Maria had kept to the exclusive company of her companion, Belle; Horatia Seymour; the Duke of Bedford; and occasionally, on unexpected afternoons such as this, Lady Clermont.

But hiding away as she had would change nothing. Time only moved forward. They could never go back. George was married now...*legally,* in the eyes of the world. And they had a child. She had cried enough tears for him, lost what had remained of her youth in a marriage that would never be considered legal. It was time for her to start living again.

As they nibbled on scones and sipped their tea, Jacko Payne showed the Duke of Bedford into the drawing room. It was raining again and his hair and face glistened with a thin patina of moisture. He brushed his gloved hand across his face to wipe away what he could and came into the room.

"Ah, Lady Clermont. What a pleasant surprise." He nodded as he removed his gloves and handed them to Jacko along with a dark wool cloak.

"Yes. I did come without an invitation. But I thought perhaps our dear Maria here could use a bit of cheer today."

"That was kind of you indeed."

"Maria is a dear girl."

"I take it then that you've heard about England's new little Princess," he said casually, taking one of the scones.

"I doubt that there is anyone in London who has not heard," Lady Clermont replied wondering how someone who claimed such great affection for Maria could be cruel enough to have spoken about it so bluntly.

But when she watched him look at her, the old woman under-

287

stood. It was all over London that the Duke of Bedford was the one who had single-handedly saved her from herself in those first dark days after the Prince of Wales's marriage.

They were said to have become the best of friends. Some people whispered that perhaps they were even more than that. Regardless of what was between them, one thing was certain. Maria did not love him.

I am an old woman and I have seen a great deal of life through these tired eyes, she thought as the Duke took a chair beside Maria, and followed her every change of expression. *When that young woman looks at him there is nothing there but gratitude. Yet the poor man is desperately in love...A shame she will never feel for anyone but the Prince of Wales what the Duke of Bedford so obviously feels for her.*

THE GOLDEN LIGHT OF A hundred candles set the house ablaze. Lively music filled the drawing room, the dining room, and all of the adjoining halls in between. Guests clustered around a table draped with white cloth and covered with a grand display of ham in Madeira wine sauce, pheasant in truffles, and almond cake. Other guests sipped wine and whispered approval of the lovely house that the Prince of Wales's dear first wife had bought entirely for herself.

After the manner in which she had been so unceremoniously discarded, she really was better off without him, most of them added... but they did so only beneath their breath.

All of the fashionable world of London had come tonight to Maria's new Tilney Street address. Lord and Lady Clermont sat speaking with the Duke of Bedford before the pistachio green tile fireplace while Richard Sheridan and his wife, Elizabeth, spoke with Maria's brother beneath a painting of their father.

Elizabeth, a small woman with pale brown curls and a turned-up nose, was laughing gayly as she stood elegantly gowned in delicate blue and white cotton. Across the room, Lord Hugh Seymour was recounting war stories and the tale of the thanks from the House of Parliament and the medal he had received for his courage at the helm of his ship, the *Leviathan*. Horatia stood beside him whispering proudly about their newest addition—Finally they had their daughter.

But most comforting to Maria in his attendance was George's own brother Frederick, the Duke of York. Through all of this ugly business he had remained her dear friend and her great supporter. ("If you're ready to take on the world again, Maria," he had said yesterday on this brief return home from the Continent, "then we shall see it is a party London shall not be allowed to forget!")

He came up now with a goblet of wine and kissed her on the cheek. "Splendid party. I knew it would be." He winked and walked back into the drawing room with windows that fronted fashionable Park Lane.

Maria was radiant in a sheer high-waisted pink gown with lace and silver borders trailed everywhere by a soft cloud of her elegant lavender perfume. Her headdress, the newest fashion, was topped strikingly with ostrich feathers. The guests watched her with admiration as she moved freely among them, smiling and nodding and checking to see that their wine glasses were kept full.

The Duke of Bedford watched her too. She was laughing at something Hugh Seymour had said and her face was glowing. Things between them had never been so intimate again as they had been that first spring night in London. But he clung full of hope to the memory of what they had shared. He also held fast to the belief, now the Prince of Wales was a father, that she would finally be able, once and for all, to let go of the dream that they might one day be reconciled.

MARIA COULD NOT STOP TREMBLING.

"She is so beautiful, she takes my breath away."

"Go on. Hold her if you like." Horatia smiled proudly as the two women peered into the cradle at the Seymours' baby daughter, their first girl, a child they had named Mary.

"Oh, I couldn't possibly. She's so small."

"You won't break her."

Maria hesitated as she looked back at the cooing infant with hair the color of her mother's, and the same wide hazel eyes. She was gowned in ivory satin and lace fit for a princess, and she smelled as sweet as a basket of spring flowers.

"Go on," Horatia encouraged. "She loves to be held."

There was no feeling in the world like holding a newborn child.

Maria had forgotten that, and she felt a sudden rush of emotion. To be a mother. It was the thing she wanted most in the world. The one thing that would have made her separation from George almost bearable.

As she held little Mary in her arms, Maria lifted a finger and instinctively the child grasped it with her whole tiny hand. "She's so strong!"

"Thank the good Lord she takes after her father."

Maria looked back at Horatia. Her chest was rising and falling with every breath. How could there be such joy and yet such utter sadness in the coming of a child? But since Mary's birth, Horatia's health had begun to worsen. She was bound to her bed much of the time and the cough she suffered had gotten worse.

"She likes you."

Maria smiled in agreement and looked back down at the little child who seemed completely contented there in her arms. "George and I thought we might have a child, once."

Her words were softly spoken but Horatia heard the longing in them. "You would have made a splendid mother."

"Yes. Well. Apparently that too is something that was just never meant to be."

Suddenly, Horatia leaned against the door frame and without warning began to falter. "Are you all right?"

"Fine," she answered, pressing a hand to her chest. "Just a bit weary. Perhaps I should lie down. But you and Mary are having such a nice visit, you're welcome to stay as long as you like."

"Thank you, my friend," Maria said with a smile, and they both knew how deeply she meant it.

Once Horatia had been helped from the nursery by her lady's maid, Maria went to the window and sat in a grand stuffed chair beside a chest of toys. The baby had already begun to nod off to sleep in her arms.

"Oh, yes. How much I wanted a little one like you," Maria said in a soft, lyrical voice as she gently rocked her. "If I had only had a child, somehow I believe all of this would have been a bit easier to bear. It would have been the one thing even the laws of England could not have taken from me."

She put her finger to the child's cheek. The feel of it was soft, so soft, and warm. Maria, transfixed, watched the little face, all inno-cence and beauty. Then all at once, as if roused from a bad dream, the child woke and began to cry.

"Hush, my little precious," Maria whispered, her heart brimming with regret. For George. For the child they would never have. For all of the love she had to give, to no one at all. "I shall stay until you fall asleep again. I won't leave you. I promise."

Maria sat like that, holding Horatia's baby, stroking her cheek, rocking her back and forth, and feeling a kind of fulfillment she had only imagined. As early-evening shadows danced on the walls, she stayed, and thought of how it might have been. How it was instead. And she tried very hard not to cry.

BENEATH A SILVERY SLIVER OF a moon, a black phaeton sat alone on Park Street facing Tilney. The carriage and two slate-colored stallions were hidden by the darkness of the night. George had chosen that carriage intentionally.

They faced a small rosy brick house with two tall sash windows exactly spaced around the door. A single light on the second floor glowed like a deep gold beacon. It must be her room. She was just beyond that window, George thought...a few feet away really, and yet by the circumstances that life had dealt them, by the choices he had made, they could not have been further apart.

It had been three days since his daughter's birth. A child with someone other than Maria was still something for which he could never forgive himself, especially knowing what motherhood had meant to her. He had lain with Caroline only in the beginning. *His duty.* That first time, their wedding night, was an event of state and a dark memory that haunted him still. It was the night he had consummated, and thus validated, a marriage that never should have been at all. When there had been no choice, and for so many reasons he had indeed married Caroline. But to make him go against his will—and his heart—George had got drunk, *very* drunk.

"Great Zeus!" Frederick had mouthed, his face paling as he first saw his flush-faced elder brother, swaying like a moored ship in the room behind the church altar. "You cannot marry like this! You can scarcely walk!"

"I was stone sober at my last wedding," George slurred. "The diversity shall be a pleasant change."

No matter how much he had drunk the night before, and that morning as well, the palliative could not erase the unpleasant image of the bride from his mind. Dark, tight curls, bulging blue eyes in a round, overly ruddy face, and that vulgar throaty laugh.

I cannot go through with it, had been his first thought that morning as he dressed. This had been a horrid miscalculation—a grand gesture he could carry through. Yet carry through with it, he did, held up quite literally at the altar by two of his brothers, and supported on either side by the two of them all the way to the marriage bed.

Both events George recalled now only through the thick, blue veil of cherry brandy that had sustained him that day. His first impressions of Caroline had proven true. She could not have been more different from Maria and that, perhaps, was a very good thing for the punishment he felt he deserved to suffer on. The coarse and bawdy sense of humor that he had witnessed at their meeting had continued, and he knew from his first conjugal touch of her bare flesh that the Brunswick princess was no virgin bride.

"Tell me what pleases you, George," she had muttered in an accent thickly laden with her Germanic roots, as she lolled beneath him in his grand poster bed. "And I shall make you forget you ever heard the name Fitzherbert!"

The laugh then, as always, guttural and harsh, stopped his heart and George's blood ran instantly cold. "You foul, foolish woman!" He moved away from her. "You have no idea a'tall, do you, how impossible that is!"

Yet forget he did. For a brief time that night he gave himself over besottedly to her flesh and his own. But each time he went to her afterward in those first blinding, drunken days, it was always the same. Maria's face came between them and remained. Her trusting expression, the essence of her kindness were like icy water, reminding him of what he had done, what he had lost, and who it was that would never escape his heart.

After only a few weeks, unable to bear the hypocrisy of the crass woman whom everyone in England (everyone but he) now considered his wife, George had gone away to Windsor. His deception to Maria had served its purpose well. The scandal about the Protestant prince and the Catholic widow had gradually subsided. The voracious rumor mill had been appeased. Lady Jersey and the Princess of Wales had taken Maria's place as the object of gossip and the subject of caricatures. But, God help him, even now after he had destroyed it, that did not stop him from desperately missing the one true love of his life.

Try as he might, George could not push the thought of her from his heart or his mind. Maria had been his touchstone, the only one who had ever mattered. Continuing to live a lie with Caroline would never change that. And so, having done his duty to Maria, and to England, he had separated from Caroline. Formally. Permanently. No matter what happened, George knew he would always have but one wife. And he had sought to make at least some part of that first marriage legal.

In the darkness, George drew a collection of papers from the pocket in his greatcoat, then opened them. He did not need to read them now for they were words burned into his mind and heart. Words he had written himself. He ran his fingers across the dried black ink.

By this, my last Will and Testament I now bequeath, give and settle at my death all my worldly property of every description, denomination and sort, personal and other, to my Maria Fitzherbert, my Wife, the Wife of my heart and soul. Although by the laws of this country she could not avail herself publicly of that name, still such she is in the eyes of Heaven, was, is and will be such in mine...

I desire that I may be buried with as little pomp as possible, and that my constant companion, the picture of my beloved Wife, my Maria Fitzherbert, may be interred with me, suspended round my neck by a ribbon as I used to wear it when I lived, and placed right upon my heart...

"This is the only consolation I deserve," he whispered, meaning the will. Gazing up at her window, he tore the velvet cord from around his neck until it snapped and the miniature of Maria tumbled into his hand. "And at that, I should be grateful."

Unable to move, he watched as a lamp in Maria's drawing room was lit. Then another, and the house was filled with warm golden light. He could see Jacko Payne through the bow window lighting a fire—it was then that he turned away; the longing in it was almost too much to bear.

George had discovered that Maria was back in London from Twickenham and she intended to stay for the season. He had appeared in all of the same places he knew she was likely to go, hoping to run into her in public since he knew she would never see him in private.

He went to the opera as he had that first night at the Theater Royal. To the Drury Lane Theater. Even to Almack's. But none of it to any avail. "This is foolish," he had told himself that last time as he had settled back into the coach seat and shaken his head, not knowing what he could possibly have said to her anyway.

George gazed back now up at her bedroom window as a shadowy figure of a woman moved toward the light. *Maria*.

He could see an elegant grass-green gown, her head held up serenely. She had not changed, he thought as a weak smile tugged at his lips. She was still like a wonderfully elegant little bird, one he had captured for a while, who had charmed his life into something exquisite. A fantasy. But, like dreams, all fantasies end, as well. Still, he had done the right thing, he reminded himself yet again, a silent mantra now.

He had found the strength to set her free when it had mattered most. It helped to remember that. Bathed in the tender glow of Maria's love, he had become a man of honor. A man who made his own choices in spite of the cost. It was what she had always wanted for him. What she believed he was capable of. The strength of spirit to be a great King. Now, at last, he was ready to take on the world.

There was only one thing he still desired more.

CHAPTER SEVENTEEN

FREDERICK BELIEVED IT BEST THAT he be the one to go to Maria—that he be the one initially to make a proposal of reconciliation. He had made the commitment to do so one evening after George had finally revealed the details of their separation, sharing with him the full and noble reason why he had been driven to set Maria free. Yet once there with her, gazing into her wounded brown eyes, Frederick found that he simply could not force himself to urge her to take his tarnished brother back into her life. The best he could do for his love of both of them was urge her at least to meet with George—to have a conversation face to face.

"But, after everything you have endured for him these past years," Frederick finally said, once the idea had finally found its way out between them, "it is a decision only you can make. What I will say is that, as my brothers have, I have always considered you George's real and only wife."

"You are a dear friend, Freddie," she said, her voice catching on her tears. "Thank you for always trying so mightily to help."

He pressed a kiss onto her forehead and tasted the sweet lavender water with which she bathed. "I wish only that I could do more."

Days passed after that. Maria was held captive emotionally, bound by her love for George and by her pain. She had promised to have him *for better, for worse* and it was a vow she had not taken lightly. By the laws of the Church, she was indeed his wife. By the law of the land, however, Caroline was his wife and—estranged or not—she was still the mother of his only child. She was also the Princess of Wales. Even Frederick's telling her that afternoon that Caroline had told him personally she knew about the situation and she hoped they could find a way to reconcile gave Maria little comfort. It still seemed an impossible situation. At the end of the day, he was still a man with two wives. By every law and moral code she knew, that was wrong.

In a curious turn in the days following Frederick's visit, other members of the royal family joined the second son with a chorus of pleading in the hope that Maria would take back the Heir. It was her duty, they said, to do so. To save him. To save the Crown.

But as what, she asked herself? *Wife? Mistress?*

"So what is it that you wish to do, child?" asked Lady Clermont as they sat together beneath an arbor bursting with sweet blooming roses in the days after Frederick's visit.

"If I only knew." She mouthed the words and each one of them was more painful than the last. "It is all so confusing."

"Your heart says one thing but your mind says another, hmm?"

Maria tried to smile. Lady Clermont was bent and withered now, a gentle remnant of another era. But this kind old woman with the traces of red rouge suffusing her ribbed, wrinkled face had come to know her so well, and there was great comfort in that. "After everything that he has done to me...to us, and with this anger inside my heart, Lord help me, how can I still care for him?"

"Dear child," she softly chuckled, and the sound alone was reassuring. "Perhaps it is because you know, and have always known on some level, that what he did, he did for love of you."

Maria turned and watched a butterfly, a bright blue fluttering creature, circling around her and then land on her sleeve. "You know the first time I ever saw him, it was on the Mall. He galloped up on a stallion, windblown and wild looking, and he flirted with me openly in my carriage."

Lady Clermont smiled a sage smile and touched Maria's knee. "That does not surprise me."

"Well, it completely unnerved *me*. I was certain he was the most handsome man I had ever seen and yet there was this winsome, childlike quality that drew me to him like no one else in my life had ever done. Everyone I had known before George was so certain of themselves. So full of predictability, of what life...and love was supposed to be about. But not George. No, not him. How I fought him every step of the way..." She paused, collecting herself. "And when we finally did come together, it was like the missing piece to a puzzle in me, a piece I didn't even realize was supposed to be there until he fought to make me see it."

"He's a very complicated man, my dear."

Maria took a deep, soulful breath. "I did not know it at first, but he was full of a great many demons when we met, elements from his past he could never quite vanquish. The need to keep things from me, to engage in deceptions he can somehow justify. I pleaded with him in Brighton to tell me why he was pulling away."

"And if he had told you it was his desire to protect you by leaving what would you have done?"

"I would have stopped him! I would have told him it was our burden to bear together!"

"He loved you enough to let you go in order to keep you safe. He could not have done that if you had remained by his side."

"He did *not* love me enough to be honest with me."

"I have come to believe the Prince did the very best, the most honorable thing for his wife, at the time." Lady Clermont patted Maria's knee gently with a bony, age-spotted hand. "And I find that I respect him for that."

Maria bit back a small smile. "How is it that you always know the right thing to say to me?"

"Age does have its privileges, my dear," she said, coming back on her feet with the help of an elegant little silver-tipped cane. "So then. Do you wish to risk a meeting with him?" she asked as they began to walk again, side by side, among the hollyhocks and the foxglove.

"Perhaps God prefers that things are left to lie."

The spirited old woman looked over at Maria and crooked an eyebrow. "So that is what is at the root of it, hmm? Your religion?"

"It is a question of bigamy this time, Lady Clermont, not faith! He has another wife, a child now!"

"That one dangerous act, his marriage to the Princess of Wales, if I may say, has given you the safety from prosecution without which you could never hope to live in peace with your George. I believe I have come to know you quite well these past years, dear heart. I know that is truly all you wish—all you have ever wished, not a royal title for yourself, nor glory, nor fame."

"I would have loved George had he been a pauper."

"Speak with your priest, Maria," she said, braiding their fingers, one hand withered, the other smooth and slender. "Seek his counsel on the matter, and if he approves, then be at peace to follow your heart, and your destiny. After all, in this life there really is nowhere else for any one of us to go, is there?"

Follow your heart, she had said in a voice of wisdom.

In her heart, Maria wanted to meet with him, once again to be with the tender, sweet George she had known at Brighton. But even a first meeting was not that simple. Nothing was that simple anymore. He was not the same man. She certainly was not the same woman. There was time and distance between them now—the problems of even considering some sort of reconciliation.

And there was the Duke of Bedford.

Francis had loved her from the beginning. He had been her greatest supporter, and yet he had asked for nothing in return. Now that she had discovered love alone was not enough, Maria could not help but wonder if she did not owe herself and Francis a chance at something more than friendship.

"At the very least, think about what I have said, child." Lady Clermont patted her shoulder.

Maria's answer was a deep sigh as she looked away. *How*, she thought, *shall I manage to think of anything else?*

CHAPTER EIGHTEEN

IN THE AUTUMN, JUST AS the leaves had begun to change, Father Nassau, the Catholic priest whom Maria had commissioned to go and lay her case before the Holy See, returned to London with a Papal Brief. His Holiness had reviewed her case and found her to be the true wife of the Prince of Wales, according to the law of the Church. He had said that if His Royal Highness was truly sincere in his promises and penitent for his sins when they met, then Maria would be free to rejoin him and to live as his wife.

On the morning after Maria had met with her priest, Horatia Seymour came to see her. She had to be helped by both Jacko and Fanny into a chair.

"I've come to say good-bye," she said, and the words were spoken with great difficulty. "I am going away."

"What do you mean, going away? Where?"

She swallowed with difficulty. "Hugh wants me to go to Madeira. It is for my health."

There was no need to explain further. The birth of her last child, the little cherub everyone now called Minney, had been the death knell that Horatia had so long feared. Her skin, once like alabaster, was now as fragile and gray as ash. Her eyes, such a lustrous hazel in her youth, had paled and now were rimmed with dark shadows. All of the powders and paints in the world could no longer disguise the fact that poor Lady Seymour was consumptive.

"Oh, Horatia." Maria came to her and took her into her arms. She kissed each of her cheeks as if she were going away forever. "I am so sorry."

Horatia managed a pale smile. "They say the air in Madeira is wonderful. Hugh holds the highest hope that after a year or two there I shall recover completely."

"Of course you shall." Maria tried to sound encouraging. "And the children?"

"They are coming with me. I'm afraid I could not do without them, Hugh being gone so much of the time. However, I shall have to learn to live without my little Minney." Horatia's gaunt face mirrored the pain of the words she had just spoken and her eyes filled with a sudden wellspring of tears. "The doctors tell me that my little one is too delicate to undergo so long a sea voyage as lies ahead of the rest of us."

"Let me take her."

Horatia looked up with surprise. "Oh, Maria, I don't think—"

"Why not? You know how much I adore that child. She could not be more well looked after in your absence!"

"I doubt if Hugh would ever approve."

"Why not? You know what a wonderful home I can give her here. Certainly no one could love her more than I."

Horatia tried unsuccessfully to keep the strain from her voice. "Will that home once again include the Prince of Wales?"

Maria sat back against the padded chair, feeling as if she had been stung. "I see that your illness has not blunted your tongue."

"Oh, Maria, forgive me. But I have my little girl's welfare of which to think. You are considering a reconciliation with him, are you not?"

"And if I were?"

"Don't make me say it, Maria, please. Our friendship is too dear to me."

Her voice was sharp with bitterness. "Say it, Horatia."

"Look, I know what you have endured with him and I am sympathetic, truly. I know it has not been easy for you. Oh, very well then,

I shall speak my mind. Maria, George is married now. Legally. He has a wife."

"And if I take him back now, people will assume I am nothing more than his mistress."

"It's not only that. I mean, Lord Seymour and I are Protestants and you know how he and most of England feel about Catholics."

A quick frown darted across her brow. "So you would surrender that lovely child as a concession, instead of giving her to me who you know and trust, and who would make a splendid home for her, simply because of what other people might think?"

"Maria, please. I must consider Minney's welfare. She is only a little girl."

"I happen to think that there is nowhere else in the world where her welfare would be more properly looked after than with me."

"I am sure you're right, but—"

"Then give me a chance, Horatia. *Please.* I would never subject that precious child to anything that would be even the slightest bit improper. You know that. She would be guided only by the Protestant faith, if that is what you desire. I would never dare to go against you and Hugh in that. As for George, no matter whether we reconcile or not, you know very well that I am not, nor never was, his mistress."

Horatia wavered. Half a smile crossed her pale, unpainted lips. "Minney does adore you, doesn't she?"

"Not half so much as I adore her."

She extended her hand to Maria. "Let me speak with Hugh this evening. I shall call on you tomorrow with his decision before we leave." They both stood. "I'm sorry to have been so harsh. It's only that...well, if I cannot return to England...if something should happen..."

Maria raised her hand. "You need say nothing more."

"I just must know that she will be properly looked after."

"All of my life I have wanted a little girl like Minney," Maria said. "Thus far, Almighty God has not seen fit to bless me in that way. I pray that, if only for a little while, He is about to change His mind."

SHE HEARD A CHILD'S LAUGHTER as Jacko Payne opened the painted black door. The sound, that next afternoon, filled the shadowy nooks and the cornices of the hollow entrance hall.

Maria sprang to her feet in the drawing room that lay just beyond. A book of poetry she had been reading tumbled to the carpet. Aided by her own footman on one side and by Lord Hugh on the other, Horatia stepped slowly into the foyer, bearing her youngest child — her precious little Minney.

Maria moved slowly across the floor and up the two carpeted steps toward them. Horatia's eyes glistened with tears as she held the wiggling child in straining arms. The two women looked at one another, knowing, sharing a bond that was deeper than friendship, older than time.

"Take good care of her," Horatia whispered as she surrendered the child into Maria's arms. Almost immediately the little tow-headed child, with light angel eyes, stopped her fussing and nestled against Maria's bosom. Maria wept. "Thank you. Thank you both."

"She is a good baby," Horatia said through her tears. "She is so little trouble."

"I promise you, Horatia, you shall not regret this."

Hugh stood beside his wife, strong and self-assured, hands linked behind his back. He was still so dashing. Only the glistening eyes gave his true feelings away. "Tell our daughter often that we love her, so she shall not forget us entirely, Maria, will you?"

"You know that I will," she assured him as the child fingered the white string of pearls around her neck. "You must concentrate on getting your wife well so that she may soon return to us."

"That I shall." He reached out and touched her shoulder in a gesture of friendship. "Thank you, Maria."

"I shall write often of her progress."

"As often as you can," Horatia implored. Then, with trembling hands, she took a small gold and ruby bracelet from her wrist and handed it to Maria. "Keep this for her, will you? My mother gave it to me the day I married Hugh. It is a piece of her heritage."

Maria took the bracelet for a moment, held it tentatively between her fingers, and then handed it back. "You give it to her. When you return."

Horatia looked at Hugh with tired eyes and he understood. He took the bracelet from his wife and pressed it back into Maria's hand. He looked down at her kindly, and something made her remember that first night when he had looked down on her in much the same way and then rescued her with a dance. What a lifetime ago that all was now.

"Come, my dear," he finally said to Horatia. "Our carriage is waiting."

Then Hugh took their baby daughter and held her one last time as the two women embraced, both of them overcome by tears.

TWO DAYS AFTER MINNEY SEYMOUR came so unexpectedly into her life, Maria consented to a meeting with George. It would be their first encounter in nearly four years.

It was to be a private meeting, supper, at a neutral location. Kempshott, a grand estate in the rolling Hampshire hills, owned by a mutual acquaintance, Sir Henry Rycroft, was finally selected. Rycroft would act as host.

Maria was shown into a grand oak-lined foyer, lit with a huge iron chandelier. George was already there, she was told, waiting with his host in the drawing room. Maria trembled with a combination of fear and excitement, realizing lately how much she really had missed him in her life. The companionship. The private moments. They were the thoughts and memories that the pain had not allowed her to feel. Until now.

The two men stood together beside the blazing fire as it cracked and popped inside a grand sixteenth-century fireplace hearth. It was crowned by a huge portrait of Henry VIII's chief minister, Cardinal Wolsey.

The manor had been unaltered since the time of the Renaissance king, and Rycroft liked it precisely that way. High ceilings carved and covered with old faded paintings. Stag horns ornamenting the paneled walls. Furniture bearing the family coat of arms.

Maria stood in the light from the hallway, her hair glistening from a fine mist of rain that lay on her chignon like tiny diamonds. George glanced up with surprise as though he had not expected to see her. They both stood looking at one another silently for several moments.

"My dear Maria," Rycroft said, as he moved toward her. "How good it is to see you again." He was a tall, dignified man with waves of milk-white hair and sharp green eyes that missed nothing. He took Maria's hand in his own and raised it to his lips.

"And you, Henry," Maria said in return but still looking at George.

His movements were stiff. Formal. As though they were strangers. They stood separated by half a length of Turkish carpet, yet between them were many miles. In her absence, George had changed. Even across the rooms she could see age's heavy hand across his face. It shook her. He moved a few steps nearer and then stopped. Their eyes were riveted on each other.

"I do hate to ask," said Henry Rycroft. "Bloody rude to my guests actually, but would you both be good enough to excuse me for just a moment? I do need to speak with the cook about this evening's menu."

The ploy had been an obvious one, but Maria still nodded politely. George did not move further. He simply stood there staring at her, making no attempt for propriety to look away. She had worn her loveliest gown, a wispy, rose-colored English cotton. It was the new style and she was not as easy in the latest fashions as she once had been. She thought that the empire waist made a lady appear fat, took away her figure. But a lady of standing had to keep current, so she had reluctantly conceded to meet the year 1800, and the turn of the century, boldly and head-on.

"You look wonderful," he said, a little surprised how little she had changed, when he knew how much he had.

She was unbending now before him, afraid. Her mouth was a hard line of defense. "What do you want from me, George?"

"I want you back in my life," he said without hesitation. Then he paused for a moment, but his gaze had already settled on her. "Perhaps I should call for some wine?"

"I do not wish anything to soften my will," Maria snapped, angry that drinking, that vice of his, had once again become an element to be spoken of. And even so, there was so much about him that was different. Even the blue eyes; those luminescent eyes that had so easily seduced her in the beginning were not so piercing as they once had been. *What is it about him that always steals my heart from me, even now, if not those eyes?* she wondered in silent anger at herself.

He stood before her wearing an elegant gray and white striped waistcoat with his ever-present high white cravat. His hair now had the first whispers of gray at the temples, just enough to give him a kind of calming grace he had not had in the beginning. He was still so handsome, though now he possessed the maturity of a man where once his youth had enticed her.

Her heart beat against her ribs, hard like a drum. Her mouth had gone dry and she was shaking. Damn! She wanted so much to remain calm now. The emotions that had swept her up in their midst so entirely six years ago must not take possession of her now. She was older. Wiser. Pain and disappointment had changed her.

"You truly do look wonderful," he said again as they stood facing one another, separated by a carved Renaissance bench.

Here alone with him like this, she remembered everything. It all flooded back to her in a barrage of memories. The blinding passion of those early years. The protective warmth of his arms. The contours of his body as he arched over her, making love to her as no one else had ever done, or ever would again.

"Damn you, George!" she blurted suddenly. "You will *not* wound me again!"

He took a step nearer to their destiny, his gaze never leaving her face. "No," he said deeply in reply. "I will not."

"You ask too much of me," she said chokingly. "...you always have."

"I tried to do the honorable thing, Maria...You always made me want to do that."

The words tore at old wounds. She sat down very slowly on the bench that a moment ago had been the only barrier between them. He loomed beside her, uncertain if she meant for him to sit as well. Good, she thought. It was better if she was not the only one filled with hesitation.

"Perhaps I *will* have that wine now," she said, still unable to keep her voice from trembling.

Henry Rycroft had done his best to see to a splendid supper for the three of them. They sat together at one end of an immensely long table that was as old as the rest of the house. Light from the two gold candelabra flickered, one at each end. Maria could not touch her supper of capon stuffed with apples, as George and Henry tried to speak with interest about current events. The continuation of the war with France. The surrender of Malta and the return from Naples of the celebrated Admiral Nelson.

As the two men tried to make conversation, Maria could not help but watch him. George took his food slowly and he drank no wine. It was a concession she had not asked for, and it was a gesture that both surprised and pleased her.

After they had eaten, Rycroft leaned back in his chair and patted his belly. "I have eaten and drunk far too much," he announced, glancing at one of them and then the other.

He had not known what to expect when he had agreed, if a little reluctantly, to host this very awkward encounter. He certainly had not expected this, neither of them speaking past a few well-chosen words and offhand inquiries about the health of the other. The tempestuous past they had shared was legendary. He gripped the edge of the table and pressed back his chair, preparing to stand.

"Well. I am afraid I am not much of a host this evening, but you must excuse me while I fetch some peppermint tea to ease this stomach of mine." He stood between them, watching them, looking for a sign that she meant to take him back. Maria looked away. George daubed his lips with a white linen napkin and finally nodded his approval that their host should go.

"I shan't be a moment," he lied before leaving them alone.

When George looked back at her, Maria was nervously fingering the base of her wineglass. She was gazing at it as though it had some intrinsic fascination, and not only that it kept her eyes from meeting his, staving off the awkward moment that would follow.

In a bold gesture, he reached out and took her hand, holding it on top of the table. The feel of it, the connection, overwhelmed him more than he had imagined.

She looked up at him again, her dark eyes wide and searching, filling quickly with tears. "It is too late for us, too much has happened."

He looked at her, his own eyes shimmering but with the old conviction in the light from the candles. "All right. We shall not mince words, Maria. Much has happened that has wounded you terribly, and for that I bear total blame. But now that there is no risk to you any longer of criminal prosecution, because I gave the King what he

306

desired, I am finally free to begin...to try to make amends..." He squeezed her hand. "To make things as they were before."

"What the King desired was that you have a legal wife, and so you do. Things can never be as they were before."

"Then they shall be better."

"This is lunacy even to consider!" She tensed again, drawing away from him.

"It is the only thing in the world that has ever been right for either of us."

"What of your daughter?" The thought of a child, the one thing she had wanted in the world, which she now had in Minney, softened her.

"If it would not bring you too much pain, I should like to see her from time to time."

"You must do that. No matter what happens between us, you cannot turn your back on her."

"Oh, Maria," he said after a little silence, taking her hand again and squeezing it desperately. "I may not always be the man you wish me to be—" His handsome face was solemn. "But all that *I* have ever wished was to be worthy of the faith I saw mirrored in your eyes."

"It is not a question of worth, George. It never has been. It is a question of two different sorts of worlds, two ways of believing, about life, about fidelity...*about honesty*."

He would not be undone by her hesitation. They had come too far. George reached up and took her shoulders, holding them tightly. "What we have, Maria, is precious, once in a lifetime. I believe we both know that there will never be anything like this for either of us, ever again. A thing of which most people can only dream..."

"But," she asked him, as he held her. "...can we truly ever find our *own* dream again?"

"If we search together very, very hard," he whispered as a tear lingered on his cheek. "Yes, I believe with all my heart that we can."

IT WOULD NOT BE PLEASANT, but it must be done.

Maria could not surrender herself fully to George until she had seen Francis. She owed him that much. She had considered calling him to her home but she thought it would be better if there was no chance of him and George seeing each other.

At least for a while the wound would still be raw. She had never lied to him, never made it out to be more than the friendship that it was. But he was in love with her and that one time between them had given him hope. She hated herself a little now for having used him like that.

"You've taken him back, haven't you?" he said as they faced each other in the gray light of early morning.

Maria felt as though she had been struck. She had not even removed her gloves. She had an elegant little speech all prepared. She was going to talk about friendship and how much he had done for her when she had needed him most. In an instant it was gone. Every word of it.

She looked directly at him, forcing the words from her mouth. "Yes, Francis, I have."

Suspecting it was not at all the same thing as hearing it from her lips. He stepped back, wounded when she confirmed what he had already heard. "I thought I would handle it better, you know," he said softly. Then he looked away, unable to bear the happiness he saw on her face. He had never made her that happy. Not even that one night when she had belonged to him completely. "I had wanted to tell you congratulations. Best of luck..."

"How did you know?" she asked quietly, and it seemed to him the most singularly inappropriate thing she could have said at a moment when his heart was breaking.

"London is really quite a small town. At least so far as it concerns pitiable news." He turned back around, pain oozing through every pore in his tall, slim body. His eyes bore the brunt of it. "I do want desperately for you to be happy, you know. I would just have preferred it to have been with me."

"Francis, I—"

"No," he held up a hand when she took a step toward him. "Save your pity, Maria. I don't believe I could bear it just now."

"I don't pity you!" she said indignantly and tried again to go to him, but sensing the barrier there now, she stopped. "I love you, dearly."

"As a friend."

"As my dearest friend."

There was a little silence and he began to drum his fingers nervously on the back of a chair. "Not much of a parting, is it? None of the congratulations and well-wishes you might have expected."

"I expected nothing from you, Francis, and yet I got so very much in return."

His laugh was bone-dry. "I suppose that is the difference between us. Try as I might to the contrary, I expected too much." He looked up at her. "I expected one day, if I were patient, that you might feel for me as much as I feel for you. Curious, isn't it? I want you but you don't want me in the same way. You, on the other hand, desire the Prince of Wales and what he really desires is other women and more money. Was that not what you told me?"

Maria put her hands firmly on her hips. Her mouth was a hard line. "Those words were spoken in confidence, Francis. Not so that you could fling them at me now because you are hurt."

He moved toward her, filling the distance between them in three quick steps. "See him for what he is, Maria! For the love of God, don't be seduced by pretty words and promises when he cannot possibly keep them!"

"I know you're hurt, Francis, but I am going to leave if you say another word against him."

He looked out of the window at the pearl gray dawn. The clouds were heavy and black. It promised to be another day of rain. Damnable rain! It was the last thing he needed when his heart was breaking.

"Forgive me," he finally said in a painful whisper.

She held his face between her hands like a precious jewel and tenderly kissed each cheek. "I must do this, Francis. Please understand. I truly believe that, come what may, it is the life which God has chosen for me."

"I am afraid for you."

"You mustn't be. I want to be with him, and I actually need him."

"Tread softly, my angel," he said and pulled her hands from his face when what he wanted more than anything in the world was to pull her closer. "And be careful of illusions."

"Do wish me luck, Francis. Please."

"Ah, yes. That," he said, unable to keep the sarcasm completely from his voice. "That is something of which, I fear, my angel, you shall need a great deal."

THERE WERE CRYSTAL VASES OF lavender everywhere. The Fitzherbert drawing room, where the guests gathered, filled with flowers, books, writing tables, armchairs and deep sofas, was a delicate mix of blue satin and saffron-yellow velvet. It was both grand and informal at the same time for the breakfast party upon which George had insisted to honor Maria.

The walls were painted with bowers of roses and jasmine. Dominating one entire wall was a full-length portrait of the Prince of Wales. His gift to Maria, George had insisted on hanging it in a position of prominence. No one would be allowed to forget by whose grace they had been invited, or whose anger they would incur by slighting her ever again.

On an ormolu table beside it was a bust of Maria's dear friend Prince Frederick. Attendants in the Prince's red and gold livery were stationed throughout the room and in the entrance hall to announce the guests. Other servants passed across priceless Aubusson carpets holding trays of candied fruit and offering them to the guests who had already arrived.

Although he had not confided it in Maria, George had every intention of making this a morning that history would not soon forget. After today, everyone would know how much the Prince of Wales adored his wife...

His *true* wife.

As he stood rocking back and forth on his heels, the height of London society was steadily streaming in through the front door. Each of the ladies, in their clingy, high-waisted gowns and unpowdered hair, *à la Grecque*, were being greeted with a long-stemmed white rose. That nuance had been Maria's touch.

Beau Brummell, the notorious London dandy, had just arrived. George watched him strutting around the drawing room like a rooster, nodding to the other guests and showing off his new silk tailcoat with brass buttons. Maria found him arrogant but George had insisted on inviting him, just the same. He found Brummell entertaining, and a mutual fascination with clothing had been the impetus for a newly formed friendship between them.

Lord and Lady Clermont were standing with Elizabeth and Richard Brinsley Sheridan beside one of the two new gold torchères.

They spoke of the seven-year war still raging with France and the dreaded Bonaparte, who was presently and so devastatingly reeking havoc with Austria. Across the room was her old friend, Anne, Lady Lindsay, who had gone away to France with her, all those years ago. She was cloistered beneath a chandelier with Georgiana, the Duchess of Devonshire, and Isabella, Lady Sefton.

"This is all really rather scandalous," Anne maliciously whispered.

"One can hardly be too critical of the poor dear," sniped an aging Georgiana in reply, her eyes fixed on those new guests who moved slowly into the elegant little room. "After all, she hasn't really gained a great deal by taking him back, has she?"

Secretly, it galled the Duchess of Devonshire beyond all reason that the mildly attractive Catholic widow had gotten yet another chance with such a firebrand as the Prince of Wales.

"She shall never be Queen," Anne forecast spitefully, poisoned by Georgiana's venom. "It would seem to me that dear Maria certainly has sacrificed her tranquility, if not her dignity, by agreeing to let that rogue back into her bed."

Just then, Maria moved down onto the last stair step, swirled in an elegant opal-colored gown. A jeweled brooch sparkled in the cleft between her breasts. Her hair was done up to perfection, a twist of pale blond spotted with tiny jewels.

"Oh, my dear, is this not just splendid?" Georgiana cooed as Maria moved into her own crowded drawing room. "You and our dear George reconciled at last!"

"It is as romantic as a fairy tale!" Anne seconded.

Maria looked over at Isabella who stood between the other two ladies, but her uncle's wife only smiled. *I believe that she learned a lesson about me the last time around,* she thought slyly. *Her silence in the face of their hypocrisy is wise.*

"I'm pleased you all could come," Maria said instead, and her voice was as sweet and sincere as if she had truly meant it.

As she turned away from them, preparing to find anyone other than that formidable trio to speak to, George caught her by the sleeve. "There you are, at last, darling," he said, kissing her cheek. "Come. I have something I want to give to you. Pardon us, will you ladies?"

He moved only a few feet, not seeking a private place away from the prying eyes of the other guests when he pulled a flat, foil-wrapped box from his tailcoat. Maria looked up at him.

"Oh, George, perhaps this is not the time—"

"On the contrary, this is precisely the time." He smiled, full of confidence. "Go ahead. Open it for everyone to see."

She looked back at him, trying to glean a bit of his courage as she unwound the wrapping. He had sought this moment intentionally. Although she did not look around again, she could hear the deafening quiet fall across the room, all of their guests watching her.

Slowly she opened the top of the box. Spread open inside, on a bed of black velvet, was a jeweled brooch, a collection of diamonds, emeralds, and gold that glistened in the room's natural light.

"The Warwick brooch," she said breathlessly.

"I gave it to you once, a long time ago, when you were not ready, and so I honored your wishes to take it back. Now, as it was then, this brooch is a symbol of my love for you. A love that shall never die." He was smiling proudly when she looked at him. "Does it please you?"

"It is exquisite."

Maria trembled as she gazed down at the sparkling jewels, which he then put into her hand. Something she had once found garish seemed the most beautiful thing in the world because now she truly did believe that he loved her.

"I worship you, Maria," he declared for all to hear. "You are the core, the very essence of my life."

Suddenly, her smile matched his own. Maria moved to embrace him but then she stopped. He saw her hesitation and moved close enough to whisper, "Please, darling, I want them all to see how happy we are. Let us show every one of these poor miserable souls how wrong they have been about us. Perhaps, by our strength, we can put an end to their vicious gossip at last."

When Maria shyly gave him a tender kiss on the cheek, the applause of the guests resounded around them. But she knew instantly that it was not enough for George. He had a point to make, and he meant to make it. Suddenly, he pulled her to his chest and kissed her as passionately as if they were making love.

She heard someone behind her gasp. She tried, but she could not break free, his arms were solid and strong around her. Maria felt his arms, his hands moving slowly upward. He touched her neck with his fingers. He touched her face. The movement was sensual, as though they were the only two people in the room. When he pulled away from her, Maria's cheeks were flushed as pink as roses.

"I do believe she has tamed the most notorious tiger in England, after all." Lady Lindsay smiled, surprising even herself.

The Duchess of Devonshire, who had not moved from the bottom of the stairs, bit her thumbnail, the muscles of her face tense and hard as a mask. "Positively sickening," she murmured beneath her breath.

"Careful, Georgiana," Lady Lindsay said in reply. "Your envy is showing."

CHAPTER NINETEEN

AS THE YEAR 1803 CAME to a close, so did a brief truce that had been forged at Amiens. Once again England and France were at war. Through the summer months all of England prepared to meet foreign invasion. Even ordinary British citizens rose up to answer the call as volunteers. Prince Frederick was assigned to lead them as Commander-in-Chief. George, however, as Heir, was barred from going.

If he could not participate in the war, then he would prepare to lead it. He and Maria returned to the seaside at Brighton. With them, he brought volumes of material on political strategy, military readiness, and diplomacy, intent on studying it all. The King's death could not be far off now, he reasoned, and with Maria once more beside him George had every intention of preparing to be the sovereign his father had always refused to let him become.

And when his time came, he knew he would have the help of his brothers. The three eldest, Frederick, Edward and William, were all devoted to him, and all adored Maria. He remembered the last time they all were together, and speaking about the war, as well as about the decline of the Whig Party. Maria fit in so easily, listening, offering opinions. She was a part of their dynasty, an integral member of the royal family.

Under Napoleon, who now was Emperor, Holland was ruled by the French. So was Italy. Spain was supplying them with men. Everything in life changed, George thought—except Maria's devotion.

"When the time comes, will you assist me?" he asked her on the long carriage ride down from London.

"Oh, darling, I do not believe that would be my place."

He ran a hand along the line of her jaw and smiled. "Are you not my partner, the woman I love, do we not share one in the same soul?"

"I like to believe that is true."

"Then there is no one's counsel I value, nor need, more. I want to be ready…I *need* to be ready when the time comes, to do battle against the skeptics who surely will doubt my ability to reign."

"Then I shall be with you," she declared. "I will be honored to do what I can."

As George had changed, so had his Brighton Pavilion. In their absence, and under the direction of the famous Henry Holland, the Prince's residence by the sea had continued its ornate and costly transformation, flinging itself further and further away from the intimate little timber-framed farmhouse that once had charmed them in its simplicity. Despite the fact that decorating in chinoiserie had not been popular since the 1760s, the Pavilion now took on an Oriental flavor. Ceramics. Furniture. Tapestry. Hand-painted wallpaper. All were done in the Chinese manner. Chinoiserie was exotic. Its return, now that it was out of fashion, suited George. It meant novelty… and George still loved to be novel.

As the Prince of Wales and his Pavilion had been transformed, so the entire town of Brighton had changed. The little fishing village at the seashore had spread its modest cottages into grand villas to the north, the east, and the west. New theaters opened. Banks and clubs sprang up to accommodate the throng of distinguished visitors who now came and spent their money so freely. But Brightonians did not forget the two who had brought them such prosperity. They honored them both in a manner neither George nor Maria had ever experienced in London.

Outside there were races, cricket matches, sea bathing, and even naval displays. Inside the newly decorated Oriental halls of the Pavilion there was an endless succession of balls, concerts, card parties, and dinners.

Servants polished silver and dusted furniture to a brilliant luster. The grand kitchens sent the delicious aroma of roasting meat through the Chinese gallery, the music room, around the new frescoes and Oriental colonnades. The long table in the newly decorated dining hall was being carefully set with silver, crystal, and Belgian lace. Fragrant spikes of lavender were set out in huge Sevres urns, it was said, because they pleased Mrs. Fitzherbert.

As the Brighton staff prepared for an evening of dining, bonfires, and fireworks across the garden at the Pavilion, George and Maria sat together on the balcony of her cozy little villa facing the sea. Minney sat at their feet, stacking building blocks and then knocking them down.

George loved to sit with her here every morning, when the air was the freshest and the gulls flocked to the deserted Steine before them. Often times, they would take tea in the afternoons here on her balcony and George would honor the townspeople who passed with a wave and smile. He was happy here. Content. Maria could see it. Everyone could. She felt blessed every day of her life that they had been given this second chance.

He turned to Maria, held her hand up, and kissed the finger that wore his ring—a ring everyone was still made to believe had been given to her by Thomas Fitzherbert. "What a glorious birthday," he said with a sigh.

Maria crooked an eyebrow as she looked at him. "But the day has barely begun, my love."

"True enough. But I have all that I could ever want, right here with me now."

"Then perhaps there is no need to give you my gift," she teased.

He pulled her to him and brushed her lips with a kiss. "Perhaps just one little gift."

Maria rose and went back into their bedchamber to a small boulle-inlaid chest of drawers beside the bed. She opened the top drawer and took out a small package wrapped in gold foil, tied with white ribbon.

"It really is more the return of something," she said as she took Minney up into her arms and sat back down beside George, "that already belongs to you."

Playfully, he shook the package first, as a child might do, and heard the clink of a single, weighty item. He smiled up at her, trying to guess what was inside, and shook it again.

Finally he untied the ribbon and then unwound the foil wrapping. Inside a small wooden box lay the locket held by a black velvet cord and bearing the miniature of herself that she had given him on their wedding day. It was the same locket he had ultimately hidden away during their separation, when seeing it had been too painful.

"Where—" he whispered as he gazed at the image of Maria, her hair curled and loose and the bust of her rose-colored gown all frills and bows. He looked back at her with tears in his sky-blue eyes. "Where did you find it?"

"You left it in London, long ago. Your new valet, Dupaquier, found it in a desk drawer when you asked him to fetch some papers. It was lying with this. He thought you might have misplaced it, since he hadn't seen you wearing the locket for some time."

Maria held out the Last Will and Testament that he had drawn up during their estrangement. It was a will in which he had not only acknowledged her as his wife but had left all of his possessions to her. "Why did you not tell me about this?"

George wiped the unexpected tears from his eyes with the back of his hand. "I have done so many impetuous things in the past to win your love, I did not want you ever to believe that this had been one of them."

"I am your wife, George, for better or for worse...now and always."

He handed the locket up to her. "Put it round my neck, will you?"

Maria smiled and leaned forward, holding the velvet cord. Then gently she slipped it over his head. "I shall not take it off again," he whispered and pressed her image to his chest. "If you've read the document already, then you know that I intend to wear it into eternity."

She tried to hand back the will to him as he looked at her. "You keep it."

"But if it should fall into the wrong hands—"

He took the hand that held the document and then kissed her fingertips. "It shall be safe with you, my darling. I know that." He touched the locket again and looked up at her. "And you have never wavered in wearing the locket I gave to you," he remembered, shaking his head softly with an air of incredulity at the breadth of her devotion to him.

Maria pulled it out of the top of her gown and held it up to him. "A day has not passed when I have ever been without it."

"Just like your faith in me," he whispered.

317

CHAPTER TWENTY

VERY SUDDENLY LITTLE MINNEY WAS an orphan.

As her mother had so often feared, the illness brought about by frequent childbirth had finally claimed her life. Maria was told in a letter, one summer afternoon, that her dearest friend had died after Lord Admiral Seymour had been forced to leave her to go to Jamaica. Mercifully, for a man who had worshiped his wife, and desperately tried to protect her, Hugh had died on the island two months later, never knowing of Horatia's death.

"I want to keep her, George," Maria said in a low voice. "Horatia left her with me and it is best if she stays here."

He tried to keep his tone gentle. "That is not what her family believes."

"But she is accustomed to us now. It would be cruel to separate us!"

In a will drawn up before Minney's birth, Lord Hugh had named his wife's sister and her husband as their children's guardians, as well as executors of his estate. Although Minney had not been specifically named, the Earl of Euston and his wife were well aware of the child's current, improper environment, as ward of the Prince of Wales's mistress. They believed it was their duty to seek full custody.

Maria took the letter she had received from the Earl of Euston, asking her to surrender Minney, and tossed it into the fire. "I'll not do it, that is all there is to it! They cannot ask me to give her up, George! I have come to love her too much!"

George understood what she felt for the child, because he felt it as well. At first it had surprised him how fond even he had become of the little minx who called him "Prinney." In so short a time, she had wrapped herself around his royal heart more securely than his own five-year-old daughter, Charlotte.

He plied Minney with gold charms, perfume, earrings, and even money to show his affection. He loved her because she was sweet and beautiful—and innocence itself. But he loved her most for the simple reason that Maria adored her. And he thought of her as the child they had, together.

"But what are we to do?" he asked as tenderly as he could. "It appears that they are well within their rights to ask for her return."

The sound of his words brought her to tears. "They have no right to Minney! She is mine! Have you forgotten what Horatia said to me? Have you?"

The previous autumn, Horatia had returned from Madeira for a brief visit with her youngest child, who had remained in England. Seeing her and Minney together, Maria had found the strength to surrender the child to her natural mother. "Don't think I could be so unfeeling as to take her from you," Horatia had said. "You are more her mother now than I." Maria thought now in retrospect how it had been almost as if Horatia knew she would not be coming back.

"Yes, I recall it," he answered her with difficulty.

"Then you know that she would not want us separated! Good God, she was right, I *am* Minney's mother now!"

Maria fell into his arms shuddering like a frightened child herself, and George held her and stroked her hair until she stopped weeping.

"Hush. There, there, my darling," he whispered. "I shall handle it."

THE COURT HAD MADE IT clear: The Seymour family was within their rights to tear little Minney from her. Maria's suitability as a guardian for the impressionable child had been a factor. However, it was not her connection to the Prince of Wales that was being ques-

319

tioned by Horatia's family, but rather her religious faith. She was still a Roman Catholic raising a Protestant child.

George's representative, Samuel Romilly, an aggressive young lawyer, countered by bringing forth a sworn affidavit signed by Maria. In it she stated that the child, now over three years old, had been and would continue to be raised in the faith of her parents.

The Prince of Wales also submitted his own affidavit stating that Lady Seymour herself had, on her brief return from England, spoken to them both as if Maria were the child's adoptive parent. He further contended that the loving environment in which she had thus far been raised was what would continue to be best for the little girl—but the Master in Chancery did not agree. The youngest child of Lord Hugh and Lady Horatia Seymour was awarded to the custody of her maternal aunt and uncle. A higher court to which the case was appealed agreed with the ruling. The last shred of hope left now to George and Maria was an appeal to the House of Lords.

It may have looked impossible just now, George told himself. There was no one and nothing in their favor. But the ever resourceful expert at deception, who had honed his skills in the best gaming houses and bedchambers of London, had one final hand yet to play.

The same evening that the verdict on the Seymour custody case was heard, the Prince of Wales left Tilney Street after Maria had been given a dose of laudanum to help her sleep. He had two social calls to pay. They would be only the beginning.

Through the dark, fog-sodden London streets, his driver led the yellow brougham first to Hertford House in Manchester Square. Francis Seymour, the second Marquess of Hertford, and Minney's eldest paternal uncle, had been told to expect him.

"Do come in, Your Royal Highness," the aging Marquess called before he fell into a courteous bow.

Beside him, his wife, Isabella, curtsied.

"Enough of that." George waved his hand as he drew near. "My business here tonight is a personal matter. We need not stand on ceremony."

"Might we offer Your Royal Highness some refreshment then?" The Marquess, a tall, slim man with waves of white hair touched with only a hint of its former chestnut, said more solicitously, "Perhaps a glass of port or a brandy to warm away the night's chill?"

George rubbed his hands together and looked at the crystal decanters on a silver tray near a wall of leatherbound books. For the first time since he had reconciled with Maria, he actually considered the option. But a clear head was better. He could afford no error in this.

"Thank you, no," he finally said.

"I suspect you've come about little Mary," surmised the Marchioness after an uncomfortable silence.

Isabella was a handsome, stately woman, heavier than her husband and far more proud, with auburn hair and a splash of gray at each of her temples. She stood straight as a plank of wood, her hands clasped before her pale blue gown, and looked directly at George when she spoke.

"I have indeed, madam," the Prince replied.

They sat before the fire in a little collection of French chairs covered in raspberry silk, and both the Marquess and his wife studied the Prince carefully. George stood and walked closer to the fire, turning his back to the flames to warm himself. He looked down at his fingers, waiting for the moment. For the inspiration.

Let me say the right thing, he was thinking. *Something, not knowing me, they will believe of the image ... Let me make no error in this ... for my Maria, and for Minney.*

"You know," he began carefully. "Horatia was a lovely young woman."

"Yes she was," agreed the Marchioness.

"Terrible tragedy, she so young and all. Did you know that she spent a great deal of time with me down at Brighton?"

The Marquess stiffened. "I was not aware of that."

"Oh, yes. With Lord Hugh away so often, I'm afraid, she was rather lonely. Ah, how many summer days and nights did we all spend together in that grand sanctuary, sea bathing, playing cricket ... It was all really rather marvelous."

He quickly scanned both of their faces. Isabella's eyes, the color and shape of two almonds, began to form the question he had hoped they would. Undaunted by what he was implying, he continued. "As those things do happen, Horatia, dear Horatia, and I grew rather close one summer there in Brighton. It must be ... yes, it would be about four years ago now."

Lord Hertford turned away with a grunt of disgust. "Are you try-ing to tell us that Your Highness and she were...*lovers?*" his wife asked more directly than he dared.

George made no move to answer nor to deny the question. The Marquess sprung to his feet. "Good God, man! She was your cousin!"

"Only by a second marriage. There was no blood tie between us," George reminded him calmly. "I realize that this is awkward but really, we are all adults here, are we not? I came to you both with this information in hopes of averting any, shall we say, embarrass-ment to your family."

Lord Hertford's tired green eyes were bright with fury as he faced the sly Prince. George stroked his chin, still in command of the encounter as he loomed over them. He must remain so if he meant to help Maria. And beyond that nothing mattered at all. *Once again, not even the truth.*

Now it was he who turned away, fingering a tall, blue Sèvres vase on the fireplace mantel. "In point of fact, I may well be the child's natural father."

Like a roll of thunder that follows a bolt of lightening, he waited for their reaction to follow his pronouncement. To his surprise, for several moments, there was only an almost eerie silence. When there was no response, George felt an icy shiver of apprehension begin to crawl upward from the base of his spine for the lie had just told. He knew what lying once long ago had cost him...but if it could keep Minney safely in Maria's arms, then even that would have been well worth the risk. When he had timed the moment as expertly as an actor in a play, George turned back around. He felt a surge of pleas-ure to see them both, frozen like statues, the Marquess having fallen back into his chair, and looks of comparable horror on both of their faces.

"It is a delicate situation, to say the least," George said with a per-fectly executed, awkward smile.

"Indeed," mouthed Lord Hertford.

"So you see, I felt I must come to you first, as you are the senior-most in her family, and therefore are naturally the one with the greatest amount of influence. I thought perhaps, after some consideration, you would find it best to keep that which is bound to come out, away from the courts...and away from the prying eyes of a less than forgiving society."

Lord Hertford let a little moan from behind the hand that covered his thin lips. Isabella looked at her husband with concern. This had been too much for him.

"Is there an equitable alternative that Your Royal Highness can see?" Lady Hertford asked, looking back up at George, still completely overwhelmed by the implications of such a scandal.

He strained to keep his voice emotionless. "Well, of course I am not well schooled in the law. However, it would seem to me, if she is indeed my child, that you and Lord Hertford would do nicely as guardians."

Isabella's painted lower lips dropped. "But she is so young! We could not possibly...what I mean is, to start all over again with one so young—"

"I understand your concern," he agreed, referring to the fact that Lord Hertford was over sixty and his wife was whispered to have been a decade behind. "But perhaps there is a compromise." George fingered his chin. "As her likely father, I would not be against the notion of the child remaining precisely where she is. Under your ultimate guardianship, of course."

A light of recognition came to her eyes. "Of course," seconded the Marchioness, who understood all to clearly now what had so cleverly been proposed.

To keep the scandal away from the House of Seymour, Lord Hertford must agree to go against the rest of the family where it concerned Hugh's youngest child. And he had made it clear that, if they refused, he, the Prince of Wales, would find a way to expose his paternity, to the detriment of them all.

For once in his life, the very way he lived that life and the gossip that had dogged him had come to some good. It doubtlessly showed them that he had no great compunction about propriety.

"I ask only that you consider the alternatives before the House of Lords next convenes," George was saying as her mind whirled with a jumble of conflicting thoughts. "There may well be an equitable solution for all concerned."

At last, Lady Hertford came to her feet, facing the Prince. Their eyes met. He could see that her reputation as a prudent woman was accurate. "It is very late, Your Highness, and I am afraid that my husband has grown weary. We shall need time to consider this, of course."

"Of course."

"Well then. May I see Your Highness to the door?"

George inclined his head, then clasped his hands behind his back. "It pains me greatly to come to you with such a tale, madam," he said beneath his breath as they strolled out into the corridor. "But if she is my child, I have an obligation, as much as the others, to see to her welfare."

"Yes. *If* she is Your Highness's child."

George stopped and turned to face her. She was looking up at him, her ruby painted lips twisted into a subtle sneer beneath a long, elegant nose. *Ah! so she could spar!* he thought. Sharp. Yes, sharp and clever. He would not have expected that. He would have to take great care to see to success in his dealing with this one. "But you do not believe that she is my child," George said with a seductive half smile.

It was the most flirtation he could manage.

"What *I* believe, Your Highness, is unimportant."

"I should like to hear, madam, whatever you have to say on the matter."

She nodded. "Then Your Highness has been duly warned."

"Point to you, madam." He smiled.

"Very well then. Although I suspect you are well accustomed to it, in future I shall not speak simply to please you."

"So noted," he said, leaning close, his smile broadening.

A footman came forward with George's hat, gloves, and cloak. "I shall speak to the Marquess again on your behalf, after he has rested." She smiled at him. "I shall be direct with his reply."

"That is all that I ask."

George took her warm hand and brought it slowly to his lips. He paused to taste her perfume. He felt her bristle at his nearness and saw the color rise in her cheeks. Good, he thought. Better she was off-guard than he.

"I suspect then we shall need to meet again to discuss the matter in greater detail."

"Yes." His blue eyes sparkled, and he felt for the moment, he was actually a point ahead. "I shall look forward to that."

AFTER LEAVING HERTFORD HOUSE THAT night, George set out on a campaign to canvas all of the members of the House of Lords for Maria. He would leave with each of them the same suspicion that he had imparted to Lord and Lady Hertford. He led them all to believe that he might well be Minney Seymour's natural father. It was the only way out of a desperate situation. Tonight, clothed in shadows, he had only enough time left to visit Lord Eldon. But tomorrow there would be half a dozen more in whom he must kindle an element of doubt. And the next day and the next until he was certain to have won a majority.

RUMOR HAD SPREAD LIKE WILDFIRE about the custody case involving the last Seymour child because the ever-scandalous Prince of Wales was now rumored to have been implicated. The House of Lords was crowded to capacity when the day came for the case to be argued. The galleries above the members, resplendent on their red morocco leather seats, were packed with those who had paid a shilling each to hear the proceedings.

Before a single peer could stand to present a bill, Lord Hertford came to his feet, leaning on a gold-tipped cane. He was a proud, arrogant-looking man, and as he rose the crowd broke into another crescendo of gossip and chatter. Finally, when the Lord Chancellor had seen the room quieted once again, Lord Hertford moved to speak. In an attempt to put an end to the gossip and turmoil, he proposed that he and his wife be made permanent guardians of the child. He further proposed that they be unfettered in the execution of this arrangement. In the end, only thirteen votes were opposed to the proposition. It was therefore decided that custody of Mary Seymour should, once and for all, be granted to Lord and Lady Hertford.

* * *

MARIA HAD MET LORD HERTFORD and his wife on perhaps a dozen occasions, never having found either of them particularly to her liking. To her mind, Lady Hertford was a forbidding and haughty woman who completely dominated her older and far less effective husband. The fact that they stood in her house now, prepared to take away her little girl, made her feel as if she were being torn in two.

Minney was sitting in an armchair beside Isabella, nervously swinging her feet in little black lace-up shoes, as Maria and George came into the library. Quiet tears were streaming down rosy cheeks that were still sprinkled with freckles. She refused to look up until Maria came into the room, and then she sprung from the chair and pressed through her gown, clinging to her thigh.

"Don't let them take me, Mama! *Please!*" she cried out and Maria's eyes mirrored the little child's pain and helplessness. Maria nodded to Lord and Lady Hertford, straining with every ounce of strength she possessed to remain civil.

"She is a lovely child, Mrs. Fitzherbert," said Isabella formally. "You have done a remarkably good job with her."

Maria stroked Minney's long brown hair and looked back at the woman who had quickly become a rival, fighting her own tears.

She hated having to be brave.

"I have loved her as if I had given life to her myself," she said softly in reply.

The two men gazed upon one another less antagonistically as Maria reached down and kissed the child's tear-stained face.

"She is such a sweet and special little girl," Maria said resignedly, with tear-brightened eyes. "Please take great care with the knowledge of that."

Lady Hertford rose to her feet in a stiff lilac gown and large, ribboned hat. Her hands hung at her sides. "My dear Mrs. Fitzherbert," she said, and the lines in her face deepened as she smiled, "we've not come to take the child from you. We've come to ask you to continue caring for our niece, just as you have been all along. We agree with His Royal Highness's assessment that it is quite in her best interest to remain where she is. That is, provided of course that you still agree to raise her as a Protestant."

"...His Highness's assessment?" Maria managed to ask.

She felt faint. Had the woman before her actually spoken those words or had her mind played on her the most evil trick imaginable? Without thinking or even breathing she pulled Minney up into her arms and the child began to kiss her face and neck.

"Oh, Mama! May I stay? May I?"

For a moment there were no other words. Only tears. George came behind Maria and put a comforting hand on her shoulder. He had made a great many mistakes in his life. He knew in his heart that he would likely err again. But for this single and brief, shining moment, George Augustus could finally say that this was one exquisitely right thing he had done. And this time, he hadn't needed to hurt his Maria to do it.

He had put his wife, the woman of his heart, and her happiness ahead of everything else. Nothing he would ever do again, even as King of England, would ever bring him such satisfaction or peace of mind as he felt at this moment.

"Are you not glad now that you came down to greet Lord and Lady Hertford yourself?" he said with a kind smile as he bent to kiss the top of Minney's head.

"But w-what about your other relations? Will they not object?" Maria asked in a whisper when her voice would not come through.

"They should not concern you, my dear," said the Marquess with a formal nod. "Whatever their private opinion on the matter, I am the eldest within our house. They have no choice but to concede to my will in this."

"Let us simply say that if we are kept happy, they will be happy," Isabella purred, implying volumes more than she had said.

Maria's lips hung open and, for the complete shock from the turn of events, no more words would come. Isabella's inference, however, was not lost on George. He was not above the use of flirtation to secure the child for Maria. After seeing the desolation on his wife's face at the prospect of losing Minney, he would have done far more to see them kept together. Lady Hertford had made it clear that she and her husband were still free at any time to change their minds and with that sort of uncertainty looming over his head, he had only one choice. He must, in some fashion, make Isabella desire to please him.

ALONE IN THEIR BED, AFTER they had gone, Maria laughed in disbelief. "You told them *what?*"

"I merely suggested that I might well be the child's father."

She moved away from his chest and sat up, the rumpled bedcovers falling away from her bare breasts. "And do you believe that you could be?" she asked, almost unable to bear hearing the reply.

George saw the shock on her face and felt a smile. She was still so gullible, so innocent in so many ways. What a jewel she was to have survived unscathed in the society by which they both were so tightly bound.

"I never touched Horatia. I simply made them believe that I had."

"You lied?"

"I thought this one time, perhaps you just might forgive me."

She bit back a smile, trying to remain stern. "You know well what honesty means to me, George."

"I swore, Maria, that I would not let you down in this, and so I did what I thought I must to keep Minney with us."

This had been, perhaps, his greatest gift to her. And in the face of that she wanted very much to overlook this one last subterfuge. Her kisses fell lightly on his gently aging, upturned face.

"Oh, George Augustus, how I do adore you, even though there are some things about you, I fear, that shall never change," she whispered, kissing his eyelids, his cheeks, and his lips again and again. Now it was Maria who pressed him back into the cool folds of Belgian linen, anxious to make them as close as she possibly could. "Yes, this one last time I do believe I shall forgive you your deception."

A scattering of thoughts, of justifications like pearls fallen free from a string, moved through his mind. He despised the pretense. And yet, what choice did he have? Isabella had made it patently clear that she had the power to snatch Minney away anytime she chose. If he did not devise some clever scheme to keep a bored, aristocratic female thinking a tryst with the future King might well be just in the offing, he had no doubt what would occur.

He tried to imagine himself going to Maria, confiding in her about

328

all of this. Asking for her counsel. But what he saw in his mind as the answer was Maria's face. It was the same pain he had seen so many times, in Brighton from the cruel caricatures, and here in London when she truly believed she was about to lose the only child she would ever have. She had endured so much more than any woman ought—to become and to remain, his wife. How could he actually do it? How could he tell her that, after all of these years, the worst was not yet over? He had no choice. In spite of the danger. There was simply no way he could tell Maria. He must handle this himself. He must play this tenuous game to keep Minney with her. And hope... *pray*, for the best.

CHAPTER TWENTY-ONE

1806 WAS A YEAR FOR deaths.

First there was William Pitt, the former Prime Minister, the man who had opposed George's financial relief and threatened Maria in the House of Commons. The man who had opposed his unconditional Regency. King George III's great ally.

The Prince of Wales's great enemy.

Only when he realized that death, like wishes, nearly always came in threes did he feel an ominous rush of fear. True to the maxim, in March, Georgiana, the saucy, opinionated Duchess of Devonshire, often his most bitter opponent, more often his dearest friend, finally succumbed to the various illnesses that had plagued her for years.

For her, George wept. No more grand parties at Devonshire House. No more impotent flirtation with the woman who had taught him how. No more coquettish entreaties for dominance over him. She had often been a nuisance. But through the years, she had also become more like a beloved sister, and with her death, an era had ended.

First William Pitt, then dear Georgiana, took with them an entire age. In those first days following her passing, George waited full of fear for the return of the dark shadow of death to revisit London.

There would be a third. That was the way it always went. It was the cold, unforgiving months of winter and he must wait with the rest of the city, cast now with a bitter pall, to discover exactly who it was to be.

CHARLES JAMES FOX HAD MADE great strides politically in the past year. His faction of Whigs, known as "Foxites," had been outspoken in advocating peace with Napoleon and with France. It had gained him a small but strong group of supporters. After the death of William Pitt in January, the King surprisingly ceased to oppose Fox in office and the new ministry became predominantly Foxite.

Charles himself became Secretary of State. His authority now was beyond question. Politically, he had survived the wars, and he was back again. He was a survivor. So it was a surprise to everyone that, just when he seemed on the brink of a real and solid base of power, his health quickly began to fail.

"How is he?" The Prince of Wales asked Fox's wife, Elizabeth, as he removed his hat and stepped into the entrance hall.

"The doctors tell me that he is as well as can be expected, Your Highness," she nodded.

It was the first time George had seen his former mistress in many years, and Elizabeth had changed. With time, her skin had lost its rosy hue, and was marred now by a network of fine wrinkles, near her eyes, her mouth. Etched into cheeks that had once been smooth as new silk. Her hair still had traces of its lush auburn red, but even that was only a shadow of what it once had been. George took her hand and kissed it as old friends do. His own mortality was laid bare to him as he looked at her, and it had unnerved him a little.

"It was good of Your Highness to come," she said.

His tone when he replied was grave. "You know I could not have stayed away."

She said nothing else but led him into the dark, stale-smelling bedchamber and then left the two old friends alone. George scarcely recognized the man he saw before him.

"How like you not to rise when I enter a room," George tried to joke when he saw Fox lying on the daybed, covered over with a mountain of blankets, his face ashen.

Fox tried to laugh but he winced instead. "Yes. Well, I am sorry about that. It has been a rather difficult few days."

"So I have heard." George moved nearer and sat in the hardback satinwood chair beside him. It was still warm from Elizabeth, who had spent her morning there.

"You know, Fox, this simply will not do. You, like this, just now when I need you the most. We've made great strides with the King these past few days. I think he may be weakening."

"I know. Rather a bore, is it not?"

He tried to sit up but required George's assistance. The Prince fluffed the small green satin bolster and then placed it gently back behind Fox's head. Then he straightened the blankets. "Might I get you anything?"

"Just another ten years." He smiled. "And perhaps a cup of water."

George scanned the room and saw a china pitcher of water and a cup on the bedside table. He moved to get it.

"Ironic," Fox said as George poured the water. "After so many years. Just when I have in my sights all of the things for which I have struggled so long and so dearly."

George looked back over his shoulder. "What is this? Talk of defeat from a man who has mastered the impossible?"

"Perhaps I have become more realistic, George. Age does curious things to a person."

"It certainly muddies the spirits. I can see that plainly enough." George brought the water and helped him drink it. He coughed a little and the Prince of Wales lovingly dotted his chin with a tip of the blanket. "Besides, there is nothing wrong with you that a good wench and a bottle of brandy would not cure."

Fox lay his head back against the satin bolster, exhausted. "Would that it were true, my friend."

"I—I know I never said it back when it really mattered," George began, finding the words harder to speak than he had thought. "But...I love you, you old Fox. I truly do."

Charles grinned peevishly. "Why, Your Highness. I never figured you for the sort."

George twisted his lips. "Don't make sport of it. You know precisely what I meant."

He reached out a trembling hand and braided his fingers with the Prince, cold ice against warm, vital flesh. "Yes, I do know what you meant."

"You were always there for me back in those early days, you and I and Sheridan setting London on its ear."

"Yes. We were a randy trio, at that, were we not?"

George's brilliant blue eyes narrowed. "And Georgiana, always baiting and tempting us. Keeping us on our toes. I miss those days. The thrill of the game..."

"Entertaining times, they were."

"But it was always more than that to me. You were like family when my own failed me as they did."

"Oh dear, Georgie." Fox gave a sad little laugh. "For your own sake, do not try to make it out to be more than it was. Sheridan and I needed your influence against the King. In those days we used you dreadfully."

Their hands tightened together, binding friendship and love, pressing out the years of estrangement. "Perhaps in the beginning that was true. But we all became so much more to one another, didn't we?"

"That we did," Fox conceded and George could see that he was beginning to tire.

"I...just want you to know that I am sorry I wasn't a better friend, what I did to you at the House of Commons—for Maria's sake."

"You love her a great deal," Fox said. "Any man worth his salt would likely have done the same thing, had he been in your shoes."

"But I lied to you about the marriage."

"I know that. But then I lied to you about Elizabeth." Fox smiled. "I bedded her long before I told you, or anyone else, that I had done it. One of your elegant little deceptions. Is that not what you fancied them?" He winked and then smiled. "So perhaps now we are even."

George's voice was strained. His eyes were rimmed with tears. "You are only trying to clear my conscience over my behavior."

"No. I am merely trying to set my house in order. It is important that you know I forgave you for all of that a long time ago. Because, all right, yes, if you must know, I love you as well. You have been the nearest thing to a friend this life ever offered me...and I do care deeply for you. Remember that always. And after you leave here today, I should like you to do something for me."

"You have only to name it."

"Have a huge cherry brandy for me. I think I shall miss that about this life even more than the sex."

Charles James Fox, orator, raconteur, puckish charmer, and friend, died later that afternoon but George drank only one sip of cherry brandy in honor of his friend. He closed his eyes and heard the sweet, funny echo of Fox's voice. The melancholy in his heart made it seem almost real. But soon it would fade with all of the other idealistic voices of his youth.

George was glad that in the end they had reconciled. Somehow it had made the loss of a mentor a little easier to bear. His greatest regret was that Charles would not be there to one day see him crowned King of England.

They had shared so much. Politics...gambling...mistresses. Now, just when they had found one another again, when they were both happy and secure with the lives they had made for themselves, he was gone again. This time, forever.

An era had ended with the death of Pitt, Georgiana, and Charles, but a new one, a grand new chapter, his own reign—with the woman he loved beside him—was close at hand.

THE DECISION BY THE HOUSE of Lords to award custody of little Mary Seymour to the Marquess of Hertford had been anything but a popular one. Although there had been a great deal of public interest in the case, the decision served to revive the old prejudice against Maria. Her religion, as it had always been, was still at issue. It was unthinkable by much of society that a Protestant child should be handed over to a Papist simply because the lady happened to be sleeping with the Prince of Wales.

The air in the city was blue with gossip, and once again the cruel caricaturists wetted their pens. This time, however, it was not exclusively Maria, but Minney Seymour against whom they scrawled their derisive barbs. The innocent little child was portrayed most cruelly in a cartoon entitled "To Be or not to Be...a Protestant."

Maria had finally learned to bear the daily onslaught of indignities against herself. It was a risk she had accepted by remaining, through the years, George's secret wife. But this, involving a child, was unacceptable.

Feeling a blinding surge of motherly protection, she decided to take Minney and spend the remainder of the summer back in the safe haven of Brighton. George agreed that she should go and that he would join them as soon as duty would permit. But there was another more dangerous reason he decided to linger in London.

Isabella's continued refusal to give George the assurance he needed about Minney began to obsess him. He invited her everywhere, hoping to woo her and thus keep her in line. Not only did she spend time at Carlton House but at Brighton as well, where, in an odd show of propriety, she would only dine if Maria were present.

In their game of cat and mouse, the clever Lady Hertford was most definitely winning. She seemed to want to keep him guessing. The devotion of the future King of England, any way she could achieve it, was a powerful chit for any ambitious Tory wife.

He wanted to be in Brighton with Maria and Minney, and whatever he needed to do to achieve that suddenly became acceptable. A dalliance would not alter his love for Maria, to his mind, it would only ensure it. After all, wasn't it the King himself who had taught him that the ends do indeed justify the means? At least that was one thing he could say he had learned from his wretched father.

"Take care, my darling," Maria whispered as they stood beside the carriage on a fog-blanketed London morning, saying their final farewells.

"Will you promise to write to me, Prinney?" asked the little girl they both loved as their own.

George scooped her into his arms in the courtyard of Carlton House and kissed her until she began to writhe with infectious giggles. "Just try to stop me!" he said into her ear. "But you must write to me in return."

"Every day," she dutifully promised.

"And see that your mama does the same."

"Oh I will, Prinney! I will!"

He set her gently back to the ground but not before her eyes were moist with tears.

"I wish you were going with us," Minney said with a sad smile.

"So do I. More than anything. But I shall join you soon."

"Do you promise?"

Her eyes, wide and filled with so much innocence, had the power to wound him as nothing else other than Maria's ever could. George felt the sudden sharp sting of regret for not having told her about Isabella and what he had been forced to do to secure her favor. But it was too late for that now. Besides, it would be easier, certainly better, to tell her everything when he had finally found a way to secure Minney's future permanently. He could, after all, not lead the amorous woman on indefinitely.

"Yes, child," he said gravely. "I promise."

George watched them settle into the carriage and then stood waving in the courtyard as they pulled out of sight, free at last of Minney's adoring eyes, and Maria's trust.

He sighed, hating himself a little for the risk he was taking. He knew what it was likely to cost him if Maria discovered the truth before he was ready to tell her. But for the love of his family, it was a risk he still must take.

CHAPTER TWENTY-TWO

MARIA SANK BACK AGAINST THE carriage seat as they wound their way through London. It was more and more difficult to return to the city now, in the autumn of 1809, with the peace of Brighton to which she could repair. Where Minney was happy. Where they both were safe.

But she and George had been apart for nearly two long weeks and she missed him desperately. And in spite of how taken up his letters said he was with some sort of vague business he never seemed to detail, she knew how lonely he would be by now. She smiled and closed her eyes. A surprise visit was just the thing. She would coax him back to Brighton with her today, whatever she needed to do.

George must have come out here, she thought, heading quickly out of Carlton House and into the garden when none of the staff seemed to know where he was. It was not that much of a surprise, knowing how he loved to be alone, to stroll in his garden, collect his thoughts.

She heard the voices first. One husky and low, a woman's. The other was familiar. It was George. Maria moved nearer. Instinct made her careful on the pink gravel to make no noise. Two people were behind a tall hedge. There was a small, painted gazebo just beyond it, draped with pale pink almond blossoms. The gazebo had been her idea, her design shortly after they married. A place for them to retreat alone.

"George, please." The woman's voice carried across the hedge. There was seduction in it. "You must understand. I simply cannot give you any greater assurance," she purred.

"Then give me, at least, a reason."

"Because it goes against everything I believe."

"That is not enough."

"Dear George. You are a Whig. I am a Tory. I am married to Lord Hertford. You are a man with two wives. I simply cannot risk the complications of giving you what you desire."

Maria felt the blood leave her face. It drained from her limbs in an excruciatingly hot rush. She faltered. Lady Hertford? He wanted *her?* Sweet Jesus in heaven above, it simply was not possible! Not what she was thinking! The woman had handed over her niece! Was this what she meant to take in return?

Maria faltered. A roar, like rushing water, rose up inside her head. Their voices grew more faint. But the need alone to hear the rest stopped her from losing consciousness entirely. For a moment there was silence between them.

Maria longed to charge at them both in that instant, for the reality of what was happening.

"You are an exceptional woman, Isabella," she could hear her husband saying. "Can you not do this one exceptional thing?"

Memories tumbled back at her through the years. Words spoken to her in a garden once. A desperate young prince. The need he had for assurance to attain what he desired. God, *was Isabella Hertford what he desired now?*

Maria moved slowly to where the hedge broke and was parted by the slim gravel path. She peered around the corner. Her heart raced so violently that she was certain any moment it meant to kill her completely. They were sitting together on a painted iron bench inside the gazebo, Isabella and George. *Her George.* The man for whom she had given up so much, and compromised the rest. The sun was behind them, bathing them in pink-and-gray silhouette. But she could see them both. See it all.

Tears streamed down Maria's cheeks as her heart beat a wild rhythm. That sound, like the tide, swelled up within her once again as she watched, through her tears, this man she loved so desperately, touch the neck of another woman, then trace a kiss where his fingers had been. This was the business? The vague reason he did not go with them to Brighton? He was trying to seduce this bulky, passionless woman, as if Maria had never even existed...As if their love, and all that they had endured, had never even happened. She felt the bile rise swiftly in her throat.

Hearing a rustling beyond the hedge, and then a tiny whimper, George glanced up and caught just enough of a glimpse behind the emerald screen to know that it was Maria. He sprang from the bench but she ran from him.

"Maria!"

The sound of him calling her name, spoken through lips that only a moment ago had touched Lady Hertford's bare flesh, stung her like venom. She moved only a few steps more before she tripped on a stone, then collapsed onto the gravel, and George swept her up into his arms.

"Darling, what on earth are you doing back in London?"

"Bastard! She seethed and beat on his chest with her fists as tears of rage blinded her. "Bloody bastard!...and you promised that it would be different this time!"

"I've done nothing! I—"

"Lying swine!"

Maria struggled to get back to her feet but he was holding her shoulders, forcing her to stay there with him. He was trying to force her to listen, not certain of what he would say if she did. "You must understand..."

She swung wildly at him again. "I understand completely! How could you do this to me yet again—*to us?*"

Maria backed away on her hands in the gravel and tried to rise. "Darling," he said, softening his voice in hopes of calming her. "Just give me a moment to explain. It isn't what it—"

When she had risen she looked down at him, her eyes blazing with pain. Her words were spoken in anger. The betrayal had been too strong for it to have been any other way. They came in little gasps of breath.

"You want to...to explain...*yet again?* How truly gracious that would be of me...And what utter lunacy! All the times we hosted her, entertained her...all those many evenings I believed you were merely showing interest in her for Minney's sake!" When he tried to take her arms again she spat at him. "That is what I think of your protestations, George! Your lies and your deceptions!"

LATER THAT EVENING, WHEN HE hoped that she would have calmed down, George went to Maria's house. He would explain what he had really been trying to get from Lady Hertford and all would be forgiven. He stood alone in the doorway of her dark bed-chamber, his lips parted in surprise.

"What are you doing?"

She was calm now, deathly calm. "Packing."

He came toward her clothed in shadows. "And might I ask where it is you mean to go?"

"I need to get away from London, and Brighton, for good. Minney and I are going to Twickenham."

"But she's our child, yours *and* mine! You cannot simply take her away!"

She was holding the last two silver scent flasks from her dressing table. She looked at him, the anger and the betrayal still burning like an onyx fire in her dark eyes. "Your Highness did see her to my care. Or do you mean to take that from me, as well?"

He raked a hand through his hair, his face was ashen. "I wish you would listen to me about this."

"There are a great many things I would have wished for as well, George. Not finding you clandestinely with Lady Hertford today, whispering to her like a lover, and kissing her neck, quite certainly would have been at the top of that list."

George lunged at her, pressed by the futile need to make her understand. "Damn it, Maria, she is *not* my mistress, not in that sense of the word! I swear that! I was seeing her for your sake!"

"For *me?*" she huffed incredulously. "That is beneath us both!"

"It is no ploy! Not this time. All right, I shall tell you the truth. All of it. Will you at least agree to hear me out?" When she did not

340

respond, he continued. "You know painfully well that the Hertfords will forever be Minney's legal guardians and, from the outset, Isabella made it clear to me that I should be mindful of that fact. She is an ambitious woman, Maria, and I was attempting to change her mind."

Her eyes, this time, did not soften with love as they had the last time he had confessed a lie, when the issue had been Minney's paternity. Now they blazed with anger. "So you thought if you simply seduced her—"

"I did think, if I could just get close enough to her, that she would come to feel some sort of...allegiance, yes. Then perhaps she would be less inclined to displease me by holding the child's custody over our heads! But I swear to you, that was all!"

She still struggled beneath his grasp but George would not let her go, knowing that if he did that now, it would be forever. "And the fact that she is just a dalliance, not some formal sort of concubine, *yet*, that makes the lying and the deception justifiable?"

The muscles in his face tensed. A moment later, he looked away.

"For the love of God, George! Can you look at me and say that you would not have made it more, if it had come to that?"

In a moment between two heartbeats, he struggled with whether or not to be honest now, to tell her what she was asking, knowing in his heart what the truth was likely to cost him.

A carriage passed by beneath her bedroom window. The clock ticked on into the strained silence between them as Maria's eyes rooted onto his.

"Yes. All right, yes! I would have done even *that* for you...and for Minney!" he blurted out. "And I was bloody well prepared to do it in spite of how ill the nearness of so wretched a cow makes me!"

George heard her gasp behind her hand, but he could not stop now. She wanted the truth. Deserved it. So she must have it. *All of it.* After all of their years, everything they had endured together, he owed her that much.

"Perhaps it was foolhardy, but I would have done anything in this world to see you happy with your child, and Minney secure...The deception was wrong, I will admit that. I was wrong not to tell you, but everything I have ever done, since that first night at Carlton

House, has been for love of you! If it is what you truly desire, then from this day on, I shall spare you nothing, not even dark details like that."

As he spoke the words they were not a lie. He meant them completely. But Maria had come to know him almost better than he knew himself. George was not capable of changing something that was so much at the core of who he was as a man, and as a prince. He was what his history, what his father—and fate, had made of him.

In his mind, the end would always justify the means. The business with Charles James Fox... Lady Jersey... Now Lady Hertford... *And tomorrow who or what would be next?*

Maria's voice was low, heartbroken. "Do not make promises you cannot keep."

She gazed out the window at the night sky, which filtered in a soft white light from the moon. She must say it and it must be now. In spite of the fear. In spite of the fact that she still loved him desperately, and always would. She must say it now as much for her own sanity as for the final shreds of dignity she had left. When she gathered the courage, all that she had left in her body, she pulled away. "I want a formal separation."

He let go of her and stepped back. "You cannot mean that."

Maria heard the shock in his voice but she did not look at him. She could not, if she meant to see this through, if she had any hope of rescuing herself. "Under the circumstances, I think it would be for the best."

"No, damn it! I shall not let this happen to us! *Not* again!"

"Do you not understand, George? We're too different, you and I. It has taken me all of this time to realize just how different our worlds are. Mother Mary! You have been lying to me about one thing or another, and then justifying it to us both, for our entire marriage!"

"That is not true—"

"In some ways, I actually understand why you do it. A part of me even loves you for going to such vile extremes to help Minney and me. But even that cannot change the fact that your methods go against everything I believe, the things I hold most sacred in the world. And if I do not have my beliefs, George. I have nothing at all."

"We're too precious, Maria. You cannot simply toss us away like yesterday's rubbish!"

"Let me go, George," she pleaded, the same elixir of anger and pain rising to the surface once again. "Let me go before every last shred of what we feel for one another is destroyed forever!"

He closed his eyes and drew in a breath. She was right. He was beaten. His life and his demons had beaten him. He could not swear in his heart that he would never use deception again in his life if it meant protecting those he loved...He would not hurt her anymore.

George touched her face with the back of his hand. The skin was still smooth, like a child's, but the expression on her face carried the weight of a lifetime...a weight for which he alone must bear the responsibility.

"So, then I suppose it is truly over between us," he said softly.

After a moment, George lifted her chin with the tip of his finger and pressed his mouth on hers. Gentle. Tender. As he tried to touch the past, the tears in her eyes mirrored his own.

"Very well then. I shall not fight you any longer. But I will *never* stop loving you, Maria," he whispered against her lips.

...And, God help me, she thought. *I know I shall never stop loving you.*

AFTER HE HAD GONE, THAT sound of his carriage clicking off into the night, Maria moved slowly, like a woman twice her age, to her bedside table. She opened it and brought out a small mahogany chest with a little brass lock. The key was beneath an oil lamp on top of the table. She opened it with a little click. This was where she kept her secret things. Things she had long considered most precious. Her yellowed and faded marriage certificate to George. A bundle of old love letters. The deed to the house on Tilney Street that she had proudly purchased for herself. The Papal Brief declaring her marriage valid.

It felt like the summation of her life.

She tossed the contents onto her bed and fanned out the papers with limp fingers, wearily searching first for the Papal Brief. Considering George's new friendship with Lord and Lady Hertford, both, Protestant Tories, and the anti-Catholic sentiment so rampant in England, she must take no chances.

Maria held the brief to her chest for a moment. She closed her eyes. This document had justified her actions. It had brought her

343

peace with God and peace with herself. But now it was a danger. She looked over at the fire. It must be surrendered to the flames. Tonight George had left her no choice. Her life was in ashes now anyway, so perhaps it was fitting. But she could not bear to watch it burn. Tossing it into the fire, she turned away.

Next she opened the marriage certificate and gazed down at the fading signatures of her brother and uncle, the two who had witnessed her felony. Now that all hope for this marriage was destroyed, she could not know that George would not seek to implicate them.

She reached for the fire again as the thoughts swirled in her mind, blending together. Colors. Memories. Images of that day. Of her and George so much in love. So impenetrable. Once, he had sworn that nothing would ever part them. Another empty promise. Yet another deception. But as she held it over the open flames, this single remaining proof of their union, she could not bring herself to destroy it. She might well have torn out her heart as rip this symbol from the pages of history. Perhaps some day someone would care that they really had been man and wife, after all.

With trembling hands, she took a pair of scissors from the top drawer of her night table. The flames in the hearth began to sputter, the Papal Brief now black as coal. She fixed her eyes back on the certificate of their union. Slowly, painfully, she cut away her brother's name. Her uncle's name followed.

If evidence of their illegal marriage was discovered one day, then so be it. As she had always said, she had married George for better or for worse. Even now that they were to separate, she remained bound by her vows. But by this act, she had seen to it that only she would ever pay the price for what she had been so moved, for love, to do.

As the small slips of paper bearing their names burned, Maria fell onto her bed, her face in her hands. But she did not cry. She could not. Not yet. Tonight the pain of losing George again was too intense, almost unreal. Having so bright and shining a dream finally at an end...yes, she would have a lifetime to mourn for that.

Part Four

I WONDER BY MY TROTH, WHAT THOU

AND I

DID TILL WE LOVED.

—JOHN DONNE

CHAPTER TWENTY-THREE

"IS YOUR MAJESTY READY THEN?"

The question came from the reed-thin, raven-haired valet, Dupaquier. George looked up, at first seeming not to hear. *Your Majesty*. It was 1821, he was fifty-nine years old, and yet how hollow that still did sound. He would never grow accustomed to the fact that now, finally after so many years of waiting in the shadows—and twelve since his final rupture with Maria, he was George IV, King of England.

His father's death, two years after the death of his mother, had not been unexpected. The old King had lived to the age of eighty-two. He was no more than the shell of the man who had ruled England through the American Revolution and also the defeat of the unrealistic Napoleon Bonaparte at Waterloo. As much as one man's end, so it was another's beginning, and for that he had little cause to grieve. But the death of George's younger brother Edward Duke of Kent, six days later, had shocked the nation.

Second in line to the throne after Frederick, Edward had been the only son of George III to have conceived a living, legitimate heir. With George's only daughter, Charlotte, dead now as well, Edward's eight-month-old little girl would likely one day wear England's Crown—as Queen Victoria.

George sat in his dressing room vested in purple and gold as Dupaquier came to him. He would open Parliament today seated on a new throne built especially for him. It was a new era for England and against the advice of his counsel, his first act would be to try to get rid of the new Queen. His *other* wife.

Since their only child, Charlotte, had died giving birth, Caroline had been abroad in Italy. Her behavior had become erratic, even scandalous, and George had enough to bear from public opinion without having to deal with a Queen who had lost her morals. He had longed to find a way to be out of the marriage since the day after the ceremony—but it had taken twenty-six years.

He knew that she meant to claim her place as Queen of England. That thought was nearly impossible to bear, since he knew, even now, that the only woman who should be standing beside him, as his partner, his Queen, was Maria. Still and always she.

He pushed back the thick crimson drapery. Once again this afternoon there was a group collected just beyond the long Ionic screen that separated Carlton House from Pall Mall. They were chanting the same thing today that they always did in Caroline's favor. "No Queen, no King!" They cried it over and over again between their hisses and their shouts against him.

"Bloody fools...You never understood," he muttered to himself. No one really ever knew the magnificent queen Maria would have made.

The list of things Caroline had done to disgrace him was endless. Gambling night after night. Attending masquerades in costumes coming no further up than her waist. And then there were the men. The most infamous and the most embarrassing was Joachim Murat, brother-in-law of England's greatest enemy, Napoleon Bonaparte.

George fingered the gold fringe along the drapery's edge and listened to the ceaseless chanting of his people beyond the wall. They were angry with him again. Angry for a thousand things. Caroline was only the icing on a very thick cake of their disillusion.

George's ministers had tried to persuade him not to attempt a divorce with sentiment against him running so high. They had even tried to bribe her to stay abroad, knowing what would occur if she returned. Their pleas only made her more insistent.

"Shall we go then, Your Majesty?" Dupaquier asked again. He held up an elegant blue cutaway tailcoat. George fingered the brocade. Rich and luxuriant, the fabric even felt costly. It made him smile. *How fortunate I am,* he thought, *to have all of the things that money can buy, since it appears I shall never again be blessed with those things which it cannot.*

His valet held out the obligatory last cherry brandy to see him through the morning, or most of it anyway. George drank it in one swallow and handed back the empty crystal glass. "Would Your Majesty like another before we go? It may make your day a bit easier to bear."

George looked at his new valet, young and lithe and too bloody attractive for a morning when he felt so dreadful. "Charles," he said, wearily. "I am afraid I have discovered the hard way that there is not enough cherry brandy in all the world to accomplish that."

"YOU WOULD NOT HAVE BELIEVED it, I tell you, Belle," Fanny said. "The crowd to see Her Majesty's return wound the whole way from Westminster Bridge to Greenwich! There was a throng of carts and carriages and horsemen three deep surrounding her coach the entire way. And they were shouting, "Long live the Queen! Long live Queen Caroline!"

Fanny stooped over a half-mended shirt at the scarred oak kitchen table. Her chapped fingers were busily pushing a needle back and forth through the fabric. A thick soup behind her on the stove filled the kitchen with the mingling aroma of boiled beef, sage, and rosemary.

Belle Pigot, frail now and doddering, sipped a cup of lukewarm tea and gazed at Fanny as she clacked on and on about Queen Caroline's triumphant return to England.

"And then I heard at the tavern last night that as Her Majesty rode up St. James's Street, she was nodding and smiling like a common whore, at all of the men who watched her from the windows of White's Club! Scandalous! Do you not think?"

"You'd best hold your tongue," Belle said in a throaty admonishment, "and remember who it is you serve."

"Oh, I'd never forget Mrs. Fitz. She's been good as gold to me all of these years."

"That she has. Remember it well too. It cannot have been easy for the King's rightful wife having Caroline of Brunswick returning to London as Queen of England."

Fanny set the shirt onto the table with a heavy sigh and rested her elbows on top of it. She had been thoughtless. Belle was right. It should have been Queen Maria whom they hailed and cheered. After all, she was the true wife before God, of England's King.

It was all so terribly confusing to those who knew or even suspected the truth. To the English, she was seen as just another infamous mistress. To the rest of the world who did not acknowledge English law, Maria Fitzherbert was his wife because she had married him before God.

"Serves him right, I say," Fanny declared, trying to make right her momentary lapse of discretion. "I hear from a friend of mine, a chambermaid at Carlton House, that the other day as His Majesty rode down the Mall they actually stoned his carriage!"

"He certainly does not possess the great allure he once did," Belle conceded. "On that we shall agree. The charm walked out of his life the day his real wife did the same."

"Poor bloody bastard. If you ask me, he deserves everything he gets for what he has done to poor Mrs. Fitz!"

"That will be quite enough. Both of you."

It was Maria, her voice strident and deep. She had been standing behind them in the open doorway since the dangerous exchange began but she had chosen not to speak up until now. The only way she ever heard anything about the Queen of England was when those who wanted to protect her did not know that she was listening.

"Ma'am!" Fanny sprang to her feet and curtsied, pulling out the sides of her black cotton gown. "I—we had no idea that you were there!"

"Apparently not."

"Forgive us," said Belle from where she sat. "We meant no harm."

Maria was as stern and unmoving as a soldier, arms at her sides.

She looked at one of her servants and then at the other, two women with such different faces, yet both filled with the same curiosity and concern. Perhaps they were entitled to a bit of gossip. All of London was abuzz with the news of the Queen's return. And Caroline *was* the Queen. No matter what girlish things she might once have hoped for in her own youth, Caroline had taken her rightful place beside England's new King.

These days, Maria consoled herself with her own quiet life. She was thankful for her bright young daughter—a beauty now, whose way in society she must oversee at each critical turn. Thank the Lord for Minney, she so often thought. That blessed child was the evidence that her tumultuous union with George had not been a complete failure, and her upbringing now had become Maria's focus.

Maria had given parties and balls in her honor since Minney was a child. Now the beautifully grown young woman with the hazel eyes and Horatia's pale brown hair, and with her continued connection to the King, was considered the most splendid catch in England. The plans that Maria had for her beloved daughter did not include a young opportunist like George Dawson.

Their recent sojourn to Paris, however, had done little to quell Minney's insistence for the young upstart. Dawson, a cavalry officer who, to his credit, had seen action at Waterloo, unfortunately was only the second son of an Irish earl. His elder brother would inherit the title and property. But even more reprehensible than the order of his birth was the factor of his reputation, and Mr. Dawson had quite a scandalous reputation with women. Ironic as it was to try to quell someone else's heart after the life she had led, Maria simply could not bear to have that fate befall her precious daughter the way it had befallen her.

That bothersome state of affairs, and finding a way out of it, occupied Maria's mind now. The two young lovers had even taken to the disagreeable behavior of meeting in secret. Maria had responded to the first news of that by fainting. She had needed to be revived with smelling salts. She could not let her darling girl end up alone, and filled with regrets, as she had.

"May I fetch you some tea, ma'am?" Fanny asked awkwardly, with her hands clasped behind her back.

Tea with my servants, thought Maria. She looked again closely at each of their faces. It would be most irregular to join them here like this. But they had lived with her every day through so much of the scandal and the heartache, and it was quite likely that at this stage of her life, Belle Pigot and Fanny Davies were the dearest friends she had left in the world. Why not have tea with them? Why not, indeed. After a moment's consideration she sat on the edge of one of the stiff walnut chairs. Fanny's green eyes widened.

"Here, ma'am?"

Maria glanced at Belle, then looked up at her with mock surprise. Only God in his Heaven knew when she might expect to see her girl again this afternoon. She had gone with George Dawson to a water-color exhibition and once again Maria had been left alone with her unsettling fold of memories and regrets. Anything would be preferable to facing that yet once again today.

It seemed as if everyone was leaving her life, a little at a time, and there was not a thing she could do about it. *Damnable age!* she thought sadly, still feeling inside like the same young woman who had first captured the heart of a prince, and set all of London ablaze with gossip—knowing that she was no longer. So many losses from her life. Horatia, then Hugh. Her own brother, Jack. Now even dear sweet Francis Russell.

She had only just last evening read of his death. She had not seen him since that morning she had reconciled with George, when his harsh reproach had made strangers of them. But she had kept informed about him through Lady Clemont, and through George's brother Edward as well.

Both of her friends had told her, sadly, that Francis had died unmarried, never having completely been able to put Maria from his heart or his mind. Only now that she had experienced that same kind of loss herself, one that had spoiled her heart for anyone else, was she truly able to understand what she had once meant to him. For that she truly grieved.

Maria glanced at Belle and then Fanny. "Did you not ask me if I would like tea?"

"Indeed I did, ma'am," Fanny replied.

"Well then. I might just as well take it here among friends as out there alone. Would you not agree?"

KING GEORGE IV DID NOT divorce his Queen. But in 1821, a year after he ascended the throne, Caroline died. Publicly, he mourned her, his *other* wife—and a virtual stranger. Three weeks was considered sufficient to stay the ire of the people before he could begin again to live the life he desired, free and unfettered by an obligation he had long ago come to regret. It was not at all the charmed, beautiful world that Maria Fitzherbert had presided over with him, and everyone knew it, but still he went again to Brighton. *Chasing Rainbows*, he called it—holding on to some few fragments of a happy past.

"No! I'll not allow it, Nash!"

George raged at his architect and tossed the plans onto the floor beside a pale yellow and black Chinese screen inside the Pavilion.

"I was very clear that this particular room was not to be altered. I made my wishes clear from the outset!"

John Nash, a gray and balding man with a barrel chest and a thin, pale line for a mouth, was not deterred by the King's rage. "But Your Majesty must listen to reason," he continued undaunted. "It will change the symmetry of the house if we do not alter this room."

"I do not care! I do not want this one changed!" George looked around at the one remaining room from the farmhouse that he had maintained for Maria. Glancing around, he saw the fabrics that he and Maria had chosen together that first summer so long ago, the table she had ordered from France, and his heart ached as if she had left yesterday.

"You may have your carpets here and bring in a few more of your bamboo chairs," he said firmly. "But beyond that the subject of this room is not open to debate."

Nash knew from hearing the servants gossip that this room was part of the original farmhouse, the only part of the house left untouched. But he had no idea, until today—until this moment really, that the King had maintained it unaltered for such strong reasons of sentiment.

There could be only one reason that he refused to surrender it now to Nash's grand scheme for the Pavilion. After all this time, His Majesty was still in love with his Catholic wife. That, he thought, was quite amazing.

"Is there nothing I can do to change Your Majesty's mind?" Nash persisted.

"As I said, John, the subject is closed. Now if you will excuse me" George nodded. "I am going for a walk in the garden."

Brighton was so beautiful in the spring. George inhaled deeply and felt the salt air replenish his tired body. As it always did. He felt rejuvenated by the air, by the sea and the freedom. But it was not the same, nor would it ever be.

"Oh, how I do love it," he said to himself with a sigh, leaning against the stone railing that separated his veranda with the neatly laid garden and the dazzling blue-green sea beyond it. Suddenly he caught a glimpse, across the garden, of Maria's house. It had been a mistake to return here this time. He knew that now.

George had done everything he could to avoid her when he was here in Brighton and, for the most part, he had been successful. But there had been a heavy price to pay for his avoidance. He no longer walked along the Steine or bathed in the cool ocean water as he so had loved to do. Nor did he commune with the eager Brightonians who strolled along the seafront before his Pavilion hoping to catch a glimpse of him as they once so freely had done. All of which had helped him feel, from those earlier years onward, like he could be, if only for a little while, just a man. A simple man, like anyone else. Free to love and be loved.

"Why not go to Windsor," his staff encouraged, seeing the pain daily in his eyes. "It's so lovely there this time of year with all of the hyacinths and the lilacs in bloom."

George drummed his fingers against the stone railing and looked out to the sea. It had been wonderful to come here again. To live in the past for a little while. But he must leave the memories behind if he had even a ghost of a chance of getting on with his life. A life with which he was trying to come to terms—*a life still without his love.*

That afternoon, two sleek black stallions led George's rattling yellow carriage toward London. As they crested the hill he glanced back for just a moment, looking at his grand creation silhouetted in the setting sun. It was the last time he would ever see his splendid, contestable Pavilion again. Somehow he knew now that this part of his life, as well, was finally over. Like Maria, however, this too was a dream that was hard to let go.

CHAPTER TWENTY-FOUR

IN THE END, IT WAS another battle Maria had lost.

In August of 1825, five years after their meeting, the marriage of Miss Minney Seymour to Colonel George Dawson would take place. Through Frederick, who as always had acted as intermediary, Maria and the King had both conspired against the union for as long as they were able. But Minney and her paramour insisted that they were in love and that they meant to be together. Considering their own scandalous past, and the way in which they had fought to be together, it was something that neither George nor Maria had the will to remain against in the end.

Now, Minney stood in Maria's bedchamber in her white canton crepe wedding gown. Tall candles and brass lamps were lit against a pearl-gray morning sky.

Her hair had been heated with tongs into soft brown curls and topped with a wreath of lily of the valley and white rosebuds. On her cheeks and lips she wore just the slightest hint of pale rose color to warm her unmarred skin. A bit of cosmetic was the one concession Maria had agreed to make to the girl whose innocence meant everything in the world to her.

They had already spoken of her duties to her husband, of what would pass between them on her wedding night. They had spoken about patience, understanding, and about devotion. Especially devotion. It seemed to Maria that it was particularly important that her daughter understand about that.

"Well?" sighed Maria from the little blue velvet settee at the end of her huge canopied bed. "Are you not going to open it?"

Minney looked down at a small satin-covered box that was tied up with silver, ivory, and rose-colored ribbons. She glanced uncertain back up at Maria. She saw the hurt in her mother's aging eyes every time Prinney sent her a gift.

Minney loved him more than her heart could bear. He was the only father she had ever known. But if he could not find the courage to be here today of all days, she really wished he had possessed the strength of conviction to have sent nothing at all. It was her wedding day and the only gift she wanted was to see, if only for a few hours, her parents reunited.

"Go on," Maria urged her. "Open your gift. We've got a hundred other things to do before you take your vows."

They had been coming for days. Packages in all shapes and sizes that now lined the second-floor drawing room. She had just yesterday received a package from Prinney's brother Frederick. Something from his old friend, the Duke of Devonshire, had followed in the afternoon. She had even received a gift from the third royal brother, William, Duke of Clarence.

Minney looked at Maria. Convinced that she must do this, she reluctantly untied the knot. The collection of ribbons fell to the floor as she unwound the satin wrapping. Inside a small box on a bed of red velvet was a glittering set of diamond earrings. "Oh, Mama!" she gasped, forgetting to appear disinterested. "Look at them!"

"They're lovely," Maria said, forcing a smile. "Put them on."

"Oh, yes, I shall wear them today. It will almost be like having Prinney here with us." She glanced up at Maria as the words fell from her lips. She touched her mouth with her fingertips but it was too late. For so many years, Minney had tried to be a conduit between the only parents she had ever known. Their reconciliation was the thing she had hoped for, prayed for. But it was not to be. "Oh, Mama. I'm so sorry. I did not mean to infer—"

Maria softly smiled. "Child, you have every reason to wish that he could be here with us today. You need not be sorry for that."

"Thank you, Mama," she said, lowering her bright, hazel eyes. *Horatia's eyes.*

"If he were here to see you, you would take his breath away. Do you know that you have never looked lovelier? No, it's true, and do you also know who you look just like, standing there before me now? You look like your mother."

Maria had always been her mother. "Lady Seymour?" she asked.

"You are the very image of her, my dear child." Maria rose slowly. "She would be so proud of the lovely young woman you have become. Almost as proud as I am."

Minney set the box down on the corner of the settee. "I do wish I had known her."

"I wish that you had as well. She was very, very special and I believe today there is something that she would have liked you to have."

As Minney watched, Maria moved slowly to her dressing table between two windows and opened a small burlwood jewelry chest that sat between bottles of lavender perfume. She searched through the old pieces of gold and silver, clinking the ruby earrings, the emerald brooch, and her two other wedding rings before she found what she was searching for. When she turned back around, she was holding a sparkling ruby-studded bracelet.

"Your mother was wearing this the day you came to live with me."

Minney fingered it in awe. "It is so lovely."

"She said that it had belonged to her mother, and that someday she would like for you to have it." Maria smiled, her heart filled to bursting with pride and with the memories of the day she had taken that bracelet reluctantly from Horatia's feeble hand. "I can think of no more special day than this."

Minney slipped it over her wrist and pressed it to her heart. "I shall wear it too. Then I shall have everyone around me who is important. At least in spirit."

Maria's face wrinkled with her smile. "That you will, child."

After Minney had gone downstairs with Fanny, Maria looked back in the box from which the King's gift had come. There, beneath the velvet, was a note that they had missed. But she stopped herself. It was not for her to read. It had been sent to Minney. She must not breech that.

After a moment, she took the ivory parchment between her fingers anyway, and she knew that George had held this in his own hand just a short time ago. It was the closest they had come to one another for a very long time.

Maria pressed the letter tenderly to her cheek, hoping to catch the scent of the civet perfume she remembered so well. How funny life was, she thought as she shook her head, that he should still wear the same fragrance, that she should still love it so much after all of these years.

The envelope came open easily. It had not been sealed with wax. She saw the familiar scrawl and knew that it had been written in George's own hand. Her eyes raced over the contents but she saw all that mattered in the very last line.

...And always be good to Maria. She shall need you now more than ever, my own dearest girl. Connected once. Connected still.

Two lives woven together forever by this precious girl.

With trembling hands, Maria placed the letter back in its envelope and set it back beneath the velvet for Minney to find. She should not have read it. She should not have cared. But she did care... and, God help her, she always would.

"Are you all right, ma'am?" Belle asked.

The old woman came in and sat beside Maria on the settee. She moaned as her old brittle bones settled into place. "I see Mistress Minney received the King's gift. He had hoped she would see it before the wedding."

Maria was startled and looked over at her companion, her lips slightly parted. "You knew that His Majesty was sending a gift?"

Belle Pigot looked at her. "Didn't you know that he would, ma'am?"

Maria lay her head against one of the carved bedposts. "Oh, Belle. I don't suppose I know what I thought."

"Perhaps you thought he would find a way to be here today."

"Yes. Perhaps that is it."

She patted Maria's knee with gnarled fingers then kept them there a moment longer. "Today it is a difficult day for you both, hmm? The love you share for that child bonds you together even though you are apart."

"Oh, if only—"

Belle's answer was a deep sigh. Then she said, "Ah yes. *If only...* We all of us have a lifetime of those to plague our hearts, don't we now?"

Maria twined the fingers of her right hand with Belle's and the two of them sat silently together. The first bit of morning sun broke through the clouds and cast a ray of sunlight across the room. The door was still open. They could hear Jacko and Fanny and all of the other servants downstairs admiring Minney in her wedding gown.

"Is he happy with her, Belle?" Maria asked unexpectedly about Elizabeth, Lady Conyngham, the King's new companion.

"I think it is more that he has finally tired of the chase, if you'll pardon me, ma'am."

"He doesn't go out into to society so much anymore. I hear so little about him."

"Perhaps that is for the best. At least where it concerns you. These past years cannot have been easy."

Maria closed her eyes. "You know, Belle, I thought once that time would help me to forget him. But it has only made the painful times the ones that are so much harder to recall."

"Time is a mixed blessing for so many things."

For a moment Maria wavered, near tears. "That it is, Belle," she finally said, and put her arm around the old woman's shoulder. "...That it is."

MARIA SEALED A LETTER TO Minney that she would mail to her on her honeymoon. Then she pushed herself slowly away from the carved, painted writing table. It was late. She reached for her glass but found that she had already drunk the rest of the brandy. She had drunk little through the years because of George. Because it once had so consumed him. But today she had made a concession. Today she had drunk a great deal.

It had been a difficult day to have endured alone.

She had always believed, on the day when Minney married, that she and George, hand in hand, would watch her become wife to some wealthy, titled nobleman of whom they both heartily approved. As with so much else in her life, this had not gone the way she had planned it. But it was not her time any longer. Nor were they her choices.

And that was the way it was meant to go. *The old die off as the new ones bloom...Life, and living it, is for the young...Memories and ghosts of all the yesterdays are what is left to those of us who must stay and grow old.*

359

CHAPTER TWENTY-FIVE

"HIS HIGHNESS HAS ARRIVED, MA'AM," Fanny announced.

Maria looked up from her writing table, a place where she spent much of her time now that Minney was again in Paris, celebrating her fifth wedding anniversary. Maria had just put her signature on another letter to her daughter when Fanny knocked on the open bedchamber door and took two tentative steps inside.

Before her, a huge, partially open window faced out onto the Steine. The breeze tossed the salt air in across her desk, ruffling all of her bills and papers. But Maria did not care. It was here at Brighton, like no other place on earth now, breathing this air, that she felt truly well.

Since Minney's marriage to George Dawson, Maria had begun to suffer bouts of rheumatism. Her early condition was made worse by the fact that the last of her friends now were dying. By their deaths, she was forced to face the reality of her own mortality.

Last spring, the irascible Lady Clermont, her friend and confidante through some of the worst events of her life, had finally gone to her grave. There were those who thought she might live forever. Maria had been one of them, and her death had been a heavy blow.

But the most difficult loss to bear had come at Christmas with the death of her dear Frederick. Dear, dear Freddie. For almost thirty years, nothing had shaken their friendship, not even her enduring problems with George. He had been a great source of strength to Maria through the toughest of times, visiting her and writing to her consistently. When he died, Maria felt she had lost her very last friend in the world. George was gone from her life.

Minney now too was married and gone, and she had never felt more alone.

Maria looked back out of the window as Fanny stood beside her. It was nearly dusk, the sky was a bonfire of color. A large crowd still gathered in anticipation near her door. The Duke and Duchess of Clarence had arrived from Dieppe and they had just landed at Chain Pier.

The pier, at the end of the Steine, had been illuminated with dozens of huge lanterns for their disembarkment. From her window, Maria could see that they had been received by the town fathers and were being escorted to her doorstep by the light of burning flambeaux, lanterns, and candles. The Brighton Steine glowed. By Frederick's death, it was William who would next be King of England after George.

She put the letter to Minney back in the desk drawer and Fanny helped her with a black Chantilly lace shawl across her shoulders. That once had been Belle's job, but like all of the others who had been so dear to her, now she too was dead. Only Jacko and Fanny remained, and they too were aging. Without another word between them, the two women went down the twisted, creaking mahogany stairs together.

"Your Highness," Maria said in introduction. The rheumatism made her curtsey difficult and William, George's second brother, kindly held out his hand to help her back up again.

Around them on the veranda and in the street a crowd still gathered to see the King's brother visit who many still believed was the true Queen of England. Maria had not yet met the Duchess of Clarence, a tall, dignified woman with a well-bred hauteur. Still, the two women embraced as if they were old friends.

"William has told me so much about you," the Duchess said as the evening breeze rustled the graying curls of her hair. "It is an honor to finely meet you, ma'am." The Duchess addressed her as she would have her Queen. Maria was struck.

"The honor is mine, Your Highness. It was good of you both to visit me while you are in Brighton."

"Ma'am," said William with devotion in his voice. "I consider it my duty."

They followed Fanny and Jacko up the steps and into the graceful brick house. Jacko closed the door but even then the crowd did not disperse. Maria was their royalty here in Brighton and they still chose to honor her that way.

Fanny set out a tray rattling with crystal decanters of port and sherry for the guests to help them shake the autumn chill. Maria watched the Duke take a glass of the sherry and sip it slowly as he sat, legs crossed, beside the fire.

William was not unlike his eldest brother in stature and appearance. He was a large man with silver hair only at his temples and the still ruddy complexion of his boyhood. As Frederick had, so did this third royal son share the same crystal-blue eyes with their King. *The haunting eyes that long ago had won her in another life, another time.*

Eighteen twenty-nine, the year past, had been a year of change for England and the old friends spent most of the evening talking about it. After years of bitter battles, Catholic Emancipation, which Maria cared deeply about, had finally been passed into law. Catholics could finally now be admitted to Parliament and they could no longer be excluded from holding any office with the exception of Regent or Lord Chancellor of England. It had been a long battle.

As they dined, William and his wife wisely avoided discussing the fact that, with the vigorous prodding of Lady Conyngham, George had opposed the measure. He had even, for a moment, threatened to abdicate rather than give his assent. In the end however, four months ago, he had signed it. There were few doubts in England as to the real reason why.

"I am glad that, at last, it has worked out this way," William said. "I know how important the measure was to you."

"There was a time when it was important to the King, as well," Maria said in reply.

"The years have changed my brother a great deal, Maria, not only his allegiances. In many ways I believe you would no longer know him," William cautiously divulged as he sipped another glass of sherry and Fanny and Jacko silently cleared the dinner dishes from the table.

Maria had heard that George was unwell. The gossip of it was all over England. But still she could not help herself from asking as she fingered her half-full goblet of wine, "And...is His Majesty well?"

William dotted his lips with a white linen napkin and leaned back in his chair. "I am certain you know that he goes out very little these days. Of late, he has suffered a number of illnesses."

"Yes. I have heard that."

"I myself have seen him only a half-dozen times in the past two years. He is kept rather closely guarded."

"By Lady Conyngham."

"As she is now Lady Steward, she is with him often, yes."

Out of deference to Maria, William did not add that for the past several years, his brother had lived like a captive in a prison of his own design. He remained almost exclusively at Windsor. All of the roads leading to Windsor Castle now were heavily guarded, thanks to Lady Conyngham's influence, and if he did ride outside the grounds, his equerries went ahead to make certain that no one was spying on him.

William also chose not to divulge that the last time he had seen his brother, George had dwelled on the past more than ever. The moment they were alone and he had spoken Maria's name, tears had come to his eyes.

Surely, William thought, there was no purpose in burdening her with that. She did not deserve any more pain. George had chosen his course. The Duke of Clarence would not be the one to bring more distress upon this dear woman who, by all rights, today should be queen.

"Do you suppose he shall ever return here to Brighton?" she found the courage to ask as they all stood and prepared to adjourn into the drawing room.

"I believe that he has wanted to for some time," he replied, taking Maria's arm as they strolled together with the Duchess of Clarence out of the dining room.

"It would be so nice for him to see this lovely little town again."

Another glass of port later the tall ebony clock near the fireplace hearth chimed midnight, and William and his Duchess stood to leave. Jacko went to fetch their cloaks and hats as Maria walked with them to the door.

"Is there anything at all I can do for you, Maria?" he asked as they stood facing one another in the small, candlelit entrance hall.

She smiled but he could see that her eyes were immeasurably sad. "Like your brother Frederick before you, William, you have given me so much just by remaining my friend through all of these years."

He reached over and kissed her cheek tenderly. "Surely you know it is so much more between us than that."

SHE WAS DOZING ON A daybed in her dressing room only to wake suddenly each time a deeper sleep was near. Every time Maria closed her eyes she thought she heard his voice as it had been in the beginning, so filled with pleading.

Maria!...Maria!...

She had left Brighton for London when the rumors of George's illness grew too pervasive to ignore. Now she waited anxiously in her elegant house across from Hyde Park, not certain of what to do. They had been estranged for so long. But that did not alter the fact that she was still, in the eyes of God, his one and only wife.

Long ago she had committed her life to him. Word that he was seriously ill changed everything. Most especially, it vanquished her pride.

Maria rose from the daybed and cast off the cashmere shawl that had covered her slim shoulders. The rheumatism made movement excruciating. It was raining again and the scent of damp air was strong even with a fire blazing. It made it such an effort even to walk back into her bedchamber. But no one hated the rain more than George.

For days she had been able to think of no one but him. Thoughts and memories stole into her mind no matter what she was doing. It was entirely mad, but she could not shake the curious feeling that she should at least try to go to Windsor. That he needed her now. But even if she could find the courage, Lady Conyngham would never allow it.

Maria paced back and forth in her bedroom. For so long she had denied her feelings to everyone—especially to herself. But he was still the only man she had ever loved.

And she knew in her heart how much he had always loved her.

Finally, Maria sat down at the little writing table where she had written so many letters to Minney this past week, and gazed down with tired eyes at a crisp blank page. Could she actually find the strength to forgive him? How many times Frederick had pleaded with her to try. Minney too. She heard the soft echo of their collective voices in her mind. *You must do it . . . you must at least try . . .*

Finally, when there was no other choice left to her by her conscience or by her heart, Maria dipped her pen in the silver well of ink and pressed it to the page. A moment later, she rang a little silver bell for Fanny.

"Yes, ma'am?"

Maria sealed the envelope with red wax and then looked up from her desk. "Fanny, I want you to see that Jacko does an errand for me. It is the most important thing I shall ever ask either of you to do. I want him to see this personally to the hand of the Duke of Clarence, and no one but the Duke."

Fanny looked down at the letter and then back at her mistress.

"You're going to see the King."

Maria took a breath, not caring how she knew. "Yes, Fanny. I am going to try."

"But is it not dangerous, ma'am? Since she was made Lady Steward of his household, Lady Conyngham's influence with His Majesty is said to be absolute."

As Maria leaned heavily on her cane, and rose to standing, her gray hair sparkled in the light as if it were threaded with real silver. "I am not without my own influence in the royal family, my friend."

Maria's maid took the sealed letter and began to turn away, then stopped. Slowly, she turned back around, her own aging face lit with a question. "Pardon me for asking. I know it is hardly my place, but do you believe the rumors that His Majesty . . . is the King dying?"

Maria sighed and felt the weight of a lifetime on her shoulders. With a heavy heart she said softly, "Oh, with all my heart, Fanny, I do so dearly hope not. Not yet. And do tell Jacko, please, to hurry."

The Lord is my Shepherd,
I shall not want.
He maketh me to lie down in green pastures.
He leadeth me beside quiet waters,
He restoreth my soul…

Reading that passage in the Bible gave George comfort that the laudanum no longer offered. If he could only put right before his death some of the wrong he had inflicted on others in his life. So much petty selfishness. So little trust in others. His life had been defined by it. And in the end it had consumed him.

He reached up and touched the locket bearing Maria's picture, which he still wore around his neck, and he felt as if he were touching her face. That precious image from so very long ago. So many years. Now his greatest consolation.

The King's physician and friend, Henry Halford, came into the bedchamber a moment later and the image of Maria receded back into the corner of his mind.

"Sit beside me, Henry." George beckoned with a trembling hand.

Halford came and sat in the chair beside the King's bed. George looked at him for a moment before he spoke. "I am to be buried wearing it," he said, clinging to the locket. "You shall see to it personally, won't you?"

It was the fourth time he had asked that morning.

"Yes, Your Majesty," Halford softly assured him once again. "It has been arranged."

"I've been so bloody foolish…about so many things. Now it is important to me that she be with me forever…at least in this one small way. Can you understand that?"

"Indeed, Your Majesty, I believe I can," Halford replied, blinking back his own tears for things that would never be for his King and the woman he had so loved.

Contented for the a little while once again, George tried to smile, then he settled back into the cool white linen. "If only I'd been granted just a little more time. If someone could have told her that… no one ever came closer to her in my heart…"

"Perhaps you should tell her yourself."

The resounding voice belonged to William. George's brother

stood at the foot of the bed beside a woman cloaked in forest-green velvet, both of them hidden by shadows. George squeezed his eyes for a moment and then opened them again, straining to make real what he dared not believe.

"Halford, light a candle," he said with a labored breath.

The surgeon now too looked up and knew at once who had accompanied the Duke of Clarence. Had he not seen it with his own eyes he would never have believed it.

Without needing to be asked, he set the freshly lit candle on the bedside table and left the room swiftly beside the Duke.

"If this is a dream then, I bid you, do not wake me," George whispered as Maria drew near.

Time and the years apart had changed her. The beautiful golden hair had gone gray, and her once flawless skin had a soft network of wrinkles. But he had known her in a heartbeat. Still so serene and elegant. The woman who should have been his Queen, his Maria...

Tears filled his dull, glazed eyes. "You...are as beautiful as ever."

"And you, I see, are as charming as ever."

He drew in a rasping breath as she sat down beside him and took his hand. It was cold, cold as ice. The feel of his flesh, once so warm and full of life, was as changed as his eyes. Once they were brilliant blue, *I thought they were as endless as the sky,* her heart reminded...*as endless as my love for you.*

Now that she was here beside him, all of it was so unimportant. All of the lies. The pain. The wasted years. None of it meant anything. Not Lady Jersey. Lady Hertford. Not even the possessive Lady Conyngham, past whom William alone had possessed the influence to see her brought.

"I do not dare to ask your forgiveness."

"I have not come for that."

He tried to smile. "Then it does not matter...why you are here, only that you are."

"Shh," she said in reply, as she ran a hand gently across his forehead, pushing back the matted snow-white hair. "Rest. You must rest now. I am here."

"Try as I have to forget you, you are still the core of me, Maria..." he said in short whispered gasps. "You are still...my soul."

367

Maria shivered, but the room was warm. A fire blazed in the hearth beside the bed and yet she was suddenly as cold as George. *Light of my life, take not so soon thy flight* ... A poet's pleading words flashed across her mind with a thousand other thoughts. Things done and not done. Said and not said.

"Oh, my dearest, dearest life," she whispered. But he did not hear her. His eyes were closed again, and for a moment she thought that he had died.

"And Mrs. Fitzherbert ... How do you find my Conservatory?" his voice broke. " ... Ah. I see you disapprove. So I shall have it razed ... first thing tomorrow." He looked at her, but the woman he suddenly saw was in a different place, different time. A lifetime ago.

"It is safer in the past, beloved. It is all right," she whispered. "Stay and dream of things as they were. Once they were sweet between us. So sweet —"

She clutched his hand more tightly, desperately, but still the warmth did not come. *Once I said that I wished I had never fallen in love with you, because of the pain, because it hurt so much to lose you,* she thought. *But I was wrong, George. I was so wrong. Loving you, being loved by you in return, was worth the cost. We loved and we married for love, whatever history makes of me, that they cannot deny.*

George closed his eyes again and she watched his drawn face as the pinched features slowly began to soften into something closer to what he once had been.

Such a magnificent face, Maria thought, even though she could see no visible traces of it. Suddenly she felt him squeeze her hand almost fiercely, as though he were trying to hold on to life. She squeezed back.

"It is all right, my darling. I am here now. I am here."

George did not open his eyes again. After a moment he seemed to want to say something. She leaned forward, a breath away. Then softly, gently, she pressed her lips to his.

"You are still ... my very soul," he whispered again and squeezed her hand. " ... my very soul."

EPILOGUE

ONCE AGAIN SHE REACHED OUT and touched the surface of the coffin. Yes, the scars were deep but the love was deeper still. It had endured.

Her voice was a whisper. "Oh my love...why was it never enough, what we had?"

Just then, a single guardsman returned and moved slowly toward her, his heels echoing across the bare plank floor. "It is time, ma'am," he said. When he extended his arm, Maria clutched it willingly. What little strength age had left her, grief had now taken.

"Your daughter is waiting for you in the courtyard," he said softly. "If you will permit me, I shall see you to her care."

She had not noticed it as she had come into the State Apartments, but lining the darkly paneled corridor was a gallery of paintings, each framed in heavy gold leaf. Each image, an echo from the past, gazed down upon her with a familiar warmth.

There was Ernest, so shy and adolescent with moppish red hair and a blush the color of camellias, then Edward. His daughter Victoria would one day carry on his legacy as queen. Maria winced. The two brothers were side by side, frozen in time. *Such innocence,* she thought as she paused to look up at them both smiling down with the carefree air of youth.

Were any of us ever so young? she wondered, mouthing the words.

Beside Edward was William, now King of England. He certainly was not the most handsome of the brothers, but his great kindness became him. History would see to that.

Beside him, as she knew it must be, was the portrait of Frederick, dressed in uniform, his head held high with the pride of his post. It was the most lifelike of the paintings. Gazing up at it, Maria fought a sharp stab of pain. She paused only a moment more. It was all that she could bear.

"How I do miss your counsel, my dear, old friend..."

She could not look at the image that she knew would be beside it in the largest, heaviest frame. Just now, that would have been too much. Instead, she moved beside the guardsman on down the long and shadowy corridor. She had done what she had come to do. She had said her farewells.

Out in the courtyard, beneath a gray sky, pillowed with heavy dark clouds, Minney and George Dawson waited for her beside their carriage. Minney, wrapped in a dark blue velvet cloak, came forward alone. She did not know—no one but William and Fanny did, that she had spent those final precious moments with the King.

"Are you all right, Mama?"

Maria held her as closely as her arms could bear. "At last, I think, he is free from his demons, darling. He has found that little bit of peace for which he searched so long."

Minney pulled away and looked down at Maria, both of them beginning to shiver from the wind and the cold. "But you, Mama. Will *you* be all right?"

Maria reached up to touch Minney's soft face. "Such a dear child you always were...right from the beginning."

"George would like you to come and stay with us for a while, Mama."

Maria tried her best to smile but it was a futile attempt. That they both should have come to love a George. Ah, there was too much irony in that for her, today of all days.

She was tired now and cold. This had been the longest day of her life. "And I thank you both," she managed to say. "but I want to go home. Truly. Jacko and Fanny will be there. And besides, I want to be in Brighton for spring. You know how lovely it is there just as spring comes with the new flowers and that ocean breeze."

"Prinney used to say Brighton had the aroma of beginnings."

Maria took a deep breath and reached up to touch a strand of Minney's pale brown hair. "That he did, child. That he did indeed."

HER HAND WOUND TIGHTLY IN Maria's, Minney reached over and lightly kissed her cheek as the carriage moved down London's busy Pall Mall. Maria seemed not to feel her daughter's touch. She was looking at the place where Carlton House had once stood. It was a vast area now, covered with terraces of houses where the palace and its gardens once punctuated the center of London. So much had begun and ended there.

He had made her remember the Conservatory most of all. After decades of costly renovations and improvements, many of which had been the cause of his financial problems, George had decided Carlton House was too old and too small for the residence of a King. How like him it was never to be content with anything, she thought.

Maria could not stop her mind from crossing yet again back through the years, to another time. She saw, through the curtain of the age, an evening in that very palace when she had begged the young impetuous Prince of Wales not to destroy his strange and grand Conservatory. It was the first time he had ever kissed her.

When she had first believed he might really come to love her.

Maria reached up and touched her lips but they held no remembrance of it. Now that evening, like the magic that had been between them, was locked safely in her memory. *Memories*, she thought sadly. *At least they still do belong to me.*

"I do believe that Prinney was trying for a very long time to find his way back to you," Minney whispered.

Maria breathed a weary sigh and looked back at her. "It does make it somehow easier to believe so."

"Well, I believe it with all of my heart. I've never stopped believing it."

She patted Minney's knee with an icy hand. "I know, child . . . I know."

371

Maria lay her head against the smooth blue velvet coach seat, listening to the sounds of London, feeling the pulse of the city that had so often maligned her. She had left Windsor resolved to recall the good things about the man who had become King George IV, the legacy he had left England, and the architectural alterations that would forever change the face of London. But there would always be more.

Finally, against the carriage seat she fell asleep, exhausted, tasting yet again the forbidden memories and the hopes of what might have been.

AUTHOR'S NOTE

The story of the locket bearing Maria's picture is a true one, as is the account of his last will and testament, in which she was formally declared to be his true wife. In spite of their tumultuous love affair, and their estrangement, George IV of England is, to this day, buried in Westminster Abbey in London, wearing around his neck the image of Maria, a woman who was his secret wife but never his Queen. Maria remained in Brighton after William ascended the throne and did indeed wear widow's black until her own death two years later. She is buried in the seaside town they loved—in the shadow of George's mythical Pavilion.